INFORMATION AND EMPIRE

Information and Empire

Mechanisms of Communication in Russia, 1600–1850

*Edited by Simon Franklin
and Katherine Bowers*

https://www.openbookpublishers.com

© 2017 Simon Franklin and Katherine Bowers.
Copyright of each chapter is maintained by the author.

This work is licenced under a Creative Commons Attribution 4.0 International license (CC BY 4.0). This license allows you to share, copy, distribute and transmit the work; to adapt the work and to make commercial use of the work providing attribution is made to the authors (but not in any way that suggests that they endorse you or your use of the work). Attribution should include the following information:

Simon Franklin and Katherine Bowers, *Information and Empire: Mechanisms of Communication in Russia, 1600–1850*. Cambridge, UK: Open Book Publishers, 2017, http://dx.doi.org/10.11647/OBP.0122

In order to access detailed and updated information on the license, please visit https://www.openbookpublishers.com/product/636#copyright

Further details about CC BY licenses are available at http://creativecommons.org/licenses/by/4.0/

All external links were active at the time of publication unless otherwise stated and have been archived via the Internet Archive Wayback Machine at https://archive.org/web

Digital material and resources associated with this volume are available at https://www.openbookpublishers.com/product/636#resources

Every effort has been made to identify and contact copyright holders and any omission or error will be corrected if notification is made to the publisher.

ISBN Paperback: 978-1-78374-373-5
ISBN Hardback: 978-1-78374-374-2
ISBN Digital (PDF): 978-1-78374-375-9
ISBN Digital ebook (epub): 978-1-78374-376-6
ISBN Digital ebook (mobi): 978-1-78374-377-3
DOI: 10.11647/OBP.0122

Cover image: Top: Clement Cruttwell, *Map of the Russian Empire*, in *Atlas to Cruttwell's Gazetteer*, 1799, image by Geographicus Fine Antique Maps (https://commons.wikimedia.org/wiki/File:1799_Clement_Cruttwell_Map_of_Russian_Empire_-_Geographicus_-_Russia-cruttwell-1799.jpg). Bottom: image from the first Italian edition of Sigismund von Herberstein's description of Muscovy (Venice, 1550), private collection.

Cover design by Katherine Bowers and Corin Throsby.

All paper used by Open Book Publishers is SFI (Sustainable Forestry Initiative), PEFC (Programme for the Endorsement of Forest Certification Schemes) and Forest Stewardship Council(r)(FSC(r) certified.

Printed in the United Kingdom, United States, and Australia
by Lightning Source for Open Book Publishers (Cambridge, UK)

Contents

Acknowledgments   1

Notes on Contributors   3

Introduction   7
Simon Franklin

I. MAP-MAKING

1. Early Mapping: The Tsardom in Manuscript   23
   Valerie Kivelson

2. New Technology and the Mapping of Empire: 59
   The Adoption of the Astrolabe
   Aleksei Golubinskii

II. INTERNATIONAL NEWS AND POST

3. Muscovy and the European Information Revolution: 77
   Creating the Mechanisms for Obtaining Foreign News
   Daniel C. Waugh and Ingrid Maier

4. How Was Western Europe Informed about Muscovy?   113
   The Razin Rebellion in Focus
   Ingrid Maier

III. NEWS AND POST IN RUSSIA

5. Communication and Obligation: The Postal System of the   155
   Russian Empire, 1700–1850
   John Randolph

6. Information and Efficiency: Russian Newspapers, 185
ca.1700–1850
Alison K. Smith

7. What Was News and How Was It Communicated 213
in Pre-Modern Russia?
Daniel C. Waugh

IV. INSTITUTIONAL KNOWLEDGE AND COMMUNICATION

8. Bureaucracy and Knowledge Creation: The Apothecary 255
Chancery
Clare Griffin

9. What Could the Empress Know About Her Money? 287
Russian Poll Tax Revenues in the Eighteenth Century
Elena Korchmina

10. Communication and Official Enlightenment: The *Journal* 311
of the Ministry of Public Education, 1834–1855
Ekaterina Basargina

V. INFORMATION AND PUBLIC DISPLAY

11. Information in Plain Sight: The Formation of the 341
Public Graphosphere
Simon Franklin

12. Experiencing Information: An Early Nineteenth-Century 369
Stroll Along Nevskii Prospekt
Katherine Bowers

Selected Further Reading 409

List of Figures 417

Index 423

Acknowledgments

This volume had its genesis in the project "Information Technologies in Russia, 1450–1850", led by Simon Franklin. We are grateful to Cambridge University and the Leverhulme Trust for their generous support of the project.

The volume grew out of the discussions at the symposium "Information Technologies and Transfer, 1450–1850", co-organised by Katherine Bowers and Simon Franklin, and held at Darwin College, Cambridge in September 2014. The symposium was made possible by a Research Network Workshop Grant from the Centre for East European Language-Based Area Studies, and funding from the Dame Elizabeth Hill Fund and the Department of Slavonic Studies at Cambridge University. We thank all of the symposium participants for facilitating such a vibrant discussion.

We wish to particularly thank Professor Don Ostrowski of Harvard University for his sage comments as we began to plan the volume, as well as the comments of the three anonymous readers who reviewed the manuscript and provided valuable feedback.

Last, but not least, we are grateful to our editor, Alessandra Tosi, who has supported this volume from its earliest stages, and her team at Open Book Publishers.

Notes on Contributors

Ekaterina Basargina is a Senior Researcher in the St Petersburg Branch of the Archive of the Russian Academy of Sciences. Her research mainly focusses on the history of the Russian Academy of Sciences. Her publications include: *The Imperial Academy of Sciences at the Turn of the 19th and 20th Centuries* (in Russian, 2008), *The Russian Academician G. H. Langsdorff and his Travels to Brazil, 1803 29* (in Russian, 2016, ed.), *The Department of Russian Language and Literature of the Imperial Academy of Sciences During the First 50 Years of its Activities, 1841–91* (in Russian, 2017, with O. Kirikova). She won the Macarius Prize in 2004.

Katherine Bowers is an Assistant Professor of Slavic Studies at the University of British Columbia. Her research interest is nineteenth-century Russian literature and cultural history, and she is currently working on a book about the influence of gothic fiction on Russian realism. Other publications include *Russian Writers at the Fin de Siècle: The Twilight of Realism* (2015, ed., with A. Kokobobo) and *A Dostoevskii Companion: Texts and Contexts* (forthcoming 2018, eds., with C. Doak and K. Holland). From 2012–14 she was Research Associate on the project, "Information Technologies in Russia, 1450–1850", led by Simon Franklin, and a Research Fellow of Darwin College, Cambridge.

Simon Franklin is Professor of Slavonic Studies at the University of Cambridge and a Fellow of Clare College, Cambridge. He has written widely on the history and culture of early Rus, Muscovy and Russia. Books include *The Emergence of Rus 700–1200* (1996, with Jonathan Shepard), *Writing, Society and Culture in Early Rus, c. 950–1300* (2002), and *National Identity in Russian Culture: an Introduction* (2004, ed., with Emma Widdis). His recent research has focussed on the social and cultural history of technologies of the word in Russia in the late medieval and early modern periods (*ca.*1450–1850).

Aleksei Golubinskii is a Lead Researcher in the Russian State Archive of Ancient Documents (since 2007) and a Junior Researcher at the Institute of Russian History of the Russian Academy of Sciences (since 2016). A specialist in eighteenth–century history, his research interests include the General Land Survey, GIS, peasant literacy, and cartography. He recently collaborated on the project *Cities of the Russian Empire from the Economic Notes of the General Land Survey* (in Russian, 2016, eds., with D. A. Chernenko and D. A. Khitrov). Currently he is a participant in the project "16th- and 17th-century Drawings of the Russian State". He also created and maintains the website of the Russian State Archive of Ancient Documents.

Clare Griffin is an Assistant Professor of the History of Science and Technology at Nazarbayev University (Astana, Kazakhstan). She is the author of 'In Search of an Audience: Popular Pharmacies and the Limits of Literate Medicine in Late Seventeenth- and Early Eighteenth-Century Russia', *Bulletin for the History of Medicine,* 89 (2015), and 'Russia and the Medical Drug Trade in the Seventeenth Century', *Social History of Medicine,* forthcoming. Her current research considers the role of the Russian Empire in early modern commodity and knowledge exchanges relating to medicaments.

Valerie Kivelson is Thomas N. Tentler Collegiate Professor and Arthur F. Thurnau Professor of History at the University of Michigan. She is the author of *Cartographies of Tsardom: The Land and Its Meanings in Seventeenth Century Russia* (2006), *Desperate Magic: The Moral Economy of Witchcraft in Seventeenth-Century Russia* (2013), and most recently, with Ronald G. Suny, *Russia's Empires* (2016). With Joan Neuberger, she edited *Picturing Russia: Explorations in Visual Culture* (2008), and her current work brings together her interest in empire and the visual.

Elena Korchmina is a Research Associate at New York University in Abu Dhabi. She has published several articles in *Rossiiskaia istoriia*, most recently under the title '"… v chest' vziatok ne davat'… ": kak "pochest'" stanovitsia "vziatkoi" v postpetrovskoi Rossii' ['… don't give bribes in honour…': how gifts became bribes in Post-Petrine Russia'] (no. 2, 2015). Her most recent publication is the chapter 'The Practice of Personal Finance and the Problem of Debt Among the Noble Elite in Eighteenth Century Russia', in *The Europeanized Elite in Russia, 1762–1825. Public Role and Subjective Self*, A. Schönle, A. Zorin, A. Evstratov, eds. (2016). Her research interests are in the economic history of eighteenth- and nineteenth-century Russia and in the history of the Russian nobility and noble self-government.

Ingrid Maier is a Professor of Russian in the Department of Modern Languages at Uppsala University. Her research interests lie in the history of Russian language and culture, especially aspects of influences between Western Europe and Russia. Some of the main topics of her recent research concern translations of European (above all German and Dutch) newspapers into Russian during the seventeenth and early eighteenth centuries ("Vesti-Kuranty") and the history of the Russian court theatre at the time of Tsar Aleksei Mikhailovich. Her most recent book is *The Court Theatre in Russia during the Seventeenth Century: New Sources* (in Russian, 2016, with Claudia Jensen).

John Randolph is a specialist in imperial Russian history, and an Associate Professor in the Department of History at the University of Illinois at Urbana-Champaign. He is the author of *The House in the Garden: The Bakunin Family and the Romance of Russian Idealism* (2007) and co-editor of *Russia in Motion: Cultures of Mobility, 1850-Present* (2012).

Alison K. Smith is a Professor in the History Department at the University of Toronto, and the author of two books: *Recipes for Russia: Food and Nationhood under the Tsars* (2008) and *For the Common Good and Their Own Well-Being: Social Estates in Imperial Russia* (2014). Her current research focuses on the palace of Gatchina and its surrounding area, examining the ways that individual subjects of the Russian Empire interacted directly with imperial authority.

Daniel Waugh, Professor Emeritus of History, International Studies and Slavic at the University of Washington (Seattle), has written extensively on Muscovite book culture, on the history of the "Great Game" rivalries over control of Central Asia, and on the historic "Silk Roads". He is co-author with Ingrid Maier of a forthcoming book on news in Muscovy, and for over a decade has edited an annual, *The Silk Road*.

Introduction

Simon Franklin

The title and subtitle of this book need some decipherment in order to focus and limit expectations regarding its contents. What is here meant by the mundane yet historically slippery word "information"? Within that, what is implied by the phrase "mechanisms of communication" in the subtitle? Easiest to locate should be the "empire" in question: it is Russia. However, the Russian state was formally designated an empire from 1721 to 1917, a period which does not at either end coincide with the chronological boundaries of the present volume, *ca.*1600–1850. This, too, will require prefatory explanation.

The study of information and communication has become central to our understanding of the world in which we live. However, this truism of modernity also has implications for our understanding of pre-modernity. The means and the mechanisms change, but systems of information and communication have always been central to the ways in which humans operate in societies and states. All ages are, in their own ways, "information ages". Therefore, prompted in part by discussion of the significance of information in the present and future, historians have increasingly turned to investigating the mechanisms, functions and significance of information in the past. Or so it appears. In fact, of course, historians have been doing so for far longer than is sometimes assumed or claimed. The study of information, of its organisation, encoding, storage, retrieval and uses, is integral to well-established fields such as the history of the book, libraries, archives, intelligence and espionage, or structures and methods of governance and administration. At the more general level, influential modern studies of the social, cultural, economic and political implications of the major pre-modern *technologies* of information—writing and printing—have long been established without necessarily labelling them as such.[1]

What is, perhaps, relatively new is the focus on the word and the concept of "information" itself. Often the word provides little more than new packaging for, or a new angle of vision on, quite traditional types of granular study.[2] More substantive, however, is the foregrounding or upgrading of claims for the importance of information as a key (for some, *the* key) to understanding major cultural phenomena and historical processes. For example, Jacob Soll titles his study of Louis XIV's Minister of Finances, Jean-Baptiste Colbert (1619–83), *The Information Master*, arguing that Colbert, with his almost obsessive appetite for acquiring and ordering information of many kinds, played an important role in the development of the modern bureaucratic state.[3] Similarly, for Edward Higgs the history of the "information state" tracks the ways in which the state has gathered information on its citizens (although Higgs stresses consensual aspects of the process).[4] By contrast, Steven G. Marks proposes that an "information nexus" was a major factor in the rise of capitalism.[5] Away from such large-scale conceptualisations, there is also a new interest in the micro-mechanisms and manipulations of information, as, for example, through rumour and gossip.[6]

In the wake of information in history comes the history of information. Does information as such have a history? Does the

---

[1] Among the seminal works (prompting discussion and modification as well as agreement) see, especially, Jack Goody, *The Domestication of the Savage Mind* (Cambridge: Cambridge University Press, 1977); and *The Logic of Writing and the Organization of Society* (Cambridge: Cambridge University Press, 1986); Elizabeth L. Eisenstein, *The Printing Press as an Agent of Change* (New York and Cambridge: Cambridge University Press, 1979).

[2] E.g., in a medieval context, Emily Steiner and Lynn Ransom, eds., *Taxonomies of Knowledge: Information and Order in Medieval Manuscripts* (Philadelphia: The University of Pennsylvania Libraries, 2015).

[3] Jacob Soll, *The Information Master. Jean-Baptiste Colbert's Secret State Intelligence System* (Ann Arbor: University of Michigan Press, 2009), p. 12.

[4] Edwards Higgs, *The Information State in England: The Central Collection of Information on Citizens since 1500* (Basingstoke: Palgrave Macmillan, 2004).

[5] Steven G. Marks, *The Information Nexus: Global Capitalism from the Renaissance to the Present* (Cambridge: Cambridge University Press, 2016).

[6] David Coast, *News and Rumour in Jacobean England: Information, Court Politics and Diplomacy 1618–1625* (Manchester: Manchester University Press, 2014).

accumulation of particular studies feed into a synthetic discipline, a historical phenomenology of information? The transition sounds obvious but is not straightforward. In the first place, no less obviously, if we want to deal with the thing itself rather than with diverse aspects of its functioning, we have to be clearer about what the thing is. The broadest definitions are far too capacious to be historically useful.[7] Almost anything *can* be deemed a container or bearer of information. Some objects that are deliberately used for information storage are designated through natural metaphors—books have always had leaves, computing now has clouds—but non-metaphorical leaves and clouds, on plants and trees and in the sky, can also be deemed to be rich sources of information, whether for botanists and climate scientists, or for anybody out for a walk or looking through a window. And that is before we begin to think of the almost mythically complex information stored chemically in the double helices of deoxyribonucleic acid. Adding to the potential confusion, there is the contiguous or overlapping but far from identical field of informatics, or information science.

It helps a little, but not enough, to apply a common distinction between information and mere data.[8] Data simply exist, information is determined by human agency. Information consists of those data or combinations of data which people choose to regard as informative. It is the "deeming" that turns data into information, not any feature of content or mode of organisation. Data become information in the process of being observed. From this point of view, information is something that is created, not just something that is. Information, to put it glibly, is a cultural construct. However, this still does not take us very far from the all-encompassing concept. Is Information History the study of changing criteria of informativeness and/or of the nature and functions and uses of the things deemed to be informative? The scope remains daunting, the opportunities for multi-disciplinary dialogue are legion, and the likelihood of unforced, persuasive theoretical cohesion seems low. It may be no accident that a collection of studies on Information

---

7   For a succinct overview of a range of approaches to the notion of information see e.g. Toni Weller, *Information History—An Introduction: Exploring an Emergent Field* (Oxford: Chandos Publishing, 2008), pp. 11–22.

8   Here, too, there is scope to make an ostensibly simple contrast complicated: see the discussion of various approaches to information and data in Jennifer Rowley, 'What is Information?', *Information Services and Use*, 18 (1998), 243–54.

History, edited by one of the pioneers and advocates of the field, was reckoned by reviewers to be, despite the framing discourse, more like a collection of studies on—once more—information *in* history.[9] The filter is disciplinary and the argument is circular.

All this is by way of an excuse, not entirely disreputable, for the lack of an overarching theoretical framework, or, if one prefers a more fundamental metaphor, for the lack of a solid theoretical base, for the chapters in the present volume. They are "aspects of...", "studies in...". However, to abjure cohesiveness and comprehensiveness is not the same as to accept (let alone justify) randomness or amorphousness. The studies here have a context and focus. While not being consistently or explicitly comparative, they can add to the wider discussion.

The chronological scope of this book reflects, approximately, what tends to be termed Russia's Early Modern period: that is, the period covering the territorial and institutional expansion of the Muscovite state and its transition to (and the further growth of) empire. Here, too, we enter a potential quagmire of questionable concepts and definitions. The label "Early Modern" is derived from conventional periodisations of the history of Western Europe. As usual, the attempt to apply a West European conceptual template to Russia is problematic.[10] Over the past couple of centuries the pendulum of interpretation has swung several times between emphasis on Russian equivalence and insistence on Russian difference. We cannot here be concerned with the theologies of Russian identity: the extent to which Russia, though individual, was essentially European, or essentially Asiatic, or whether it was entirely distinctive, *sui generis*, a "Eurasian" phenomenon all of its own. Comparative studies of empires have brought a more nuanced appreciation of multiple affinities and differences.[11] Notwithstanding, in the present context the principal area of comparison, both implied and, in places, explicit, is Western Europe. Many of the information

---

[9] Weller, ed., *Information History in the Modern World. Histories of the Information Age* (Basingstoke: Palgrave Macmillan, 2011): see the reviews by Colin Higgins in *Journal of Librarianship and Information Science*, 43.4 (2011), 271, and by Anne Welsh in *Rare Books Newsletter*, 92 (July 2012), 26–27.

[10] On approaches to "modernity" in relation to Russia see Simon Dixon, *The Modernisation of Russia 1676–1825* (Cambridge: Cambridge University Press, 1999), pp. 1–24.

[11] See esp. Dominic Lieven, *Empire. The Russian Empire and its Rivals* (London: John Murray, 2000).

structures and practices here explored were to varying degrees expressly derived from West European models. This does not mean that information practices in Russia straightforwardly mirrored their putative prototypes. In several cases the process of "translation" entailed quite radical functional transformations. The mutations of cultural transfer are as informative as the ostensible equivalences.

As an exercise in very crude modelling, we can imagine two types of information flow in relation to the state. One type of information flow involves information gathered to or emanating from the state, the other type involves information travelling between points within the state (or across borders at the non-state level). The first type might be visualised as vertical, or as radial, depending on whether one chooses to see the state as the summit or the centre. The "radial" notion better accommodates cross-border information flow to or from the state, since the relevant lines can simply be continued outwards. The second type—information flow contained within the state—can be seen as lateral, horizontal. Broadly speaking, when Soll discusses information in relation to the emergence of the "modern administrative state", he is dealing predominantly with vertical or radial flow, whereas Steven Marks's notion of an "information nexus" in the rise of capitalism is concerned predominantly with lateral flows. Variations in the nature of each and in the balance between the two may reflect and/or contribute to distinctive features of information structures and communicative mechanisms in a given society. Again at the level of very crude generalisation, in Russia the dominant mode was vertical or radial for most of the relevant period. Horizontal information flow, though not entirely negligible, began to develop rapidly only from the end of the eighteenth century.

Some of the nuances and manifestations of this changing relationship emerge from the case studies in the present volume. However, two contextual points should be signalled in advance. One of them relates to space and geopolitical structures, the other relates to technology.

The geopolitical aspect is the formation and growth of the Russian Empire. From the mid-sixteenth to the mid-nineteenth century Russia was transformed from the moderate-sized, land-locked Muscovite principality into the largest empire on earth, or at any rate the largest to be based on a continuous land-mass, without overseas territories or colonies (except for Alaska). As one would expect in an expanding state, the same period saw the growth of an administrative apparatus. From the late fifteenth century to the end of the seventeenth century the administrative functions were allocated to chanceries (*prikazy*). Overall a total of some 150 chanceries were founded. Some were short-lived, others became permanent institutions. Over the course of the seventeenth century there was an average of around sixty to seventy active chanceries at any given time. Hardy perennials included those responsible for gathering census data (the earliest of which date from the late fifteenth century) and the Diplomatic Chancery (or "Ambassadorial" Chancery—*posol'skii prikaz*). The chanceries varied hugely in size and in specificity of function. For example, in the late seventeenth century the Apothecary Chancery (*aptekarskii prikaz*) employed, apart from its medical specialists, just two clerks, while the Service Land Chancery (*pomestnyi prikaz*) employed almost five hundred clerks.[12] In a series of measures between 1717 and 1720 Peter I streamlined the structure of Imperial administration by setting up, in place of the chanceries, a far smaller number of "colleges" (initially nine, then twelve). In 1802 Alexander I replaced the colleges with ministries. The case studies in the present volume consider aspects of the functioning of all three — seventeenth-century chanceries, eighteenth-century colleges, and nineteenth-century ministries—in the dynamics of information in the service of the state.

As regards the *technologies* of information, Russia lacked, or failed to make equivalent use of, some of the tools often associated with the emergence of the empires of Western Europe. In Russia there was no early modern "print revolution". The complex and far-reaching cultural, economic and social phenomena associated with the proliferation of printing presses across Europe in the late fifteenth and early sixteenth centuries have no equivalent in Russia. Although printed books were imported and used in Russia at least from the late fifteenth century (for example, as sources for the creation of the first full Slavonic text of the Bible, completed in Novgorod in 1499), Muscovite printing did not begin until the 1550s, and it remained sporadic until the early seventeenth

---

12   See the tables in Peter B. Brown, 'How Muscovy Governed: Seventeenth-Century Russian Central Administration', *Russian History*, 36 (2009), 459–529 (pp. 496–501). For an overview of the chanceries see D. V. Liseitsev, N. M. Rogozhin, Iu. M. Eskin, *Prikazy Moskovskogo gosudarstva XVI–XVII vv. Slovar'-spravochnik* (Moscow and St Petersburg: IRI RAH; RGADA, Tsentr gumanitarnykh initsiativ, 2015).

century. However, the disparity of chronology is not the main point. A major factor, perhaps *the* major factor, contributing to the disparities between the spread and impact of print in Russia and in Western Europe can be traced to differences not in chronology but in structure. The extraordinary proliferation of printing presses across Western Europe was market-driven: driven, that is, not by a market for any particular products (few could have afforded Johannes Gutenberg's Bibles, even if they had desired to possess one), but by a market in the technology itself. The skills of printers were available for hire, whether to ambitious patrons or to any client prepared to pay for a job, however small. In contrast, in Muscovy, and in the Russian Empire almost until the end of the eighteenth century, there was a market in some of the products, but not in the technology itself. Presses were subject to financial constraints, but not to market forces. The means of production were in monopoly ownership.

From the mid-sixteenth century until the early eighteenth century there was, for most of the time, just one printing house in Muscovy, owned by the state, subject to a chancery, producing materials almost exclusively for the Church.[13] Between the 1720s and the 1770s a handful of additional presses were licensed to institutions—the Academy of Sciences, the Holy Synod, the Senate, various cadet corps, Moscow University—but market-driven proliferation only began when the restrictions on ownership were relaxed in the 1780s.[14] The issue here is not censorship. On the contrary, regular and regulated institutions of censorship only developed *after* the end of monopoly ownership.[15] The issue is structural. Although handwriting was, of course, available

---

13 See e.g. A. A. Sidorov, 'Rukopisnost'—pechatnost'—knizhnost'', in *Rukopisnaia i pechatnaia kniga*, ed. by T. B. Kniazevskaia *et al.* (Moscow: Nauka, 1975), pp. 227–45 (p. 231). For a range of perspectives on early Muscovite printing see e.g. I. V. Pozdeeva, 'The Activity of the Moscow Printing House in the First Half of the Seventeenth Century', *Solanus*, 6 (1992), 27–55; Edward L. Keenan, 'Ivan the Terrible and Book Culture: Fact, Fancy, and Fog: Remarks on Early Muscovite Printing', *Solanus*, 18 (2004), 28–50; Robert Mathiesen, 'Cosmology and the Puzzle of Early Printing in Old Cyrillic', *Solanus* 18 (2004), 5–27. See also the essays in *Canadian-American Slavic Studies* 51 (2017), 173–408.
14 See esp. Gary Marker, *Publishing, Printing, and the Origins of Intellectual Life in Russia, 1700–1800* (Princeton: Princeton University Press, 1985).
15 On censorship initiatives in the late eighteenth century see Marker, *Publishing*, pp. 212–32; on formal censorship before the mid-nineteenth century see G. V. Zhirkov, *Istoriia tsenzury v Rossii XIX–XX vv.* (Moscow: Aspekt Press, 2001), esp. pp. 7–64.

and not susceptible to the restrictions of monopoly ownership, the lack of a market in the technology of print had implications for the balance between vertical and horizontal information flow in Muscovy and the Russian Empire. In France, for example, nearly six thousand printings of royal acts have been identified from the period before 1600, a substantial proportion of which were produced on the initiative of commercial bookseller-publishers rather than through the royal printers.[16] In Russia before the early eighteenth century the Moscow Print Yard issued just one compilation of laws and just one separate governmental decree (on customs dues), in 1649 and 1654 respectively.[17] In this aspect of its information resources, despite the *leitmotif* of contacts with and borrowings from Western Europe, Russia was generically closer to other empires which had extensive territory without distributed technology, such as the Ottoman Empire or China.[18] Therefore, although several of the studies in the present volume highlight printed materials, the history of print as such does not figure as a major theme.

The case studies in this book mainly consider aspects of the vertical or radial flows of information—information to, from and for the state—although they also explore areas where the balance to some extent shifted, areas in which, rather late in the narrative, patterns of horizontal information flow began to become established. Apart from the direction, the particular focus of the volume is on the means: on mechanisms of communication. Like "information", the notion of "mechanisms of communication" needs parameters in order to be useful in this context. For the most part, the "mechanisms" here are the institutional and procedural structures through which information was conveyed: the bureaucratic structures charged with the task (chanceries, colleges, ministries), the infrastructural networks set up for

---

16 Lauren Jee-Su Kim, *French Royal Acts Printed Before 1600: A Bibliographical Study* (Ph.D. dissertation, University of St Andrews, 2008), p. 115 ff.

17 The 1649 *Ulozhenie* and the 1654 *Tamozhennaia ustavnaia gramota*. On the latter see Simon Franklin, 'K voprosu o malykh zhanrakh kirillicheskoi pechati', in *450 let Apostolu Ivana Fedorova. Istoriia rannego knigopechataniia v Rossii (pamiatniki, istochniki, traditsii izucheniia)*, ed. by D. N. Ramazanova (Moscow: Pashkov dom, 2016), pp. 428–39.

18 For the supposition that in China the arrested development of printing with moveable type (and of other technologies) is attributable to the role of the state, see Manuel Castells, *The Information Age: Economy, Society and Culture. Volume I, The Rise of the Network Society*, 2nd ed. (Chichester: Wiley-Blackwell, 2010), pp. 7–10.

the purpose (postal services), the outward-facing media distributed or displayed for the purpose (newspapers, signboards). The underlying questions are simple. How did the growing state inform itself about itself—its physical and human geography, its economic activities? What mechanisms did it establish, when and how, for the flow of information from beyond its borders? When and how did it develop procedures for projecting information from or about itself, both internally and externally? How and when did autonomous (non-state) means emerge for the communication of information? What was the relationship between institutional structures and more traditional, informal modes of gathering and disseminating information?

The studies in this volume are organised into five sections. *Section I* charts the history of mapping. The first chapter (by Valerie Kivelson) considers the early and often informal attempts at map-making during the period of Russia's expansion across Siberia, and analyses their implications for the way the nascent empire envisioned itself. These were not maps for publication and distribution, but mainly for reconnaissance and intelligence, and to clarify claims to property. The second chapter (by Aleksei Golubinskii) considers the next phase, imperial map-making from the mid-eighteenth century as an official enterprise, using scientific methods and instruments. The central episode, symbolically and practically, was the systematic import, and then the local manufacture, of West European (principally English) geodesic astrolabes (graphometers, semi-circumpherentors), the instruments reckoned essential for the first projected large-scale survey of the empire.

Section II explores the flow of information from and to Western Europe. In Chapter 3 Daniel C. Waugh and Ingrid Maier consider how, over the seventeenth century, a system emerged for the regular import of Western (mainly German and Dutch) newspapers. This was not in order to feed any public demand for the acquisition and dissemination of news, but rather the opposite. As they crossed the borders into Muscovy, the imported papers changed their function and their genre. Instead of broadening access to information, they were narrowly channelled into providing material for intelligence reports for the tsar. In Chapter 4 Maier introduces a case-study in the movement of information in the opposite direction, examining how Western reports of the insurrection, capture and execution of the infamous Cossack rebel, Stepan ("Stenka") Razin, were, to an appreciable extent, informed by quite effective Muscovite propaganda.

In *Section III* the focus shifts to internal networks of news and communication. John Randolph examines the development, expansion and thickening, over the eighteenth and early nineteenth centuries, of Russia's postal system, by horse relay. Apart from its principal function as the transport network that enabled communication of, and travel on, state business, the chapter highlights an aspect that has tended to receive little attention. The postal relays were supported through obligations imposed on local communities along the routes. There were social costs in the development of an information infrastructure. In Chapter 6 Alison K. Smith picks up the story of newspapers within Russia—that is, of Russian papers designed to disseminate "news", rather than of foreign papers used as intelligence sources. The chapter highlights ways in which, especially as printing and publishing became more diffuse and more commercially orientated, successive governments tried to maintain the view that newspapers should "play roles in policing information". In Chapter 7 Daniel C. Waugh steps back from the analysis of formal institutions, networks and publications. What sorts of information did a broader public consider to be newsworthy, and what were the informal means of transmission—including, for example, gossip and rumour—through which such unofficial "news" was disseminated? The chapter concludes with a study of how, once more in relation to the Razin revolt, the government investigation itself relied on such informal sources. Here again it becomes hard to draw a meaningful distinction between news and state information gathering or intelligence.

The three chapters in *Section IV* consider aspects of the bureaucracy as a medium for the gathering and/or dissemination of information. In chronological sequence, Clare Griffin (Chapter 8) shows how the Apothecary Chancery in the seventeenth century, though primarily serving the tsar and his family and entourage, also played a role in the creation and dissemination of medical knowledge in Russia. In Chapter 9 Elena Korchmina turns to the Imperial finances in the mid-eighteenth century. Through a detailed study of sources relating to the collection of the poll tax in the 1730s, she shows that the Imperial government was woefully under-informed about the dispersed processes and details of collection, but that this does not necessarily imply that Russia was "undergoverned", since local cash-flows could nevertheless appear to be adequate. The study by Ekaterina Basargina (Chapter 10) is again about the dissemination rather than the gathering of information. Her subject is a remarkable journal, issued by the Ministry of Public Education (or, as one might more tendentiously translate it, the Ministry for the Enlightenment of the People). For a while in the second quarter of the nineteenth century, under the editorship of Count Sergei Uvarov, the *Journal of the Ministry of Public Education* extended its role beyond that of a repository of official information and discussion about education in Russia. Its mission to "enlighten" meant also conveying the fruits of learning, reflecting and publicising the scientific and scholarly preoccupations of the time.

Section V turns from networks and institutions to public space, and asks the question: what kinds of information were communicated through open display in the urban environment? The "public graphosphere" of my contribution (Chapter 11) is formed by the writing visible in the outdoor spaces of the city, from tombstones and inscribed monuments to street signs and shop signs. The chapter surveys the emergence and growth of a public graphosphere in Russia and considers some of the main institutional impulses for its various stages of development from the mute spaces of the later Middle Ages to the relatively dense graphosphere of the mid-nineteenth century. In the final chapter (Chapter 12), Katherine Bowers moves from broad processes to the exploration of a specific graphospheric location at a particular time: Nevskii Prospekt, in St Petersburg, in the 1820s and 1830s. Based on a close reading of a contemporary lithographed "panorama" of Nevskii Prospekt, she sets out on a "virtual stroll" along St Petersburg's most fashionable thoroughfare, taking in the shop-front information as part of the urban experience.

It would be premature to convert these few case studies into an integrated chronological narrative. Gaps gape. The sample analyses of a few administrative structures for information fall a very long way short of "coverage". The surveys of postal systems presuppose the existence of the relevant roads, but otherwise lacking is any discussion of the physical infrastructures that enabled (or hindered) the movement of people and hence of information: rivers, roads, eventually railways. Because of the emphasis on "mechanisms of communication", institutions for information storage and organisation (archives, libraries) do not figure, nor do changes in methods of recording, storage and retrieval such as the shift from archival scrolls to codices.[19] The history of print is briefly summarised only in these introductory remarks, not backed up with a case study of its own. The history of handwriting—still the most common medium for the storage and distribution of non-spoken information right through to the mid-nineteenth century—is barely mentioned.

Nevertheless, some potential patterns suggest themselves. Until the end of the seventeenth century the organised mechanisms of communication were designed to gather, organise and convey information almost exclusively inwards and upwards to and for the state. This was a principal function of the chancery system. During this period the authorities paid relatively little attention to establishing means for channelling information outwards or downwards, apart from traditional modes of projection through images (as on coins, for example) and public ritual. The only institution with a network or locations and personnel geared to directing verbal messages outwards was the Church. Indeed, the one state chancery whose specific purpose was ostensibly the production and dissemination of information—the Print Chancery (*prikaz knigopechatnogo dela*), in charge of the Moscow Print Yard—in fact operated almost exclusively on behalf of the Church. Chanceries were not hermetically sealed, so some outward and downward seepage did occur, whether from the narratives in the *kuranty* or from the expertise of the doctors at the Apothecary Chancery, for example, but this tended to be a by-product of the institutional structure, not a consequence of consistent policy and focussed efforts. More research is needed on the extent to which the Ambassadorial Chancery engaged in the manipulation of information sent abroad, but Maier's investigation of the reports of the Razin rebellion raises intriguing possibilities.

Mechanisms to enhance the downward flow of information on the vertical axis from state to people (or, if one prefers, the outward flow on the radial axis) began to be developed from the early eighteenth century: through the institution of an official printed bulletin or state newspaper,

---

19 See e.g. V. N. Avtokratov, 'K istorii zameny stolbtsovoi formy deloproizvodstva—tetradnoi v nachale XVIII v.', *Problemy istochnikovedeniia*, VII (1959), 274–86.

through the prescribed printing and public posting of laws, through the systematic production of engravings illustrating state occasions and achievements, through the lavish staging of public state celebrations along with printed commentaries on their meanings, and more widely with the expansion of print into the non-ecclesiastical sphere (while maintaining a tight control on ownership). As for lateral information flow, structures of communication that had been established in the service of the state—in particular, the postal system—came to serve also as networks linking and serving a wider population. Autonomous structures of communication from and for non-state actors (aside from traditional informal means) developed quite intensively from the very end of the eighteenth century or the turn of the nineteenth century: newspapers whose principal purposes were not linked to official announcements; commercial signage; commercial and provincial publishing.

None of the studies in the present book strays much beyond the middle of the nineteenth century. This cut-off point, *ca.*1850, is not justified with reference to any particular event or set of events that mark a conventional division between epochs. Nor, however, is the break entirely arbitrary. In the first place, the main emphasis here is on emergence and establishment rather than on continuation. In the mid-nineteenth century the empire reached pretty much its maximum size, especially with its expansion into Central Asia. The mechanisms of communication that had accompanied, facilitated and been stimulated by its growth were structurally embedded. Secondly, and more pertinently for the theme of the volume, in the middle decades of the nineteenth century new technologies, structures and mechanisms of communication were emerging, with far-reaching implications: infrastructural innovations such as railways, technical transformations of traditional technologies such as steam-driven rotary presses, plus the fundamentally new technology of the telegraph. Taken together, these phenomena can indeed be seen as providing impetus for a fresh phase in the history of information and mechanisms of communication in Russia, material for a somewhat different volume.

I.
MAP-MAKING

1. Early Mapping:
The Tsardom in Manuscript

Valerie Kivelson

In some ways, the maps produced in Russia from the mid-fourteenth to the early eighteenth centuries fit uncomfortably in a volume devoted to the study of information and mechanisms of communication. To a modern viewer, or even to an educated European of the early modern period, the expected cartographic formulae are distinctly lacking, replaced by colourful drawings of little houses, churches, and trees. The maps' visual vocabulary is more pictorial than graphic, their content more fanciful than informative. Not anchored by unified perspective or scale, often without a fixed point of orientation, they show a topsy-turvy landscape of villages and forests pointing up, down, and sidewise. On first impression, these maps strike the eye as childish and naïve, a far cry from the cool abstractions that we tend to associate with cartography today. The information they contain would seem, therefore, to be minimal. As a mode of communication, early modern Russian maps were even more severely limited. Appropriately called "sketches" (*chertezhi*) rather than "maps" in Russian, these hand-made drawings were never printed and were not created with any view toward wide dissemination. For example, only *one* map of the city of Moscow was printed in Russia prior to 1741, and that was a small map included in the frontispiece to a 1663 Bible. This experiment in publication inspired no imitators.¹ Rather than print and circulate maps, Russian authorities understood maps as potentially dangerous and militantly controlled their production and distribution.

Isaac Massa, a Dutch merchant who lived in Moscow in the early seventeenth century, reported that although he was eager to obtain a map of the city, he would never have dared ask for one, "because they would have quickly seized me and delivered me over for torture, thinking that in making such a request I must be contemplating treason. This people is so suspicious in this regard that nobody would have been so bold as to undertake the task". A Russian friend explained the risk involved in sharing cartographic information, telling Massa: "I would be in danger of my life if anyone knew that I had made a drawing of the town of Moscow, and that I had given it to a foreigner. I would be killed as a traitor".² With this story of punitive state censorship, Massa reinforces one of the most persistent ideas about Russia, enduring powerfully until today; that is, rather than encourage the collection and circulation of information, the Russian state preferred to monopolise both of these spheres of activity and to quash communication.

At the same time, however, Massa's saga exposes the limits to this picture of state censorship: in spite of the obvious risks involved, Massa ultimately succeeded in gathering a good deal of cartographic information from his Russian contacts and his fellow expatriates. He even prevailed on the same fearful Russian friend to draw a map for him, though on condition of utter secrecy. The Dutchman is associated with four splendid maps of Russia: the one of the city of Moscow that his friend entrusted to him; one of the Southern regions of Muscovy reaching down to the Crimea and the Northern coast of the Black Sea; a general map of all of European Russia; and a particularly valuable one of the Northern coast of Russia and Siberia, which retained its value as a reference to this little known region into the eighteenth century.

---

1   Simon Franklin, 'Printing Moscow: Significances of the Frontispiece to the 1663 Bible', *Slavonic and East European Review*, 88. 1/2 (2010), 73–95, esp. pp. 93–94.
2   The map drawn by Massa's friend survives and is reproduced from the manuscript in G. Edward Orchard's English translation of Massa. Isaac Massa, *A Short History of the Beginnings and Origins of These Present Wars in Moscow under the Reign of Various Sovereigns down to the Year 1610*, trans. and intro. by G. Edward Orchard (Toronto: University of Toronto Press, 1982), p. 130.

Figure 1: Willem Janszoon Blaeu, *Tabula Russiae* (1635). Map and inset of the city of Moscow based on Isaac Massa's maps.

Figure 2: Isaac Massa, *Russiæ, vulgo Moscovia, Pars Australis* [The Southern part of Russia, called Muscovy] (1645).

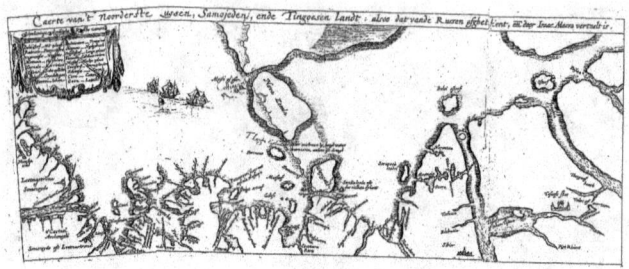

Figure 3: Isaac Massa, *Caerte van't Noorderste Russen, Samojeden, ende Tingoesen Landt: alsoo dat vand Russen afghetekent* [Map of the northern-most Russian, Samoyed, and Tungusic land, as copied from the Russians] (1610).

Two of the maps of Russia most frequently reprinted in European atlases of the early modern era bear his name. *Novissima Rvssiae Tabula* and *Rvssia vulgo Moscoviae Pars Avstralis* are both clearly attributed to him: "Auctore Isaaco Massa".[3] Richly populated with Russian toponyms, the maps confirm Massa's acknowledgement of the generous contributions of Russian informants to his sense of the local geography.

Massa was not alone in suggesting that, regardless of the fearful punishments they might incur, Muscovites and foreigners exchanged geographic information at a considerable rate. The Habsburg envoy Sigmund von Herberstein reported a parallel experience during his two visits nearly a century earlier. Unlike Massa, he was unable to convince his friends to provide him with actual maps—none would dare—but with the assistance of knowledgeable Russian and European informants, he accumulated the geographic information that made possible the publication of his map of Muscovy in copper engravings accompanying his *Notes upon Russia* in Vienna in 1549. In subsequent decades, the work appeared in multiple editions and translations, and adaptations of the map were included in various world atlases.[4]

---

3 Although Leo Bagrow suggests that none of the maps were actually Massa's work: *A History of Russian Cartography up to 1800*, ed. by Henry W. Castner (Wolfe Island, ON: The Walker Press, 1975), pp. 51–58.

4 Leo Bagrow, 'The First Russian Maps of Siberia and Their Influence on West-European Cartography of North East Asia', *Imago Mundi*, 9 (1952), 83–95; A. V. Efimov, *Atlas geograficheskikh otkrytii v Sibiri i v severo-zapadnoi Amerike XVII–XVIII vv.* (Moscow: Nauka, 1964), pp. vii–viii; Carl Moreland and David Bannister, *Antique Maps: A Collector's Guide*, 3rd ed. (Oxford: Phaidon Christie's, 1989), p.

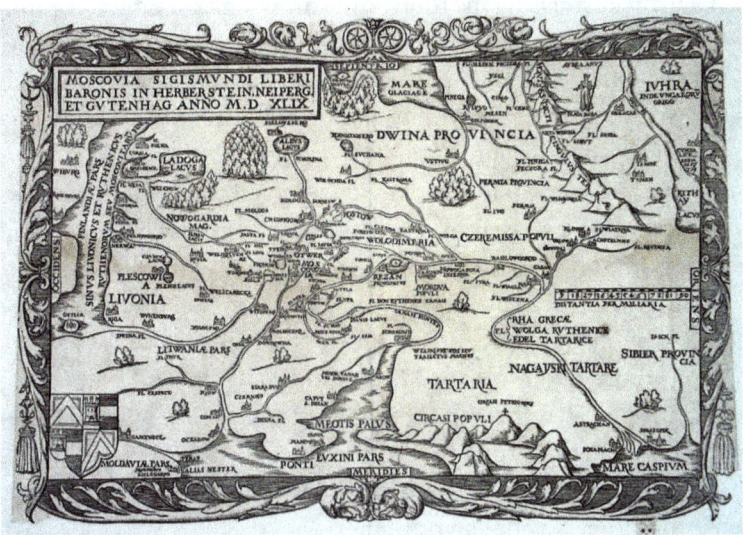

Figure 4: Map of Moscovia, Sigismund von Herberstein (1549).

These foreigners' travails, just two of many tales of cartographic adventure, illuminate the complexities involved in tracking the flows of cartographic information and communication in early modern Russia. Their reports demonstrate that, already by the time of Herberstein's visits in the early sixteenth century, Muscovites had developed a strong and effective cartographic sensibility and had collected a cache of geographic information sufficient to support the production of maps. Further, foreigners recognised the value of Muscovite geographic knowledge and of the maps themselves. Russia's pictorial sketches followed different models than the scientific survey mapping beginning to characterise European cartography in the sixteenth and seventeenth centuries, but nonetheless they conveyed valuable spatial information much sought after by both the tsarist state and the foreigners interested

---

238; A. V. Postnikov, *Karty zemel' rossiiskikh: ocherk istorii geograficheskogo izucheniia i kartografirovaniia nashego otechestva* [also in English as *Russia in Maps: A History of the Geographical Study and Cartography of the Country*] (Moscow: Nash dom and L'Âge d'Homme, 1996); A. I. Andreev, 'Chertezhi i karty Rossii XVII v., naidennye v poslevoennye gody', *Trudy Leningradskogo otdeleniia Instituta istorii AN SSSR*, no. 2 (Leningrad: AN SSSR, 1960), 88–90; W. E. D. Allen, 'The Caspian', in *The Hakluyt Handbook*, vol. I, ed. by David B. Quinn, issue 144 (Burlington, VT: Ashgate, 1974), pp. 168–175.

in it.[5] Far from dismissing the funny little drawings, foreigners scrambled to get their hands on them, with some success. Although maps were a controlled substance and publication remained out of the question, this information circulated widely and built cumulatively on the pooled knowledge of diverse contributors.

This chapter draws on my previous work on Muscovite maps but with a quite different analytical focus.[6] Where my earlier cartographic research primarily explores Muscovite political and religious culture, this chapter pursues the themes of this volume: information and communication. In this context, the following pages investigate the kinds of information conveyed in Muscovite maps, the ways the maps communicated meaning, the interplay of Muscovite and foreign cartographers and informants, and the ways these precious documents circulated in the politically charged climate of the seventeenth century, when publication was not an option.

Muscovite Sketch Maps and How to Read Them

Maps as physical artefacts, schematic representations of the world in two dimensions, are not inevitable or natural correlates of a geographic sensibility or awareness of one's place in the world relative to other locations. Maps remained exceptional in most parts of Europe, for instance, until the fifteenth century, when they began to catch on, although the Chinese already could boast an established mapping tradition perhaps as early as the second century BCE. In Russia, researchers have discovered a single rough sketch of the layout of the compound of the Kirill-Belozerskii Monastery from the 1360s and rare

---

5 Of course, pictorial mapping was never eradicated in Western Europe or elsewhere, but in the context of official, state mapping or publication, scaled survey mapping became the norm in most places by the seventeenth century. See for instance, discussions and illustrations in Roger J. P. Kain and Elizabeth Baigent, *The Cadastral Map in the Service of the State: A History of Property Mapping* (Chicago: University of Chicago Press, 1992); Peter Sahlins, *Boundaries: The Making of France and Spain in the Pyrenees* (Berkeley and Los Angeles: University of California Press, 1989).

6 Valerie Kivelson, *Cartographies of Tsardom: Maps and their Meanings in Seventeenth Century Russia* (Ithaca: Cornell University Press, 2007).

mentions of maps surface in texts from the fifteenth century,[7] but they do not appear to have been made with any regularity until the late sixteenth century, and they do not survive in significant numbers until the seventeenth century. When they show up, they fall into two general categories: sketches of very local terrain, drawn up to establish property lines or chart the state of military defences; and depictions of great swaths of the tsardom drafted for diplomatic, military, and strategic use. Since the local maps appeared earlier, we will begin with those and then move to the more comprehensive maps of the realm.[8]

One of the very earliest surviving maps illustrates the nature of the local property maps. A few lines scratched in ink on paper documents a sale of land transacted in 1533.

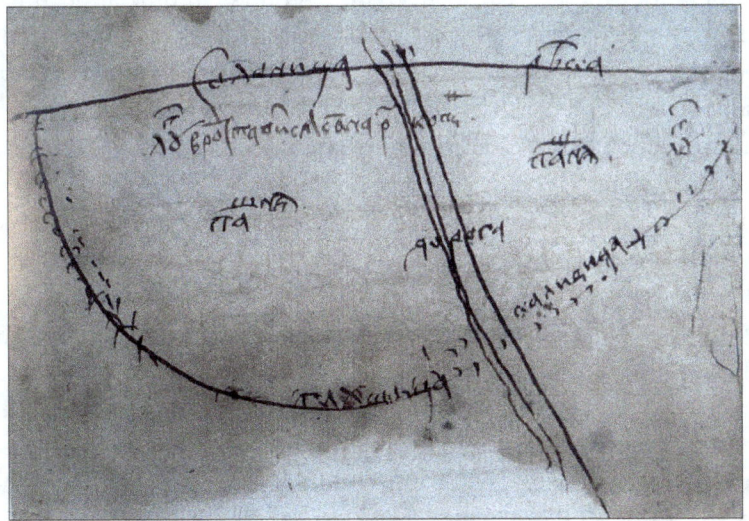

Figure 5: Drawing of the Lands of the River Solonitsa.

---

7   *Entsiklopediia russkogo igumena XIV–XV vv. Sbornik prepodobnogo Kirilla Belozerskogo. Rossiiskaia Natsional'naia Biblioteka, Kirillo-Belozerskoe sobranie, no. XII*, ed. by G. M. Prokhorov (St Petersburg: Izd. Olega Abyshko, 2003), pp. 19–26; map on p. 19.

8   Maps on icons form a subset of local maps beginning in the late sixteenth century. I will not address these fascinating maps here, but they are discussed in V. S. Kusov, *Kartograficheskoe iskusstvo Russkogo gosudarstva* (Moscow: Nedra, 1989), pp. 43–56. On the history of early mapping in Russia, see Leonid A. Gol'denberg, 'Russian Cartography to ca. 1700', in *The History of Cartography*, vol. 3, pt. 2, *Cartography in the European Renaissance* (Chicago: University of Chicago Press, 2007), pp. 1852–1903. For a valuable catalogue of Russian maps with important commentary, see: V. S. Kusov, *Chertezhi zemli russkoi XVI–XVII vv.* (Moscow: Russkii mir, 1993).

A double line indicates a road transecting a semi-circular arable field that abuts a river. Text on the obverse side describes the purchase of the field in question by the Trinity St Sergius Monastery. Unimpressive in its degree of cartographic expertise, the sketch nonetheless conveys all the information relevant to the exchange. The drawing situates the field in question along the appropriate river (the Solonitsa) and relative to the road; it notes the positioning of fields and meadows; and it records the value of the land with a terse reference to "a crop of 100 haystacks".[9] Efficient and unpretentious, the sketch demonstrates a command of relative positioning and cartographic vision fully adequate to the needs of the moment.

Written sources record little about the early development of visual mapping, but the few early surviving mentions in official documents suggest that officials of the grand prince initiated the gradual incorporation of maps as an administrative and juridical tool and as a supplement to their abundant textual records. Fleeting references in administrative records demonstrate that the initiative came from above in pursuit of entirely practical ends. For instance, orders were sent from Moscow to provincial officials in 1534 and 1535 instructing them to study the conflicting claims of rival litigants and to send maps of the properties in question back to the authorities in the Kremlin. In the 1534 case, an order issued in the name of the grand prince (the four-year-old Ivan IV) required a local official in Beloozero Province to examine the lay of the land in connection with a suit between the same Kirillov Monastery, mentioned earlier, and two peasant brothers. He was to "sketch a map of the disputed land, and having written up his judgment and the results of his investigation truthfully and having sketched the map, report to me, the grand prince, and bring before me both of the litigants for a face-to-face [literally, eye-to-eye] confrontation".[10]

---

9   First reported by S. M. Kashtanov, 'Chertezh zemel'nogo uchastka 16 v.', *Trudy Moskovskogo gosudarstvennogo istoriko-arkhivnogo instituta*, vol. 17 (1963), 429–36; reproduced in high quality colour in Postnikov, *Russia in Maps*, pp. 11–12.

10 Sanktpeterburgskii filial Instituta rossiiskoi istorii RAN, coll. 41 [Collection of N. Golovin], no. 56. A second order to draw up a map was sent to the same official the following year. *Ibid.*, coll. 41, no. 57. A copy of the same document is preserved in the Russian National Library, in a Kirillov copybook: Rossiiskaia Natsional'naia Biblioteka, St Petersburg, Manuscript Division, the Collection of St Petersburg Spiritual Academy [Dukhovnaia Akademiia], A. I/16, fol. 495–495v. I am grateful to M. M. Krom for these citations.

Although the officials' handiwork does not survive, they presumably produced sketch maps similar to the surviving 1533 map, the precursor of the more elaborate and numerous property litigation maps of the seventeenth century.

In the seventeenth century, and particularly the final third of that century, the production and use of maps proliferated, along with a generalised expansion of administrative record-keeping and increasingly dense webs of interaction between state officials and society. As the tsars extended their military lines to the South and East, the Chancery of Military Affairs ordered maps prepared to identify the most effective placement of fortresses. Maps were used for the extensive projects of town planning undertaken in the seventeenth century by the Muscovite state.[11] Sketch maps became fairly standard elements in the lawsuits over real estate that filled the tsars' courts. Sometimes the litigants would take the initiative and produce their own rival maps in support of their opposing claims, leaving the officers of the court to sort out the contradictions. More commonly, the courts would commission a city clerk or retired soldier, any passably literate man of good reputation, to go out to the land in question and make a map.

The men entrusted with the job were not formally trained in cartography, and the fruits of their labour display a variety of approaches, but they all share a pictorial vision rather than a geometric one, and a sense of orientation rooted in the embodied presence of a human passing through the landscape rather than an abstract, homogeneous, planimetric or "god's eye" view from above. A few examples will give a sense of this embedded vision and picture-book aesthetic. A vivid map from Aleksin Province, in the far South, dated 1671, situates the viewer in space by sketching out a rough framework of rivers (in green) and roads (in brick red).

---

11 A. P. Gudzinskaia and N. G. Mikhailova, 'Novye materialy po istorii drevnerusskikh gorodov', *Istoriia SSSR*, 1970, no. 4, pp. 199–202; G. V. Alferova, *Russkie goroda XVI–XVII vekov* (Moscow: Stroiizdat, 1989); Bagrow, *History of the Cartography of Russia up to 1800*, pp. 1–17; N. F. Gulianitskii, ed., *Gradostroitel'sto Moskovskogo gosudarstva XVI–XVII vekov* (Moscow: Stroiizdat, 1994), *passim*; A. V. Postnikov, *Razvitie krupnomasshtabnoi kartografii v Rossii* (Moscow: Nauka, 1989), pp. 5–10; B. A. Rybakov, *Russkie karty Moskovii XV-nachala XVI veka* (Moscow: Nauka, 1974), pp. 7–20; Leonid A. Gol'denberg, *Russian Maps and Atlases as Historical Sources*, trans. by James R. Gibson (Toronto: B. V. Gutsell, Dept. of Geography, York University, 1971).

Figure 6: Map of Aleksin (1671).

Two little villages are indicated by tiny houses. One village is surrounded by a walled enclosure; a colourfully striped church distinguishes the other. Uninhabited arable fields (*pustoshi*) are drawn in as rounded blobs distributed unevenly along the rivers and roads, and each landmark is labelled with clarifying text. The bulk of the artist's work, however, was devoted to filling the page with a forest of fantastic trees, painted in riotous colours.[12] The trees point this way and that, most angling woozily to one side, but others radiating out from roads and rivers, following along a navigable itinerary and reflecting the vantage point of a human traveller. It places human incursions as insignificant traces within an exuberantly wooded landscape.

This lavishly decorated cartographic painting was made by or on the order of Lazar Lavrov, Governor of Iaroslav-Maloi, for the practical purpose of determining ownership of some uninhabited fields claimed by two local landholders, and yet its visual composition seems engaged with an altogether different, perhaps more fantastical or metaphysical plane. It is hard to recognise in this work of art a pragmatic piece of legal-bureaucratic documentation. Nonetheless, it is a map, and a fully serviceable one at that. Through the distracting exuberance of irrelevant and eye-catching embellishment, the mapmaker conveyed enough

---

12 RGADA, coll. 1209, Aleksin stlb. 31 494, fol. 115.

information about relative locations to allow the courts to decide who should rightfully control which plot of land.

Like all the sketch maps, this one lacks geographic precision and the structuring geometry that European maps of the same era would likely contain: latitude or longitude markers, grid layouts, wind roses (although it should be noted that through the sixteenth century, European map makers still oriented their maps in a variety of directions, not only with the North at the top).

Among historians of cartography, the question of orientation of Muscovite maps is disputed, with each scholar asserting his or her position with great certainty. Leo Bagrow declared authoritatively that seventeenth century Russian maps were "always" oriented to the South; V. S. Kusov noted significant variation, with the majority oriented to the East, followed by a significant minority oriented to the South, and only a few oriented to the North. S. I. Sotnikova also allowed for a degree of arbitrariness in orientation, although from a small sample she identified a preference for a Northern orientation, with a minority oriented to the South.[13] As this cacophony indicates, no consensus has been achieved. That fine scholars could reach such disparate conclusions suggests that perhaps they are asking the wrong question. As medieval historian Carol Symes points out, documents can coach us in how they want to be read. Sometimes, she says, they scream out their instructions. The maps themselves tell us that they care very little about orientation. In this case, the sketch maps urge us to set aside our presumption that documents necessarily have a clear up and down, a right and wrong way of viewing them.[14] They invite us instead to delight in their pictured landscape in any direction we choose, and in multiple directions at once.

---

13   Bagrow, *History of Russian Cartography up to 1800*, p. 34; V. S. Kusov, *Kartograficheskoe iskusstvo Russkogo gosudarstva*, p. 27; S. I. Sotnikova, 'Pamiatniki otechestvennoi kartografii XVII v.', *Pamiatniki nauki i tekhniki, 1987–1988*, 1989, no. 6, pp. 176–201 (pp. 181, 186, 196, 198). Also, Franklin, 'Printing Moscow', p. 87. On *chertezhi*, see also Lutz Häfner, 'Europa ohne Grenzen? Zu Wandel und Funktion der russlandbezogenen Kartographie vom Moskauer Reich bis zur Mitte des 18. Jahrhunderts', in *Osteuropa kartiert—Mapping Eastern Europe*, ed. Jörn Happel (Münster: LIT, 2010), pp. 87–112.

14   Carol Symes, 'The "Desire of Deeds": Sensuality, Nostalgia, and the Affective Effects of Medieval Documentation', talk presented at the Eisenberg Institute for Historical Studies, University of Michigan, Ann Arbor, 1 October 2015. The talk comes from her current project, *The Mediated Text: Documentary Initiatives and Their Agents in Medieval Europe*.

This invitation is underscored by the fact that cardinal directions usually (though not always) go unmarked in the maps. More frequently, Muscovite *chertezhi* took their structure from the landscape itself and from the human itineraries that passed through it, orienting more to the courses of major rivers or paths of important roads than to abstract compass points. This is not to suggest that Muscovites had no understanding of the cardinal directions, quite the contrary, but rather to note that they chose not to indicate them in any way on their maps. The makers and viewers would have had no difficulty knowing which way was North.[15] Still, many of the maps would have presented them with the same conundrum we face in trying to resolve how they were meant to hold the map, in other words, which way was up.

The polyphonic impulses of the mapmakers come through when one attends to the visual evidence of the maps themselves, with their jumble of orientations of images and textual annotations. The point of view of the traveller along the road is signalled by the trees bristling outward; the horizontal span of the paper accommodates the flow of a river; the layout of a village around a nodal focus such as a church or a path determines the splayed depiction of houses with their roofs pointing out from the centre. Mixed perspective presents architectural complexes from multiple viewpoints simultaneously, suggesting the movement of the human viewer around the walls of a building or compound.[16] The visual impact of mixed perspective is augmented in large maps, where the artists or scribes faced the purely logistical problem of the limited reach of the human arm. Oversized maps composed of multiple sheets glued together required the mapmaker to circle around and work from different sides of the paper.

It is true that sometimes the artefacts themselves provide clues to their intended orientation. Occasionally, maps make some effort to

---

15 It is worth noting that magical spells, an illicit but popular genre, invoked the cardinal directions as part of their ritual, evidence that the points of the compass were part of common knowledge, even if the compass was not.

16 Gottfried Hagen identifies similar practices in seventeenth-century Ottoman cartography, which assumes "an observer in motion along the surface of the earth, and renders his dynamic and contextual perspective". Like Muscovite *chertezhi*, Ottoman maps are easily "derided as an 'abyss of cartographic barbarity'", but, Hagen shows, they should be read in their own terms. 'Kātip Çelabi's Maps and the Visualization of Space in Ottoman Culture', *Journal of Ottoman Studies*, 40 (2012), 283–93 (289; 285); quoting Hans von Mžik, 'Ptolemaeus und die Karten der arabischen Geographen', *Mitteilungen der geographischen Gesellschaft Wien*, 58 (1915), 152–76 (p. 168).

indicate direction themselves by the placement of the rising or setting sun, as in a lively map of Borovsk, where a summer sunrise to the right and a summer sunset to the left indicate a Northern orientation.[17] Some sketch maps, particularly the small ones contained on a single piece of paper, declare an unambiguous directionality by showing all the trees pointing in a single direction consistent with all the text. Others show a *preponderant* orientation, with *most* of the trees and text pointing in a single direction. Signatures collected from local witnesses, or from the mapmaker himself, may appear on the back of a map to add to its veracity and documentary power, and Leonid Chekin stresses that they march along the back of the page in horizontal lines, obeying a disciplined sense of up and down.[18]

Figure 7: Signatures on obverse of a map of lands along the Kamenka and the Urshma rivers in Suzdal Province. The signatures are aligned horizontally across the page, indicating a clear orientation for viewing. The document dates to 1688 or 1689.[19]

---

17   RGADA, coll. 192, descr. 1, Kaluzhskaia guberniia, no. 1. Leonid S. Chekin corrects my discussion of the orientation of this map, which he dates to 1675, in 'Russian Maps and Spatial Thinking in the Seventeenth Century', *The Portolan*, 68 (Spring 2007), 51–58 (p. 56). This is an interesting though uncharitable review of my book, *Cartographies of Tsardom*.

18   Chekin 'Russian Maps and Spatial Thinking in the Seventeenth Century', p. 56.

19   RGADA, coll. 1209, Suzdal' stlb. 27955, ch. 1, l. 73b.

This is sometimes the case (in other cases signatures run every which way), but did that regulated linearity on the back determine how Muscovites read the looser structures of the pictorial front?

These highly localised sketch maps were not concerned with situating their position in a broader world, relative to an abstract pole, an international border, or a metropolitan centre; that was not their purpose. They were created to illustrate the location of a great double-headed pine with a state agent's official boundary mark or blaze, a dark X, burned into it, or the place where a church used to stand or a graveyard lay in ruins, in order to clarify particular property lines.[20]

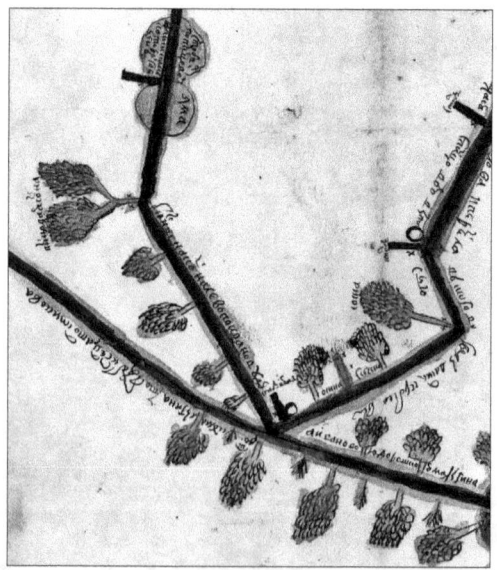

Figure 8: Map of the lands along the river Lakhost near the village of Tolstikova in Suzdal Province. The sketch documents the mapmaker's concern with the details of the local landscape and the official markers that register property lines. It demonstrates little concern with orientation or with situating the local in a broader world.[21]

The particularity of their focus is evident in the plethora of minuscule details that they record. On a map from Iurev Polskoi from 1672, a textual label above the two dark circles just right of centre notes: "In

---

20 RGADA, coll. 1209, Murom, stlb. 36032, fol. 182; 183; 184; RGADA, coll. 1209, Uglich, stlb. 35730, Ch. 1, fol. 57.
21 RGADA, coll. 1209, Suzdal' stlb. 28043, ch. 1, fol. 142.

the uninhabited arable field Tiapkova are two pits, and raspberries and nettles are growing in them, and around them is the ploughed land of the uninhabited arable field Tiapkova".[22]

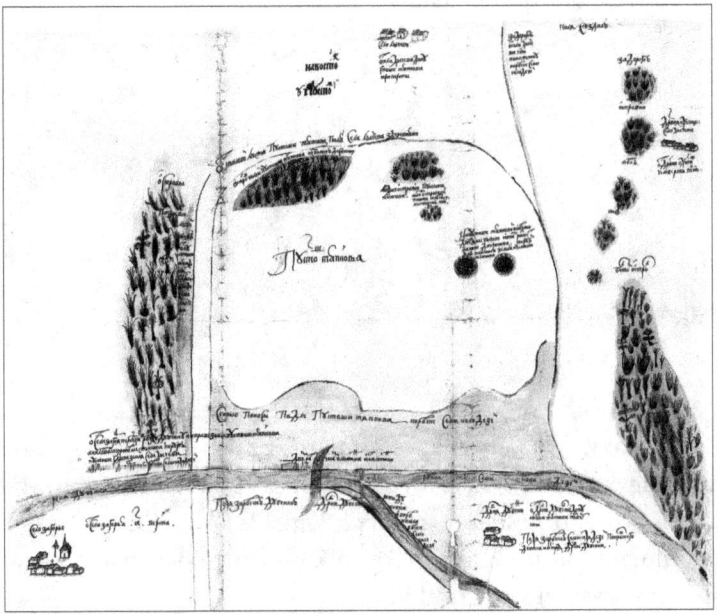

Figure 9: Map of the land along the river Sem Kolodezei in Iurev Polskoi Province, 1670-72. "The ploughed land of the uninhabited arable field Tiapkova". Like the previous map, this one focuses exclusively on local landmarks.[23]

These were the facts that would determine the outcome of a case and would allow the tsar's officials to resolve questions of boundary lines and ownership claims. The idiosyncrasies of the local landscape served the purpose far more usefully than did any abstract, generalised orientation. Modern scholars may be convinced they know the "right" way to orient these maps, but in their handiwork, seventeenth-century mapmakers show themselves to have been supremely uninterested in the question.

The sketches may have served their purpose in helping judges to issue their rulings, but that does not necessarily mean that the information they provided was accurate. A colourful sketch map drawn

---

22   RGADA, coll. 1209, Iur'ev Pol'skoi, stlb. 34253, Ch. 1, fol. 132.
23   RGADA, coll. 1209, Iur'ev Pol'skoi, stlb. 34253, Ch. 1, l. 132.

up in connection with a dispute over property in the neighbourhood of Borovsk, a town to the Southwest of Moscow, provides surprising evidence in support of the claim that these amusing little pictograms conveyed locations quite reliably.

Figure 10: Borovsk.[24]

The map shows a network of implausibly sinuous rivers snaking through the region. Oversized vegetation edges the rivers. Little houses line the roads and nestle in small settlements. All in all, it looks again like an illustration from a book of folk motifs rather than a document capable of conveying practical information.

Yet, as Chekin points out, a close comparison with a satellite photo available through Google Earth proves that our man in Borovsk knew his business.

Figure 11: Borovsk, satellite view from Google Maps (2017).

---

24   RGADA, coll. 192, descr. 1, Kaluzhskaia guberniia, no. 1.

The topography of the region and the location of identifiable landmarks line up with an impressive degree of accuracy. Chekin deduces that the mapmaker began with the town of Borovsk as his main point of reference and then worked his way through the region, dividing the territory into "manageable segments", and then using the intricate grid of rivers and roads to "further subdivide the area". He placed landmarks close to Borovsk quite accurately, while places farther afield, presumably less immediately relevant to the task at hand, were placed in the general vicinity of their actual location.[25] Untrained in Western scientific cartographic practices, unacquainted with the techniques of mathematical surveying, the Muscovite men who were haphazardly rounded into service as mapmakers nonetheless succeeded remarkably well in putting on paper usable guides to the natural and built landscape they inhabited.

State Mapping Projects: The Great Sketch Map and Atlases of Siberia

If Muscovite mapmakers could capture the fine-grained topography of small areas, how did those working on a larger canvas fare? For maps of the tsardom writ large, two major sets of sources survive: a set of documents related to the *Book of the Great Sketch Map* (*Kniga Bol'shomu chertezhu*); and a sizable collection of maps of Siberia composed from the 1660s through to the early 1700s.[26]

At the very end of the sixteenth or beginning of the seventeenth century, Tsar Boris Godunov ordered the production of a great map, the *Bol'shoi chertezh*, of the lands of the tsardom to the West of the Urals. In preparation, reports were sent to Moscow from the localities, drawing on local informants with knowledge of the major landmarks, rivers and

---

25 Chekin, 'Russian Maps and Spatial Thinking in the Seventeenth Century', 56–57. The map in question is RGADA, coll. 192, Kaluzhskaia guberniia, no. 1. A. P. Gudzinskaia and N. G. Mikhailova make an equally compelling argument for the precision and accuracy of architectural representations on *chertezhi*. See their 'Graficheskie materialy, kak istochnik po istorii arkhitektury pomeshchich'ei i krest'ianskoi usadeb v Rossii XVII v.', *Istoriia SSSR*, 5 (1971), pp. 214–27.

26 I will not address here B. A. Rybakov's not entirely convincing argument for the creation of a map of Muscovy in the fifteenth century. See his *Russkie karty Moskovii XV-nachala XVI veka* and his 'Russian Maps of the Fifteenth and Sixteenth Centuries', trans. by James A. Gibson, *The Canadian Cartographer*, 14 (1977), 10–23.

roads, forts, lookouts, wells and supply-points. The welter of strategic information was collated into a single book, the *Book of the Great Sketch Map*. From the reports, regional maps were drawn up and then pasted together into a single huge wall map. By 1627 Kremlin scribes reported the original map was "dilapidated, it was no longer possible to see landmarks on it, it was all worn out and falling apart".[27] To address the problem, in that same year Tsar Mikhail Romanov commanded his scribes to make a copy of the book and to recreate the map itself on the basis of the information it preserved. He added that a supplemental map should be made showing the territories to the South, the Ukrainian borderlands and the dangerous routes that the Tatars followed to and from the Crimea. The new *Great Sketch Map* seems to have followed its predecessor to oblivion, but the map of the Ukrainian lands survives in multiple later copies made by foreigners and circulated abroad.

This brief history of the fate of the *Great Sketch Map* further supports the notion that neither Moscow's protective monopoly on cartographic information nor its preference for manuscript over printed formats precluded active use or even dissemination. The map had been consulted frequently in the Kremlin chanceries, becoming dog-eared and faded through constant use. It had passed through many hands in the decades since it was compiled.[28] Further, we know the sketch map of the Ukrainian lands from copies made and circulated outside of the tsardom by Germans and Swedes. Their ability to find and copy such a strategic and closely held asset demonstrates beyond a doubt that, however much the Kremlin wished to hoard its cartographic information, the pressures of dissemination were greater. Classified information leaked out, then as now, and the forces of communication overrode the pressure for secrecy.[29]

---

27 *Kniga Bol'shomu chertezhu*, ed. K. N. Serbina (Moscow: AN SSSR, 1950), p. 49 (fol. lv of reproduced text). Some scholars date the original map to the reign of Ivan IV.
28 Simon Franklin provides a model of how to read manuscripts for material traces of reading practices. See his "Dirty Old Books", in *Picturing Russia: Explorations in Visual Culture*, ed. by Valerie A. Kivelson and Joan Neuberger (New Haven: Yale University Press, 2008), pp. 12–16.
29 On the *Bol'shoi chertezh*, and for reproductions of some late copies of the Ukrainian maps, see Bagrow, *History of the Cartography of Russia up to 1800*, pp. 4–12; Serbina, *Kniga Bol'shomu chertezhu*; Postnikov, *Razvitie krupnomasshtabnoi kartografii v Rossii*, pp. 20–22; Kusov, *Kartograficheskoe iskusstvo Russkogo gosudarstva*, pp. 75–77.

Similar dynamics emerge in the arc of Siberian mapping. Muscovites first crossed the Ural Mountains and clashed with the Tatars of Western Siberia in the early 1580s, under Ivan IV. Half a century later, they had reached the Pacific Ocean. As they explored, conquered, and attempted to exploit and rule the populations and resources of their vast new holdings, they recognised the importance of mapping the terrain. They had little cartographic tradition to build on in Siberia.

The Eastern reaches of Eurasia had appeared on European world maps since the revival of Ptolemaic geography in the early fifteenth century.[30] Martin Waldseemüller's famous wall map, *Universalis Cosmographia* of 1507, for instance, labels both "Tartaria" and "Sarmatia Asiatica", though not Muscovy, in its largely fanciful sweep across the continent to the Pacific. A Ptolemaic framework and a set of classical toponyms still shaped Waldseemüller's vision of Eurasia, even though he knew they were outdated and despite his pioneering revision of the world with his inclusion of America, the land of Amerigo Vespucci, as a new and separate continent.

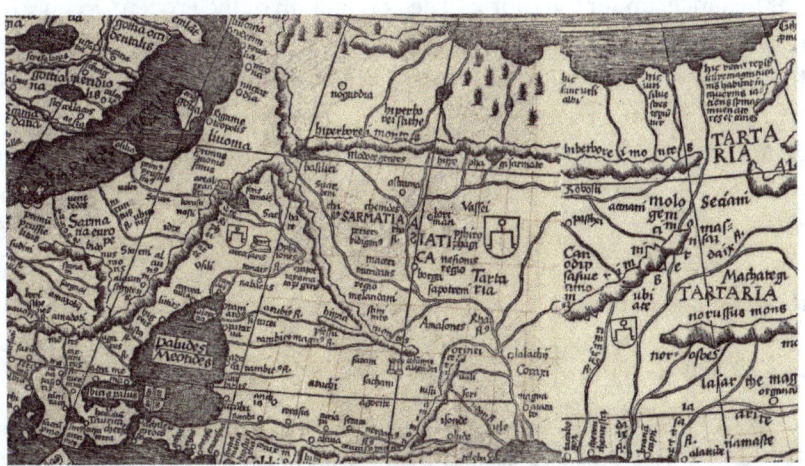

Figure 12: Martin Waldseemüller, *Universalis Cosmographia* (1507), detail. The Hyperborean Mountains run horizontally across this section of the map. "Paludes Meotides," at the bottom left, is an oversized Sea of Azov.

---

30   The rediscovery of the work of the ancient geographer, astronomer, and mathematician, Claudius Ptolemy (100–160 CE), revolutionised European understandings of cartography. His *Geography* set out principles of measurement of latitude and longitude and methods for calculating the diameter of the globe.

As Katharina N. Piechocki points out, the classical misconception about the Riphean and Hyperborean mountain ranges that purportedly ran East-West across the narrow belt of land imagined as the limit of the earth to the North of the Black Sea remained in place until dispelled by the Polish scholar Maciej Miechowita in his 1517 *Tractatus de duabus Sarmatiis Asiana et Europiana*, "the first European treatise to overtly challenge the existence of the Riphean mountains". Countering ancient mythology with up-to-date reports, Miechowita declared, "We know for certain and have seen that the Hyperborean, Riphean, and Alan mountains do not exist".[31]

Miechowita stresses the corrective power of first-hand, eyewitness accounts, and the maps produced by Europeans in the following centuries benefited from precisely this kind of information, drawn together from the travel reports of foreign merchants and envoys and from conversations with geographically savvy Russians. In the geographic descriptions in his *Notes Upon Russia*, Herberstein acknowledged the crucial information divulged by Russian contacts. For instance, under the rubric "The Navigation of the Frozen Ocean", he noted that when he was at the court in Moscow, "there happened to be there Gregory Istoma, the interpreter of that prince, an industrious man, [...] and as he had been sent by his prince in the year 1496 to the King of Denmark, [....] he gave me a short account of his journey".[32] On the basis of many such reports, once back at home, Herberstein commissioned a map of Muscovy. A form cutter named Augustin Hirsvogel produced an early version in 1546. It was reprinted in 1549 in a smaller format to accompany the first edition of *Notes Upon Russia*, and from there it "went viral", enjoying an active afterlife in subsequent editions and reprintings in atlas compilations.[33]

---

31 Katharina N. Piechocki, 'Erroneous Mappings: Ptolemy and the Visualization of Europe's East', in *Early Modern Cultures of Translation*, ed. by Karen Newman and Jane Tylus (Philadelphia: University of Pennsylvania Press, 2015), p. 86. Piechocki notes that Miechowita never travelled to the lands he described but drew on interviews with people who had been there. On Waldseemüller and the Ptolemaic model, see also John W. Hessler, *The Naming of America* (Washington, D.C.: Library of Congress, 2008), pp. 18–25.

32 Sigmund Freiherr von Herberstein, *Notes Upon Russia*, 2 vols, Elibron Classics Reprint of the 1852 publication by the London's Hakluyt Society (Adamant Media, 2005), vol. 2, p. 105, https://archive.org/details/notesuponrussiab02herbuoft

33 Leo Bagrow, *History of Cartography up to 1600*, ed. by Henry W. Castner (Wolfe Island, ON: The Walker Press, 1975), p. 60, pp. 70–72.

Herberstein was one of the early contributors to a sixteenth-century boom in European mapping of Muscovy and Western Siberia, generally designated Tartaria or Asian Scythia.[34] Muscovites contributed to this boom by sharing geographic information with their Western acquaintances, but in their own cartographic work, they adopted a distinctive approach. As Alexey Postnikov and Marvin Falk write, "the early charts of the territories of Siberia and the Northeastern regions of Eurasia produced cartography outside the Western European scientific framework of the time. Even in their appearance the Siberian charts of the seventeenth to early eighteenth century sharply differed from contemporary maps created within Ptolemy's paradigm that was then dominant in European geography". Visually distinctive in style, often oriented to the South rather than the North, and sometimes composed with the help of compass readings and chain measurements of distance, but without the benefit of a "geographic net and consistent scale and projection for all parts of the cartographic image", these Russian maps were nonetheless packed with valuable information and accompanied by textual descriptions that filled in additional context.[35]

The first map of all Siberia known to have been made within the tsardom by Russians is known as the Godunov map of 1666–67. As with the maps produced in conjunction with the *Book of the Great Sketch Map*, the Godunov map itself does not survive or has not yet been found, but its imprint is detectable in later renditions, drawn by Russians following in Godunov's tradition and by foreigners who copied it in secret. A textual lozenge appears on later copies informing the viewer that the map was made "In the year 1666–67 by order of Great Sovereign, Tsar, and Grand Prince Aleksei Mikhailovich, Autocrat of all Great, Small,

---

34 Among the earliest in this boom was a map made by Battista Agnese on the basis of information provided by the Russian ambassador to Rome, Dmitrii Gerasimov, in 1525. Gerasimov was a source for Herberstein as well. Another early map was made by Ivan Liatskoi in 1542. See for instance, discussions in Bagrow, *History of Cartography up to 1600*, pp. 61–135; Krystyna Szykuła, 'Anthony Jenkinson's Unique Wall Map of Russia (1562) and its Influence on European Cartography', *Belgeo* (2008), pp. 3–4, http://belgeo.revues.org/8827; Samuel H. Baron, 'The Lost Jenkinson Map of Russia (1562) Recovered, Redated and Retitled', *Terrae Incognitae: The Journal of the Society for the History of Discoveries*, 25. 1 (1993), 53–66.

35 Alexey Postnikov and Marvin Falk, *Exploring and Mapping Alaska: The Russian America Era, 1741–1867*, trans. by Lydia Black (Fairbanks: University of Alaska Press, 2015), pp. 17–18. See also Leonid A. Gol'denberg and A. V. Postnikov, 'The Development of Mapping Methods in Russia', *Imago Mundi*, 37 (1985), 63–80.

and White Russia" and composed "with great care" by Governor Petr Ivanovich Godunov from information collected in Tobolsk, the capital city of Western Siberia.

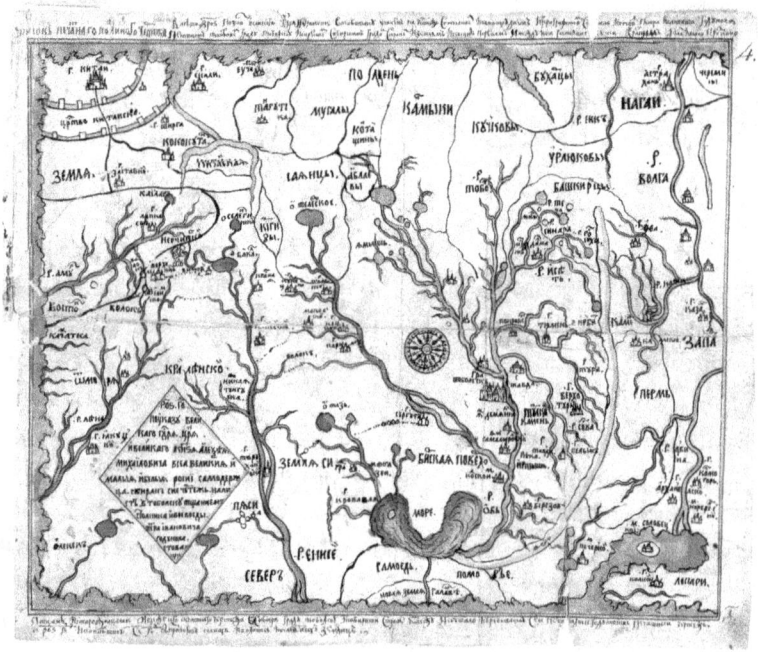

Figure 13: S. U. Remezov's copy of the Godunov map of 1666–67, from his *Chorographic Sketch Book*. The map is oriented to the south: China is indicated by concentric curves of the Great Wall in the top left corner and the Pacific Ocean frames the map at the left margin. The Arctic Ocean runs along the bottom.

Along with the textual cartouche, the surviving copies include a compass rose, underscoring the use of this directional technology in the map's composition. Named for this Siberian administrator (and not the more famous Tsar Boris Godunov), the map reflects the governor's on-going work with maps. In 1661 Godunov oversaw the construction of fortifications along the River Tobol, following "a map and description provided by well-informed people".[36] The input of

---

36 Leo Bagrow, 'Semyon Remezov: A Siberian Cartographer', *Imago Mundi*, 11 (1954), 111–25 (p. 112); cites N. N. Ogloblin, comp., *Obozrenie stolbtsov i knig Sibirskogo prikaza, 1592-1768*, book 2, in *Chteniia v Obshchestve istorii i drevnostei rossiiskikh pri Moskovskom universitete* (Moscow, 1895), vol. 173, p. 249; and S. V. Bakhrushin,

"well-informed people" contributed to this first map of all of Siberia as it had for the mapmakers back in central Russia as they laboured to sketch the bounds of landholders' estates by drawing on the expertise of "long-time residents".³⁷

Given the crudeness, in terms of scientific measurement, of Godunov's sketch, one might wonder why foreigners would take the risks involved in attempting to purloin copies. The answer points precisely to the nature of the information it conveyed and the value that contemporaries put upon it. Knowledge of river routes and linkages offered the key to travel and transportation. Henry R. Huttenbach explains the simplicity of the map's content and the emphasis on rivers to the exclusion of other features of the landscape: "For the most part these *chertezhi* resemble road maps that show points of interest on or near the road. What lies off the highway is not shown; similarly the *chertezhi* of Siberia virtually ignore the interior other than in terms of the course of the river".³⁸

The same hydrographic grid characterised the work of the extraordinary Siberian cartographer of the end of the seventeenth and beginning of the eighteenth century, Semen Ulianovich Remezov.³⁹ In creating his three atlases and many maps of Siberia, Remezov drew on the same kind of pooled knowledge that had allowed his predecessors to chart the territory. He was responsible for drawing the earliest surviving

---

    Ocherki po istorii kolonizatsii Sibiri v 16-om i 17-om vv. (Moscow: Izd. M. and S. Sabashnikovykh, 1927), 17–19 ff. Bagrow notes that Godunov supervised another ambitious mapping project in 1668, 'Information on the Land of China and on the Depths of India Provided by Petr Ivanovich Godunov'.

37 *Khorograficheskaia kniga Sibiri* [Chorographic Sketch-book of Siberia], MS Russ 72 (6). Houghton Library, Harvard University, Cambridge, MA, ff. 5v-6, https://iiif.lib.harvard.edu/manifests/view/drs:18273155$10i. On Petr Godunov's cartographic work and on this map, see Gregory Afinogenov, 'The Eye of the Tsar: Intelligence-Gathering and Geopolitics in Eighteenth-Century Eurasia' (Ph.D. dissertation, Harvard University, 2016), pp. 40–45.

38 Henry Huttenbach, 'Hydrography and the Origins of Russian Cartography', *Five Hundred Years of Nautical Science, 1400–1900, Proceedings of the Third International Reunion for the History of Nautical Science and Hydrography held at the National Maritime Museum, Greenwich, 24–28 September 1979*, ed. by Derek House (Greenwich: National Maritime Museum, 1981), pp. 142–52 (p. 148).

39 On Remezov, see L. A. Gol'denberg, *Izograf zemli sibirskoi* (Magadan: Magadanskoe knizhnoe Izd., 1991); and his *Semen Ul'ianovich Remezov, sibirskii kartograf i geograf, 1642-posle 1720 gg.* (Moscow: Nauka, 1965); Kivelson, *Cartographies of Tsardom*; A. V. Postnikov, 'Kartografirovanie Sibiri v XVII–nachale XVIII veka. Semen Ul'ianovich Remezov i ego rukopisnye atlasy', in *Chertezhnaia kniga Sibiri, sostavlennaia tobol'skim synom boiarskim Semenom Remezovym v 1701 godu*, ed. by A. A. Drazhniuk, *et al.*, 2 vols, vol. 2: *Issledovaniia* (Moscow: PKO 'Kartografiia', 2003), pp. 7–19.

Russian copies of the 1666–67 Godunov map, and he laboured to update and enrich it. A mid-level servitor, icon-painter, and administrator in Tobolsk, Remezov fulfilled increasingly ambitious orders from Moscow to map first the region around Tobolsk, then a broader swath of the surrounding steppe, and finally, in 1698, to create a new map of all of Siberia. In order to do so, he was to explore and map on his own, and he did so extensively, noting "directional measurements from a compass",[40] but he was also instructed to gather reports and maps from anyone who might have useful knowledge. His own explanation of his work acknowledges that maps and reports came to him from all over, from Russian and Cossack trappers and traders, explorers and adventurers, from military men, and from native peoples. He questioned travellers about their journeys to determine "the dimensions of lands, the route distances of towns and their villages and districts, about rivers, streams, lakes, bays, islands, and fishing, about mountains and forests, and about all landmarks that have not been plotted on previous maps".[41]

As his preface to the *Working Sketch-book* (*Sluzhebnaia chertezhnaia kniga Sibiri*), one of his three atlases of Siberia, explains, he and his sons were ordered by the head of the Siberian Chancery to compile their atlas from "pictures of twenty-three Siberian towns brought to the Siberian Chancery in Moscow". In the *Chorographic Sketch-book* (*Khorograficheskaia chertezhnaia kniga*) he explains that he used "many town maps, whatever had been sent over the years to Moscow".[42] Remezov, thus, did not work in isolation, and the resulting atlases are as much cobbled together from earlier Muscovite efforts as representative of his own, individual inspiration.[43] Notably, all of these varied people

---

40 Rossiiskaia gosudarstvennaia biblioteka, Moscow, Rukopisnyi otdel, coll. 256, Rumiantsev Collection, no. 346; published in a facsimile edition as *Chertezhnaia kniga Sibiri, sostavlennaia tobol'skim synom boiarskim S. Remezovym v 1701 godu*, 2 vols (Moscow: FGUP, PKO Kartografiia, 2003), p. 10.

41 *Chertezhnaia kniga Sibiri*, 4; discussed in V. N. Fedchina, 'Central Asia on Russian Maps of the Seventeenth Century', *The Canadian Cartographer*, 10. 2 (1973), 95–105 (102).

42 Rossiiskaia natsional'naia biblioteka, St Petersburg, Ermitazhnoe sobranie, no. 237, *Sluzhebnaia chertezhnaia kniga Remezova*, fol. 1; Remezov, Semen Ul'ianovich, 1642-ca. 1720. *Khorograficheskaia kniga*, f. 1v.

43 On the gathering of maps from many mapmakers, see, for instance, *Chertezhnaia kniga*, fol. 3, which explains that the tsar ordered the mapping of Siberia in 7177 (1668–69), and maps were collected between that year and 7209 (1700–01). Some maps in the atlas acknowledge their original authors, as, for example, *Khorograficheskaia*

had sufficient geographic interest and cartographic understanding to make important contributions to the Siberian mapping project, and the state and its delegates recognised the value of their knowledge. Some of Remezov's maps acknowledge his sources by name; others simply draw on the reports that flowed into Moscow and Tobolsk. The first map of Kamchatka, commissioned by the governor of Iakutsk, Dorofei Traurnicht, and brought back by the intrepid explorer and vicious conqueror Vladimir Atlasov, made its way into one of Remezov's atlases, with full attribution.[44]

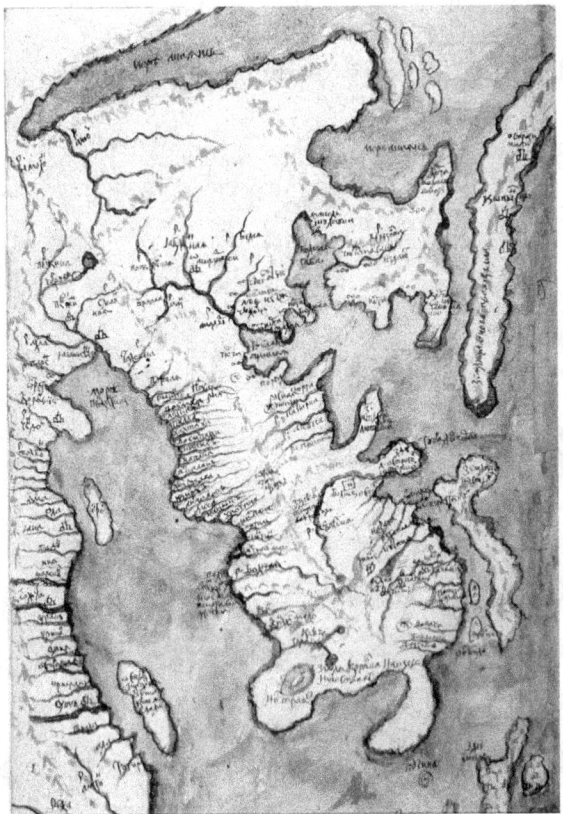

Figure 14: Kamchatka. Map of Kamchatka included in S. U. Remezov's *Working Sketch Book*. Remezov attributes the map to Dorofei Traurnich.

---

kniga, f. 147, which credits Lieutenant of the Daur Regiment Afonasii Ivanov syn Baikov with a sketch of the Amur River, China, Nerchinsk, and Irkutsk.

44   *Sluzhebnaia chertezhnaia kniga Remezova*, fol. 102v.

In his depiction of the hydrographic features of the Far East, Remezov drew on information provided by Nicolae Milescu Spathary (or Spafarii), who described and mapped the Sino-Siberian frontier in the course of a diplomatic mission to China in 1675–76 on behalf of the Muscovites.[45] Spafarii's work in turn relied heavily on the work of Jesuits, from whom he freely plagiarised, as well as on Chinese, Kazakh and Manchu informants. As Gregory Afinogenov writes, "These texts were the product of networks ensnaring Junghars, Kazakhs, Mongols, Manchus, Chinese, and even the Jesuits themselves, and as such reveal the delicate interdependencies and striking human stories that characterized Russia's presence in this borderland".[46]

With all of these streams of information flowing into his workshop in Tobolsk, Remezov and his assistants were able to create a far more densely annotated version of the Godunov map that identified hundreds more Siberian locales and refined his sense of geography, culminating in his large, stand-alone *Map of All Siberia*.

Figure 15: Remezov, *Map of All Siberia*.

---

45 Marina Tolmacheva, 'The Early Russian Exploration and Mapping of the Chinese Frontier', *Cahiers du Monde russe*, 41. 1 (2000), 41–56 (pp. 44–46).

46 Afinogenov, 'Eye of the Tsar', pp. 47–51 (on Spafarii); p. 8 (quotation). Afinogenov reconstructs the Eastern contributions to the communications networks through which information on Siberia and China circulated and explores the world of intelligence gathering in which Russia played a part.

In the bulk of his work, he followed the same general template as that used in the local real estate maps. He employed the branching network of rivers and mountains to provide the basic scaffolding, and then introduced pictorial elements to indicate Russian cities, fortified outposts, native settlements, and natural features of the landscape. Remezov abjured use of scale or precise direction, providing instead a functional itinerary, indicating which river to follow and which branch to take to a specific endpoint. Annotations on the maps augmented their practical application. Distances between set points might be indicated in *versts*[47] or days and nights. Travel between one outpost and another would take three days by ship or ten days on land. Travel to another destination would take a week by river and would be impossible by land. Although Remezov's atlases were not published until centuries later and survived as unique exemplars, he created them with the idea that they could be of practical use to travellers crossing Siberia's endless landscape. In the terms of this volume, although it is difficult to trace direct avenues of communication and dissemination, his hand-drawn atlases nonetheless both drew on and influenced a lively Eurasian exchange of critical geographic information.

Circuitous Borrowing: Information Flows and Communication in the Clandestine World of Early Modern Cartography

The familiar themes of cartographic secrecy and clandestine exchange that we have encountered before run through the story of Siberian mapping as well. The Godunov map, for instance, survives not only in the multiple copies by Remezov but also in at least three separate copies smuggled out by foreign diplomats. A recent book by Postnikov and Falk catalogues the circulation of the Godunov map through unlawful back channels. Lieutenant Colonel Fritz Cronman, Swedish ambassador to Muscovy, purloined a copy when he was in Moscow in February 1667. Cronman wrote to his monarch, Charles XI, "The map of all these Siberian lands up to China, which recently was sent here

---

47 A *verst* is roughly equivalent to a kilometre; see Chapters 5 and 11 for more information.

on His Majesty's orders by Tobolsk commander Godunov, was shown me and having received permission to keep it over night, I copied it". Cronman's countryman Claes Johanssen Prytz made another copy. In his report on his mission, Prytz wrote, "The appended land map of Siberia and adjacent lands I copied 8 January 1669 from a poorly preserved original which was loaned to me for a few hours by Prince Ivan Alekseevich Vorotynskii on the condition that I may examine it but under no circumstances copy it".[48] The report makes one wonder if the prince issued his warning with a knowing wink, creating for himself a cover of plausible deniability.

The Swedes were particularly assiduous and particularly successful in their efforts to obtain secret cartographic documents, but they were not the only ones who reported access to the Godunov map. Nicholas Witsen, a Dutchman with extensive experience in Moscow and with highly placed contacts at court, also obtained a copy of the Godunov map, together with a map of Novaia Zemblia, from one of those Kremlin insiders. Witsen with some pride wrote that he had "assembled volumes of diaries and notes in which are the names of mountains, rivers, cities and towns, together with a magnitude of drawings executed by my order".[49] In 1991 Postnikov identified the *Carte générale de la Sibierie et la Grande Tartaria*, a French map in the collection of the Newberry Library in Chicago, as a copy of a Russian original drawn in the mode of the Godunov map, dating to the late 1670s or early 1680s.[50]

The spiral of creation and copying, the back and forth between Russians and foreigners, continued apace throughout the century. An updated version of the Godunov map enjoyed a similar international transmission. Postnikov and Falk say this map was composed under the auspices of Metropolitan Kornelii in Tobolsk in 1673. It bears a close resemblance to Remezov's *Map of All Siberia*, although the dynamics of the relationship remain unclear. It survives in at least three copies.

---

48 Postnikov and Falk, *Exploring and Mapping Alaska*, p. 19.
49 *Ibid.* Witsen's source was Stanislav Loputskii, described by Postnikov and Falk as "an artist at the court of Tsar Alexei Mikhailovich". Witsen created his own quite extraordinary map of Siberia. See Johannes Keuning, 'Nicolaas Witsen as a Cartographer', *Imago Mundi*, 11 (1954), 95–110.
50 Newberry Library, Chicago, 'Carte générale de la Siberie et de la Grande Tatarie', in Cartes Marines, Edward Everett Ayer Collection; discussed in A. V. Postnikov, 'Russian Cartographic Treasures of the Newberry Library', *Mapline*, 61–62 (1991), 6–8.

The sole extant Russian version has annotations in both Russian and Latin, suggesting the cooperation of locals and foreigners. The Swedish representative Eric Palmquist managed to make a copy in that same year, as did his countryman Johann Gabriel Sparwenfeld, another Swedish *chargé d'affaires* who spent time in Moscow as part of a later mission. Palmquist collected a valuable set of documents pertaining to Russia, "among them sixteen geographic maps and plans of cities, including the general Siberian charts of 1667 and 1673". He echoed the earlier reports of the covert nature of his work, stressing the "effort and difficulties" involved, and he wrote that "I personally observed and drew maps in various places, risking my life, and also received information from Russian subjects in return for money".[51] The foreigners' reports confirm both the obstacles and the possibilities of obtaining maps and geographic information from Russia, and incorporating that knowledge into their own pictures of the world.

Adding more evidence of covert borrowings and circulation, Bagrow identified a German manuscript map entitled *Abzeichnung der gantzen Nord- und Ost- gegend von den Moschovischen grentzen durch Sibirien biss zu dem grossen Reich Kitai sonst China* at the Westdeutsche Bibliothek, Marburg/Lahn, as a copy of Remezov's *Map of All Siberia*, indicating another mysterious incident of copying and transportation, perhaps smuggling, of this hand-drawn translation.[52] All of these cloak-and-dagger escapades show that the highly classified Godunov map and its later derivatives were hotly sought after in Europe. In spite of the close guard kept on the manuscript exemplars, maps of Siberia escaped the confines of Muscovite control and circulated in a broader world of cartographic information.

Information flowed in multiple directions. At the same time that Europeans obtained classified maps through subterfuge, bribery, and friendship and set them loose in manuscript and in print abroad,

---

51 Postnikov and Falk, *Exploring and Mapping Alaska*, 19. See also Leo Bagrow, 'Sparwenfeld's Map of Siberia', *Imago Mundi*, 4 (1947), foldout plate following p. 68; J. G. *Sparwenfeld's Diary of a Journey to Russia 1684–1687*, ed. by U. Birgegard (Stockholm: Kungl. Vitterhets Historie och Antikvitets Akademien, 2002); and Erich Palmquist, *Zametki o Rossii, sdelannye Ėrikom Pal'mkvistom v 1674 godu*, ed. by Anatolii Sekerin and Gennadii Kovalenko, English trans. by Martin Naylor (Moscow: Lomonosov, 2012).

52 The German version is reproduced in Bagrow, 'Remezov', pp. 124–25.

Muscovites followed developments in Western cartography with considerable interest. The tsars' libraries and those of the Diplomatic and Siberian Chanceries acquired editions of the first world atlases published by Abraham Ortelius and Gerhard Mercator in the late sixteenth century and the somewhat later (first edition 1635) atlas produced by the father-son team Willem and Joan Blaeu, along with editions of Miechowita and other works imported from Poland. Appetite for geographic compendia was apparently not confined to the court. From the 1630s on, atlases became among the most popular and widely copied translated texts in Russia. Partial translations into Russian of several European "cosmographies", geographic histories of the world, demonstrate significant interest in keeping up with Western scholarship and technology, although most were left incomplete and none were published in the seventeenth century.[53] Omissions and amendments, particularly in the sections devoted to Muscovy itself, demonstrate active engagement with these imported sources. The first four volumes of the Blaeu atlas were translated from various editions into Russian between 1655 and 1657. According to N. A. Kazakova, the section on Muscovy is left as blank pages in Russian translations of Blaeu, suggesting that the treatment of the motherland required special consideration and was perhaps a bit too hot to handle.[54]

The path of borrowing zigzags between Russia and Europe, with each iteration informing subsequent productions. Herberstein's story epitomises the dizzying geographic and cartographic exchanges that

---

53 S. M. Gluskina, '"Kosmografiia" 1637 goda kak russkaia pererabotka "Atlasa" Merkatora', in *Geograficheskii sbornik*, 3 (Moscow-Leningrad, 1954), pp. 79–99; N. A. Kazakova, 'Russkii perevod XVII v. truda Blau "Theatrum Orbis Terrarum sive Atlas Novus"', *Vospomogatel'nye istoricheskie distsipliny*, 17 (1986), pp. 161–78; idem., 'Russkii perevod XVII v. "Theatrum Orbis Terrarum" A. Orteliia', *Vospomogatel'nye istoricheskie distsipliny*, 18 (1987), 121–31; B. E. Raikov, *Ocherki po istorii geliotsentricheskogo mirovozzreniia v Rossii* (Moscow-Leningrad, 1947), pp. 79–90.

54 Kazakova, 'Russkii perevod XVII v. truda Blau', p. 169. On the translations, see also Francis J. Thomson, 'Slavonic Translations Available in Muscovy: The Cause of Old Russia's Intellectual Silence and a Contributing Factor to Muscovite Cultural Autarky', in *Christianity and the Eastern Slavs*, vol. I: *Slavic Cultures in the Middle Ages*, ed. by B. Gasparov, Olga Raevsky-Hughes, California Slavic Studies 16 (Berkeley and Los Angeles: University of California Press, 1993), pp. 193–94; p. 212, n. 211. For an account of the sources of early European cosmographic treatments of Russia, see Marshall T. Poe, 'Muscovy in European Cosmographies, 1517–1544', *Russian History/Histoire Russe*, 25. 1–2 (1998), 89–106.

characterised this period. Herberstein, the Habsburg envoy, drew on information provided by a Russian court translator (Gregory Istoma), a Russian diplomat (by the name of Dmitrii Gerasimov), and a defector from Muscovy to Lithuania (Ivan Liatskoi) among others. Their reports informed Herberstein's geographic account and dictated the contours of the map cut by Augustin Hirsvogel in Vienna. Mercator's atlas, which incorporated Herberstein's description of Russia along with his map, brought the Habsburg envoy's impressions back to Muscovy, where they would resonate in Russians' self-descriptions and serve as a source of information about their own religion and practice for centuries to come.[55]

The case, I hope, has been made here that, despite the apparent paucity of cartographic information of any scientific or utilitarian value, the inherent limits on communication in a manuscript culture, and the deliberate obstruction of knowledge transfer, actual practices of mapping and flow of information overturn those initial assumptions. From the sixteenth century onward, Russians and Europeans participated jointly in an energetic exercise in collecting, recording and circulating practical geographic knowledge and maps.

Remezov's Maps: Information, Exchange, and the Strategic Value of Russian *Chertezhi*

As a closing example, I return to Semen Remezov, the Siberian cartographer who worked in Tobolsk in the late seventeenth and early eighteenth century. He has been described as the last great representative of a purely Muscovite cartographic tradition, the "swan-song" of an uncontaminated indigenous Russian cartography.[56]

Yet Remezov exemplifies the very pattern of ecumenical collection and dissemination of information that we have traced to this point. Enjoying one of the very first state-funded research leaves in Russian history, Remezov benefited from exposure to Western publications during the three months he spent in Moscow studying imported European

---

55 Irena Gross, 'The Tangled Tradition: Custine, Herberstein, Karamzin and the Critique of Russia', *Slavic Review*, 50 (1991), 989–98.

56 Postnikov, *Russia in Maps*, p. 24.

maps and cosmographical atlases, mostly of Dutch provenance, in the archives and libraries of the Kremlin. He appreciated all that he learned, and once back in Tobolsk, he penned enthusiastic descriptions of the wonders of the magnetic compass, of the linear scale, and of the all the "clever sciences" on offer in Europe.[57] He tested his skill in reproducing foreign maps, creating splendid copies by hand. In one atlas he included a copy of Blaeu's 1635 "Tataria sive magni Chami imperium", complete with longitude and latitude lines, camels and turbaned Muslims in the cartouches, and devils and dragons populating the "Lop Desert" just outside the Great Wall of China. He also copied a Polish map, probably a version of Anthony Jenkinson's 1562 map, complete with its Polish title and an image of the mythological Zlata Baba, Golden Woman, in the far Northeast corner.[58] Marina Tolmacheva notes wryly that Remezov's goal in copying these European maps of Siberia was "to present the state of knowledge prevailing elsewhere, which is frankly estimated at *nemnogo* ('not much')".[59]

In spite of his familiarity with the latest cartographic works from Amsterdam and elsewhere, Remezov maintained many of the techniques familiar from the Russian mapping traditions examined here. Although Remezov's small scale maps of large territories were usually oriented to the South with cardinal directions noted in the Western style, Daniel C. Waugh observes that his "large scale, detailed [maps]… most often were oriented to take full advantage of the largest (horizontal) dimension of a rectangular sheet of paper. This enabled him to follow rivers along their entire length, for indeed, as with the Book of the Great Map, the basic structure for what we might term Remezov's practical or functional maps and atlases was river routes".[60] Almost any page from his *Khorograficheskaia chertezhnaia kniga*, an atlas of sketches of small sections of Siberia, exemplifies this observation nicely. A map of

---

57 Remezov, *Sluzhebnaia chertezhnaia kniga*, fol. 12 ('Do laskovago chitatelia'); Remezov, *Khorograficheskaia kniga*, ff. 8v-9.
58 Remezov, *Sluzhebnaia chertezhnaia kniga*, fols. 22v-23 (includes Zlata Baba); fol. 107, 'Chertezh zemli khanskago velichestva', with cartouches, vignettes, and Latin labels. See also Remezov, *Khorograficheskaia kniga*, f.v., two-hemisphere map.
59 Tolmacheva, 'Early Russian Exploration and Mapping of the Chinese Frontier', p. 50.
60 Daniel C. Waugh, 'The View from the North: Muscovite Cartography of Inner Asia', *Journal of Asian History*, 49 (2015), 69–96, quote on p. 82.

a segment of the Tura River, for instance, accommodates the rivers to fit to the horizontal width of the page.⁶¹

Figure 16: Map of a segment of the Tura River, from S. U. Remezov's *Working Sketch Book*.

The paper is marked with a grid, but one used to guide the artist rather than to indicate scientifically measured position.

"Even though Remezov's maps were not composed according to the rules of Western-European cartography", Kees Boterbloem writes, "their exquisite rendering of Siberia made it undoubtedly much more feasible to traverse its vastness for travellers and to asses the extent of their domination for Russian administrators".⁶² Remezov's approach was pragmatic and suited to communicating important information about relative location.

---

61 Remezov, *Khorograficheskaia kniga*, f. 48.
62 Kees Boterbloem, *Modernizer of Russia: Andrei Vinius, 1641–1716* (Houndsmills, Basingstoke, Hampshire: Palgrave Macmillan, 2013), p. 166. Some scholars note a similarity with Chinese mapping. See Fedchina, 'Central Asia on Russian Maps of the Seventeenth Century', 104; Waugh, 'View from the North', p. 82; Tolmacheva, 'Early Russian Exploration and Mapping of the Chinese Frontier', pp. 41–56. For a pair of maps by Kalmyk cartographers of the eighteenth century, displaying yet another cartographic imaginary, see Nicholas Poppe, 'Renat's Kalmuck Maps', *Imago Mundi*, 12 (1955), 155–59. The maps are viewable online at http://goran.baarnhielm.net/Renat/index.html

The state agencies in Moscow understood the value of the maps of Siberia that Remezov produced, and they hounded him to send them the products of his work. Foreigners also tried to secure copies for publication in the West. The manuscript original of his *Sketch-book of Siberia* (*Chertezhnaia kniga*) testifies to this shared interest. All the labels appear in both Russian and Dutch. Most scholars agree that Dutch was added under the auspices of Andrei Vinius, the Russian-born son of a Dutch merchant, who served the tsarist state in various important capacities: as a diplomat, as postmaster, as head of the Apothecary Chancery, and, most relevant, as head of the Siberian Chancery. Vinius likely worked with Remezov to prepare the *Sketch-book* for publication abroad, but the plan never reached fruition. Various scenarios have been proposed: Vinius intended to smuggle the atlas out of the country but was caught, or, alternatively, he had a licence to publish it abroad.

In a study of Vinius, Botterbloem suggests a different reading: "one wonders whether Vinius was annotating the maps to dispatch a Dutch copy to [his second cousin, the Dutch statesman, merchant, and scholar Nicholaes] Witsen, in order to help his cousin fine-tune the second edition of his *Noord- en Ost-Tatarien*".[63] Witsen had published his own treatise on Muscovy and Tataria, this same *Noord- en Ost-Tatarien*, in 1690, including a map, probably modelled on originals by Remezov, Vinius, or both. As presented by Witsen, the map maintains a Muscovite Southern orientation but adds for the first time a geographic grid, though still one that is purely symbolic rather than carrying geodesic meaning.[64]

If we follow the path of borrowing and circulation further, it grows even more tortuous. Bagrow describes a head-spinning circuit of exchange and transmission, syncopated with blockages and censorship, around the publication of these late-seventeenth-century Siberian maps. In 1698, Bagrow tells us, Vinius befriended the Austrian ambassador to Moscow, Gvarienti, and in September of the following year, Vinius sent Gvarienti a map of Siberia, presumably his own or one of Remezov's, with the proposition that his friend should publish it. The plan came to naught, and a few years later, Vinius was convicted of accepting bribes and fell from grace. Bagrow intimates (on the basis of nothing more

---

63 Boterbloem, *Modernizer of Russia*, p. 166.
64 Postnikov and Falk, *Exploring and Mapping Alaska*, p. 9; Bagrow, 'Remezov', p. 125.

than coincidental timing) that his disgrace may have had something to do with the Remezov atlas that he had so assiduously patronised and then annotated.[65]

The whirl of names and whiff of scandal that cling to Bagrow's description confirm the central findings of this survey of early Russian maps. Neither the restrictive regime of secrecy nor the fact that Muscovite maps existed only in manuscript form prevented the circulation of geographic knowledge. Moreover, despite the absence of advanced scientific measurement techniques, Muscovites commanded significant knowledge of their tsardom's terrain. However naïve in rendition, Muscovite *chertezhi*, on both local and grand scale, were rich in valuable geographic information, and, as such, became tactical assets, objects of forbidden desire. They were sought after, bought, smuggled, adapted, and published abroad, while Muscovite mapmakers in turn incorporated foreign geographic ideas into their own work, participating in a vibrant web of information exchange.

The history of mapping in early modern Russia shows a state "more rather than less open to foreign infiltration, more rather than less tolerant of cultural hybridity and textual circulation".[66] Intensely interested in geographic and ethnographic knowledge, Muscovites gathered, recorded, sorted, and mapped information cobbled together from multifarious sources, ranging from their own active observations and measurements, to reports from an international cast of interlocutors, to published treatises. Their communication network ranged from China to England, and swept in any potential informants in between. Communication, as is its wont, went in all directions. The secretive Muscovite regime, despite its efforts at controlling the message, participated in a world of lively exchange of information. As Afinogenov aptly observes, "Muscovy still has the ability to surprise us, both with the unexpected inventiveness of its intelligence-gathering practices and with the unintentional—and eagerly-exploited—porosity of the apparatus that was meant to keep them secret".[67]

---

65   Bagrow, 'Remezov', pp. 124–25.
66   Afinogenov, 'Eye of the Tsar', p. 32.
67   *Ibid.*, p. 34.

2. New Technology and the Mapping of Empire: The Adoption of the Astrolabe

Aleksei Golubinskii[1]

In the eighteenth century, interest in and the intensification of support for science became a part of everyday life in the courts of Europe. Russia, too, was caught up in a fascination with science from the Petrine era onwards. Besides scientific exchange, signs of scientific interest were apparent in a variety of areas of Russian life, from the introduction of new ideas, books, and instruments, to the systematic invitation of foreign scientists and academics to act as consultants, advisors, and teachers.[2] As a result, Russia's role in international affairs became more pronounced, and the representation of Russian territories became increasingly important for geographers both in Russia and abroad.[3] To a notable extent the achievements of the St Petersburg Academy of Sciences in the interrelated fields of geography and astronomy contributed to this. The links between the scientific communities in

---

1   Translated by Elizabeth Harrison.
2   See, Anthony Cross, *By the Banks of the Neva. Chapters from the Lives and Careers of the British in Eighteenth-Century Russia* (Cambridge: Cambridge University Press, 1997); *Frantsuzy v nauchnoi i intellektual'noi zhizni Rossii XVIII–XX vv.*, ed. A. O. Chubarian, F.-D. Lishtenan (Moscow: OLMA Media Group, 2010).
3   See Leo Bagrow, *History of Cartography*, 2 vols, ed. by Henry W. Castner (Wolfe Island, ON: The Walker Press, 1975); V. F. Gnucheva, *Geograficheskii departament Akademii nauk XVIII veka* (Moscow: Izd-vo AN SSSR, 1946).

the Russian Empire and abroad stabilised, but, at the same time, were shaped by external political affairs.[4]

As this chapter will discuss, the purchase of British astrolabes[5] by the Russian Empire demonstrates non-commercial international cooperation during the period when the signing of the Westminster Treaty in 1756 had significantly complicated relations between Russia and Great Britain. While the details of Russia's procurement of complex technology during this period have not as yet attracted the sustained attention of historians, this case study is a key episode in the "scientific" turn in Russian cartography, which follows on from Valerie Kivelson's study of pre-modern mapping techniques in the previous chapter of this volume. As this chapter demonstrates, the introduction of geodesic astrolabes, first from abroad, then through local manufacture, enabled the modern mapping of empire in the eighteenth and nineteenth centuries. Astrolabes were essential to determine directions (angles) accurately and to calculate areas. They enabled Russian and European cartographers to produce relatively precise maps. Accurate mapping was of interest not only to geographers but also to astronomers, physicists, biologists and ethnographers, indeed to all who espoused the

---

4   M. Iu. Anisimov, 'Rossiia v sisteme mezhdunarodnykh otnoshenii v 1749–56 gg.' (Kand. dissertation, Institut rossiiskoi istorii RAN, 2005); L. M. Grankov, 'Morskoi torgovyi flot i vneshnetorgovaia politika Rossii, XVIII–pervaia polovina XX vv: istoricheskii aspekt issledovaniia' (Kand. dissertation, Rossiiskaia ekonomicheskaia akademiia, 2009). With Great Britain: M. Iu. Rodzinskaia, 'Russko-angliiskie otnosheniia v shestidesiatykh godakh XVIII v.', in *Trudy Moskovskogo gosudarstvennogo istoriko-arkhivnogo instituta*, 21 (1965), pp. 241-69; Iu. S. Medvedev, 'Russko-angliiskie otnosheniia v seredine XVIII veka (1748–63)' (Kand. dissertation, Rossiiskii universitet druzhby narodov, 2004). With France: E. E. El'ts, 'Franko-russkie kul'turnye sviazi vo vtoroi polovine XVIII v.' (Kand. dissertation, Sankt-Peterburgskii gosudarstvennyi universitet, 2007). With the Netherlands: I. V. Kolosova, 'Formirovanie i razvitie otnoshenii mezhdu Rossiiskoi imperiei i Niderlandami: XVIII–I polovina XIX v.' (Kand. dissertation, Diplomaticheskaia akademiia MID Rossii, 2007).

5   The "astrolabes" in this chapter are surveying instruments, not planispheric astrolabes. This is consistent with Russian terminology (*astroliabiia*) from the eighteenth century onwards. We retain the terminology, although the relevant instruments might also be designated in English as circumferentors, or semi-circumferentors, or graphometers. See W. F. Ryan, 'Some Observations on the History of the Astrolabe and of Two Russian Words: *astroljabija* and *matka*', in *Studies in Slavic Linguistics and Poetics in Honor of Boris O. Unbegaun* (New York and London: New York University Press and University of London Press Ltd., 1968), pp. 155–61. The editors are grateful to Professor Ryan for his advice on the term.

encyclopedic approach to scholarship that was typical of the eighteenth century. Precise representation of territory helped to enhance the orderliness of territorial administration and provided better information for use at the state level.

The production of astrolabes was quite knowledge-intensive. It required high-quality raw materials (metal and wood), a well developed manufacturing culture, precise measuring instruments, and well trained staff. In order for astrolabes to be produced in Russia in large quantities, improvements were needed in all these areas. The processes through which astrolabes were in the first instance acquired from abroad, and then manufactured in Russia, stand as an example of international exchange and of the adoption of technical expertise in an important area of information technology.

The Russian Imperial procurement of astrolabes from abroad made possible the creation of the largest government project to describe the territories of the Russian Empire, the Russian General Land Survey, which commenced from the middle of the eighteenth century. Over the course of the survey, six hundred thousand maps were produced in the scale 1:8400, as well as a total of more than 1.3 million documents. Generalised maps of Russia created on the basis of these maps began to filter into the West, and became the first relatively sound evidence for the actual configuration of land in Northeast Eurasia.

Attempts to carry out a universal survey of Russia's territories had also taken place in the first quarter of the eighteenth century. However, this survey still depended on mapping instruments inherited from the seventeenth century, which were not up to the standard required in the new era. Thus, during the Petrine period, the Academy of Sciences in St Petersburg began to attract foreign scholars who could help to introduce a modern culture of science.[6] Among them was the French astronomer and geographer Joseph-Nicolas Delisle. His name and that of Senate Ober-Secretary I. K. Kirilov are linked with the first attempts to create generalised (that is small-scale, general) maps of Russia. Among Delisle's proposals was the greater use of astronomical observations in order to increase the accuracy in defining geographical coordinates, and a wider distribution of instrumental land surveys. His work also

---

6 See G. N. Teterin, *Istoriia goedezii v Rossii (do 1917 g.)* (Novosibirsk: NIIGAiK, 1992).

included the creation of new instruments, for which the French master of instruments Pierre Vignon was brought to Russia along with Delisle.

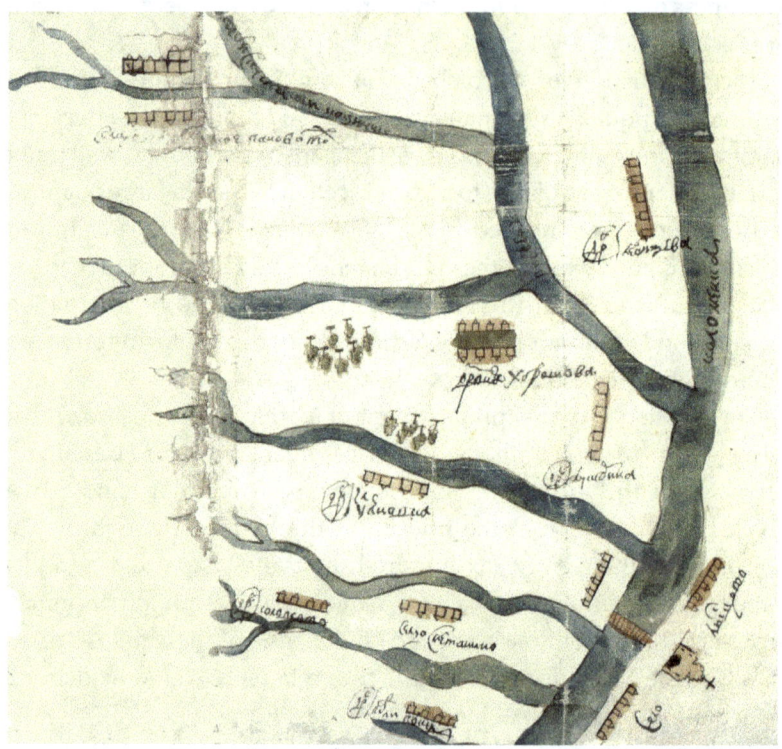

Figure 1: Plan of 1699 of the environs of Kolomna. Fragment.[7]

Towards the middle of the century, the demand for maps of Russia was so great that there was international competition for the rights to astronomical and geographical data on the Russian Empire. The publication of material about Delisle's new geographic data precipitated a scandal since publication had been expressly forbidden by the Senate. In 1752 Delisle prepared a new map of Russian exploration that included

---

[7] RGADA, coll. 1209, descr. 77, file 25186. For more detail about maps in the seventeenth century, see Valerie Kivelson, *Cartographies of Tsardom. The Land and its Meanings in Seventeenth-Century Russia* (Ithaca and London: Cornell University Press, 2006).

the results of his first and second Kamchatka expeditions.[8] G. F. Müller, one of the academicians of the Academy of Science in St Petersburg, was ordered, under threat of dismissal, to compose a "thorough refutation" for foreign journals and to concentrate on publishing new maps as soon as possible—both a general map and various specialised maps—taking into account the latest discoveries, of which Delisle could not know. Leonhard Euler, also a distinguished member of the Academy, was forced to distribute this letter to various scientific journals under threat of being deprived of his pension.[9] Another example of such competitiveness occurred in relation to a discussion of the fourth volume of *Novi Commentarii Academiae Scientiarum Imperialis Petropolitanae*, the official periodical publication of the St Petersburg Academy of Sciences. A. N. Grishov, the director of the Astronomical Observatory, requested the early publication of his research into the parallax of the moon according to observations from St Petersburg in 1752 and the coinciding observations at the Cape of Good Hope, so that French scholars could not beat Russian scientists to it.[10]

In view of this situation, the Russian government began to turn its own attention to surveying. However, in addition to knowledge of how to make accurate measurements of the land, instruments themselves were required. Among these, the most important was the astrolabe, the device required for measuring angles and hence for producing calculations which are crucial for defining boundaries between pieces of land.[11] Astrolabes may have appeared in Russia long before the era of Peter the Great, but they achieved comparatively widespread use during his reign. The first specimens of seventeenth-century astrolabes that appeared in Russia most likely resembled that illustrated in Figure 2:

---

8   J.-N. Delisle, *Explication de la carte des nouvelles découvertes au Nord de la Mer du Sud* (Paris, 1752).
9   *Letopis' rossiiskoi Akademii Nauk* (St Petersburg: Nauka, 2001), p. 406.
10   *Ibid.*, p. 421.
11   T. V. Il'iushina, 'Ot bussoli do astroliabii', in *Nauka v Rossii*, 3 (2007), 97–101; V. S. Kusov, *Izmerenie zemli: Istoriia geodezicheskikh instrumentov* (Moscow: Dizain. Informatsiia. Kartographiia, 2009).

Figure 2: A universal astrolabe (semicircumferentor) with compass. Manufactured in the middle of the seventeenth century.[12]

The type and precise specification of astrolabes used for carrying out the General Land Survey is unknown. No examples of surveying equipment from the first half of the eighteenth century have been preserved either in the collections of the Moscow State University of Geodesy and Cartography, or in the Military-Historical Museum of Artillery, Engineer and Signal Corps in St Petersburg. The impression of what astrolabes of the period looked like is based on drawings found on the decorative borders of maps of Russian districts (*uezdy*) and towns.

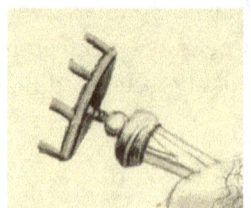  

Figure 3: Depiction of astrolabes (circumferentors) on the maps of the General Land Survey.[13]

---

12   *Rossiia i Gollandiia: Prostranstvo vzaimodeistviia, XVI–pervaia tret' XIX veka* (Moscow: Kuchkovo pole, 2013), p. 311.

13   *Plan of the city of Tver with its villages*, RGADA, coll. 1356, descr. 1, file 6057; *Plan of the city of Vesegonsk with its villages*, RGADA, coll. 1356, descr. 1, file 6027; Plan of Tver province, RGADA, coll. 1356, descr. 1, file 5949.

2. New Technology and the Mapping of Empire: The Adoption of the Astrolabe 65

In the first instance the astrolabe is depicted in profile, and the two other examples show that the astrolabe with compass was used, i.e. the type that could produce a measurement not only of angles between two lines, but also in relation to the position of the earth.[14]

Before the beginning of the General Land Survey, there was not enough equipment to carry out the project. For the creation of a full equipage of astrolabes and to assist the studies of future surveyors, four astrolabes and measuring chains were purchased by the Admiralty College (*Admiralteistv-Kollegiia*) in 1754.[15] At first astrolabes were bought to Moscow to the Provincial Office of Surveying, and afterwards were placed at the Admiralty school.[16]

Figure 4: The Surveying Process. Two surveyors, armed with an astrolabe, apparently corresponding to those imported from England, measure the boundaries between plots of land. The head of the surveying party (with a sword) looks at the astrolabe and his assistant with a field notebook adjusts it. On their left is a man with a cane (the attorney of the landowner) and in the left corner of the picture is a peasant with a measuring chain ten fathoms in length. Fragment of a map of Iaroslavl Province.[17]

---

14 This is confirmed by the fact that on the plans and field notes, angles between two lines are fixed, as is the direction of the line in relation to the points of the compass.
15 Twenty-two rubles and forty-eight kopeks per astrolabe. RGADA, coll. 248, descr. 82, file 6740, fol. 1258 and 1258a; file 5949.
16 RGADA, coll. 248, descr. 82, file 6740, fol. 1264.
17 *Map of Iaroslavl Province*, RGADA, coll. 1356, descr. 1, file 6735.

At the same time, the question arose of Russian and foreign involvement in the production of astrolabes. Initially, in May 1754, the Senate sent the Academy of Sciences and the Admiralty College an order to manufacture two hundred astrolabes.[18] It was clear that the Russian makers of astrolabes could not keep up with demand, so the only solution was to turn to makers abroad. The Russian ambassador in London, Count P. G. Chernyshev, received an order (*ukaz*): "we must get a hundred astrolabes without spirit levels from England [...] with geodesic instruments", and "having bought the requested geodesic instruments, send them here at once at the Crown's expense".[19] The reference to geodesic instruments in the first message refers to both astrolabes and measuring chains, but, as became apparent later, with regard to chains, the Russian makers could achieve the required volume manufacture on their own. Emphasising the urgency of the work, the Senate added: "And if the one hundred astrolabes required cannot be bought at once, then buy as many as you can now, and the rest later, but buy them as soon as possible, because they are extremely necessary and their absence from this summer's delivery has meant that in Moscow Province the surveyors have had to halt work".[20]

Were the astrolabes that had been ordered up to standard with the current level of technological development? In answering this question, it is necessary to say that in France at roughly the same time, the same type of instruments were in general use. These were distinguished by their simplicity, and the absence of additional elements such as a spyglass or telescope, for example. The most necessary accessory to the astrolabe was a compass, which had been requested in order to increase the accuracy of measurements.[21]

In the Academy of Sciences, three astrolabes were already nearly finished. Immediately after their completion at the Academy, the Senate paid two hundred rubles to increase production.[22] Metal for the astrolabes was ordered from the director of the Schlisselburg copper

---

18   RGADA, coll. 248, descr. 82, file 6740, fol. 1231.
19   RGADA, coll. 248, descr. 82, file 6740, fol. 1306.
20   RGADA, coll. 248, descr. 82, file 6740, fol. 1305.
21   Il'iushina, 'Ot bussoli do astroliabii', p. 101.
22   RGADA, coll. 248, descr. 82, file 6740, fol. 1268. See also: P. P. Papkovskii, *Iz istorii geodezii, topografii i kartografii v Rossii* (Moscow: Nauka, 1983); Kusov, *Izmerenie zemli*.

factory, Franz Ludwig Popp. Having agreed to make the astrolabes in the rough, i.e. without wooden parts (oak or palm wood) and without detailed finishing touches, he asked that for every *pood* (approx. 16.3 kilograms), he be given eleven rubles and ninety kopeks for all large-scale detail and sixteen rubles each for fine finishing detail.

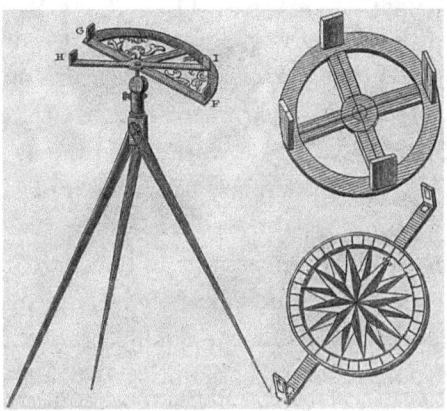

Figure 5: Engraving from *Recueil de planches sur les sciences, les arts libéraux et les arts méchaniques* (1765–72).[23]

Further work on the astrolabes, including the addition of wooden parts, occurred at the Academy of Sciences. The government's perception of the order's importance can be seen in the speed of payment: the instruments were paid for from the Treasury (the College of State Expenses—*Shtats-Kontor-Kollegiia*) almost at once.[24] As a result of such urgency, the manufacturers had to make the simplest instruments with dioptras [a surveying tool originating in the ancient world], omitting any telescopic elements.[25]

Almost immediately the problem of a lack of skilled personnel became apparent. The Academy did not have sufficient engineers with the necessary qualifications. An order from this period reads, "Due to the lack in the Academy of the type of craftsmen skilled in making scientific instruments, send Filip Tiriutin to other institutions so he can seek out those capable of this type of work, and investigate those he

---

23 *Artistes de la carte de la Renaissance au XXIe siècle* (Paris: Autrement, 2012), p. 85.
24 RGADA, coll. 248, descr. 82, file 6740, fol. 1278. On July 20, 2,120 rubles were paid.
25 *Ibid.*

finds with a level of skill and availability; moreover, he should seek out free craftsmen, and reach an agreement with them at the chancery about the price per item and set them to work".[26] The team of workers was gathered from many government institutions, "Tiriutin's apprentices made a report to the office of the Academy of Sciences declaring that they found qualified workers in state positions to help make astrolabes, specifically: in the main artillery, the instrument-maker Aleksei Dmitriev; the two coppersmiths, the Spiridon Kukin brothers; in the Naval Academy, the instrument maker Grigorii Mogilev, and the turner Petr Spalskoi".[27] Those working on the astrolabes were not permitted days off, and by January 1755 twenty-four astrolabes had been completed.[28]

Meanwhile the Russian Ambassador to London, Chernyshev, wrote that "...although I have continuously visited a large quantity of London mathematical experts famous for the quality of their work, [...] I have not found a corresponding number of finished astrolabes and additional instruments".[29] It became clear that sending the pieces from London that year as ordered would not work. The distribution of orders between different craftsmen did not help. The timely dispatch of the astrolabes was also an important issue in light of the late thawing of ice in the port of St Petersburg. Delays for this and other logistical reasons were entirely possible, so Chernyshev suggested that they be sent "to Hamburg, Lübeck or Danzig by water, and shipped from there to St Petersburg over dry land, since by this method they may arrive by the beginning of the following spring".[30] Another reason to hasten the delivery was the absence of customs duties, which occurred with other government deliveries and even sometimes in cases of private procurement in which the state was particularly interested.[31] Insufficient financial means was also an obstacle to the speedy fulfilment of the order: the initial deposit

---

26 *Ibid.*
27 RGADA, coll. 248, descr. 82, file 6740, fol. 1278v.
28 RGADA, coll. 248, descr. 82, file 6741, fol. 22.
29 RGADA, coll. 248, descr. 82, file 6740, fol. 1308.
30 RGADA, coll. 248, descr. 82, file 6740, fol. 1308v.
31 The same policy was carried out from the reign of Peter I in relation to private apothecaries (in the beginning of the Petrine era medicines were without customs duties, then duties began to be paid through the Apothecary Chancery). See M. B. Mirskii, *Ocherki istorii meditsiny v Rossii XVI–XVIII vv.* (Vladikavkaz: Goskomizdat RSD-A, 1995), pp. 42, 64.

2. New Technology and the Mapping of Empire: The Adoption of the Astrolabe 69

"of a thousand rubles from the College of Foreign Affairs for the transfer still require[d] a bit less than twice that sum".[32]

In July 1755 a discussion took place in the Senate about which method of delivery to choose. The State Surveyor General-in-Chief and Cavalryman Count Petr Ivanovich Shuvalov said that importing one hundred astrolabes from England together with the Øresund customs duty (for passage across the Strait of Øresund) would cost twenty-one rubles and sixty-seven and a quarter kopeks for each, while the astrolabes made in the Academy of Sciences cost around forty rubles apiece. In connection with this, he suggested the Academy of Sciences should not make any more astrolabes, apart from finishing those on which work had already begun.[33] As a result, the idea of ordering another nine hundred astrolabes from England came about, but "to send as many as can be found in parts and prepared without making known the full number required… so that they will not increase the price".[34]

The new Ambassador to England, A. M. Golitsyn, wrote that "the craftsmen there do not at present have the finished astrolabes, and they cannot complete even a small proportion of them for dispatch by the maritime route. The contracts signed with them stipulate that all the astrolabes should be made with the appropriate protractors; that they be of the same quality and in the same working order as those that were previously sent from there; and that they should not cost more than the previous price, that is, four pounds and ten shillings sterling each; that these craftsmen should produce a total of one hundred and thirty astrolabes per month; thus it is expected that all nine hundred should be ready by April of 1756".[35] The total cost of the contract stood at 20,773 rubles and forty kopeks and was paid by the Treasury from a sum which had been designated for "emergency expenditure".[36]

In order to imagine the magnitude of this sum, we can turn to a contemporary example. Jean Armand de L'Estocq, director of the Medical Chancery during Elizabeth's reign, asked to be provided with an assistant doctor "experienced in administrative matters, for the

---

32 RGADA, coll. 248, descr. 82, file 6740, fol. 1306.
33 RGADA, coll. 248, descr. 82, file 6741, fol. 974.
34 RGADA, coll. 248, descr. 82, file 6741, fol. 974v.
35 RGADA, coll. 248, descr. 82, file 6741, fol. 1194v.
36 RGADA, coll. 248, descr. 82, file 6742, fol. 167.

administration of the office of medical affairs under my direction", and also to confirm the new budget, "an overall sum for salaries and for the maintenance of that chancery and of the pharmacies" (medicine was for the most part obtained from abroad). To cover the cost of sixty employees in St Petersburg and Moscow and other expenses, 7,431 rubles was required.[37] In another example, on 16 March 1755, the rector of Moscow University, A. M. Argamakov, said that the empress was bestowing four thousand rubles on the university library and asked the professors for advice on obtaining books. The sum of one thousand rubles was additionally to be spent on the acquisition of equipment.[38] However, despite its magnitude, the cost of the contract for the astrolabes was no more than 0.5% of English imports to Russia, so scholars who analyse export and import, dividing it into up to twenty categories, do not separate out the import of goods connected with knowledge-based technology.[39]

The precise date of the delivery of the instruments is unknown, but the report on the execution of the order, presented on 27 August 1756, includes information that "recently these astrolabes arrived".[40] The government had in vain tried to hurry Chernyshev and Golitsyn following the January 1756 signing of the Westminster Treaty by Great Britain and Prussia. Great Britain, which had been an ally of Russia for more than twenty years, thereby became its rival. Even in the period of armed conflict during the Napoleonic Wars, trade between Russia and Great Britain was maintained via so-called "licences",[41] but the threat of deliveries ceasing was very real.[42] In 1791, in connection with the Ochakov Crisis during the Russo-Turkish War, the English side laid an embargo on the sale of equipment, and problems occurred putting into

---

37 Mirskii, *Ocherki istorii meditsiny XVI–XVIII vv*, p. 94.
38 *Letopis'*, p. 426.
39 In particular, N. N. Repin, 'Vneshniaia torgovlia Rossii cherez Arkhangel'sk i Peterburg v 1700-nachale 60-kh gg XVIII v.' (Dokt. dissertation, Institut istorii SSSR (Leningradskoe otdelenie), 1986), pp. 20–21.
40 RGADA, coll. 248, descr. 82, file 6742, fol. 167–8v. This report discusses a return of 642 rubles and 6 kopeks.
41 V. G. Sirotkin, 'Kontinental'naia blokada i russkaia ekonomika (Obzor frantsuzskoi i sovetskoi literatury)', in *Voprosy voennoi istorii Rossii* (Moscow: Nauka, 1969), pp. 54–77 (p. 65).
42 On the other hand, on 29 July 1756, in the company of the president, the English envoy W. Henbury visited the Academy (See *Letopis'*, p. 440.)

operation a machine for pumping water, for which the necessary parts were lacking.⁴³

At the same time, of the two hundred astrolabes being made in the Academy of Sciences, only fifty were completed, while the remainder had only been started. The original resolution of the Senate meant the cessation of work on the unfinished devices, but in the Academy it was declared, that "the palm wood and oak, leather for the cases and other things have been bought and are already in a state of manufacture, and so it is impossible to leave the astrolabes unfinished, because otherwise the Treasury's funds will have been spent in vain…"⁴⁴ These manufacturers therefore denied the government the choice, insisting on the continuation of the work. Moreover, by this point, the price of one astrolabe had sunk by nearly a quarter: "the astrolabes being made at present at the Academy now cost thirty rubles and twenty-five kopeks apiece, including materials and labour, but that price is not final, rather it is only approximate or estimated by the manufacturers themselves, and the actual cost will become known only when all two hundred astrolabes have been completed […]".⁴⁵

When work on the General Land Survey began in 1765,⁴⁶ the Main Surveying Chancery had about twelve hundred astrolabes in its toolroom. This was more than enough for carrying out surveying work and training future surveyors. Moreover, this supply played an important role in the development of their own manufacturing capability. Apart from the manufacture of astrolabes in the Academy of Sciences, active training of personnel for manufacture of high technology had begun and skilled foreign craftsmen had already arrived as teachers. Discussing the conditions for a new contract with the Academy of Arts in 1776, the Englishman Francis Morgan spoke of his six students, who, with varying degrees of skill, might make astrolabes, electrical machines, telescopes, microscopes, or other instruments.⁴⁷ There was a growing preference for a native skills base. Among the responsibilities of the Chief Surveying Chancery was the recruitment of personnel for

---

43 Cross, *By the Banks of the Neva*, p. 245.
44 RGADA, coll. 248, descr. 82, file 6741, fol. 1236v.
45 Ibid.
46 The General Land Survey was renewed by Catherine II in 1765 after re-thinking.
47 Cross, *By the Banks of the Neva*, p. 234

future surveys. As opposed to other areas of life, where fashion was dictated by foreigners (for example, medicine),[48] the odds were at once in favour of Russian surveyors being chosen. By the end of the eighteenth century orders were being supplied by the workshop of the Academy of Sciences, headed by Ivan Petrovich Kulibin, and at the beginning of the nineteenth century the manufacture of geodesic equipment began in the Mechanical Institute of the General Staff under the direction of Kornelius Khristianovich Reissig.[49] From the middle of the nineteenth century, orders for surveying equipment were placed exclusively with Russian producers.[50] The reason was not protectionism, but that Russian firms were by then among the most advanced manufactures of surveying equipment. The leading producer was the Russian company Boelau (Gustav Boelau was a second generation Russian craftsman).[51]

As "the sole scale by which to create general maps from specialised maps",[52] a Russian-English hybrid was devised: one *sazhen* (seven feet) to an inch. It was invented by General Lieutenant William Fermor,[53] the Russian-born son of an immigrant from England, together with Ober-Secretary Glebov in the role of senate advisor. Officially the *sazhen* was introduced in 1797 as the principal unit for measuring distances, on the insistence of Charles Gascoigne, the director of the state iron foundries in Petrozavodsk, in a statute about weights and measures, and it remained the main scale in use until the survey office ceased to function as a result of the Revolution of October 1917.[54]

---

48 A. A. Golubinskii, 'Stepan Khrulev: Sud'ba zemlemera', in *Rus', Rossiia, Srednevekov'e i Novoe vremia, vypusk III, Tret'i chteniia pamiati akademika RAN L. V. Milova* (Moscow: Orgkomitet Chtenii pamiati akademika RAN L. V. Milova, 2013), pp. 404–10.
49 P. P. Papkovskii, *Iz istorii geodezii, topografii i kartografii v Rossii* (Moscow: Nauka, 1983), pp. 11–12.
50 RGADA, coll. 1294, file 40218.
51 RGIA, coll. 1350, descr. 88, file 362, fol. 1–21.
52 RGADA, coll. 248, descr. 82, file 6741, fol. 80.
53 In the very beginning of its existence, during the reign of Elizaveta Petrovna, the Chief Surveying Chancery was headed by William Fermor. See *Russkii Biographicheskii Slovar'*, vol. 21 (St Petersburg: Tip. S. N. Skorokhodova, 1901), p. 53. In 1743–44 Fermor was appointed to conduct an audit and a census, and also to survey peasant lands in St Petersburg and Ingria.
54 Cross, *By the Banks of the Neva*, p. 237.

2. New Technology and the Mapping of Empire: The Adoption of the Astrolabe 73

Figure 6: Fragment of map of the town of Klin.[55] An astrolabe with compass is visible, a measuring chain and also a scale rule in yards per inch of the type adopted by the General Land Survey.

The fates of the astrolabes that were imported to Russia were varied. The majority of them were kept in working order until 1765, the beginning of the survey under Catherine II. Until that time, the main reserve of instruments in the Senate consisted of 611 astrolabes, a quantity of measuring chains (in Moscow alone 500 were made), plus tools for technical drawing. Moreover, in the College of Estates (*Votchinnaia kollegiia*) there were 206 Russian and British astrolabes. The total of British and Russian tools in the Chief Surveying Chancery came to 1,087 items.[56] A considerable number of these were perfectly serviceable until the end of the eighteenth century, when, on the one hand because of their age,[57] and on the other, because of obsolescence (astrolabes with spyglasses had begun to appear), they went out of use. Most of the astrolabes perished during the occupation of Moscow by Napoleon's

---
55 *Plan of the city of Klin with its villages*, RGADA, coll. 1356, descr. 1, file 2463.
56 G. N. Teterin, *Istoriia geodezii v Rossii (do 1917 g.)* (Novosibirsk: SGGA, 1992).
57 RGADA, coll. 1294, file 15335.

troops. A barge, loaded with the possessions of the Survey Expedition, tried and failed to escape the city. Its cargo included 183 astrolabes, which were burnt and dispatched to the depths of the Moscow River.[58]

The results of boundary surveys carried out with the aid of Russian and British instruments transferred across to maps of state land allocations, which in their turn became the basis for maps of districts and provinces. The results of the surveying project were brought together for the first time in the *Atlas of the Russian Empire* in 1792. This atlas, while not free of inaccuracies and errors (especially in the Eastern part of the country, where there had not yet been a survey) became the basis for the much more complete atlas by V. P. Piadyshev that was issued from 1821. Piadyshev's atlas, in turn, became a source for the ways in which, for much of the nineteenth century, the territory of Russia was conceptualised. Thus, the import and eventual domestic manufacture of the astrolabe led the Russian Empire to collect and process geographic information in a modern, scientific manner. This new-found knowledge both aligned the empire more closely with Europe and its cartographic technologies, and enabled Russia to see its own territory more clearly and accurately.

---

[58] RGADA, coll. 1294, descr. 2. According to the index the file number is 27015, but the file itself has been destroyed.

II.
INTERNATIONAL NEWS AND POST

3. Muscovy and the European Information Revolution: Creating the Mechanisms for Obtaining Foreign News

Daniel C. Waugh and Ingrid Maier[1]

Treatments of the emergence of European "modernity" invariably emphasise the development of mechanisms for the rapid dissemination of knowledge. The establishment of postal networks and in the seventeenth century the rapid proliferation of printed newspapers made possible the sharing of news across political and social boundaries, thus contributing to a growing sense of "contemporaneity" on, eventually, a Europe-wide scale.[2] The degree to which Muscovite Russia participated in this "information revolution" has been debated, though the impression persists that cultural barriers and conscious choice to a considerable degree limited any meaningful connection prior to the era of Tsar Peter I "The Great" (r. 1682–1725).

---

1   The authors gratefully acknowledge the support provided by The Swedish Foundation for Humanities and Social Sciences (Riksbankens jubileumsfond, project no. RFP12–0055:1).
2   Wolfgang Behringer, *Im Zeichen des Merkur. Reichspost und Kommunikationsrevolution in der Frühen Neuzeit*. Veröffentlichungen des Max-Planck-Instituts für Geschichte, Bd. 189 (Göttingen: Vandenhoeck & Ruprecht, 2003); Brendan Dooley, 'Die Entstehung von Gleichzeitigkeit im europäischen Bewusstsein auf der Grundlage der politischen Nachrichtenpresse', in *Presse und Geschichte: Leistungen und Perspektiven der historischen Presseforschung*, ed. by Astrid Blome and Holger Böning (Bremen: Edition lumière, 2008), 49–66; *The Dissemination of News and the Emergence of Contemporaneity in Early Modern Europe*, ed. by Brendan Dooley (Farnham, Surrey and Burlington, VT: Ashgate, 2010).

© 2017 Daniel C. Waugh and Ingrid Maier, CC BY 4.0   https://doi.org/10.11647/OBP.0122.03

The issue here is not whether there was some degree of "Westernisation" prior to Peter, affecting primarily a small segment of the Russian elite. That such was the case has long been well known. This "Westernisation" involved translation of foreign books, acquisition of knowledge about history and geography, adoption of foreign fashion or artistic norms, and much more. Our subject here is the acquisition of current foreign news in a regular and timely fashion, a process that would require establishing a connection with what we might term the "state-of-the-art" communications mechanisms shared across much of Europe and which could not, ultimately, depend on irregular and unpredictable contacts. In the first instance, the evidence is to be found in the so-called *kuranty*, translations and summaries of foreign news produced for the Muscovite government. This chapter will trace the history of their development and contextualise them with reference to the broader European communications revolution of the seventeenth century.

Down through history, governments have prioritised the acquisition of foreign news that might be relevant to political or military concerns. With the development in Muscovy of formal bureaucratic institutions and record-keeping, starting in the late fifteenth century, we can begin to trace how its government was kept informed of foreign affairs. In the first instance, this was through the reports brought back by the infrequent embassies sent abroad, or those obtained from foreign visitors to Moscow. Military intelligence obtained along the borders presumably contributed in important ways to knowledge about immediate neighbours but this can be difficult to document. Developments which, elsewhere in Europe, were already beginning to revolutionise communication—the establishment of the Habsburg Imperial Post, the development of extensive networks of correspondents, especially for commercial intelligence, and the beginnings of permanent diplomatic representation at foreign courts—had as yet no impact in Muscovy. Nonetheless, it is possible to document a growing Muscovite awareness of the importance of obtaining foreign news. By the middle of the sixteenth century, instructions to ambassadors would regularly include the requirement to learn about foreign alliances and alignments.[3] Even

---

3   Knud Rasmussen, 'On the Information Level of the Muscovite Posol'skij prikaz in the Sixteenth Century', *Forschungen zur Osteuropäische Geschichte*, 24 (1978), 88–99.

if there was no regular courier network to ensure rapid communication, for extended periods there were, in effect, resident Muscovite diplomatic agents in the Crimea, who would report in some detail both on Crimean affairs and more broadly about the Ottoman Empire.[4] To the degree that the acquisition of foreign news was deemed important, it was solely for the use of the government, not a response to any kind of demand or curiosity on the part of society at large. In this regard, throughout the seventeenth century, Muscovy continued to differ from the rest of Europe, where private initiatives and the commercialisation of news and information networks formed an important part of the communications revolution. Except for news which might pertain to immediate neighbours of Muscovy, its government only very gradually acquired more than a vague understanding of current events farther afield and felt no particular urgency to have news of them which might be fresh enough to have operative value.

As Andrew Pettegree has emphasised, news in early modern Europe might be transmitted in various media: it would be a mistake to assert, as historians of the periodical press have tended to do, that the development of printed newspapers (first known from 1605) defines the subject.[5] In fact, some of the major centres of news acquisition and dissemination (Venice being an important example) did not have regularly published newspapers, relying rather on irregular separates devoted to events of particular significance. There was a large market for broadsides and pamphlets, whose content complemented the generally dry "objective" political communications in newspaper articles. The separates might emphasise religious dispute, contain political polemics, or illustrate paranormal or natural wonders. Serious economic information was often

---

4   Aleksei V. Vinogradov, *Russko-krymskie otnosheniia 50-e–vtoraia polovina 70-kh godov XVI veka*, 2 v. (Moscow: Institut rossiiskoi istorii RAN, 2007).

5   Andrew Pettegree, *The Invention of News: How the World Came to Know about Itself* (New Haven and London: Yale University Press, 2014); cf. Holger Böning, *Welteroberung durch ein neues Publikum. Die deutsche Presse und der Weg zur Aufklärung. Hamburg und Altona als Beispiel*. Presse und Geschichte—Neue Beiträge. Bd. 5 (Bremen: Edition lumière, 2002), and *idem*, 'Ohne Zeitung keine Aufklärung', in *Presse und Geschichte*, ed. by Blome and Böning, pp. 141–78. Previous to Pettegree's recent synthesis, various authors have adopted a more balanced view about the importance of media other than just printed periodical newspapers. See, for example, several of the essays in *Die Entstehung des Zeitungswesens im 17. Jahrhundert: Ein neues Medium und seine Folgen für das Kommunikationssystem der Frühen Neuzeit*, ed. by Volker Bauer and Holger Böning (Bremen: Edition lumière, 2011).

left to the extensive networks of private, handwritten letters. Even those who were interested mainly in international politics often preferred to rely on information from such trusted correspondents, rather than on printed sources. Oral communication of rumour—which, of course, is difficult to document—continued to be important. It is essential to keep this picture in mind in assessing Muscovite foreign news, especially given the fact that before the early eighteenth century there was no such thing as a printed newspaper produced in Russia.

The analysis which follows here is limited by the uneven state of the preservation and publication of the primary sources. Prior to the seventeenth century, we have only a handful of news pamphlets that made their way to Russia and were translated. They are not without interest—for example, a report about an earthquake and even a pamphlet devoted to Columbus's discovery of America—but their acquisition surely was a matter of chance.[6] There is no reason to suspect that they hint at any significantly larger body of such news pamphlets which Muscovy might have acquired.

Of greater value here are the reports of Muscovite ambassadors, whose files date from the late fifteenth century. What came to be termed the *stateinye spiski* were written reports filed at the end of an embassy.[7] The earliest ones tend to be rather cryptic, probably reflecting the fact that much which was transmitted orally was not committed to writing, but from the beginning of the second half of the sixteenth century, they become increasingly detailed. In the first instance, such reports were intended to show that the ambassador had fulfilled precisely his instructions and ensured that the honour of his ruler was not in any way impugned. Thus we find specifics of diplomatic exchanges and descriptions of ceremonies and, occasionally, entertainments. Since instructions to ambassadors regularly required that they learn of alliances and alignments of the court to which they were sent, the *stateinye spiski* contain often cryptic, formulaic indications about who

---

6   Nataliia A. Kazakova, *Zapadnaia Evropa v russkoi pis'mennosti XV–XVI vekov. Iz istorii mezhdunarodnykh kul'turnykh sviazei Rossii* (Leningrad: Nauka, 1980).

7   For a sampling of the texts, see *Puteshestviia russkikh poslov*, ed. by Dmitrii S. Likhachev (Moscow: Izdatel'stvo Akademii nauk SSSR, 1954); on the procedures for composing the reports, see Aleksei A. Novosel'skii, 'Raznovidnosti krymskikh stateinykh spiskov XVII v. i priemy ikh sostavleniia', *Problemy istochnikovedeniia*, 9 (1961), 182–94.

was friends with whom, hostile to whom, etc. From the end of the sixteenth century, the *stateinye spiski* sometimes include appendices with translations of foreign news reports.

By themselves though, the *stateinye spiski* sketch an imperfect picture of Muscovite news acquisition.[8] They inform only on the occasion of the dispatch of an embassy. Such foreign missions were infrequent and irregular, even though they grew in number during the seventeenth century. Since the ambassadors reported only at the end of an embassy (until the last third of the seventeenth century, when the European postal networks made possible the release of regular dispatches to Moscow), the news they brought might be very dated and have little operative value by the time it reached the Kremlin. Granted, during any negotiation, either abroad or in Moscow, news might be communicated in ways that could influence the outcome. That was more likely to be the case where foreign embassies were in Moscow than in situations where the Russian representatives were abroad, handcuffed by instructions that gave them little flexibility to agree on anything of substance without first consulting Moscow.

Since only a small portion of the very extensive archival files of reports sent to Moscow by its military governors (*voevody*) in the seventeenth century has been published, it is difficult to document exactly how significant such reports were in the acquisition of foreign news. Clearly though, these commanders were critical providers of information regarding what was going on adjacent to the Muscovite borders.[9] Its sources could be merchants, other travellers (including, in the South, Balkan clerics hoping to obtain financial support in Muscovy), and spies sent specifically to gather foreign intelligence. Important news generally would be communicated by courier, which meant it might arrive in

---

8 Cf. Mikhail A. Alpatov, 'Chto znal Posol'skii prikaz o Zapadnoi Evrope vo vtoroi polovine XVII v.?', in *Istoriia i istoriki. Istoriografiia vseobshchei istorii. Sbornik statei* (Moscow: Nauka, 1966), 89–129, who relies primarily on them in his assessment of the information level of the Ambassadorial Chancery in the seventeenth century. Noteworthy among those who have attempted to broaden the perspective offered by Alpatov is the late Elena I. Kobzareva, 'Izvestiia o sobytiiakh v Zapadnoi Evrope v dokumentakh Posol'skogo prikaza XVII veka' (Kand. dissertation, Moskovskii gosudarstvennyi universitet, 1988). Her specific examples focus on information about England; she pays considerable attention to the *kuranty*.

9 Nikolai Ogloblin, 'Voevodskie vestovye otpiski XVII v. kak material po istorii Malorossii', *Kievskaia starina*, 12 (1885), 365–416.

timely fashion. While in the first instance the *voevody* reported to the *Razriadnyi prikaz* (which was in charge of military service appointments), news of particular interest regarding foreign affairs might also be quickly forwarded to the Ambassadorial Chancery (*Posol'skii prikaz*) or one of the departments with regional competence such as the Chancery for Ukrainian Affairs (*Malorossiiskii prikaz*). While systematic study of such material is a task for the future, arguably the reports by the border commanders constituted perhaps the single most significant source of foreign news for the Kremlin, focussed as they were on matters directly relevant to the state's security. While such reports might include news from further afield, the government needed to develop mechanisms which would ensure its regular and timely acquisition. In this then lies the story of the Muscovite *kuranty*, which is inseparable from the history of Muscovy's foreign post.

The term *kuranty* here will be used as a shorthand to designate a wide range of translated news sources acquired in Muscovy during the seventeenth century. In the Muscovite context, the term first appears around 1650, borrowed from the titles of some (especially Dutch) newspapers,[10] but in fact the acquisition of such sources and their translation has an earlier history.

Since the *kuranty* had first become known to scholars only from fragmentary publication of a few texts, there was little serious study of these news sources until the last decades of the twentieth century. To the degree that there had been any interest, the focus was on the question of whether they presaged the first publication of newspapers in Russia initiated under Tsar Peter I.[11] The mistaken notion that they were the equivalent of a "newspaper" is one we question in our conclusion. In his Ph.D. dissertation, Daniel Waugh devoted a chapter to the *kuranty*, exploring in a limited way the relationship between the translations

---

10 Daniel Clarke Waugh, 'Seventeenth-Century Muscovite Pamphlets with Turkish Themes: Toward a Study of Muscovite Literary Culture in Its European Setting' (Ph.D. dissertation, Harvard University, 1972), App. IIa, pp. 447–51, http://faculty.washington.edu/dwaugh/publications/kurantyterminologydissappIIa.pdf; Stepan M. Shamin, 'Slovo "kuranty" v russkom iazyke XVII–XVIII v.', *Russkii iazyk v nauchnom osveshchenii*, 1. 13 (2007), 119–52.

11 A. N. Shlosberg, 'Nachalo periodicheskoi pechati v Rossii', *Zhurnal Ministerstva narodnogo prosveshcheniia*, 35. 2 (September 1911), 63–135; Aleksei A. Pokrovskii, 'K istorii gazety v Rossii', in *Vedomosti vremeni Petra Velikogo*, vyp. 2: 1709–19 gg. (Moskva: Sinodal'naia tipografiia, 1906), pp. 1–98.

and some of their sources, and in the context of examining Muscovite writings about the Turks looked more broadly at a range of translated pamphlets which seemed to have been produced in conjunction with the Muscovite acquisition of foreign news.[12] One real obstacle to meaningful study of the texts had been the limited knowledge of their foreign sources. What turned out to be extensive files of Western newspapers acquired in seventeenth-century Moscow had lain largely untouched in the Russian archives, and the labour-intensive process of locating additional sources in multiple repositories outside Russia had not begun. The publication of a few of the original newspapers in the *vesti-kuranty* series launched in 1972 (see below) enabled Roland Schibli to write a detailed monograph exploring the translation techniques at least for a limited period in the first half of the seventeenth century.[13] The work of Ingrid Maier has opened a new era in the study of the texts, as, almost single-handedly, she has been responsible for locating many of the originals the translators used and thus has been able substantially to expand our knowledge about virtually every aspect of the way the sources were processed by the translators in Muscovy. Her work for the first time provided a meaningful comparative perspective from the history of the European press, and her monograph-length treatment of the subject accompanies the first major compendium of the foreign source texts.[14] Fortunately, on the Russian side, we also now have the contributions of Stepan Shamin, whose published *kandidat* dissertation on the *kuranty* in the time of Tsar Fedor Alekseevich (r. 1676–82) provides valuable information about the process of news acquisition, the content of texts, the instances where it is possible to document dissemination of texts outside the chancery milieu and more.[15]

---

12   Waugh, 'Muscovite Pamphlets', Ch. 2, http://faculty.washington.edu/dwaugh/publications/muscovitekurantydissch2text.pdf and http://faculty.washington.edu/dwaugh/publications/muscovitekurantydissch2notes.pdf. For his publications based on the dissertation, see citations in various notes below.

13   Roland Schibli, *Die ältesten russischen Zeitungsübersetzungen (Vesti-Kuranty), 1600–50. Quellenkunde, Lehnwortschatz und Toponomastik*. Slavica Helvetica, Bd. 29 (Bern and New York: Peter Lang, 1988).

14   See her 'Vvodnaia chast'', introduction to V-K VI/2, whose full citation is in n. 16. Many of her other publications are cited below.

15   Stepan M. Shamin, *Kuranty XVII stoletiia. Evropeiskaia pressa v Rossii i vozniknovenie russkoi periodicheskoi pechati* (Moscow and St Petersburg: Al'ians-Arkheo, 2011).

The systematic publication of the texts began in 1972 in a series given the generic title *Vesti-kuranty*, reflecting the fact that often the news (*vesti*) came not from published newspapers but from manuscript newsletters or other sources.[16] Unfortunately, decisions about what to include in the *Vesti-kuranty* series (hereafter abbreviated to its generic title V-K) mean that it is far from a complete record of foreign news arriving and translated in Moscow, since many of the archival foreign relations files have not been systematically explored to identify relevant material. That said, the *kuranty* that are available offer a reasonable approximation of the flow of foreign news and clear evidence as to how it was processed.

Documents in the first five volumes of the series (ostensibly covering the period from 1600 through the 1650s) leave us with the impression that news acquisition was unpredictable, vacillating between some periods of intensive and regular communication, and long periods when there was nothing (perhaps, of course, a reflection of poor preservation, rather than an indication of an actual void). Frequently the Russian translations of that period were based on news handed over to the Muscovite authorities by foreign merchants or agents, their sources being either printed newspapers or manuscript newsletters. Dutch merchants and entrepreneurs—Isaac Massa, Georg Klenck (Iurii Klink) and Carp Demulin are among them—provided a good many of the early foreign news sources.[17] These sources often provide no information regarding the initiative for the supplying of such news: surely many of the foreigners voluntarily provided it, presumably in the hope of solidifying their position in the eyes of the Muscovite authorities, but one also has to imagine that pressures were exerted to ensure that information received through private correspondence was shared with

---

16 The volumes are: *Vesti-kuranty*: vols 1–5: I (1600–39); II (1642–44); III (1645–46, 1648); IV (1648–50); V (1651–52, 1654–55, 1658–60), ed. by N. I. Tarabasova, V. G. Dem'ianov et al. (Moscow: Nauka, 1972; 1976; 1980; 1983; 1996) [hereafter abbreviated V-K I, II, etc.], vol. 6, pt. 1, *Russkie teksty*, 1656, 1660–62, 1664–70, ed. by A. M. Moldovan and Ingrid Maier (Moscow: Rukopisnye pamiatniki drevnei Rusi, 2009) [hereafter: V-K VI/1], vol. 6, pt. 2, *Inostrannye originaly k russkim tekstam*, ed. by Ingrid Maier (Moscow: Iazyki slavianskikh kul'tur, 2008) [hereafter: V-K VI/2]. For a detailed review of V-K I, see Daniel C. Waugh, 'The Publication of Muscovite *Kuranty*', *Kritika*, 9. 3 (1973), 104–20; a detailed review of V-K V, by Vadim Borisovich Krys'ko and Ingrid Maier, in *Russian Linguistics*, 21 (1997), 301–10. It was only with publication of V-K VI that the deficiencies noted in those reviews began to be addressed.

17 See V-K I, *passim*. For a review of the transmission and processing of foreign news in this period, see Schibli, *Die ältesten russischen Zeitungsübersetzungen*, esp. Ch. 2.

the Russian officials. It was a normal procedure that foreigners would be interrogated on arrival in Muscovy. Since such news often came into Muscovy via the Northern route from the White Sea, by the time reports about events in Western Europe reached the Kremlin, they might be several months old. Furthermore, navigation via the Northern route extended only over a relatively short period of summer months.

News arriving via Arkhangelsk would continue to be translated in subsequent decades. However, improvements to this irregular and slow transit would perforce involve more direct routes via the Baltic, taking advantage of the developing Northern European postal and merchant networks. Annotations on many of the news compilations indicate that they were forwarded from Pskov or Novgorod. In 1631, a certain Melchior Beckmann sent newsletters from Stockholm.[18] For more than a decade beginning in 1636, a Swedish resident in Moscow, Peter Krusbjörn, supplied a substantial number of news reports.[19] His successor Karl Pommering took up where Krusbjörn left off.[20] There were opportunities for the Muscovite Ambassadorial Chancery to hire agents who might supply news on a regular basis. A Rigan, who wrote under the *nom-de-plume* of Justus Filimonatus, offered to send news to Moscow, and in fact over more than half a year between late 1643 and mid-1644 submitted a series of reports from Riga and Danzig.[21] In the 1640s, we increasingly see Peter Marselis, an important Danish entrepreneur, among those supplying news. His sons would later, for a brief period, run the Muscovite foreign post. John Hebdon, who subsequently would carry out commissions for Tsar Aleksei Mikhailovich, also became a supplier of news in the 1640s. One of the impressive instances of intensive news acquisition came when a Muscovite embassy was in Stockholm between June and October 1649, from which it transmitted translations of foreign news via courier on a weekly basis over several months. Twenty of these translations have been preserved.[22] The most important source was the

---

18 *V-K* I, pp. 133–38, 161–62.
19 *V-K* I, pp. 167–76, 182–92, 204–07, 209–14; *V-K* II, pp. 11–14, 50, 88–91, 122–23, 125–26, 207–09; *V-K* III, pp. 78–82, 121–30.
20 E.g., *V-K* III, pp. 190–96.
21 *V-K* II, pp. 40–43, 54–55, 59–74, 76–80, 83–84, 97–103, 109–13, 126, 131–38, 146–47, 167–72, 178–83.
22 *V-K* IV, pp. 97–169. For an analysis, see Ingrid Maier, 'Newspaper Translations in Seventeenth-Century Muscovy. About the Sources, Topics and Periodicity of *Kuranty* "Made in Stockholm" (1649)', in *Explorare necesse est. Hyllningsskrift till*

Wochentliche Zeitung published in Hamburg. Overall, despite some gaps we might attribute to vagaries of preservation, the quantity and coverage of foreign news received in Moscow in the 1640s is impressive.

Even if their acquisition was irregular, strikingly the first foreign newspapers made their way to Russia within a relatively short time after they had first begun to appear on a regular basis in the West.[23] The earliest evidence for a weekly newspaper in Europe is from 1605, with the earliest known examples from 1609. By 1620, there were already several regularly published German and Dutch newspapers and the first in English and French (printed in the Netherlands). As early as 1621, only three years after the first appearance of a Dutch weekly newspaper, at least a couple of numbers had arrived in Moscow where they were translated. Translations into Russian from German newspapers also date from this year. During the first half of the seventeenth century, it seems that the German newspapers, primarily those published in Hamburg, were much more often the sources for *kuranty* than were the Dutch (primarily from Amsterdam). The Russian archival files preserve only occasional copies of the foreign newspapers which served as sources for the *kuranty* during the first half of the seventeenth century, the earliest German example dating from 1631 and earliest Dutch newspaper from 1646. Yet it was precisely these files that first drew the attention of historians in the first half of the nineteenth century to the Muscovite acquisition of foreign news. For the second half of the seventeenth century, the state of preservation is substantially better — over 2600 individual numbers of the German papers, most of which are unique copies not preserved in other European collections, and more than 650 numbers of Dutch newspapers.[24]

In the circumstances in which it seems relatively few of the newspapers were making their way to Moscow, the initial response of the Ambassadorial Chancery seems to have been to translate large

---

Barbro Nilsson. Acta Universitatis Stockholmensis. Stockholm Slavic Studies, vol. 28 (Stockholm: Almqvist & Wiksell, 2002), 181–90.

23   Maier, 'Vvodnaia chast'', introduction to *V-K* VI/2, pp. 29, 53–57.
24   V. I. Simonov, 'Deutsche Zeitungen des 17. Jahrhunderts im Zentralen Staatsarchiv für alte Akten (CGADA), Moskau', *Gutenberg-Jahrbuch* (1979), 210–20; Ingrid Maier, 'Niederländische Zeitungen ('Couranten') des 17. Jahrhunderts im Russischen Staatsarchiv für alte Akten (RGADA), Moskau', *Gutenberg-Jahrbuch* (2004), 191–218.

portions of them, if not necessarily their entirety.²⁵ The result was the availability in Russian of a substantial collection of news about the events of the Thirty Years War, often containing detail that surely would have been meaningless to a reader in Muscovy and of no direct relevance for the shaping of Muscovite foreign policy. By the time of the Russian embassy in Stockholm in 1649, clearly the translators were being selective, using parts of some articles, omitting others, and combining material from several sources.²⁶ In addition to the newspaper accounts, the officials in the Kremlin received and had translated larger separates. They had the entire texts of treaties, including the Swedish-Danish treaty of Brömsebro²⁷ in 1645, the treaty between the Netherlands and Spain of January 1648 in Münster, and that between the German Empire and Sweden in summer 1648 in Osnabrück—thus, two of the three treaties which ended the Thirty Years War in 1648.²⁸ They obtained texts of pamphlets with the famous appeal of King Charles I and later a description of his execution in 1649, an event which offended the tsar's government and resulted in the curbing of English trading privileges.²⁹ Since copies happened to be received (not, it seems, consciously sought out by the chancery) of extended accounts concerning the miraculous cures effected at the waters of the much-frequented Protestant spa at Hornhausen in Northern Germany, those too were translated.³⁰ Surely this material would have struck a chord amongst those in Moscow

---

25   See the analysis by Schibli, *Die ältesten russischen Zeitungsübersetzungen*.
26   Maier, 'Newspaper Translations', p. 188.
27   *V-K* III, pp. 21–39. See Ingrid Maier, *Verbalrektion in den 'Vesti Kuranty' (1600–60). Eine historischphilologische Untersuchung zur mittelrussischen Syntax*. Acta Universitatis Upsaliensis. Studia Slavica Upsaliensia, 38 (Uppsala: Acta Universitatis Upsaliensis, 1997), pp. 37–41.
28   *V-K* III, pp. 161–79; *V-K* IV, pp. 13–64. See Maier, *Verbalrektion*, pp. 41–60.
29   *V-K* III, pp. 159–61; *V-K* IV, pp. 82–85. On the translation of Charles I's 'Declaration to all His Subjects', see Ingrid Maier and Nikita Mikhaylov, '"Korolevskii izvet ko vsem ego poddannym" (1648 g.) — pervyi russkii perevod angliiskogo pechatnogo teksta?', *Russian Linguistics*, 33 (2009), 289–317.
30   *V-K* III, nos. 48–49, pp. 133–42, and nos. P8–9, pp. 241–51. The first of these texts, no. 48 (see Maier, *Verbalrektion*, pp. 72–74), is a complete translation of *Gründlicher unnd Warhaffter Bericht/ von dem Wundersamen Heilbrunnen/ so newlicher Zeit auß sonderbahrer Göttlicher Gnade/ in dem Stifft Halberstadt bey einem Dorff Hornhausen genant* [...] (n.p., n.d. [1646]). The second text, no. 49, is an almost complete translation of *Weiterer Bericht Von dem wundersamen Heyl-Brunnen/ Welcher von einem Knaben/ als derselbe am fünfften Martii auß der Schuel gegangen/ zuerst erfunden worden* [...] (n.p., 1646).

familiar with the listings of cures appended to saints' lives and tales about miracle-working icons. Indeed, accounts of the paranormal, including prognostications by self-proclaimed holy men, formed part of the output of the translators in the Ambassadorial Chancery, alongside propaganda that included fictive missives from the Ottoman sultan threatening death and destruction to Christian Europe.[31]

The real push to regularise the acquisition of foreign news dates from the reign of the second Romanov, Tsar Aleksei Mikhailovich (1645–76). An important reason for this appears to have been the personality and intellectual interests of the tsar himself. While we lack details, we know that part of his youthful education included exposure to European broadsides. The inventory of his Privy Chancery (*Prikaz tainykh del*), which had been created at the beginning of the long war against Poland in 1655 and was disbanded only after the tsar's death in 1676, offers ample evidence about his broad interests.[32] Among the files were many *stateinye spiski* and, significanctly, long runs of the *kuranty*. In an instruction to his chief foreign affairs adviser Afanasii Ordin-Nashchokin in 1659, the tsar indicated he wanted to be supplied with foreign news on a monthly basis.[33] Soon afterwards, a Russian embassy to England and Italy was tasked with exploring the possibilities of engaging regular correspondents to send news to Moscow, though it seems no concrete arrangements followed. It is hardly a surprise that when the Muscovite foreign post was finally established in 1665, it was under the auspices of Aleksei Mikhailovich's Privy Chancery, with the

---

31 Stepan M. Shamin, '"Skazanie o dvukh startsakh": K voprosu o bytovanii evropeiskogo eskhatologicheskogo prorochestva v Rossii', *Vestnik tserkovnoi istorii*, 2008, 2 (10), 221–48; D. K. Uo [Daniel C. Waugh], *Istoriia odnoi knigi: Viatka i "nesovremennost'" v russkoi kul'ture Petrovskogo vremeni* (St Petersburg: Dmitrii Bulanin, 2003), pp. 48–53, 100–02, 294–95, 298–301; Daniel C. Waugh, *The Great Turkes Defiance: On the History of the Apocryphal Correspondence of the Ottoman Sultan in Its Muscovite and Russian Variants*, with a foreword by Academician Dmitrii Sergeevich Likhachev (Columbus, OH: Slavica Publishers, 1978).

32 Daniel C. Waugh, 'The Library of Aleksei Mikhailovich', *Forschungen zur osteuropäischen Geschichte*, 38 (1986), 299–324; idem, 'Azbuka znakami lits: Egyptian Hieroglyphs in the Privy Chancellery Archive', *Oxford Slavonic Papers*, 10 (1977), 46–50 [with four plates]; idem, 'Tekst o nebesnom znamenii 1672 g. (k istorii evropeiskikh sviazei moskovskoi kul'tury poslednei treti XVII v.)', in *Problemy izucheniia kul'turnogo naslediia* (Moscow: Nauka, 1985), 201–08.

33 Shamin, *Kuranty*, pp. 83–84.

explicit purpose of obtaining foreign news on a regular basis.[34] Some credit the initiative to Ordin-Nashchokin, although direct evidence is lacking. He certainly had shown initiative earlier in establishing his own network of correspondents across the Northern borders, and had been one of the suppliers of foreign news to the tsar.

In May 1665, a postal contract was drawn up with the Dutch entrepreneur Johann van Sweeden, who had for some time been active in Muscovy.[35] He was to be paid a lump sum each year to maintain a postal route to Riga with predictable bi-weekly deliveries of foreign news. Van Sweeden's system was independent of the long-standing Muscovite network of horse relays (the *iamskaia gon'ba*). His riders had to wear uniform clearly marked with postal insignia. It was his responsibility to negotiate with the postmaster in Swedish-held Riga the details of the schedule and what news was to be acquired.

This arrangement through a private contractor was not unusual in the larger context of the various efforts by the Muscovite government in the seventeenth century to tap foreign expertise, which in the first instance had been for the improvement of the Muscovite military by hiring mercenaries and raising arms production to a more efficient and technically advanced level. Nor was it unusual elsewhere in Europe when new postal networks were being established, to contract them to entrepreneurs who might have had some previous experience in managing such a system.[36] Just as in Muscovy, so elsewhere in Europe the development of the post and the dissemination of news went hand in hand: European postmasters often were the collectors and

---

34 For details on the early history of the Muscovite post, see D. Uo [Waugh] 'Istoki sozdaniia mezhdunarodnoi pochtovoi sluzhby Moskovskogo gosudarstva v evropeiskom kontekste', *Ocherki feodal'noi Rossii*, 19 (2017), 394–442. A good overview of Muscovy's Riga postal connection is Enn Küng, 'Postal Relations Between Riga and Moscow in the Second Half of the 17th Century', *Past: Special Issue on the History of Estonia* (Tartu-Tallinn: National Archives, 2009), 59–81. The still unsurpassed history of the Muscovite post throughout the second half of the seventeenth century is I. P. Kozlovskii, *Pervye pochty i pervye pochtmeistery v moskovskom gosudarstve*, 2 vols (Warsaw: Tip. Varshavskogo uchebnogo okruga, 1913), in which vol. 2 contains most of the important archival documents.

35 For the text, Waugh, 'Muscovite Pamphlets', App. IIc, pp. 510–12, http://faculty.washington.edu/dwaugh/publications/vansweedencontractdissappIIc.pdf. On van Sweeden, see Kozlovskii, *Pervye pochty*, vol. 1, pp. 60–62.

36 See, e.g., Karl Heinz Kremer, *Johann von den Birghden 1582–1645. Kaiserlicher und königlich-schwedischer Postmeister zu Frankfurt am Main* (Bremen: Edition lumière, 2005).

purveyors (even publishers) of newspapers. A generation earlier, a Muscovite foreign post probably would have been impossible, given the fragmented and often contentious nature of the various postal services in Northeastern Europe. Even if there were still improvements to be made and conflicts to be adjudicated, by the 1660s the postal networks in the Baltic region, which extended through the Northern German states West to Antwerp, South into Italy, and North into Sweden, were in place.[37] To connect Muscovy via Riga, between which there had already been quite regular communication, was a logical next step.

Despite the fact that van Sweeden seems to have had no previous experience in running a postal network, as near as we can tell he did manage to fulfill the terms of his contract and provide news from Riga on a bi-weekly basis.[38] Even though van Sweeden's contract was renewed in 1668, in that same year the management of the post was abruptly handed over instead to the Marselis family, who enjoyed the favour of Ordin-Nashchokin. Apart from personal loyalties, the move may in part reflect an effort by Ordin-Nashchokin, now in charge of the Ambassadorial Chancery, to streamline the management of Muscovite foreign affairs. The post was now delivered to his department, not routed first to the tsar's Privy Chancery. When Ordin-Nashchokin lost his position in 1671, the post was handed over to Andrei Vinius, only to have it come back to Leonhardt Marselis when Vinius was sent abroad on a foreign embassy that lasted from 1672 to 1674.

Under the Marselises, there was a substantial reorganisation (and upgrading) of the service, with the posts running weekly to both Riga and Vilna. The latter route was necessitated by the Truce of Andrusovo (1667), which established diplomatic residents of Poland-Lithuania and Muscovy in the respective capitals, requiring that they be able to communicate on a regular basis with their superiors. Moreover, the post was no longer to be an independent, private transport service; instead it was to use the Muscovite horse relays, within which system some carriers

---

37 See Pārsla Pētersone, 'Entstehung und Moderisierung der Post- und Verkehrsverbindungen im Baltikum im 17. Jahrhundert', *Liber Annalis Institut Baltici* (Acta Baltica, 35) (Königstein im Taunus, 1997), 199–218; Küng, 'Postal Relations'; Magnus Linnarsson, 'The Development of the Swedish Post Office, c. 1600–1721', in Heiko Droste, ed., *Connecting the Baltic Area: The Swedish Postal System in the Seventeenth Century* (Stockholm: Södertörns högskola, 2011), pp. 25–47.

38 For details, see Uo, 'Istoki sozdaniia'.

were to be assigned specifically to postal duties and expected to keep to a regular schedule. Maintaining the schedule was not always easy, the initial targets for transit times were overly optimistic, the riders often incompetent (or drunk), and weather and road conditions hindered speedy travel.[39] However, it seems that the Marselises did manage to establish a regular schedule, if with somewhat slower delivery than had originally been envisaged. An English embassy in Moscow in 1669 was able to send weekly reports back to London through the post.[40] Under optimal conditions, those letters spent a little over a month in transit. A year or so later, a Swedish resident in Moscow, the Reval-born merchant Christoff Koch (later ennobled von Kochen), began to send weekly reports via Novgorod (which was on the Riga postal route) to Narva, which were copied there and sent to Reval, Stockholm and probably to other places.[41] The Swedish diplomat Johann Kilburger, writing in detail about Muscovy and its trade in 1674, indicated that the elapsed time for mail between Riga and Moscow was nine to eleven days, which was certainly faster than had been possible a few years earlier.[42] Nine days may be somewhat optimistic. In the 1690s, for which we have a decent run of statistics for the route, it seemed to deliver the mail between the

---

39 See Kozlovskii, *Pervye pochty*, for much of the relevant documentation. Weather could interrupt the normally regular postal deliveries elsewhere in Europe as described in reports sent to London by English agents in Hamburg. The winter of 1667 seems to have been especially severe. On 26 January 1667, the English agent reported "The northern posts for the most are yet to come w-ch. delay is onely caus'd by the great quantity of snow in Suedeland & the Danish streames frozen" (National Archives, London, SP 101/39, unpaginated, newsletter addressed to Joseph Williamson at Whitehall, probably sent from Hamburg on the same date).

40 The reports from the embassy headed by Sir Peter Wyche between June and October are in the National Archives, London, SP 91/3. While there are a few gaps (possibly due simply to the loss of a letter), the dates suggest weekly communication.

41 For the early part of the communications which Koch sent from Moscow to the Swedish governor in Narva on nearly a weekly basis, see Riksarkivet (Stockholm), E4304, Bengt Horns Samling. A forthcoming article by Heiko Droste and Ingrid Maier, 'Christoff Koch (1637–1711)—Sweden's Man in Moscow' (forthcoming in *Travelling Chronicles: Episodes in the History of News and Newspapers from the Early Modern Period to the Eighteenth Century*, ed. by Siv Gøril Brandtzæg, Paul Goring and Christine Watson), will discuss his reports and this network; see also Maier's chapter on the reports about Stepan Razin in the present volume.

42 See Boris G. Kurts, *Sochinenie Kil'burgera o russkoi torgovle v tsarstvovanie Alekseia Mikhailovicha* (Kiev: Tip. I. I. Chokolova, 1915), p. 160.

two cities in about eleven days with reasonable consistency (counting the day of departure and day of arrival).[43]

The Vilna route also ran efficiently for a time and certainly was actively used by Vasilii Tiapkin during his residency in Poland from 1673 to 1677.[44] However once he left (and the Polish resident also had departed Moscow) the route became increasingly problematic, maintained in the first instance because of the continuing negotiations between the two countries which would result in the "Permanent Peace" of 1686.

In the final quarter of the seventeenth century, the Muscovite foreign post was managed by Andrei Vinius, whose Dutch father had come to Muscovy as an entrepreneur. The younger Vinius was probably born in Moscow, must have grown up bilingual, and from an early age, starting in the mid-1660s, served as a translator in the Ambassadorial Chancery.[45] He surely would have been involved in the translation of Dutch and probably also German newspapers; we have a number of other translations written during his long career in Russian service, which lasted until his death in 1717. Even before he became postmaster, Vinius would have been one of the best informed Muscovite officials regarding European affairs; that, plus his language competence, would explain why he was selected to travel as an ambassador to several European states in 1672 in what would prove to be an unsuccessful effort to build a European coalition to fight the Turks.[46] On his return, he assumed the postmastership, eventually taking on other important administrative responsibilities. So busy had he become in the 1690s that for a time his son Matvei officially took over the post, even though there is good reason to believe that his father continued to manage it.

---

43 Daniel C. Waugh, 'The Best Connected Man in Muscovy? Patrick Gordon's Evidence Regarding Communications in Muscovy in the 17th Century', *Journal of Irish and Scottish Studies*, 7. 2 (2014 [2015]), 61–124 (pp. 96–97).

44 Aleksandr N. Popov, *Russkoe posol'stvo v Pol'she v 1673–1677 godakh. Neskol'ko let iz istorii otnoshenii drevnei Rossii k evropeiskim derzhavam* (St Petersburg: Tip. Morskogo kadetskago korpusa, 1854).

45 For Vinius's management of the post, the fundamental work remains Kozlovskii, *Pervye pochty*, starting with Ch. 4. More generally for his biography, the fullest treatment is Igor' N. Iurkin, *Andrei Andreevich Vinius, 1641–1716* (Moscow: Nauka, 2007).

46 Nataliia A. Kazakova, 'A. A. Vinius i stateinyi spisok ego posol'stva v Angliiu, Frantsii i Ispaniiu v 1672–74 g.', *Trudy Otdela drevnerusskoi literatury*, 39 (1985), 348–64.

In Muscovy, Vinius never could assume the role sometimes taken by foreign postmasters, simultaneously becoming the publisher of a newspaper. However, there is good reason to think that Vinius was a key figure in the processing and dissemination of foreign news in Muscovy, beyond his obvious involvement in acquiring the foreign news materials and facilitating their translation and summary. Insights into Vinius's role in news dissemination can be gained from the diary of the Scottish mercenary Patrick Gordon. When in Moscow, Gordon would often meet with him; when abroad, Gordon sent Vinius reports on a regular basis, and when posted in Ukraine, through his correspondence with Vinius back in Moscow, Gordon regularly received news, sometimes in the form of published newspapers. In general, there seems to have been extensive exchange of foreign news amongst the Muscovite elite connected with the court. Arguably, Vinius stood at the centre of this web of information.

The documents relating to Vinius's management of the posts make it clear that he understood their significance for the acquisition of foreign news. When he was arguing for the closure of the Vilna route in 1681, on the basis of its being little used and too costly, he buttressed his case by stating:

> And the Imperial and Dutch newspapers, which formerly were sent through the Vilna post, are now sent as well from Königsberg through Riga, and in addition, according to my agreement with the printer of the Riga newspapers, a third set of newspapers—the Riga ones—are now being sent, which never were received previously. And in these newspapers there is always more Polish and Swedish news than in the Königsberg or Dutch ones.[47]

In the summer of 1683 he added:

> And since 1681 only the Riga post has been running, and they have undertaken to send through the Riga post every week without interruption all the news of what is happening in Europe and in some parts of Asia.[48]

These comments highlight shifts in the importance of various foreign news sources as the seventeenth century progressed, even if Vinius

---

47 Kozlovskii, *Pervye pochty*, vol. 2, pp. 57–58.
48 *Ibid.*, p. 69.

might have stretched the facts in order to strengthen his argument. Oddly, during the first year Tiapkin was in Poland, hardly any foreign newspapers arrived via the Vilna route, a fact Shamin explains by suggesting Tiapkin's own reports superseded them.[49] While some of the Dutch papers continued to be received and excerpted regularly, we know that amongst the German newspapers, those published in Berlin were extremely popular in Moscow in the period between 1668 and 1676.[50] Königsberg papers similarly became very significant as sources for news in Muscovy, since, until the appearance of published newspapers in Riga (from 1681, at the latest), they were issued closest to the Muscovite borders, were full of news directly relevant to Muscovite interests, and could be obtained rapidly via the Vilna post. Kilburger specifically mentions in 1674 the regular receipt and translation of Hamburg, Königsberg and Dutch printed newspapers as well as manuscript newsletters.[51] To the degree that statistics of preserved copies of the German papers from this period in the Moscow archives might reflect their relative popularity, newpapers published in Danzig were third behind those of Berlin and Königsberg. So far there is no reason to think that what we know about the composition of the sources for the *kuranty* translations during 1671–72 (those years to be covered in the next volume of the V-K series) will change significantly for succeeding years of the seventeenth century.

With the regularisation of the acquisition of foreign news (as a result of the establishment of the foreign post) clear patterns emerge in the way the Kremlin dealt with what was now, for Muscovy, a constant surfeit of information.[52] When both the Riga and Vilna posts were functioning according to schedule, from six to eight news deliveries a month might arrive in Moscow. The translators had no choice but to be very selective if the news was to be made available in Russian without delay as soon as it had arrived through the mail.

While there are exceptions involving the translation of foreign reports undertaken by members of a Muscovite embassy abroad or

---

49 Shamin, *Kuranty*, p. 89.
50 Maier, 'Vvodnaia chast'', pp. 77–81; Simonov, 'Deutsche Zeitungen'.
51 Kurts, *Sochinenie Kil'burgera*, p. 161.
52 Maier, 'Vvodnaia chast'', Chs. 4, 5; Shamin, *Kuranty*, pp. 88 and *passim*.

at border posts,[53] for the most part the foreign news was processed in Moscow. After a short-lived contretemps in which Leonhardt Marselis was reprimanded for having opened the mailbags before handing them over to the Ambassadorial Chancery, the normal procedure was for them to be delivered sealed, even if private correspondence might then be handed unsealed to the postmaster for local delivery. Marselis also incurred the ire of the translators by suggesting to them the articles they should translate; he was told in no uncertain terms that it was none of his business, as the translators themselves had the expertise to decide. Of course in the absence of hard evidence this leaves open the question of how exactly decisions were made regarding what news was important. We can but assume that the translators, if regularly reading the foreign news sources as they arrived (and given the fact that at least some of them would have had a network of contacts in Moscow from which they could have acquired other information), would have an ongoing sense of the important developments across Europe. Presumably it did not take much to know the current priorities of Muscovite foreign policy and to have a sense therefore of what news should be deemed most relevant. Extant copies of the foreign newspapers in the Moscow archives often contain marginal markings which apparently specify which news might be of the greatest interest. And some copies of the papers were additionally annotated as having been translated or, on the contrary, containing nothing of particular interest since they duplicated information already in hand.

What "translation" really meant, though, needs some close examination.[54] There are some serious methodological challenges to be addressed before it is possible to determine how the translators dealt with their sources. They generally would indicate in the heading for each set of the *kuranty* whether the source was printed or handwritten, in German or Dutch, both, or, rarely, in some other language. However,

---

53 Maier, 'Newspaper Translations'; Shamin, *Kuranty*, pp. 97–98. When Peter the Great was in Holland in 1697, his translators were translating foreign news reports and sending them back to Moscow alongside the original newspapers. See Ingrid Maier, 'Presseberichte am Zarenhof im 17. Jahrhundert. Ein Beitrag zur Vorgeschichte der gedruckten Zeitung in Russland', *Jahrbuch für Kommunikationsgeschichte*, 6 (2004), 103–29 (p. 109).

54 For further details on the challenges of identifying the original Russian texts and the features of the translations in the cases where the sources are now known cf. Maier, 'Vvodnaia chast'', esp. Chs. 4–6.

in some instances, it seems that an indication of sources in both German and Dutch is erroneous, as in fact news was drawn from only one. In the absence of such headings, translation from a single language might be assumed. With rare exceptions (generally in the first half of the century, when whole newspapers might be translated), there is no indication of place, date or publisher of the original. Pamphlet titles might be translated, but not the titles of newspapers: the sources are generally termed simply *kuranty*, sometimes with the qualifier that they included both handwritten and printed items. While in a very few instances the translators selected from a single newspaper, which might make it easier to match the translation with the original (assuming there is an extant copy), more often any given set of the *kuranty* was compiled from reports in several separate issues of the foreign newspapers, and that information in turn might be supplemented with handwritten sources which have not yet been identified.

While they tended to condense and often simply to paraphrase their sources, at least in the early part of the century the translators generally would draw any given news item in a set of the *kuranty* from only one or perhaps two foreign sources. Later, our task of identifying sources becomes ever more complicated as they proliferated in Moscow and the translators tended to combine information from several different reports under a single date. Often there would be more than one newspaper containing a similar report but with the same dateline as in other papers that contained the same news.

It is important to keep in mind here that the average German newspaper of the period, printed in quarto (4°), would contain half a dozen to a dozen articles.[55] The Dutch papers, published in small folio, with smaller font and generally with much shorter articles, might contain two dozen or more news items. There are a few examples where as many as half a dozen datelined articles in a single set of the *kuranty* can be traced to a single Dutch newspaper. Given the relatively poor preservation of the German newspaper originals for the 1660s, it is difficult to generalise about the degree of selectivity by the translators for any given number of a German newspaper.[56]

---

55 Maier, 'Vvodnaia chast'', pp. 89–91.
56 *Ibid.*, pp. 141–42.

In short, all of these considerations, compounded by the fragmentary and scattered preservation of the original sources, render analysis of the translation techniques extremely difficult. That said, it is possible to suggest why, in many cases, material from the original was omitted or simplified. In the first instance, material deemed peripheral to the substance of the news report (or not at all relevant to the Muscovite government's understanding of foreign affairs) might be deleted. The translator might deem irrelevant qualifications in the original news report regarding the degree to which a particular report was reliable. Of course, omitting such doubts would make the information in the resulting "translation" seem more authoritative than it was. Translators might omit or elide passages they could not understand (for example, quotations or words in Latin, which often found their way into the Dutch or German texts). Unfamiliar geographical locations might be dropped, although there also developed a practice of providing marginal glosses to those that remained but that might be assumed unfamiliar to the tsar or his boyars (nobles) when the texts were read to them. On the other hand, in such cases translators might add explanations in the text and might, on occasion, even update an entry with information that had not been known to the foreign writer or publisher.

Apart from editorial techniques, the accuracy of the translations (or summaries) is of considerable importance.[57] Sometimes, in the process of transcription, foreign names were garbled beyond recognition. Syntactical constructions in the originals might be misunderstood; words might be mistaken for ones of similar appearance but with a totally different meaning. Occasionally the lexical errors are surprising, as we would assume the words involved should have been familiar. While instances of such errors add up, on the whole the translations were not badly done, especially considering the haste with which they were produced. The translators seem to have had a decent knowledge of the Russian vernacular; their failings might have been due to their apparent lack of formal education in the foreign languages they were translating. It would be easy to explain this if, as seems to have been the case, some of the translators grew up in Moscow, learning Russian while young, speaking the family (foreign) language at home, but never

---

57   This is the subject of *ibid.*, Ch. 5.

having had the opportunity to acquire much formal schooling in it. Only infrequently does a *kuranty* text identify who translated it, but whether linguistic analysis of those translations can help us to identify who undertook other, anonymous, ones is questionable. Given the small number of those who knew Dutch, we might venture to guess who was responsible for translating the Dutch newspapers, but for German, there are more possibilities.

Normally at most two or three copies of the *kuranty* translations were made. In some instances, we have both the draft copy, replete with crossed out text, corrections, etc., as well as the clean copy which presumably would have been taken to the tsar. There seems to have been a process where the translation was reviewed for possible further correction by a different individual before it was finalised.

The manuscripts occasionally have inscriptions added on the reverse indicating they had been read to the tsar, and even more rarely, "while the boyars listened in the antechamber". Shamin suggests that it was the normal procedure for this to happen within a day or two of the receipt of the foreign post.[58] In instances where the tsar was out of town, the *kuranty* might be taken to him, though this could involve some days' delay. During the seventeenth century it seems that the interest of the rulers in hearing the news fluctuated, depending on the individual and on particular circumstances. While obviously interested in the news, Peter the Great, always impatient, began to require short summaries based on the longer compendia, so we begin to see such condensations in the last years of the seventeenth century. All in all, it is reasonable to suggest that the processes by which rulers and their advisers acquainted themselves with foreign news back in the seventeenth century were not vastly different from the processes today. Yes, political leaders may view, listen directly to, or read news sources, but at the same time, most of them have to rely on summaries of intelligence prepared by their staffs. Of course this process has the inherent danger that the staffers may not always select the right thing, may tell their bosses what they think they want to hear, or may deliberately skew their selection so as to influence decision-making.

---

58 Shamin, *Kuranty*, pp. 112–16, 123–28.

After the establishment of the foreign post in 1665, the *kuranty* files are sufficiently complete to indicate the government priorities in obtaining foreign news. Here we can assume that the texts reflect a conscious policy of selection, not simply a possibly random compilation of whatever happened to be available. There are few surprises: by definition, news tends to be that which its consumers perceive to be relevant to their particular interests. In the Muscovite case, in the first instance this was information relating to its immediate neighbours, those states with which it had relations (whether friendly or hostile), and news about other states which might affect Muscovite security, political or economic interests. The most common topics in the 1660s included: news about Poland, the Ottoman Empire and its vassals; news relating to the competition for control of Ukraine; the Ottoman wars against Venice and the Austrian Habsburgs; events in Hungary and Transylvania; reports about Muscovy; and news relating to political and commercial matters in the Baltic region, involving Sweden, Denmark, Holland and England.[59] The reports about Poland and Ukraine frequently focus on the rebellion by the Polish magnate Lubomirski and on the complicated politics involving the Cossacks. The Anglo-Dutch war was of considerable interest, since it affected Baltic trade; some reports translated from Dutch newspapers were cargo lists for the East Indies fleets which had recently arrived in Amsterdam. There are reports in the *kuranty* about the peregrinations of the Swedish Queen Christina after she had abdicated, a subject that seems to have intrigued many followers of the news throughout Europe. An interesting view of what was being obtained in Moscow during this period can be seen in a scrapbook kept by Andrei Vinius, where amongst a broad range of visual material is an engraving of the great fire of London in 1666 and several engravings from news broadsides devoted to the Venetian naval wars against the Ottomans in defence of Crete.[60]

---

59 See Maier, 'Vvodnaia chast'', pp. 91–108.
60 On the Vinius scrapbook (album), which Daniel Waugh has examined *de visu*, see N. Levinson, 'Al'bom "Kniga Viniusa" — Pamiatnik khudozhestvennogo sobiratel'stva v Moskve XVII veka', *Ezhegodnik Gosudarstvennogo istoricheskogo muzeia. 1961 god* (Moscow: Gosudarstvennyi istoricheskii muzei, 1962), 71–98. Amidst considerable controversy in Russia, the album was recently sent to the Netherlands for restoration; a facsimile edition, which we have not seen, has been published: *Al'bom Viniusa*, ed. and intro. by I. M. Beliaeva and E. A. Savel'eva (St Petersburg: BAN and Al'faret, 2010).

To a considerable degree, these emphases in the *kuranty* of the 1660s were similar to the material one finds in the German-language newspapers published in Northern Europe; the same information also tended to dominate the handwritten newsletters being sent regularly to London by the English residents in Hamburg, whose sources included regular reports out of Poland and from Vienna.[61] Those foreign reports rarely included news from Moscow, perhaps because little was to be had, but also possibly because it was simply of less interest than it seems to have been in Moscow itself (see below).

Certain subjects were of such interest that entire separate pamphlets were translated (in addition to whatever shorter notices were in the periodical press).[62] Noteworthy among them were reports about the treaty between the Netherlands and the Archbishopric of Münster in 1666; the abdication of Polish King Jan Kazimierz in 1668 and the election of his successor Michał Wiśnowiecki in 1669; a pamphlet containing a fictive threatening letter by the Ottoman sultan addressing the Habsburg Emperor in 1663; and the disorders in the Ottoman Empire in Arabia, especially during the brief period in 1665 and 1666 when, throughout Europe, attention was focussed on the Jewish false messiah Shabbetai Zevi. Some of the translated separates are of interest for the fact that at least a few copies of them eventually found their way into wider circulation beyond the Ambassadorial Chancery: this is the case with the account about the Polish election and the fictive letter by the sultan.[63] Probably the most intensively reported event, concerning the Ottoman disorders and Shabbetai Zevi, did not get into wider circulation. Throughout Europe it was a true news sensation,

---

61 See the files in National Archives, London, SP 101/39, 101/42 and 101/43. These newsletters were presumably sent under the cover of the letters between the Hamburg residents and their correspondents in London, now filed as SP 82.

62 See the overview in Maier, 'Vvodnaia chast'', pp. 108–31.

63 For the fictive letters of the sultan, see Waugh, *Great Turkes*; Daniel Waugh, 'The Russian versions of the apocryphal correspondence with the Ottoman sultan', in *Christian-Muslim Relations. A Bibliographical History, Volume 8. Northern and Eastern Europe (1600–1700)*, ed. by David Thomas and John Chesworth (Leiden: Brill, 2016), pp. 981–88; Ingrid Maier and Stepan Shamin, 'Legendarnoe poslanie turetskogo sultana nemetskim vladeteliam i vsem khristianam' (1663–64 g.). K voprosu o rasprostranenii perevodov evropeiskikh pamfletov iz Posol'skogo prikaza v rukopisnykh sbornikakh', *Drevniaia Rus'. Voprosy medievistiki*, 30. 4 (2007), 80–89. Maier located the Dutch original for the translation of 1664, a broadside brought to Moscow by Dutch merchants via Arkhangelsk.

not only unsettling Jewish communities everywhere and thus affecting commerce, but connecting with the eschatological concerns of various religious groups. The *kuranty* contain both translations of newspaper articles (notably from the *Oprechte Haerlemse Courant*) and translations from separate broadsides and pamphlets about the false messiah.[64] The interest in Moscow may in part be explained by the fact that anything that would unsettle the Ottoman Empire could have a bearing on whether the Turks might be able to pursue an aggressive policy in Southern Poland and Ukraine; similarly, Shabbetaian unrest clearly had the potential to destabilise Poland. It is also reasonable to assume that the atmosphere in Moscow involving the Church Schism and the concurrent eschatological expectations would have created an environment conducive to the spread of news about Shabbetai. In fact though, this may explain why the news never made it out of the chanceries (except in a separately produced anti-Jewish polemical book published somewhat later in Ukraine[65]): the Orthodox authorities and the Muscovite government seem to have been particularly concerned to suppress any manifestations of "popular religion" (including eschatological agitation) that could not be controlled and directed by the Church.

Not surprisingly, the coverage by the *kuranty* of foreign political news in the 1670s and 1680s seems to have been little different from that of the preceding decade, given that Muscovite foreign policy concerned itself with the same issues. News out of Poland and Ukraine and anything relating to the wars against the Turks and Tatars was of particular importance at a time when there were few periods of peace. Considerable diplomatic attention was devoted to the creation of a broad European coalition to fight the Turks, but any agreement with Poland about this was hindered by the historical legacy of its hostility with Muscovy, suspicions of deceit, and the as yet only tentative nature of the Truce of Andrusovo of 1667, which ongoing negotiations would

---

64   Daniel C. Waugh, 'News of the False Messiah: Reports on Shabbetai Zevi in Ukraine and Muscovy', *Jewish Social Studies*, 41. 3–4 (1979), 301–22; Ingrid Maier and Wouter Pilger, 'Polnische Fabelzeitung über Sabbatai Zwi, übersetzt für den russischen Zaren', *Zeitschrift für slavische Philologie*, 62. 1 (2003), 1–39; Ingrid Maier and Daniel C. Waugh, '"The Blowing of the Messiah's Trumpet". Reports about Sabbatai Sevi and Jewish Unrest in 1665–1667', in *Dissemination*, ed. by Dooley, pp. 137–52.

65   Ioanikii Haliatovs'kyi, *Mesia Pravdivyi Isus Khristos Syn Bozhii…* (Kiev, 1669).

succeed in converting into a "Permanent Peace" only in 1686. Following the military disaster of the loss of Chyhyryn in 1678, Muscovy achieved a temporary respite by signing a peace with the Tatars in 1681, but it was again drawn into the Ottoman wars following the Turkish failure at Vienna in 1683, which began a long and successful military effort to push the Turks out of East-Central Europe. Among the noteworthy events of this long conflict that were reported in the Russian translations from the European press were: the destruction of the Parthenon during its siege by the anti-Ottoman forces in 1687; and, a decade later, the important victory over the Ottomans achieved by the Habsburg armies under Eugene of Savoy at Zenta.[66] The first of these events, which had little strategic significance, probably attracted little attention when it was reported in the *kuranty* (nor would its cultural importance have been understood), but the second was the subject of several reports which made their way out of the confines of the chanceries and into wider circulation. In general, these decades were ones in which such translated items as the fictive letters of the sultan found wider audiences in Muscovy, although how we explain their appeal is uncertain. Was it because of the widespread concern over the Ottoman threat, or because of their being analogous to other polemical texts that circulated in Muscovy, or might there be some other explanation?

In his study of the *kuranty*, which focusses on the period of the 1670s and 1680s, Stepan Shamin delineates a number of topics (beyond the political reportage) which help us to appreciate the breadth of subject matter covered in the translations of foreign news and may thereby enhance our appreciation of why the *kuranty* would have interested the Muscovite elite. His focus is on what the news reports would have informed their Muscovite readers about various aspects of daily life and culture in Europe.[67]

Even today, by its very nature, the news often focusses on what threatens lives and livelihoods. In the world of the seventeenth century,

---

66 Daniel C. Waugh, 'News Sensations from the Front: Reportage in Late Muscovy concerning the Ottoman Wars', in *Rude & Barbarous Kingdom Revisited: Essays in Russian History and Culture in Honor of Robert O. Crummey*, ed. by Chester Dunning, Russell Martin and Daniel Rowland (Bloomington: Kritika, 2008), pp. 491–506 [with 2 plates]. The material there about the reports on Zenta needs substantial revision, to incorporate unpublished texts in the Russian archives.

67 For what follows here, see Shamin, *Kuranty*, Ch. 4.

understandably there was considerable attention devoted to reports of epidemics and disasters inflicted by severe weather. Of course, writing about such matters had a long history in Russia (as can be seen in chronicles and miracle tales). The news reports of the seventeenth century might cite them as evidence of divine dispensation (punishment for sins) or it might avoid such indications entirely. Reports sometimes specifically cast doubt on superstitious interpretations. For Muscovy, the news about epidemics was particularly significant, and we have evidence the government would quickly act to establish quarantines at borders if there was any indication of the spread of contagion.[68] This is one of the clearest indications of how the news in the *kuranty* was actually used, and how its timely receipt was important.

Phenomena of nature such as comets or meteor showers were a traditional source of concern; during earlier times in Russia and elsewhere these were often interpreted as warnings of some impending doom.[69] There was no clear distinction between what we term scientific astronomy and astrology. In this fertile soil for speculation and superstition, the occasional newspaper reports and often dramatically illustrated pamphlet separates or broadsides would resonate. A good many such accounts were translated, and the emphasis seems to have been on those that related the natural phenomena to impending disaster.[70] It is of interest in this regard to compare the *kuranty* reports

---

68 Apart from the examples cited by Shamin, one should note that the news about the major plague outbreak of 1665, translated for the *kuranty*, was marked by enclosing the relevant articles in boxes and placing crosses in the margins to indicate how important this news was. See RGADA, coll. 155, descr. 1, 1666 g., no. 11, fols. 56–57, 59; published in *V-K* VI/1, no. 65, pp. 231–32. Presumably these markings, undoubtedly contemporary, were to indicate items that were to be copied or cited in warnings to be sent to border commanders.

69 See, for example, Wolfgang Harms, *Das illustrierte Flugblatt in der Kultur der Frühen Neuzeit: Wolfenbüttler Arbeitsgespräch 1997* (Frankfurt am Main: Peter Lang, 1998). For a thought-provoking analysis of the changing interpretations of "natural wonders", see Katharine Park and Lorraine J. Daston. 'Unnatural Conceptions: The Study of Monsters in Sixteenth- and Seventeenth-Century France and England', *Past and Present*, 92 (1981), 20–54, and the same authors' *Wonders and the Order of Nature, 1150–1750* (New York and Cambridge, MA: Zone Press, 1998).

70 Apart from Shamin's *Kuranty*, pp. 216–31, see, e.g., Stepan Shamin and Andrei P. Bogdanov, 'Prirodnye iavleniia v tsarstvovanie Fedora Alekseevicha i chelovecheskoe soznanie (po gazetnoi informatsii Posol'skogo prikaza)', in *Istoricheskaia ekologiia i istoricheskaia demografiia* (Moscow: ROSSPEN, 2003), pp. 239–55 (pp. 244–46).

of the widely viewed comet of 1680 with reports about the same comet which Sir Peter Wyche, the English resident in Hamburg, sent home. The Russian texts (one apparently translated from an illustrated broadside) include, seemingly without comment or expression of doubt, the popular perceptions of the comet as a warning of disaster whose appearance coincided with other paranormal phenomena. The educated Wyche, who made it clear "my assent is not easily wonne to Wonders", nonetheless reported all these prognostications and stories about other supernatural phenomena. However, as a member of the Royal Society, he also recorded scientific observations about the comet and asked that they be sent on for the Society to use.[71]

Just as the reports on Shabbetai Zevi could not have been welcomed by the authorities if they threatened the stable order and official religious controls, likewise we find evidence that prognostications based on abnormal events in nature might be actively suppressed, for example in the period of political unrest following the death of Tsar Fedor Alekseevich in 1682. Of course not all of the real or imagined heavenly phenomena lent themselves to negative interpretations—one example, known to have entered Muscovy via Ukraine, was based on an apparently popular depiction of signs in the heavens interpreted to foretell the ultimate defeat of the Turks.[72] Some copies of this escaped the chanceries, perhaps with the support of someone in a high place, since propaganda to drum up support for the wars against the Ottomans would undoubtedly have had official encouragement.

There is no clear line to be drawn between some of the texts relating to the Ottoman wars, "heavenly" phenomena or other reports of unnatural events (for example, "monstrous births"), and a broader range of translated material in the *kuranty* that touches on various aspects of European religious affairs. The machinations of the Devil

---

71 National Archives, London, SP 82/16, containing letters of Sir Peter Wyche, English resident in Hamburg, to Sir Lionell Jenkins, here fol. 241, page 3 of letter sent 14/24 January 1681. Wyche's reports about the comet and what was being said about it begin on 23 November 1680 (Old Style) and continue through 21 January.

72 Waugh, 'Tekst'. For significant new information and a different interpretation regarding the origins of the text and its illustration, see Iurii D. Rykov and Stepan Shamin, 'Novye dannye o bytovanii perevodnogo izvestiia o Vengerskom nebesnom znamenii 1672 g. v russkoi rukopisnoi traditsii XVII veka', in *Istoriografiia, istochnikovedenie, istoriia Rossii X–XX vv.* (Moscow: Iazyki slavianskikh kul'tur, 2008), pp. 263–308.

lurked in some reports, alongside others that clearly focussed on matters of secular political import. Readers of the *kuranty* could in fact find out a lot about Protestant vs. Catholic conflicts, Papal policies, and disputes within the Catholic Church, in addition to material about the confrontation between the world of Islam and Christian Europe. The intentions of the Papacy regarding the Orthodox world were clearly of concern in considering potential alliances to fight the "common enemy of Christianity".

Public ceremonies, generally involving royalty and the European elite, were frequently reported in the Western news: celebrations of weddings, births, birthdays, military victories, and funerals. It is thanks to this interest that we have some valuable reports that have helped to rewrite the history of the first court theatre in Moscow.[73] While by no means all such reports made their way into the *kuranty* translations, this news was of interest if for no reason other than the fact that the Muscovite government kept close track of ceremonies that might in some way involve its own honour and prestige. This was not merely a matter of how one's own ambassadors might be received, but whether others were given more lavish treatment. In addition, there surely has to have been some interest in the possibility of emulating entertainments that were common to other major courts. The fact that fireworks were already a part of some celebrations in Muscovy in the late seventeenth century is one indication of such an interest. By the time of Peter's conquest of Azov in 1696, it is clear that in Moscow there was already a very good sense of the Baroque ceremonial celebration of military victories. One can at least posit that knowledge of the role of theatre and dance in court entertainment (even if not specifically derived from translated reports in the *kuranty*) had a bearing on the creation of the court theatre for Aleksei Mikhailovich.

Much has been made of the Muscovite government's concern over protocol in diplomacy, including in particular the accurate rendering of the tsar's titles. Frequently, negotiations foundered upon disputes

---

[73] See Claudia Jensen and Ingrid Maier, 'Orpheus and Pickleherring in the Kremlin: The "Ballet" for the Tsar of February 1672', *Scando-Slavica*, 59. 2 (2013), 145–84; idem, 'Pickleherring Returns to the Kremlin: More New Sources on the Pre-History of the Russian Court Theater', *Scando-Slavica*, 61. 1 (2015), 7–56. Both articles with some revisions have now been published together: see Klaudiia Dzhensen and Ingrid Maier, *Pridvornyi teatr v Rossii XVII veka. Novye istochniki* (Moscow: "Indrik", 2016).

over titulature. Such concerns were hardly unique to the Kremlin, any more than concerns other governments would express over the way their affairs were reported in the news. One might think that there was no particular value to the Kremlin in translating from foreign news reports about Muscovite business—after all, they could learn nothing of a factual nature about what was going on at home beyond what they already knew. Yet in fact there is a significant amount of material in the *kuranty* containing reports from Moscow.[74] There are well-known examples when, as the result of the publication of some report in the West, the tsar's government lodged an official protest, demanding that the offending publications be destroyed and their authors or publishers punished. One suspects that some of these incidents were deliberately blown out of proportion to serve some other diplomatic aim; of course, if there was little that could be done to curb private publishers, the response from the recipients of the complaints might be inaction. Only in rare instances did foreign authorities attempt to comply with what Moscow demanded.[75]

There is considerable evidence of widespread concern in Europe over the accuracy of reporting. English agents in the Baltic region would complain about what Dutch or German newspapers said about English affairs and constantly prodded their controllers in Whitehall to provide English versions of events that could be used in the foreign capitals to counter adverse propaganda. Sir Peter Wyche wrote to Sir Lionell Jenkins from Hamburg on 3 September 1680 (OS),

> I am in continuall Warre against the Impudent Libellers, But I must confesse I yet can not bethincke my selfe how to putt in practice Your Commands, to buy off the Gazettiers, to speake neither good nor bad of Our affaires. With all humble submission I thincke they are to bee more roughly handled and every Minister in his Post is to oblige the Government where he is, not to allow them to print the scandalous advices... I have complained, and will have the Printer severely punisht...[76]

The attitude expressed here and the action it proposed are little different from what we find the Kremlin doing if a foreign news report offended it.

---

74 There is an extended discussion of this material in Shamin, *Kuranty*, Ch. 3.
75 E.g., *ibid.*, p. 151.
76 National Archives, London, SP 82/16, fols. 175-175v.

Apart from anything that would have been of concern to the Muscovite government, in Muscovy the Scottish General Patrick Gordon, a passionate adherent of the Catholic Stuarts, was distressed when he received news (probably based on Dutch reports) about the invasion of William of Orange in 1688 that led to the "glorious revolution" that toppled King James II and VII.[77] To him those reports were biased, even if, as he admitted, they had some element of truth about the weakness of the Royalists' efforts to put James back on the throne. What Gordon may not fully have appreciated was the degree to which the Dutch Resident in Moscow, Baron von Keller, was perhaps manipulating the news he received (quite apart from the events of 1688) and was transmitting to the Muscovite officials, in ways that worked against English interests.[78]

This history opens up for us the possibility that by the 1680s, if not earlier, the acquisition and dissemination of foreign news in the elite circles in Moscow might have a significant political impact. The official acquisition of foreign news and its translation contributed to this awareness of contemporary events in Europe, but it was surely only part of the reason why there was a level of knowledge within the Foreign Suburb, and in the regular interactions between the foreigners and the arbiters of Muscovite affairs, that far exceeded what it might have been only a generation earlier. It was not merely an awareness of the value of factual reporting, but of the usefulness of manipulating the news for one's own advantage. Indeed, as Shamin has suggested, there is some indication that foreign news stories were manipulated in translation to serve even domestic purposes, and by the mid-1660s there is evidence the Muscovite government was arranging to have stories planted in the Western press that would reflect favourably on Muscovy. While we have no proof it was acted on, a Swedish merchant in Lübeck, Johann van Horn, made a concrete proposal in 1667 to Ordin-Nashchokin whereby he would have become, in effect, Muscovy's press agent in the West.[79] In any event, the planting of favourable stories had become a common practice by the time of Peter, which undoubtedly helps to explain why he created the published *Vedomosti*, so that the government would have

---

77   Waugh, 'The Best Connected Man', p. 112.
78   Thomas Eekmann, 'Muscovy's International Relations in the Late Seventeenth Century: Johan van Keller's Observations', *California Slavic Studies*, 14 (1992), 44–67.
79   Shamin, *Kuranty*, pp. 152–53, no.18.

its own organ for spreading internally the news that would support the tsar's policies.

In processing the flow of foreign news, the Muscovite functionaries quickly developed a sense that careful selection was imperative, as was the awareness that timeliness in receipt was significant if the information was to have any operative value. This may have been less significant than the dramatic transformation in Europe that resulted from the communications revolution, during which, as Wolfgang Behringer points out, people began to mark time by the postal schedules, and a common salutation might be "What's news?"[80] At very least though, it is clear that being saturated with news did not mean accepting all of it uncritically.

Certainly there was a relationship between the acquisition of foreign news and the making of foreign policy. Yet there are very few direct indications that foreign policy decisions followed upon receipt of a particular news item via the *kuranty*, or depended on the receipt of such news. Of course this could merely reflect a convention whereby such indications would not have made it into the written record, especially where that written record all too rarely provides any insight into the actual deliberations that resulted in the adoption of a particular policy. Another possibility, though, is that news sources other than the *kuranty* were more significant, since at least for neighbouring countries they might be more current and/or accurate. Where historians have paid close attention (which is all too rarely) to the acquisition of news and its relationship to the making of foreign policy (a noteworthy exception is the negotiations leading to the Permanent Peace with Poland in 1686), the evidence suggests that information obtained by well-placed agents played a crucial role, rather than the news reports coming out of Poland that were commonly printed in the newspapers.[81] Might it not be, as evidence from Western Europe continues to remind us, that the handwritten reports of trusted agents were much more likely to be valued by those in power than anything in the newspapers? Perhaps Baron Mayerberg's sneer about how the benighted Muscovites in the 1660s believed anything they read in the printed foreign newspapers is

---

80 Behringer, *Im Zeichen des Merkur*, pp. 106–07, p. 117.
81 Kirill A. Kochegarov, *Rech' Pospolitaia i Rossiia v 1680–1686 godakh. Zakliuchenie dogovora o Vechnom mire* (Moscow: INDRIK, 2008).

totally wrong: when it came to practical policies, they may have believed little of it.[82] At the very least, they were selective in what they actually used. At best, we might posit that the importance of the *kuranty* lay in what they contained about the broader context of European affairs which was not usually to be found in the more localised intelligence reports. Yet the evidence shows that in the process of selecting what news to translate, the Kremlin functionaries often deliberately narrowed the focus to the subjects that lay closest to home.

The pre-eminent historian of the Muscovite post, I. P. Kozlovskii, articulated clearly the idea that the foreign post was, at least potentially, of immense cultural significance for Russia. Yet, by the end of the seventeenth century, when so few Russians were actually using it, he had to confess that its cultural impact had been disappointing. If we are to assess the cultural impact of the *kuranty*, whose history is inseparable from that of the post, we might be forced to reach the same conclusion, which is hardly at odds with what we already know about cultural change in late Muscovy. We must stress again that the *kuranty* were never *intended* for broad distribution; the news in them was deemed confidential, for the eyes and ears of the tsar and his close advisers. However, there is something to be said about the impact of the post and the *kuranty* beyond the circles of the court in Moscow.

Certainly one can trace the spread of a rather small number of manuscript copies of some of the translations that were part of the corpus of the *kuranty*.[83] Even as early as the late fifteenth and the first half of the sixteenth century, the few translated foreign pamphlets we have in Muscovy are to be found exclusively in a few monastic miscellanies. Whether it is sufficient to conclude, as Shamin does, that they therefore "left a noteworthy mark on the cultural and religious life of sixteenth-century Russia" may, of course, be debated.[84] One then has to jump ahead to the second quarter of the seventeenth century to find

---

82 Avgustin Meierberg, "Puteshestvie v Moskoviiu Barona Avgustina Meierberga", in *Utverzhdenie dinastii. Andrei Rode. Avgustin Meierberg. Samuel' Kollins. Iakov Reitenfel's (Istoriia Rossii i Doma Romanovykh v memuarakh sovremennikov XVII–XX vv.)* (Moscow: Fond Sergeia Dubova. Rita-Print, 1997), p. 90.

83 Shamin, *Kuranty*, brings together an overview of such material in his concluding Chapter 5; he has elaborated on the history of several texts in various articles cited there and in work that continues to appear as he mines the Russian manuscript collections.

84 Cf. *ibid.*, p. 283.

evidence about the spread of translated "news pamphlets", evidence that, significantly, may be found in documents concerning government investigations about possible sedition or religious deviance. Rare are the instances in which we encounter more than an isolated copy of a text in some manuscript miscellany. Exceptions include the apocryphal letters of the sultan and a few pamphlets with prognostications based on wonder signs. Undoubtedly, people with close connections to the Ambassadorial Chancery somehow facilitated the making of copies that made their way outside the chancery milieu, even if it is difficult to identify who the individuals were. There are rare instances in which, on receipt of news about, say, an important victory of a Muscovite ally, the authorities would deliberately disseminate that news in order that the event be celebrated publicly. Unofficial channels may have circumvented the Ambassadorial Chancery (for example, if texts were translated in Ukraine). Whatever exactly the processes, what we really want to know is whether any of the translated brochures or occasional news reports of political or military events might have changed the worldview of Russian readers. To the extent that we can identify who owned the manuscripts, the "readership" would seem in the first instance to involve those who might already have been in a position to acquire a broader outlook than the ordinary peasant or villager. The content and number of the texts is so limited that they could hardly have done much to open up a wider world and provide their owners or readers with a sense of contemporaneity. If anything, arguably they generated interest because they connected with contemporary preconceptions and fitted comfortably within the framework of existing Muscovite culture.

Were we to follow the lead of some historians of the European press, we might wish to make the case that the *kuranty* provide evidence for increasing rationalism and secularism that are deemed to be hallmarks of modernity. Yet, even for other parts of Europe, such an emphasis has come under question, as scholars explore more broadly the ways in which news was transmitted and the content of the various popular genres transmitting it. Certainly there is no lack of material in the *kuranty* regarding the paranormal or natural wonders, and, as we have seen, some of what there is might be understood most persuasively within a context of traditional religious culture. Just because the *kuranty* were the province of a court elite does not mean then that this elite had moved far from the cultural milieu in which they were raised, any more than the readers of Western newspapers in, say, Hamburg, can be assumed to have abandoned a providential view of the world inspired by deep religious devotion. The spread of *kuranty* texts may be significant as an indication of change in the patterns of Muscovite interaction with its neighbours and some kind of greater integration of Muscovy in Europe, but we should be very cautious in drawing any conclusions from such limited evidence regarding what the foreign news could possibly have meant for those who read or heard it. To have possessed a few of the translated reports hardly makes the owners of the manuscripts "readers of the foreign news" in any meaningful sense.[85]

Since earlier studies of the *kuranty* focussed on their relationship to the first published newspaper in Russia, Peter's *Vedomosti*, a few concluding comments on that subject are in order. Clearly the *kuranty* were *not* "Russia's first newspaper", if by newspaper we mean a publicly available periodical publication communicating news about current events. The *kuranty* were not published. They were not created to meet some broader demand from society at large to be informed regularly and rapidly about current events. Therefore, despite the fact that very occasionally items from the *kuranty* made it into wider circulation, it is impossible to speak of their having a role in the creation of a "public sphere", as Jürgen Habermas argued (problematically) for the European newspapers of the seventeenth and early eighteenth centuries. That said, it is clear that the mechanisms that were in place and functioning well by the last decades of the seventeenth century, connecting Muscovy with the European news networks, were essential to the creation of the *Vedomosti*, whose first issue (not extant in printed form) seems to have appeared in 1702.[86] That is, to the degree that foreign reports made it into the new printed newspapers in Russia, they were supplied in a way

---

85   Cf. *ibid.*, p. 302.
86   There is a common misperception that the first printed *Vedomosti* date from 1703, but as K. V. Kharlampovich convincingly argued, even though no printed copies are extant, manuscript copies suggest that the first two numbers appeared near the end of 1702. See Konstantin V. Kharlampovich 'Vedomosti Moskovskogo gosudarstva 1702 goda', *Izvestiia Otdeleniia russkogo iazyka i slovesnosti Rossiiskoi Akademii nauk*, 23. 1 (1918), 1–18. Kharlampovich's argument seems to have been accepted by the compilers of the standard bibliography of Petrine imprints in Slavonic type, T. A. Bykova and M. M. Gurevich, in *Opisanie izdanii, napechatannykh kirillitsei. 1689-ianvar' 1725 g.* (Moscow and Leningrad: Izdatel'stvo Akademii nauk SSSR, 1958), p. 83. Those unique copies are in the manuscript which is the subject of Waugh, *Istoriia odnoi knigi*.

that differed little from what had become Muscovite practice. What Peter and his advisers knew about the nature and role of the European press, knowledge acquired in part through the *kuranty*, surely provided the inspiration for a regular, published organ of news controlled by the government and intended as a tool for generating support for Peter's policies. The European experience certainly contained examples of a politically controlled press alongside the more abundant and freewheeling private news publications, which were nonetheless not immune to censorship and proscription. Was Peter's goal in creating the *Vedomosti* to educate its readers and listeners and not merely to whip up enthusiasm for his policies? Possibly. But such a goal cannot be read into the history of the creation and development of the *kuranty*. As with so many other developments, the history of the *kuranty* is indeed part of the story of Russia's "Europeanisation" or "modernisation", but inevitably we need to recognise that developments we can trace both in Russia and elsewhere in Europe generally do not move in synchrony. Newspapers in Russia only began to play the role attributed to them in the West in a later era.

4. How Was Western Europe Informed about Muscovy? The Razin Rebellion in Focus

Ingrid Maier[1]

The Cossack peasant rebellion under the leadership of Stepan Razin, with its culmination in the year 1670, was not only a major event in Muscovy; it was also an exceptional media sensation. West European newspapers printed the latest reports from the battlefront with great regularity, as well as rumours about the leader, Razin, and his plans and military alliances. When no news had arrived at the publisher's desk, this very lack of information was considered to be worth mentioning, for instance with the remark "About Razin there is no news, beyond that he is neither dead nor captured", found in a Dutch newspaper

---

1   The research for this chapter was provided primarily by The Swedish Foundation for Humanities and Social Sciences (*Riksbankens jubileumsfond*, 'Cross-Cultural Exchange in Early Modern Europe', RFP12–0055:1). Moreover, the author is most grateful to the National Endowment for the Humanities (RZ-51635–13) who helped to fund several research trips to London, Stockholm, and Bremen. Any views, findings, or conclusions expressed in this chapter do not necessarily represent those of the funding organisations. Holger Böning and Michael Nagel at the research institute *Deutsche Presseforschung* have made my extended stays in Bremen both productive and enjoyable, providing help in both scholarly and practical issues. My frequent co-author, Daniel Waugh (Seattle), has read two draft versions of this chapter and made numerous very helpful comments; he also pointed out many relevant documents. I also offer my warm thanks to Claudia Jensen, for her editorial help, and to Gleb Kazakov for the discussions, particularly relating to Fig. 2 in the present chapter.

printed in Haarlem.² One of the reasons for the unparalleled interest in all matters concerning the Razin uprising is the fact that the rebellion had a negative influence on trade, not only within Russia (or between Muscovy proper and the region of the Don Cossacks, beyond the "Don steppe frontier"³), but also between Muscovy and Western Europe. Merchants from Holland, England and Hamburg were discouraged from trading with Russia during the peak of the uprising, and thus there was a risk that trade between Russia and Western Europe would come to a standstill. The real culmination of the Razin rebellion, however, was reached several months earlier than the peak of the corresponding media hype in West European newspapers and pamphlets.

The reporting on the Razin rebellion is an excellent example to illustrate how news was collected in Moscow and transmitted to the West. The important research questions include: how did the publishers get the reports from Muscovy that ended up in their newspapers? Who were the authors, and how was the news transmitted to the West? The hypothesis is that there is some kind of connection between diplomatic correspondence and printed (or handwritten⁴) newspapers—a connection that has actually been demonstrated for a slightly earlier time period, viz. the early 1650s, when the Swedish resident in Moscow, Johan de Rodes, was sending regular reports to Queen Christina of Sweden, and the content of some of these letters could also be traced in printed Hamburg newspapers.⁵ Granted, we still do not know whether de Rodes himself had the necessary contacts with traders of news;

---

2   *Oprechte Haerlemse Dingsdaegse Courant* 1671, no. 18 (National Archives London, SP 119/53, fol. 53v), in a news item datelined Moscow, 26 March 1671. Most of the surviving historical Dutch newspapers are now available online at http://kranten.delpher.nl/

3   The term is borrowed from Brian J. Boeck's monograph *Imperial Boundaries. Cossack Communities and Empire-Building in the Age of Peter the Great* (New York: Cambridge University Press, 2009).

4   I am focussing on printed newspapers because I have not studied manuscript newspapers—which also played an important role at the time—in any systematic way.

5   See Martin Welke, 'Rußland in der deutschen Publizistik des 17. Jahrhunderts (1613–1689)', *Forschungen zur osteuropäischen Geschichte*, 23 (1976), 105–276 (pp. 151–53 and 255–64).

possibly the letters to the Swedish heartland were copied somewhere en route (for instance, in Narva).

While my main focus here is on Swedish diplomatic correspondence, I will first review how Razin's rebellion was mirrored in the periodical press of the time, focussing above all on German-language newspapers from Hamburg, with only occasional examples from papers issued in other languages or from other countries. The German newspapers, especially the ones from Hamburg, are of particular interest, since they contain more—and also more detailed—articles about the uprising than other papers (including the Latin newspaper from Cologne).

The Razin Rebellion as a Media Sensation

According to the German press historian Martin Welke, the Razin rebellion was one of the most frequently reported subjects in the German-language press of the years 1670–71: between September 1670 and August 1671, on average, there was news about this rebellion in every third or fourth newspaper issue available to him. He found a total of 180 items in that timespan that contained news about Razin. Another 40 items, dealing with the Muscovite government's—usually successful—attempts to defeat the rebellion, after the execution of its leader had become known in the Western press, were found in papers printed between September 1671 and February 1672.[6] The "media peak" thus started around the time when the actual uprising was more or less over: Razin had won his last military victories—at Saratov and

---

6 *Ibid.*, p. 203. Welke studied all the issues of printed newspapers in German for the relevant period that were available in the research institute *Deutsche Presseforschung* in Bremen, which houses copies of more than 60,000 different newspaper issues. When Welke's dissertation appeared in print, in 1976, the huge collection of German newspapers kept at the *Rossiiskii gosudarstvennyi arkhiv drevnikh aktov* (RGADA) in Moscow was not yet known in Germany; copies were received in Bremen only at the very end of the 1970s. See V. I. Simonov, 'Deutsche Zeitungen des 17. Jahrhunderts im Zentralen Staatsarchiv für alte Akten (CGADA), Moskau', *Gutenberg-Jahrbuch*, 54 (1979), 210–20. Simonov lists all German-language newspaper issues that have survived in RGADA. To the 640 issues from the period September 1670 until August 1671 which Welke studied we can now add several dozen unique copies printed during the relevant time period in the Eastern part of the German-language territory, above all in Königsberg and in Berlin (*ibid.*, pp. 215, 217).

Samara—in August 1670; in a decisive battle near Simbirsk the rebel was wounded and "disappeared from the scene until his final capture", which took place on 14 April 1671.[7] As noted already, the "culmination" of the rebellion in West European newspapers was "delayed", in comparison with the historical facts. The earliest item published in A. G. Mankov's chapter about "Reports from newspapers and chronicles" is datelined Moscow, 14 August [1670],[8] an exceptionally long article about Razin's seizure of Astrakhan and a discussion of the consequences for Moscow's supply of fish, salt and horses from that region.[9] The reason for this paradox cannot be explained exclusively by the transmission time; that is, it would normally take only about five to six weeks for news from Moscow to arrive at the newspaper publishers in Hamburg[10]

---

7   The date 14 April is mentioned in the verdict, read aloud publicly on the day of Stepan Razin's execution; see the publication of this text in *Krest'ianskaia voina pod predvoditel'stvom Stepana Razina*, vols 1–4 (Moscow: Izdatel'stvo Akademii nauk, 1954–1976), here vol. 3, no. 81, p. 87. See also André Berelowitch, 'Stenka Razin's Rebellion: The Eyewitnesses and their Blind Spot', in *From Mutual Observation to Propaganda War: Premodern Revolts in their Transnational Representations*, ed. by Malte Griesse (Bielefeld: Transcript Verlag, 2014), pp. 93–124 (p. 105).

8   *Inostrannye izvestiia o vosstanii Stepana Razina. Materialy i issledovaniia*, ed. by A. G. Man'kov (Leningrad: Nauka, 1975), pp. 92–93.

9   "[…] and trade with Prussia and Russia will probably come to a sudden standstill, and Moscow will be in great disorder because all salted fish—which is so important for this nation, because of a high number of fasting-days—and also the salt used to come here [from that place], and every year 40 000 horses from that region were brought to the tsar […]" (Man'kov, *Inostrannye izvestiia*, p. 93). The number of horses seems very high, and generally numbers (e.g., of Razin's followers, or of those killed) given in newspaper articles are far too high. On the other hand, the information about the consequences for trade within Muscovy makes it clear that the author of that correspondence from Moscow must have had a very good knowledge of Muscovite trade. Cf. also the partially overlapping information in *Nordischer Mercurius*, pp. 587–88 (quoted Man'kov, p. 95).

10 Cf. Daniel C. Waugh and Ingrid Maier, 'How Well Was Muscovy Connected with the World?', in *Imperienvergleich. Beispiele und Ansätze aus osteuropäischer Perspektive. Festschrift für Andreas Kappeler*, ed. by Guido Hausmann and Angela Rustemeyer, Forschungen zur osteuropäischen Geschichte, vol. 75 (Wiesbaden: Harrassowitz, 2009), pp. 17–38 (pp. 31, 33). The timespan of twenty or, at most, twenty-one days for mail from Moscow to reach Hamburg, mentioned in a news item in *Nordischer Mercurius*, datelined Moscow, 17 August 1668, is quite optimistic; only under optimal conditions could a letter from Moscow to Hamburg reach its addressee so fast. Some years later, in 1674, Philipp Kilburger gives the same optimistic view regarding the transmission time from Moscow to Hamburg: twenty-one days via Vilna and twenty-three days via Riga; see B. G. Kurts, *Sochinenie Kil'burgera o russkoi torgovle v tsarstvovanie Alekseia Mikhailovicha* (Kiev: Tip. I. I. Chokolova, 1915), p. 160.

or Amsterdam (and some additional time for it to have reached the Russian capital in the first place), not several months. Another part of the explanation may lie in the fact that the "disappearance" of Razin from the battlefield constituted fertile ground for speculations, rumour and hearsay, much of which was published in Western news media. These news items often had very little in common with the actual events.

According to Welke, as many as twenty-one newspaper items had as their subject Razin's execution;[11] moreover, two German-language "execution pamphlets" are known (see below, especially note 40). A number of pamphlets about the rebellion (and, above all, about Razin's execution in Moscow on 6 June 1671) also appeared in other countries: in Holland, in the Holy Roman Empire, in England, and finally in France.[12] All known contemporary Razin-related pamphlets, and also a small portion of contemporary newspaper items, were republished during the Soviet era.[13] Prior to these publications of printed sources from other countries, a multi-volume edition of Russian-language archival documents about the rebellion had been published by the Historical Institute of the Soviet Academy of Sciences, under the generic title "The peasant war under the leadership of Stepan Razin".[14]

How Reliable was the Printed Razin News?

The newspaper publishers and printers (in the first century of the printed newspaper this was often the same person) faced a rather difficult task in choosing the news items that they found most interesting for their readership, and most trustworthy, from among the incoming commercial newsletters, or from previously printed papers.[15]

---

11   Welke, 'Rußland', p. 204, no. 444.
12   See A. L. Gol'dberg, 'K istorii soobshcheniia o vosstanii Stepana Razina', in *Zapiski inostrantsev o vosstanii Stepana Razina*, ed. by A. G. Man'kov (Leningrad: Nauka, 1968), pp. 157–65; Berelowitch, 'Stenka Razin's Rebellion', p. 97.
13   Man'kov, *Zapiski inostrantsev* and *Inostrannye izvestiia*.
14   *Krest'ianskaia voina*.
15   A very insightful treatment of the development of the news market is in the recent book by Andrew Pettegree, *The Invention of News. How the World Came to Know about Itself* (New Haven and London: Yale University Press, 2014). About the problem of "establishing the veracity of news reports" (regarding commercial manuscript newsletters), see especially pp. 2–3 and 115–16.

To determine the reliability of news was a constant challenge, and not only with regard to news from Russia: how could a publisher decide which of the reported stories might later prove to be true, and which would turn out to have been mere gossip and hearsay? One option was, of course, to wait for independent congruent information from other sources. However, in this case the scrupulous publisher would risk being scooped by another paper whose editor was not so careful about verification. News from Muscovy sometimes had to pass through many mouths (and pens) before ending up in a printed newspaper. If one person in this information chain, which stretched between a faraway eyewitness and the publisher (or, for that matter, the copyist of a manuscript paper), invented a few spicy details in order to make the news more interesting and therefore more "saleable", the person at the end of the chain had no means whatsoever to detect this. The truth could be determined only in retrospect. The people who traded in news were very much aware of this problem, as can be shown on the basis of the following examples from printed newspaper articles, in which these difficulties are mentioned explicitly either by the author or by the editor.

In a news item from Hamburg, 17 February 1671, published in the Berlin-based newspaper *Mittwochischer Mercurius* and dealing mainly with the uncertainty of incoming information about a conflict in nearby Braunschweig (also situated in the Northern part of the German Empire), the Hamburg correspondent makes a most telling comparison: "To sum up: nobody knows what is the truth in this question. How could we ever, in such circumstances, have any trustworthy information from Moscow, situated some 400 miles away?"[16] This journalist was clearly addressing the permanent uncertainty concerning news about the Razin rebellion, when numerous contradictory reports could be read in the press. The problem that no one could guarantee the truth of any specific news item describing the current state of affairs in far-away Muscovy was regularly addressed in the articles. According

---

16 *Mittwochischer Mercurius, zur 8. Woche 1671 gehörig*, news item "Ein anders/ vom vorigen" (= Hamburg, 17 Feb.) on p. [2]. The only surviving original is in Moscow (RGADA, coll. 155, descr. 1, 1671, no. 3, fol. 22v). There is a cross mark in the margins exactly next to this sentence—apparently, this is a translator's mark.

to Welke, thirty-nine of the news items studied by him (from the period up to the first reliable reports about Razin's execution) explicitly talked about the fact that there was contradictory news, that a previously printed news item had proven to be wrong, or that the latest news had not yet been confirmed.[17] In the example quoted above the problem had been addressed by the author of the news item, but we have evidence for the same kind of awareness among some newspaper publishers. Without any doubt the editor and publisher of the Hamburg-based paper *Nordischer Mercurius*, Georg Greflinger, took the lead in this race, constantly emphasising the uncertainty of all incoming news from Muscovy. Browsing the complete collections of the years 1670–71[18] gives plenty of examples, such as the following news item, datelined *"Nider-Elbe vom 9. May"* ("Lower Elbe, 9 May" [1671]): "Letters from Moscow itself of 31 March Old Style do not mention any particular disturbances in connection with the rebels. They confirm that a leading member of Razin's party was captured, his hands and feet were severed, and finally he was hanged. Other [letters] report something different. Time will be witness to everything".[19] All news items containing the place name *"Nider-Elbe"* were apparently put together in Hamburg, and we can make a qualified guess that the "Lower-Elbe" items printed in the *Nordischer Mercurius* were composed by Greflinger himself, generally using material from several incoming newsletters sent from different places.

---

17 Welke, 'Rußland', p. 203.
18 The regular newspaper issues have a continuous pagination for the whole year, and title pages only for every new month and new year; other issues indicate only the year and the current month in the same line (for instance, "Anno 1671. Majus".). This "yearbook character" might have been the reason for the fact that some complete year collections of the *Nordischer Mercurius* have survived: the newspaper was not always used to wrap sandwiches, but at least some subscribers kept all their issues and took them to the book binder at the end of the year. For the year 1671 two complete collections are known, one in *Deichmanske bibliotek* in Oslo, the other in the Royal Library of Copenhagen (signature: 147.15); there are copies, as always, in Bremen (*Deutsche Presseforschung*). The entire Bremen collection has been digitised over the past few years and is now available at http://brema.suub.uni-bremen.de/zeitungen17/
19 *Nordischer Mercurius*, May 1671, p. 288. The source here alludes to the fact that Muscovy, in common with many parts of Western Europe, still used the Julian calendar (the 'old style'), in contrast with the Gregorian calendar (the 'new style') that had been introduced for most Catholic countries in 1582.

News Directly from Moscow, and from "Passionate Places"

Comments by Greflinger in his *Nordischer Mercurius* suggest he considered news that was communicated in letters directly from Moscow to be more trustworthy than news composed in other places. The reason for this might be previous experience, for instance, that fewer *post-factum* corrections were needed for news that came directly from Moscow, compared with newsletters composed—less frequently—in Pskov or Novgorod, or beyond the Muscovite borders.

News items about the Razin rebellion composed in Moscow during the first six months of 1671 report, as a rule, that the situation was under control (which is more or less according to the historical facts), whereas ones that had been written in Riga, Stockholm, Vilna, Warsaw, Lemberg (today Lviv, Ukraine), Danzig etc.—that is, by authors from Sweden and Poland-Lithuania, Russia's potential enemies—tended to present the Russian state as weakened by the rebellion and to exaggerate Razin's successes up to the very day of his execution[20] and even beyond that date. So, for instance, we have a Russian translation of a news item from Hamburg, 6 June 1671, stating that "Couriers report from Livonia and from Moscow that the traitor Razin is again gathering his forces and seizing cities".[21] Ironically, 6 June was actually the day of Razin's execution in Moscow. Almost two months prior to this he had been captured near Kagalnik (a village situated eight kilometres from Azov) by Kornei Iakovlev, the *ataman* (Cossack leader) of the Don Host (who was loyal to the tsar).[22] Another item, datelined Warsaw 31 January [1671] and also translated for the Muscovite government, is in a printed Dutch newspaper from The Hague: "The news from Muscovy reports that the rebellion there is still going on and that the colonel [i.e., Razin]

---

20   Cf. also Welke, 'Rußland', p. 203f.
21   The Russian translation is in RGADA, coll. 155, descr. 1, 1671, no. 7, fol. 158. The *kuranty* (compilations of foreign news that were produced regularly at the Ambassadorial Chancery) for the years 1671–72 are being prepared for publication under the title *Vesti-Kuranty 1671–1672 gg.* and will be printed in 2017. I have *not* been able to locate the original news item in German, which presumably was in a printed newspaper from Berlin or Königsberg that has not survived, so my translation is from the Russian version. The relevant printed papers had arrived in Moscow via the Vilna postal line on 6 July 1671; see RGADA, *ibid.*, fol. 155.
22   *Krest'ianskaia voina*, vol. 3, no. 56, p. 62 and no. 58, p. 64.

and his followers have conquered not only Astrakhan and Kazan, but also about 50 other important places. Their troops are said to consist of about 200,000 men. An envoy from the Swedish crown is said to have arrived there with letters, in which he [Razin] calls himself the Tsar of Astrakhan, to treat with him. Allegedly the Persian [shah] also is interfering in this rebellion on account of differences [with Russia] over the Caspian Sea".[23] The numbers in this news item are heavily exaggerated, and it is exactly the kind of report about which the publisher of *Nordischer Mercurius*, Greflinger, would have commented with the explanation that it had come from a "passionate place" (that is, the news is biased). Why such patently ridiculous articles were translated for the *kuranty* when the tsar, of course, had much better, more up-to-date, and more reliable sources about the current situation, has already been discussed in another article.[24] It is well known that the Muscovite government was interested in foreign reporting about Muscovy, especially if it was false and could be protested. The tsar's colonel, Nicolaus von Staden, wrote from Novgorod on 24 September (probably 1672) to a representative of the Swedish crown:[25] "[…] Regarding the protest, which his Tsarish majesty has directed to the Swedish crown in connection with printed newspapers: it can be answered truly — as Count Tott also said in his answer to me — that neither in Sweden, nor in Riga, nor in any other territory belonging to his Royal Majesty [of Sweden] are any newspapers in German being printed. It is impossible to protect oneself from such deceitful people [*falsche leute*], who write down such lies and hardly control them, God forgive them. The old Marselis,[26] who receives the newspapers, and

---

23 The slightly abbreviated Russian translation is in RGADA, coll. 155, descr. 1, 1671, no. 7, fol. 6v-7, the Dutch original in *Haegse Dynsdaeghse Post-tydinge* no. 14, preserved in RGADA, coll. 155, descr. 1, 1671, file 5, fol. 8. My translation is made from the Dutch original, not from the Russian version. Cf. also Ingrid Maier and Stepan Shamin, '"Revolts" in the *Kuranty* of March-July 1671', in *From Mutual Observation to Propaganda War*, ed. by Griesse, pp. 181–203 (p. 193, with an English translation of the *kuranty* version).
24 Maier and Shamin, '"Revolts" in the *Kuranty*'.
25 Swedish State Archives in Stockholm (SSAS), Diplomatica Muscovitica, vol. 83 (not paginated). Since the letter to the (anonymous) "*Hochgeehrter H. Bruder*" ('highly honoured brother') was preserved among Adolf Eberschildt's letters to the Swedish king, it is most likely that the diplomat Eberschildt was the addressee.
26 Peter Marselis, who had administrated the Russian post for a couple of years.

always immediately makes translations of news from Sweden directed against Moscow, has only caused problems because of that".

We find the very first authentic (*post-factum*) information about Razin's capture in a news item from Hamburg ("*Nider-Elbe*") dated 20 June, in which the editor (Greflinger) refers to newsletters directly from Moscow: "Letters of 16 May Old Style from Moscow itself confirm that the rebel Razin has been captured, and that he is being brought to the tsar very slowly. However, there are still no details about the manner in which he was captured and taken from his army. Some [letters] add that all lost cities, except Astrakhan, are again in the possession of the tsar".[27] The first sentence may well be based upon a dispatch from Moscow sent to governor Simon Grundel-Helmfelt in Narva from the same date, quoted below (see p. 138).

The newspapers occasionally referred explicitly to the fact that a news item's reliability might depend on its place of origin. Several authors, as well as the publisher Greflinger, speak about "passionate places" ("*passionierte Orte*"), which should be understood as "partial, biased, one-sided" in this context. Examples are an item from Danzig, dated 7 April 1671: "Some [authors] talk again about the rebel Razin's big successes, although this news for the most parts originates from 'passionate' places",[28] or another, datelined "*Nider-Elbe vom 9. April*" (that is, most certainly containing Greflinger's own voice): "There is news via Danzig saying that [those of] the Don Cossacks, whom Moscow is trying to win for money, are now on the side of the main rebel, Stepan Razin. However, some [people] think this is biased news" ["*vor eine passionierte Zeitung gehalten wird*"].[29]

Many strongly biased news reports from "passionate places" can be found in the Cologne-based Latin newspaper *Ordinariæ Relationes*. For example, the following item from Lemberg (Lviv):

> Lemberg, 27 March. [...] From Muscovy we have learned that the rebellion is growing stronger and uglier from day to day, and that the rebels threaten to kill the Muscovite Grand Prince. Peasants and [people] belonging to the lowest layer of men flee in growing numbers to the army of the rebel Stepan Razin [*Stephani Raninii*] because they see that

---

27 *Nordischer Mercurius* (June 1671), p. 380.
28 *Nordischer Mercurius* (April 1671), p. 217.
29 Ibid., p. 253.

4. How Was Western Europe Informed about Muscovy? 123

the Muscovite Prince is inferior in the defensive struggle, and that they will be living more safely under Stepan's leadership than under the rule of the [Grand] Prince.[30]

Most suspicious of all, at least in Greflinger's opinion, seemed to be those newsletters about the rebellion which were sent from Riga. International mail from Moscow was usually sent via the Riga postal line, which had been established in 1665; Riga was thus an important transfer point for news out of Moscow. When the Moscow news arrived in Riga, it was usually "completed" with information from other places—and probably with a great deal of hearsay. Greflinger summarises the difference between Moscow news and Riga news in an item from "Nider-Elbe" (Hamburg), dated 3 February: "Letters from Muscovy dated 24 December report that everything is calm, whereas Livonian letters say it is all bad".[31] That much faked news was sent out from Riga can be explained in part by a conscious disinformation campaign carried out by the tsar's Riga-born colonel, Nicolaus von Staden, in the spring of 1671. A news item from Riga, dated 6 March 1671, reports his arrival and then continues: "Moreover we hear from this envoy's people that the well-known rebel Stepan Razin has been completely defeated. 20,000 of his former followers were hanged, the same amount captured and killed by sword, and about 50,000 have been drowned".[32] This news was biased, and the numbers of people killed are heavily exaggerated. This can be compared with earlier information from "passionate places", according to which Razin had assembled an army of 100,000 men. It may well be that Nicolaus von Staden's "disinformation campaign", conducted while he was in Riga in the spring of 1671 (undoubtedly on the tsar's

---

30 *Ordinariæ Relationes* 1671, no. 36 (printing date: 5 May 1671). The complete year collection is in private possession, at the Castle of Herdringen in Arnsberg, Westphalia (shelf number: Fü 3301a). The original Latin text reads: "Lembergo, 27. Martii. [...] Ex Moscovia resciimus rebellionem indies turpiorem accrescere, & mortem Magno Moscorum Principi rebelles minari: agricolæ & ex infima hominum fœce quamplurimi ad castra rebellantis Stephani Raninii confugiunt, vident enim Moscorum Principem resistendo imparem, seseque sub moderamine Stephani quam Principis imperio tutius victuros". My thanks to the owner, Baron Wennemar von Fürstenberg, for letting me work with his unique collection on several occasions, and to Winfried Schumacher (Cologne) for his help with the translation from the Latin.
31 *Nordischer Mercurius* (February 1671), p. 74.
32 *Nordischer Mercurius* (March 1671), p. 188.

orders), was one of the reasons why Moscow news "made in Riga" was not very trustworthy. Ironically, von Staden was also on the payroll of the Swedish state, although probably this began some months later.[33]

Greflinger usually published corrections and modifications of news printed during the previous month on the verso of the title page at the beginning of the new month. During January 1671, in his "*Correctio Nicht erfolgender Sachen im Decembri 1670*" ("*Correction of News from December 1670 that Could Not be Confirmed*"), he writes: "The Muscovite news items are still very uncertain, therefore their correction will have to wait until the next month". Most telling is a news item from the Hamburg region, "*Nider-Elbe vom 17. Febr*"., two thirds of which deals with the situation in Russia:

> The news about the events in Muscovy varies so much that one is almost afraid of reporting anything [...] Letters of 11 January Old Style from the city of Moscow itself report that nothing was known there about any rebellion, and the tsar is planning to marry again, within six weeks. Other [letters] of 5 January from the same city, that have arrived in Danzig, say that a lot of news is coming from the Muscovite army, but there is no reliable information. Older letters of the last of December 1670 inform that the rebel has been repulsed to such a degree that a hundred miles are paved with poor killed people, former soldiers of the rebel's army. Letters from Riga of 31 January New Style mention that no news had come in from Moscow these last days, and they therefore still do not presume anything positive. Everybody is invited to believe whatever he wants about all this [...].[34]

---

33 At a meeting of the Swedish Council of the Realm on Saturday, 29 July 1671, the councillor of the realm and governor general of Swedish Livonia, Count Clas Åkesson Tott Junior (1630–74), informed his colleagues that he, at the order of the king, had awarded von Staden a pension of 1000 *dalers*. The payment was for von Staden's successful attempts in making "Artemon" favourably disposed towards Sweden. This refers to Artamon Sergeevich Matveev, head of the Ambassadorial Chancery since spring 1671. The council decided that a bill of exchange of 500 *dalers* should be sent to Inspector Möller in Riga, apparently to hand the money over to von Staden at his next visit to his home town. See SSAS, Odelade kansli, Riksrådsprotokoll, vol. 58. My thanks to Heiko Droste for a transcription of the quoted protocol. See also von Staden's letter sent from Novgorod and dated 24 September (no year; probably 1672), signed by him personally, which was quoted on p. 121. Count Tott—with whom von Staden had been in contact—and "Stenca Raisin" are mentioned. See SSAS, Diplomatica Muscovitica, vol. 83 (not foliated; among letters from autumn 1672).

34 *Nordischer Mercurius* (February 1671), p. 104.

Contradictory news from Muscovy arrived throughout the whole first half of the year 1671 and was published, very often with a comment by Greflinger saying that the reader could not be certain of anything. The situation changed only in the second half of 1671, from mid-July, when the first reliable news about the execution had arrived in Hamburg. However, at first the publisher of the *Nordischer Mercurius* remains somewhat cautious, as we read in a news item datelined *"Nider-Elbe vom 11. Juli"*: "We now have so many newsletters from Moscow [stating] that the rebel Razin has been seized, that one can no longer have any doubts about it, although the letters are still controversial. See some of them here [below]".[35] This announcement is followed by three news items, the first one from Pleskau (today Pskov) dated 20 May: "The Don Cossacks who have remained on the side of Moscow have captured the rebel with a special trick. He is being brought to the emperor [*Käyser*] to get his reward". The second is datelined *"Novigrodt"* (Novgorod), 29 May. It describes a great fire in Moscow and another in Tver. About Razin we read: "The rebel has been brought to Moscow as a captive. This, however, does not mean that the uprising has come to an end: they believe that there will be more disturbances". Finally, the most recent—and therefore most updated—news item (from Moscow, dated 8 June) reads: "On the third of this month the rebel was brought here, and on the sixth he was thrown to the dogs, very mutilated. More details will follow as soon as possible".[36] The only minor mistake in this Moscow news item, when it comes to historical facts, is the date when Razin was brought to the capital: this happened on 2 June, not on the 3rd.[37] But generally the information is correct—for instance, the date of the execution was indeed 6 June. The news item from Pskov is also absolutely correct, and the one from Novgorod contains only one minor mistake: on 29 May, Razin had not yet been brought to Moscow, for on that date he was still on his way. The newsletter from Moscow dated 8 June had made its way to Hamburg very quickly, within around

---

35 *Nordischer Mercurius* (July 1671), p. 417 [recte: 427].
36 *Ibid.*, p. 428.
37 The date 2 June is mentioned in *Krest'ianskaia voina*, vol. 3, no. 99, p. 106 and no. 104, p. 114. We have the same date in Christoff Koch's eyewitness report of 6 June 1671, sent to the Swedish governor general in Narva, Simon Grundel-Helmfelt (SSAS, Livonica II, vol. 180, Moscow attachment of 6 June 1671).

thirty-four days, since Greflinger could publish it around 12 July,[38] and 10–11 July was apparently the time when the first information about Razin's execution had reached Hamburg (both Moscow and Hamburg used the Julian calendar). Incidentally, in this specific case we can be quite sure that the printing date was 12 July, because the obligatory weather observations at the end of the issue cover the period between 8 and 11 July,[39] and generally we can presume that the printing day would have been one day after the issue's "Lower-Elbe" item. On the basis of Greflinger's "More details will follow as soon as possible", we can extrapolate that he already *had* these details on 11 July. However, he could not insert a detailed description of what had happened in Moscow on 6 June into the current issue, which was already filled with all kinds of other news, the major portion of which most probably had already been typeset when the Moscow news came in. All he could do was insert that very short "post-execution" message. Immediately after the weather observations is another notification, an advertisement: "*Hierbey wird etwas sonderliches verkaufft*" ("In connection with this, an additional separate [publication] is being sold"). Although this phrase does not say explicitly that this "additional separate publication" was to cover Razin's execution, it seems likely that this was the intent.

A Printed German-Language Report About the Execution

Two anonymous German-language quarto pamphlets about Razin's execution are known, one of them containing a (very unrealistic) "portrait" of the rebel.[40]

---

38 The issues of the *Nordischer Mercurius* did not have a printing date on them, which was quite normal for seventeenth-century German-language newspapers from the Holy Roman Empire, whereas the printing date was usually given in Dutch papers, and also in the Latin-language paper published in Cologne.

39 *Nordischer Mercurius* (July 1671), p. 428.

40 "Umständiger Bericht Von deß grossen Rebellen wider Moßkau STEPHAN RAZINS Hinrichtung; Geschehen in der Stadt Moßkau den 6. Junij st. v. 1671. Dabey auch seine gewesene Gestalt abgebildet ist" ("Detailed report about the great rebel against Moscow, Stepan Razin's, execution, which took place in the city of Moscow on 6 June 1671 Old Style. With a picture of his previous appearance"); see Fig. 1. The portrait is on the verso of the title page. The only surviving copy I could locate is within the Copenhagen volume of the *Nordischer Mercurius*

4. How Was Western Europe Informed about Muscovy?

Figure 1. An (invented) portrait of a turbaned Razin with a marshal's baton in his right hand from a German-language pamphlet.⁴¹

According to Mankov, this pamphlet probably was an appendix (*prilozhenie*) to the *Nordischer Mercurius*,⁴² whereas Welke thinks that the "Razin issue" belongs to *another* Hamburg-based paper, *Wöchentliche Zeitung auß mehrerley örther*.⁴³ In my estimation, it was not an appendix at all, but just a separate pamphlet. One additional

---

    1671, where the pamphlet is placed between p. 436 and p. 437. This imprint is not in VD17. The other edition, without the portrait, is registered in VD17 and available as full text at http://www.gbv.de/vd/vd17/12:629466X (The title in VD17 is erroneously given as *Umständlicher Bericht*, instead of *Umständiger Bericht*.) The first part of the title is the same as in the edition with the portrait, including the date, "6. Junij st. v. 1671" although the information about the portrait is, of course, missing here. The only known copy is in the Bavarian State Library in Munich, signature Res 4 Crim. 140, 18.

41 The woodcut portrait is based on a copper engraving printed in Nuremberg at the late Paulus Fürst's printing house; see Gleb Kazakov, 'Through Glory and Death: Portraying Razin the Rebel in Western Media', in *Iconic Revolts: Political Violence in Early Modern Imagery*, ed. by Malte Griesse (forthcoming). The Fürst portrait is available at http://russiapedia.rt.com/prominent-russians/history-and-mythology/stepan-stenka-razin/

42 *Inostrannye izvestiia*, ed. by Man'kov, p. 84.

43 Welke, *Rußland*, p. 204, no. 444. In 1671 the original title from 1618 (when this newspaper was founded) was no longer in use; at that time, the series published on different days of the week had different titles: *Ordinari Diengstags Zeitung* resp. *Wochentliche Donnerstags Zeitung*. Welke even gives a concrete ordinary number to which he thinks it belongs: "Prima zu Nr. 29" (which is synonymous with *Ordinari Diengstags Zeitung*, no. 29). There is no announcement about any special issue on the last page, as would usually be the case when a "special" had been issued; see http://brema.suub.uni-bremen.de/zeitungen17/periodical/pageview/1143975

textually identical version was published in an ordinary number of *Europæische Montags Zeitung* (issued in Hanover[44]), under the headline "Moßkau den 20. Junij/ styl. nov." There are minor differences in spelling and punctuation between all three versions. Mankov reprints the text.[45] Partially different versions (although some fragments always overlap with the "original" version, from 1671) were reprinted in later years, in chronicle books and historical encyclopedias such as *Diarium Europæum* (in German) or *Hollandtsche Mercurius* (in Dutch).[46] Could it be that both scholars are right, and two Hamburg publishers issued one supplement each? In this case one might presume that the edition with the portrait was issued by Greflinger, the publisher of *Nordischer Mercurius*, because there is an advertisement on the last page of a February issue reading "In connection with this [*hierbey*] the portrait of Stepan Razin, the main rebel against Moscow, is being sold"[47]—which means that Greflinger actually was in possession of the "portrait" (an invented portrait, imitating a copper engraving from the workshop of the late Paulus Fürst, Nuremberg; see note 41).

---

44   See Else Bogel and Elger Blühm, et al., *Die deutschen Zeitungen des 17 Jahrhunderts. Ein Bestandsverzeichnis mit historischen und bibliographischen Angaben*, vol. 1 (Bremen: Schünemann Universitätsverlag, 1971), pp. 191–93. The relevant issue is number XXX of 1671, pp. [3]-[4] (signature in *Deutsche Presseforschung*, Bremen: Z161).

45   Man'kov, *Inostrannye izvestiia*, pp. 96–97. The text is *not* identical to any of the two pamphlets described above, in note 40, nor with the version in the periodical newspaper. According to the authors of this introductory section (A. G. Man'kov, A. L. Gol'dberg, and S. Ia. Marlinskii), the transcription was made from a copy in the city archives of Stralsund, "apparently, an appendix [*prilozhenie*] to the *Nordischer Mercurius*", kept in the archive "within a volume of Hamburg newspapers of the year 1671" (*ibid.*, p. 84). I find this information very confusing and suppose that it is based on a misunderstanding. It is true that the city archives of Stralsund house more or less complete collections of *two* Hamburg newspapers for a long series of years, among them the year 1671 (signature E.511 o), but *Nordischer Mercurius* is *not* among them—see Bogel and Blühm, *Die deutsche Zeitungen*, vol. 3, (Munich: Saur, 1985), p. 114—and I could not find this "appendix" in Stralsund. Apparently, the Russian scholars had not seen any original newspapers and pamphlets kept outside the Soviet Union and the German Democratic Republic, but were relying upon copies received from the Bremen scholars Elger Blühm and Martin Welke (Man'kov, *Inostrannye izvestiia*, p. 81). It would have been logical to look for this imprint in Stralsund if Welke's hypothesis had been correct (see note 43), but in this case there would not be any connection whatsoever between the imprint and the *Nordischer Mercurius*.

46   See *ibid.*, pp. 82–84, 100–01, 104–05.

47   *Nordischer Mercurius* (February 1671), p. 110.

Although it seems impossible to prove whether one of the pamphlets was connected to *Nordischer Mercurius* in some way, at least one more note about the execution was printed in an ordinary issue of that newspaper. Under the headline "*Nider-Elbe vom 1. Augusti*" we read: "How the rebel Razin was executed has been drawn by hand in Moscow, and the description about it is in Greek letters. Arms and legs are on poles, and the head and the trunk, too, whereas the intestines have been thrown to the dogs".[48] This note apparently describes the colour drawing from Moscow (see Figure 2); either the author of this note (probably Greflinger himself) or somebody else must have *seen* a version of the drawing, not only heard about its existence, since the body parts that had been set up on poles correspond to the *drawing*, not to the actual facts: in all eyewitness reports about the execution only *five* body parts (arms, legs, and head) had been set up, whereas the trunk had been left on the ground for the dogs. We will return to this question below.

---

48   *Nordischer Mercurius* (August 1671), p. 474. The German press historian Else Bogel apparently thought that this note was related to the quarto pamphlet about the execution; see her hand-written note on the Bremen copy of the pamphlet, referring to p. 474 of "Z20" (= *Nordischer Mercurius*; the Bremen copies were made from the Copenhagen volume, where the pamphlet is placed after p. 436 of the newspaper): http://brema.suub.uni-bremen.de/zeitungen17/periodical/pageview/1001356 However, Bogel is wrong; the small news item on p. 474 talks very explicitly about a *drawing by hand* (not an imprint), and the description is in "Greek letters" (= Cyrillic; see also below). Unfortunately, as a consequence of this mistake, the pamphlet was digitised together with the *Nordischer Mercurius*, where it was placed after p. 474. One strong indication for my hypothesis that the Razin brochure is not an integral part of the *Mercurius* is the format: in order to fit into the octavo volume of the *Mercurius*, the quarto pamphlet had to be folded twice, something that is quite obvious for a reader of the originals in Copenhagen, but impossible to see from the Bremen copies. The ultimate proof that the anonymous imprint does not belong to the periodical *Mercurius* is the fact that the Oslo volume does not contain this pamphlet. It contains another pamphlet, one that also does not belong to the periodical newspaper. I offer my thanks to Ole Skimmeland from *Deichmanske bibliotek* in Oslo for checking this for me and sending photographs in September 2016; see also note 18 about the two surviving complete year collections. A reasonable explanation is that the seventeenth-century newspaper reader and collector added the Razin pamphlet to his full-year collection of *Nordischer Mercurius*, apparently because of the thematic connection. This does not mean, however, that I would exclude Georg Greflinger from the possible publishers of this pamphlet. On the contrary, I think he is one of the stronger candidates, but more research is needed in order to corroborate such a hypothesis.

Razin's Rebellion in Swedish Diplomatic Correspondence

Let us now return to the research question formulated in the introduction to this chapter: who were the authors of the Muscovite items in the West European newspapers, and how was the news transmitted to the West? It has already been mentioned that Johan de Rodes, the Swedish commercial agent in Moscow in the first half of the 1650s, may have been the purveyor of news that ended up in printed German newspapers, so one hypothesis is that the situation was still just about the same in the early 1670s. During the period in which many Western newspapers quite regularly printed news about the Razin rebellion, another Swedish citizen, Christoff Koch—actually Johan de Rodes's brother-in-law—was sending regular reports to the governor general of Swedish Ingria in Narva, Simon Grundel-Helmfelt (1617–77).[49] Although I have not yet found any longer verbatim passages in that "Swedish correspondent's" letters and in German-language newspapers, it seems very likely that some of the printed information about Razin had originally been assembled by Koch. He was born in Reval in 1637 to German-speaking parents[50] and there are no indications that he knew much Swedish; all his letters, which have been preserved primarily in the Swedish State Archives in Stockholm, are written in German. Koch came to Moscow in 1655 aged eighteen, together with his brother-in-law Johan de Rodes, and stayed there for most of his life. He must have earned his living in Moscow first and foremost as a merchant, but he also received both money and recognition in Sweden for sending regular reports to Swedish court officials. His early letters sent to Helmfelt, from the 1670s, are always anonymous, but since a lot of later letters have also been preserved, signed by him personally (although usually not written by his own hand), we can be fairly sure that the earlier, unsigned communications were also written by him. A strong argument for this assumption is Koch's particular use of German (for instance, the frequent appearance of Low German words,

---

49   I will for the most part use "Helmfelt" as a short form of his name.
50   For more details about Koch's biography, kinship relations, and activities, see Heiko Droste and Ingrid Maier, 'Christoff Koch (1637–1711)—Sweden's Man in Moscow', in *Travelling Chronicles: Episodes in the History of News and Newspapers from the Early Modern Period to the Eighteenth Century*, ed. by Siv Gøril Brandtzæg, Paul Goring and Christine Watson (forthcoming).

and Low German influences on his grammar and spelling); another is that no other regular "correspondent" from Moscow at the time is known. Moreover, the governor, Helmfelt, to whom the letters were sent, often mentions "my correspondent" or "the usual correspondent in Moscow", and sometimes he even mentions Koch by name (in the Swedish form, Kock).

One of Helmfelt's tasks was to send regular reports to the Swedish government about everything that was happening in Muscovy. His reports were officially addressed to King Charles XI, who had not yet attained his majority. Together with his own letters Helmfelt would also send attachments. Most of the attachments preserved in the archives are reports written by Koch, but Koch would also send other materials to Narva—for instance, official Muscovite documents, such as a peace treaty. He seems to have written to Helmfelt once a week, and apparently Helmfelt also wrote one letter every week to the king. Of course, many of these letters, and possibly even more of the attachments, are now lost.

Helmfelt received such correspondence not only from Moscow, but also from Novgorod and Pskov, although more rarely. If nothing had been received from any of these places he would mention this too, for instance with the words "no news has come in from the neighbourhood"[51]—Narva was very close to the Muscovite border—and he would still report about the state of affairs in Muscovy in a sentence or two. The governor's letters are usually very short, in some cases because he had not received any reports. On other occasions he would offer a brief summary and mention that more details could be read in the attachment(s). Presumably Helmfelt normally did not forward the originals received from Moscow (written by Koch's secretary), but had his own secretary make copies. However, some of the communications that were forwarded to Stockholm from Narva may well have been the originals from Moscow.

The Moscow correspondence from the relevant timespan can be found in three modern archival files at the Swedish State Archives in Stockholm: Livonica II, vol. 179, containing Helmfelt's letters (usually with attachments) to his king from the years 1668–70; vol. 180, comprising the years 1671–73; and the Bengt Horn collection, E4304,

---

51 SSAS, Livonica II, vol. 180, *passim*.

with letters—and attachments—from Helmfelt to Bengt Horn, the governor of Estonia from 1656. Interestingly enough (although not very surprisingly), several "Moscow attachments" in the "Livonica files" and in the Horn collection not only contain exactly the same reports, but are also written by the same hand; in these cases we can be sure that both copies were made by Helmfelt's secretary, because the Moscow correspondent would not have sent two copies of the same letter to Narva.

The first letter to the Swedish king in which Helmfelt mentions the rebellion of Stepan Razin is dated Narva, 14 July 1670.[52] In addition, the attachments from Novgorod and Moscow also contain "Razin news".[53] In the following archival file, vol. 180, probably all the Moscow attachments had been sent to Narva by Christoff Koch. The oldest report from Moscow in this file is the "*Extract schreiben auß Muscou d. 13. Xbris 670*" ("Summary letter from Moscow, 13 December 1670").[54] It was sent from Narva to Stockholm together with an accompanying letter of 5 January 1671 addressed to the king and signed by Helmfelt. About two-thirds of the "Extract" deal with Razin: "From Astrakhan we do not have any other news, beyond that it is still occupied by Razin's army. He has sent the harvest of this year, such as wine, melons, and other fruit, to his majesty [the tsar], that is, he has sent everything to Simbirsk, and the *voevoda* [military commander] has dispatched [a courier] to his majesty, asking whether he would like him to forward the merchandise to Moscow. Thereupon they consulted the patriarch, whose recommendation was to pour the wine into the Volga river, because Stenka could have poisoned it [...]". The letter is quite typical for Koch's correspondence: many details are given, not only about Razin, but also—towards the end—about the new customs system which the

---

52 See Livonica II, vol. 179 (not foliated), Helmfelt's letter to the king from Narva, 13 December 1670. Many thanks to Heiko Droste for sharing his notes on vol. 179 with me.

53 The attachment from Moscow was possibly not by Christoff Koch, who seems to have spent part of the year 1670 in Reval.

54 SSAS, Livonica II, vol. 180 (not foliated); most of the quoted letters by Koch and Helmfelt are from this volume. It is generally safe to assume that correspondence from Moscow was written by Koch. There is a microscopic theoretical possibility that some of the Moscow reports could have been written by somebody else (since they are anonymous), and only forwarded by Koch, but for most of the reports from Moscow this seems unlikely.

Muscovite government was about to introduce. First and foremost, Koch was a merchant who would have been attentive to such details. The report also contains some typical examples of "Koch syntax", such as *"von Stenca Raisins seinem Volcke [...] besetzet"*.⁵⁵ Also included is a report from Novgorod (thus not written by Koch; we can only make a qualified guess that the Novgorod item was composed by the Swedish commercial representative to Novgorod), which is dated 25 December. Presumably, the Novgorod author also had other sources, since he underlines the uncertainty of the situation: "[...] About Razin different news has been received, so that nothing certain can be communicated. Some think that he is in Astrakhan, others that he is in Simbirsk, and although a letter which arrived here on 21 December tries to make the common populace believe that he has been wounded, this was only a rumour, because we were informed for sure by a secretary from the Chancery [*auß der Pricase*] that he is still healthy and is encamped near Simbirsk [...]". As we see, this Novgorod item contains exactly the same type of contradictory news as we could read in the newspaper items presented above.

In the next letter to the Swedish king, dated 12 January 1671, Helmfelt mentions an attachment, "which is a letter sent by the tsar to the *voivods* in Novgorod [*Naugorodt*] and Pskov [*Plesco*], in which the tsar himself reports in great detail what has happened since 1668, when this unrest started, until 6 December 1670, the date of the letter". A letter to the military commander of Novgorod, M. Morozov, is published in *Krest'ianskaia voina*.⁵⁶ It does not have an exact date on it, as only the month is indicated (November). The ending of this letter to Morozov gives some insight into how its contents might have become known to the Swedes and other foreigners: "When you have received our great ruler's letter [*gramota*], you should order it to be read aloud more than once to the inhabitants of Great Novgorod, whatever rank they might be, in the administrative office [office of the provincial *voevoda-prikaznaia izba*], so that they will get word about the victory, won by our great ruler's soldiers, over the rebel, apostate and traitor Stenka

---

55   In normal High German either *"von Stenca Raisins Volcke"*, or (colloquially) *"von Stenca Raisin seinem Volcke"* would be acceptable, but marking possession using both a genitive -s and the pronominal form *seinem* is unusual.

56   *Krest'ianskaia voina*, vol. 2, part 1, no. 277, pp. 339–42.

Razin and his allies".[57] This is a very interesting example of the way the government wanted to get its version of the news out, presumably in the first instance for internal Muscovite consumption, but possibly also with foreign merchants and others in mind as a second target group.

Helmfelt continues his short summary of the tsar's *gramota* with the words "At the end he [the tsar] mentions that their Razin [*Raisin*] is wounded and had to retreat.[58] The tsar orders that this letter be publicly read in the *pricasse*, or Chancery [*Cantzleystube*] [...]". There cannot be any doubt that both the commander of Novgorod and Helmfelt received essentially the same document. What we do not know is who sent or handed over the document to Helmfelt. Presumably the tsar's letter was first sent (or given) to Helmfelt in Russian, and most probably Helmfelt forwarded the original Russian text to Stockholm, although we cannot exclude the possibility that the translation was made in Novgorod or in Narva, and Helmfelt received a Swedish translation. Since the handwriting of the Swedish version is the same as in many other translations from Russian that are preserved in the Swedish archives, it is more logical to presume that it was made by one of the translators for the Swedish crown in Stockholm. In the archival box there is no Russian version, only a Swedish one. Another attachment forwarded to the king by Helmfelt on the same occasion is the full twenty-eight-page text of the 1667 treaty of Andrusovo between Muscovy and Poland. The letter and the attachments were apparently sewn together in Stockholm; today, some folios have become loosened from the rest. In this way the official view of the Muscovite government might have found its way into a printed newspaper, via people like Koch and Helmfelt.

An example for which we only have the Russian translation in the *kuranty* is a Moscow item of 26 January 1671 from a Dutch newspaper: "Here there are letters from the regiments of his Majesty the Tsar which write how the bandit Stenka Razin has arrived at the city of Simbirsk with 20,000 men. And from 4 September through 3 October they launched 15 terrible assaults on the city. [...]".[59] The reader is told

---

57 *Ibid.*, p. 342.
58 *Ibid.* The Russian document here reads: "And this rebel and apostate fled away from Simbirsk, heavily wounded, down on the Volga river with a few boats and with a small group of his men".
59 RGADA, coll. 155, descr. 1, 1671, file 7, fol. 40v, and see also the complete English translation of this *kuranty* item in Maier and Shamin, '"Revolts" in the *Kuranty*',

about the boldness of General Ivan Miloslavskii and about the joining of forces with Prince Iurii Bariatinskii, who had arrived from Kazan. The newspaper article also tells us that the tsar promoted Miloslavskii to a high rank for this victory. We read about Razin being wounded and that he "barely escaped in a boat, and only a few people escaped with him.[60] Five hundred people were taken alive and executed on the spot [...] And this disorder has now completely ended, and the merchants can once again set out for this state".[61] The last sentence confirms that it was very important for the tsar to communicate to merchants in Western Europe that it was now safe again to take up trade with Muscovy. On 26 January 1671, three to four months had passed since the deciding battles, and such a "news" item would only make sense in the context of a summarising official statement, of the same type as the communiqué dated 6 December discussed above. I could not find such a summary in the published Russian documents, although there are plenty of reports about military action, which were sent separately as events were occurring. My hypothesis is that the government had made a compilation at the beginning of December 1670, and this compilation was either handed over to some foreigner or it leaked out. Eventually a version of this compilation was published in The Hague, and it came back to Moscow in a news summary, as a news item in the *kuranty*.

In his letter of 3 March 1671 Helmfelt informs the king that the tsar's colonel, Nicolaus von Staden, is on his way to Riga, via Novgorod, and he also mentions two attachments about Razin, which were marked with the letters "A" and "B" respectively. About attachment "B" Helmfelt writes: "I am sending to Your Majesty, under letter B, what has been made public by the Russian side in the form of a report about the recent course of events concerning Stenka Razin [*Stencka Raisin*]". Unfortunately, only the missive marked with the letter "A" is in the document box; the other attachment might have been filed somewhere else in the archive, or it might be lost altogether. But it is very clear

---

    p. 198. The authors say that the newspaper item must be based on "an official communication of the Russian authorities" (*ibid.*), but it was not yet known, at the time that article was written, that the Russian government really did spread its official viewpoint via foreign residents in Moscow, possibly above all foreign merchants, such as the Swedish citizen Koch.

60 Compare this with the Russian document quoted in note 58.
61 Maier and Shamin, '"Revolts" in the *Kuranty*', p. 198.

from Helmfelt's letter that the tsar actively spread his communications to the foreigner Koch in Moscow, who forwarded them to Helmfelt in Narva. The most likely person to have contacted Koch was Artamon Sergeevich Matveev, the man who was to become the new head of the Ambassadorial Chancery, after Afanasii Ordin-Nashchokin had been removed in 1671.[62] There are several letters from Moscow, mostly from the following year, 1672, in which Koch writes that he had been invited to take a meal with A. S. Matveev.[63] Yet as early as 21 March 1671 Koch sent Helmfelt a very positive assessment of Matveev, and it is also clear from this and several other letters that Koch visited the Chancery quite regularly: "He [Matveev] is intelligent [*gutes Verstandes*], he makes quick decisions, and he helps the rich and the poor to obtain justice. [...] Yesterday I saw him making more than thirty decisions [*Urteil*] within five hours. I have never experienced anything similar before. Probably he will climb high here".

In a letter from Narva of 15 March, Helmfelt reports that "the news, according to which Stenka Razin had been brought to Moscow in chains, has not been confirmed"—the Russian side had spread this rumour prematurely, when it was already quite clear that the rebel would soon be seized.[64] In the same letter Helmfelt also informs the

---

62   Cf. an attachment, datelined Moscow 24 January 1671 and forwarded from Narva to the Swedish king on 3 February: "It's over with Nashchokin, because the affair between Poland and the tsar has come to such a bad end". The author understands clearly that Nashchokin is being removed for political reasons; eventually he took monastic orders.

63   Koch and Matveev had a close relationship, at least during the years 1671–72. For more details see Droste and Maier, 'Christoff Koch' (forthcoming).

64   Already on 4 January 1671 the *ataman* of the Don host, Kornei Iakovlev, reported to the Ambassadorial Chancery about an attempt to capture Razin, who, however, had escaped to Tsaritsyn; see *Krest'ianskaia voina*, vol. 2, part 2, no. 74, pp. 94–95. A missive dated 5 March (received in Moscow on 16 March), sent from G. Romodanovskii, the commander of the Belgorod regiment which was on the frontier with Ukraine, indicates that the capture of the Razin brothers by Kornei Iakovlev has occurred, but that the cossacks are holding him somewhere for reasons Romodanovskii has not been able to establish, so he is sending orders to find Razin and to have him sent on to Moscow without further delay. (See *Krest'ianskaia voina*, vol. 3, no. 22, p. 29.) This reveals the level of uncertainty even among the best-informed Muscovite officials. In fact, it seems that Razin had *not* yet been seized, since an instruction sent out to Romodanovskii on 4 March to send reinforcements against Razin mentions a report by Iakovlev of 28 February, which stated that Razin was still at large near Cherkassk, and that there were not sufficient forces to capture him (*ibid.*, no. 21, pp. 27–28). Clearly there were Cossack rebels still on the loose, as we see in no. 34, pp. 41–42, a report written between 30 March and 3 April by the military commander of

king that "Artaman Sergeevich [*Sergeiewitz*] has been installed at the Ambassadorial Chancery [*Posolski pricas*] instead of Nashchokin, because the latter has to go to Poland as an envoy". Incidentally, the news about Nashchokin going to Poland was also premature, because, in his correspondence of 21 March, Koch writes that Ivan Ivanovich Chaadaev, Dementii Minich Bashmakov, and a secretary are going to Poland as envoys, instead of Nashchokin.

In his letter of 19 April to the king Helmfelt gives a short summary of the included attachment, a report from Moscow dated 4 April, in which Koch writes: "They say, concerning the rebel Razin [*Raisin*], that he has been in Saratov not long ago and that he has substantial forces. They also say secretly [*auch wird heimlich geredet*] that he is planning to hand over Astrakhan to the Turks". Helmfelt's next letter to the king, dated 8 May, contains an attachment from Moscow with Razin news (as usual, among many other subjects), dated 11 April: "The rebel is said to have united his forces with the Calmucks, the Bashkirians, and the cossacks from Zaporozh'e, and he is on his way to Simbirsk with powerful forces. Borotinskoi has been sent to Simbirsk with his forces, and Petr Vasilevich Sheremetev [*Peter Wasilowitz Scheremetoff*] has received orders to go to the Don with his army". The confusing information is probably based on the equally confused state of the Russian authorities (cf. note 64). Koch makes it quite clear that this news has not been confirmed; he is reporting the rumours that were circulating in Moscow.

After Helmfelt's letter of 8 May there is a gap in the archival file. His next letter to the Swedish king is from 1 June. In the archive, this letter is filed together with attachments from Moscow of 16, 23, and 30 May.[65] Helmfelt comments on his long silence by observing that there were

---

Korotoiak. On 1 April, Romodanovskii was sent further instructions to learn about Razin's camp on the Don (no. 35, pp. 42–43), and on the same day Romodanovskii wrote about Razin's intentions to march against the Ukrainian towns, for whose defence there were insufficient forces; this letter was received and read to the tsar on 6 April (no. 36, p. 44). A report of 8 April indicates that Razin had still not been captured, but his brother was under arrest in Tsaritsyn (no. 40, pp. 47–48). On April 13, instructions were sent out referring to the danger that Razin was intending to march on Voronezh and Korotoiak (no. 44, p. 52). I am very grateful to Dan Waugh, who directed my attention to these documents and discussed their significance with me in great detail.

65 The dispatch from Moscow dated 30 May cannot have been in Narva on 1 June, so the order in the archive might be inaccurate in more cases than this.

several posts that did not contain any news about Muscovy, or, if they did, the news they contained was not worth mentioning. However, in another archival file,[66] containing Helmfelt's reports to the governor of Estonia in Reval, Bengt Horn, there is a letter from the following day, 2 June, with a Moscow attachment of 9 May. This is the earliest "Koch report", in which we read about the seizure of Razin by the Cossack Kornei Iakovlev. However, Koch is still a bit skeptical: "Last Thursday a messenger arrived from the Don Cossacks, reporting that the rebel Razin was captured by a Don *ataman*, called Corneli *Jacoblef*, and he is said to be brought here as soon as possible. On the following Friday this news was confirmed by two written communications [*2. posten*] and spread among the most noble as well as the common people. Time will show, whether the same thing as happened lately will be repeated again". The recent event was undoubtedly the occasion on which a previous report about Razin's capture had to be disclaimed later on.

In his letter of 16 May[67] Koch confirms once more that Razin had been seized; among other things, he writes: "Not only several letters [*etzliche Posten*], but also fourteen Don Cossacks, who had been sent to Moscow five days ago especially for this reason, confirmed that an old ataman of the Don Host, whose name is Corneli *Jacofloff*, has actually captured the rebel, and he will soon be brought here [i.e., to Moscow]".[68] The next Koch report, of 23 May, confirms this fact once more: "It was confirmed that Razin really has been seized. Count *Grigori Grigoriewitz Romodannofskoj* has sent some troops to meet up with them, so that those [Cossacks], who are with him, can advance safely". In his letter of 30 May Koch communicates that the rebel and his brother will be delivered to Moscow "this coming Friday", which also would prove to be correct: Koch usually wrote his letters on Tuesdays; the next Friday after Tuesday, 30 May, was in fact 2 June, the day on which Stepan and Frol Razin were brought publicly to Moscow, a scene very well known from several descriptions.

---

66   SSAS, E 4304.
67   Now again in SSAS, Livonica II, vol. 180.
68   A letter by ataman L. Semenov of 25 April about the seizure of Stepan and Frol Razin, published in *Krest'ianskaia voina* (vol. 3, no. 52, p. 59), is a good candidate for one of the four "posts" mentioned by Koch in his newsletter of 16 May. Kornei Iakovlev is mentioned, and the letter states that the rebels are being brought to Moscow.

Stepan Razin's execution: a previously unknown illustrated description

Towards the end of June, Helmfelt sent two letters to the king, this time from Nyen (not from Narva, as usual), one on 24 and one on 30 June. The latter is very important for our purpose. Here Helmfelt mentions that the rebel Razin is dead, and that all details can be read and seen in the attached "relations and drawing". Indeed, there are *two* "relations" in the Stockholm archives, in other words, two of Koch's reports, written 6 and 13 June respectively, both with the headline *"Extract Schreibens auß Musco"* and the date, and one coloured drawing. The drawing must have been made in Moscow, probably at the initiative of A. S. Matveev, the head of the tsar's Ambassadorial Chancery, as proof that the rebellion was over. In the archive, the three attachments are sewn together with Helmfelt's letter.[69]

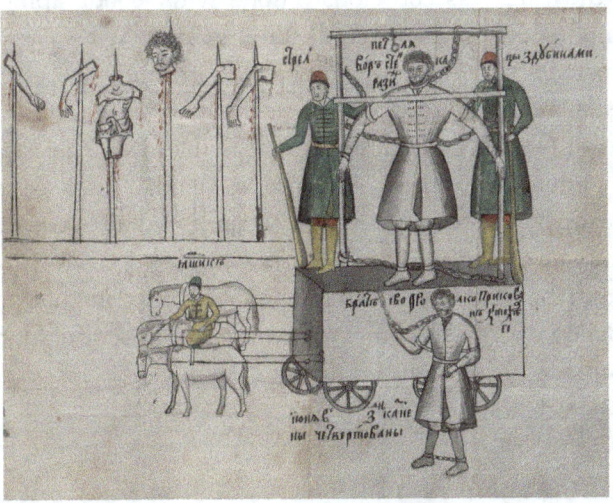

Figure 2. Coloured drawing of Razin's execution (originally from Moscow), 1671.

---

69 For a complete translation into Russian of Koch's two "relations" about the Razin brothers' delivery to Moscow and Stepan's execution, as well as a comparison of Koch's reports with other descriptions of these events, see Gleb Kazakov and Ingrid Maier, 'Inostrannye istochniki o kazni Stepana Razina. Novye dokumenty iz stokgol'mskogo arkhiva' (forthcoming in *Slovene*).

The drawing shows two separate scenes: in the right half we see Stepan Razin on a cart and his brother Frol chained to the cart, four days before the execution, when the two brothers were brought to Moscow. (On the day of the execution the same cart was apparently used again.) In the left half, above the horses with the carter (*iamshchik*), Stepan's body parts are shown, set up on poles: arms, legs, trunk, and head. The first scene (on the right) is apparently presented in a realistic way and must have been produced by someone who had seen how the two Razin brothers were delivered to Moscow on 2 June. Many people had seen this event, and an artist from a Muscovite chancery must have produced an illustration (or rather several copies, since they seem to have ended up in at least three countries; see below).

The drawing was made by an artist who was not familiar with Western perspective: the perspective of the cart is not shown correctly, and all persons are shown from the front. Of course, it is also possible that the drawing was consciously done with iconographic inverted perspective, and we cannot exclude the scenario that it was produced in the first instance for a Muscovite, not a Western, audience, even if copies were then sent to the West. Moreover, the manner in which the cart is attached to the horses is technically impossible. Nonetheless, this is an extremely interesting piece of evidence, since not a single other portrait of Razin drawn from life exists.[70] We had supposed that portraits printed in other countries were all based on pure imagination. However, it now appears that the portrait on the folding plate printed in London in 1672[71] was modelled on this eyewitness drawing, so the London portrait, too, is based on reality, albeit at second hand.

---

70 See Gleb Kazakov, 'Through Glory and Death' (forthcoming).

71 *A Relation Concerning the Particulars of the Rebellion Lately raised in Muscovy by Stenko Razin; its Rise, Progress, and Stop; together with the manner of taking that Rebel [...]*. Published by Authority. In the Savoy: Printed by Tho. Newcomb, 1672. Wing R774 (British Library, shelf no. b.32.g.42). The folding plate measures 295 x 184 mm (printing plate: 280 x 163 mm). Both the folding plate (see Fig. 3) and the complete text (pp. 3–18) are available online via Early English Books Online (EEBO). One more copy, also held at the British Library, was placed in front of another imprint about Razin when it was bound, viz. *A Narrative Of the greatest Victory Known in the memory of man [...]*. London: Nath. Crouch, 1671 (no. C.194.a.635(16); I could not find the latter imprint in EEBO, 02/02/2016). The following pamphlet in this collection is *A Relation Concerning...* (see above).

Figure 3. Folding plate, printed in London (1672).[72]

The engraving is a mirror image of the prototype from Moscow, the logical result of an engraving copied from an original and then reversed when printed. The engraver of the folding plate apparently tried to adjust the Muscovite original so that it was presented in something closer to Western artistic language. Although the perspective of the cart is quite odd even here, the human figures are shown from different angles (front, profile, back), and the horses—or rather donkeys, or mules—are attached to the cart in a realistic way. The artist's intention was certainly not to make an exact copy of the Moscow drawing, indeed there are additional differences between the images. For instance, on the engraving Razin's brother wears a cap; the carter is not sitting on one of the horses, but standing next to them, and the musketeers hold halberds, not clubs, in their hands. The "post-execution scene", with the skewered body parts, is missing altogether on the London folding plate. But all in all there are so many similarities between the two pictures that we can safely exclude the possibility that the engraving could have been made without access to a copy of the drawing from Moscow. Of course, the drawing that was sent to England would not necessarily have been identical to the one kept in the Swedish archives; it is possible that some of the differences in the London image, relative to that in the Swedish archives, might have resulted from the production of multiple copies (for instance, perhaps the version used for the London illustration did not include the impaled body parts at all).

---

72 With thanks to Dan Waugh, who made this photograph at the British Library, from the copy in no. C.194.a.635(16).

In any event, the London engraving is proof that drawings—as "hard-copy evidence" for Razin's execution—were given to several persons in Moscow: beyond the original drawing preserved in Sweden we have indirect indications that a version ended up in England (the London engraving), and one copy must also have been delivered to Hamburg, since what was described in the small article in *Nordischer Mercurius*—"drawn by hand in Moscow", with a description in Greek letters (actually Cyrillic), is nothing other than the colour drawing made in Moscow (see the full quotation above, p. 129).

The scene with the cart and the two brothers corresponds very well to the eyewitness reports about how the rebels were brought to the city. In several descriptions the construction to which Stepan is fastened with chains is called "a gallows".[73] This is shown by the (tiny) loop on the upper horizontal wooden beam and the word "*petlia*" ("loop"). The musketeers are shown with clubs in their hands—not with halberds, as they are shown on other Muscovite pictures and on the London engraving. The Russian text also says explicitly "*strel'tsy z dubinami*" ("musketeers with clubs"). Under the loop we can see the words "*vor Stenka Razin*" ("the rebel S. R."), and on the left side of the cart, next to the portrait of Frol Razin, "*brat evo Frolko prikovan k telege*" ("his brother Frolko, attached to the cart"). At the bottom we are informed— erroneously—that both persons were executed and quartered on 7 June ("*kazneny chetvertovany iiunia v 7 den'*").

A striking detail about this unique historical document is that it must have been produced *before* the execution had actually taken place. There is no absolute proof, but we have three indications for this statement. First, the date of the execution is not correct: the text on the drawing

---

73 See, for instance, the description of Jacob Reutenfels (or Rautenfels, which was his real name) in his book *De Rebus Moschoviticis ad Serenissimum Magnum Hetruriæ Ducem Cosmum Tertium* (Padua, 1680), Liber secundus, p. 148: "Intrabat perduellis ille urbem, catenis patibulo alligatus [...]" ("That rebel entered the city, chained to a gallows"). Thomas Hebdon used the same word in his letter to Richard Daniell, dated Moscow, 6 June, 1671: "Razin himself placed upon a scaffold under a gallows". The letter, which is kept at the National Archives in London, SP 91/3, was published by S. Konovalov, 'Razin's Execution: Two Contemporary Documents', *Oxford Slavonic Papers*, 12 (1965), 92–98 (pp. 97–98). The folio number given by Konovalov, 204, is wrong; the correct folio number is 202. I am grateful to Arthur der Weduwen for a photograph of the letter. Both the English text and a Russian translation of Hebdon's letter are in Man'kov, *Zapiski inostrantsev*, pp. 129–31.

says 7 June, instead of 6 June. (There seems to have been some confusion regarding the exact day and manner of the execution; see below.) Moreover, the text wrongly states that *both* rebels had been executed and quartered, although Frol's life was to be spared for another five years,[74] and finally, Razin's trunk is among the impaled body parts, whereas all our descriptions agree upon the fact that the trunk had been left on the ground.

Koch's "relation" dated 6 June is a very detailed — and hitherto unknown — description of Razin's execution. It comprises five pages, of which I will provide but a summary here. First Koch describes how the two rebels were "taken in miserably last Friday, that is, on the 2nd of this month, here into Moscow, through the Tver Gates, and brought to the Land Court[75] in the Red Wall. The cart had four tall wheels, and it had a platform on top". The description corresponds so well to the drawing that one may wonder whether Koch was describing the scene from his own memory, or, instead, from the drawing he had in front of him. He also mentions the "gallows":

> In the middle on that cart there was a gallows, about one span taller than himself; in this the poor hero Razin [*Raisin*] was fastened with iron chains. He was hanging in it like a fly in a spiderweb. First of all, his head was fastened on that same gallows with a chain; he was also fastened at both shoulders, at his arms, and on both posts of the gallows, with handcuffs on both hands that were forged to the posts of the gallows. The middle part of his body was also fastened with chains, and last but not least, below, both his legs were fastened on both sides of the posts, with chains. In front of his chest there was a horizontal wooden pole, onto which he could sometimes lean forward. Thus he had to make his entrance on such a Triumphal Chariot, standing, fastened to a gallows, as described above. His brother was fastened on the left side of the cart with a long chain. His legs were also bound together quite closely.

So far everything is exactly as in the drawing. According to the written text, four musketeers were standing on the cart, one in each corner,

---

74 The Brandenburg resident in Moscow, Hermann Dietrich Hesse, reported in his letter of 24 May 1676 to the Kurfürst in Berlin that Stenka Razin's brother had been beheaded the previous Thursday. (Geheimes Staatsarchiv Preußischer Kulturbesitz Berlin, I HA (Geheimer Rat), Rep. 11 (Auswärtiges), Nr. 6572.) My thanks to Heiko Droste for sharing his archival notes with me.

75 Koch writes "auff den Semschen Hofe", which must be *Zemskii dvor*.

whereas the drawing shows only two of them; similarly, on the three horses "three unhandsome boys were sitting in torn clothes", whereas there is only one horseman in the drawing. The written text mentions that musketeers were riding on horses in front of the cart, as well as the Cossack *ataman* Kornei Iakovlev with five of his closest men, followed by another eighty Cossacks. Koch characterizes Razin as quite a tall person with large shoulders, light brown curly dense hair, covering half of his ears, and a "short, roundish dense beard". His face looks strong and bold (*frech*); he appears to be in his mid to late thirties. His brother's appearance is quite similar, his age about 26 years. Koch also describes the first torture session of 2 June; since he cannot have been an eyewitness to the torture, his report does not contain anything new on this subject. Then, however, we get some interesting and hitherto partially unknown information: on Saturday 3 June, two blocks—one each for the execution of the two brothers—were set up on Red Square, as well as five sharpened poles for each of them, for their heads, legs, and arms. At ten o'clock the execution was to take place, and the foreigners had been assigned a special spot from which they could see everything. However, the execution was delayed, because the two brothers were to be tortured once more. Apparently, no new date for the execution was given immediately, which might explain why the author of the drawing indicated the wrong date. Finally, "today" (6 June), at twelve o'clock, the Razin brothers were brought to Red Square, where Razin's "wicked deed" and the verdict were read aloud; the public reading took about half an hour.[76] "I will try to get this [text] and send it over", Koch writes further down in this same report. Upon the command given by the "Chancellor *Larrivan Ivanofvitz*" (Larion Ivanov, who became a *dumnyi d'iak*, or state secretary, in 1669)[77] to quarter the rebel, Stepan walked courageously towards the blocks, prayed, made the sign of the cross, and lay down on his belly. His right arm was axed off to the elbow, his left leg to the knee, then his left arm and his right leg, and finally his head. All five severed body parts were set up on poles; the remainder, the trunk, however, was left on the ground. Upon this, Stepan's brother

---

76 A copy of the document is kept in the *Donskie dela* files at RGADA. It was published in *Krest'ianskaia voina*, vol. 3, no. 81, pp. 83–87.

77 See N. F. Demidova, *Sluzhilaia biurokratiia v Rossii XVII v. i ee rol' v formirovanii absoliutizma* (Moscow: Nauka, 1987), p. 225.

said that he had something more to tell. He was conducted to the Land Court for a new session of torture, during which he lost consciousness. Like other eyewitnesses, Koch underlines that Stepan did not show any emotions during the torture, whereas his brother cried and was reproached by Stepan: "You son of a bitch, why do you cry? Remember, that you won much honour together with me, and that we had ruled over not only all of the Don, but also over the whole Volga". The last twelve or thirteen lines of Koch's correspondence contain other information: a courier is said to have arrived from Count Romodanovskii[78]—one of the field commanders fighting against the rebelling Cossacks—with word that "Astrakhan and all places that had been won by Razin were now brought back to his Majesty the tsar, and they are asking for mercy".[79] The last two sentences of the letter are dedicated to other issues.

The second "relation" mentioned by Helmfelt and also attached to his own letter of 30 June was written one week later, on 13 June. It contains the well-known story (a rumour?) about the treasure trove of gold, silver, and other precious things hidden near Tsaritsyn, reported by Frol Razin, a story that is also known from a Russian document.[80] The men who had dug the hole had all been killed, and now Frol was the only remaining person who knew where it was. We learn that the five poles with Razin's body parts were brought to the "swamp" (*Bollota*) on the other side of the Moscow River, and set up again, whereas the trunk was put on the ground, as before. Koch highlights the fact that he had seen all this "three days ago" (which would have been 10 June). We also get some background information about how Razin was taken prisoner by Kornei Iakovlev and his 2000 Don Cossacks, and that the

---

78 Grigorii Grigor'evich Romodanovskii, killed during the uprising of 1682 in Moscow.
79 Among the published documents there are plenty of reports from military commanders about places retaken from the rebellious Cossacks (see for instance vol. 2, part 2, no. 78, pp. 102–03), but I have not found a specific document about Astrakhan.
80 This story, which is included in a report from an interrogation of Frol Razin on 8 June, is in *Krest'ianskaia voina*, vol. 3, no. 85, p. 94. Frol talked about silk and other fabrics, but nothing about "treasures of gold and silver" as such; these things were given to the Metropolitan (Archbishop) of Astrakhan to guard them for Stepan, thus there was no buried treasure, which is why I think that the treasure story might have been based on hearsay. My thanks to Dan Waugh for bringing this reference to my attention.

ataman was richly rewarded by the tsar.[81] The final—fourth—page is about other issues (for instance, a Polish embassy is expected). All in all, both attachments are typical examples of Koch's detailed reports from Moscow.

Conclusion

Let us now return to the question of how the newspaper publishers in Western Europe were informed about Muscovy, through the prism of this specific case of the Razin rebellion. We have been able to document *some* overlap between Koch's correspondence to Helmfelt, and articles in printed newspapers, but so far, we have found no longer fragments or whole news reports that are virtually identical in the two types of source. As was mentioned above, for another time period—the early 1650s—it has been shown that certain parts of reports to Queen Christina of Sweden, written by Johan de Rodes while he was a Swedish resident in Moscow, also ended up in printed German newspapers, sometimes verbatim, although we still do not know how: did Rodes have contacts with any news agencies, or did the news "leak out" somewhere during the transmission, for instance, in Narva? My hypothesis is that not much had changed when Koch, Rodes's brother-in-law, was sending his correspondence to Narva in the early 1670s; that is, I think that parts of Koch's dispatches also ended up in the European news market. It is very difficult to prove this unequivocally as so many numbers of printed seventeenth-century newspapers are lost forever.

A major difference between the 1650s and the 1670s is, of course, the fact that in the meantime an international postal line between Muscovy and Western Europe had been established. For Koch this meant, on the one hand, that he could send his reports to governor Helmfelt in Narva—from which point they were forwarded both to other Swedish-Baltic provinces and to the Swedish government in Stockholm—in a very timely fashion, once a week, every Tuesday; Koch did not have to wait for the next merchant or diplomat to cross the Russian borders, as would have been the case in the 1650s. Since Koch's correspondence

---

81 Rewards to Cossacks who helped fight Razin are mentioned in *Krest'ianskaia voina*, vol. 3, no. 99, pp. 106–08. On what was given to Iakovlev as a reward, see especially p. 107.

was conveyed by Muscovite officials, this also meant that his dispatches could be opened, read and translated into Russian. He could therefore have written—or rather dictated—slightly different versions to Helmfelt, on the one side, and to a news agent, on the other side, to make certain he would not be blamed personally for any "inconvenient" news about Muscovy that had made its way into the international European press.[82] However, in this case modern scholars, too, might never be able to really prove any direct or indirect connections between Koch and the news market. Even if we do not have, at this moment, any strong evidence that Koch's reports in one way or another ended up in European newspapers, we can be fairly sure that the news market was being fed with Moscow news by men like Koch—well-informed merchants and diplomats with good relations to the tsar's entourage, who were gathering news, in the first place, for the governments in their respective home countries. Koch, with his superb knowledge of Russian politics and culture, with his knowledge of the Russian language, and his (at that time) excellent relationship with the Russian political elite (especially Matveev), would have been an ideal person to gather news about Muscovy.[83]

Koch's newsletters—at least the ones we have found in the Swedish archives—were sent to Narva, and we know that copies were made in Narva: not only the Swedish government in Stockholm, but also Governor Horn in Reval, and quite certainly the governors in the other Swedish provinces on the Baltic littoral, were provided with copies of the reports that Helmfelt received from Moscow, Novgorod, and Pskov. Both the Narva copyist and those who received the new copies might have handed over "Koch news" to a news agent, so even if we eventually find overlapping verbatim passages in Koch's newsletters and in the press, we still will not know the exact connection: was it Koch personally who fed the "Moscow news market" with his information, or was it somebody who had seen, or copied, his reports?

An important result of this study is that we know the Russian authorities, during the reign of Tsar Aleksei Mikhailovich, were more

---

82 In this paper I have focussed only on German newspapers, although I am, of course, aware of the fact that the news market was international; see, for instance, Pettegree, *The Invention of News*.

83 See also Droste and Maier, 'Christoff Koch' (forthcoming).

actively engaged in spreading their viewpoints (or their talking points) to foreigners living in Muscovy than we used to think, and, as a result, we might have to reconsider Muscovy's "information policy" during this period. It has long been known that the Ambassadorial Chancery collected news from abroad (for instance, among other sources, via translations of handwritten and printed newspapers from Germany and the Netherlands; see the chapters by Waugh, and Waugh and Maier, in this volume). However, very little has been known about the manner and the degree to which the Kremlin actively manipulated Muscovy's image in Western Europe. We have read about the tsar's attempts to create a better image of Russia in the world by soliciting foreign governments to reprimand their gazetteers, or even punish them, if those writers had printed any "lies" about the tsar or his country.[84] These attempts never worked out well, because, among other reasons, the Russian government's ability to influence the press in countries like the Dutch Republic and the German Empire was very limited. Perhaps people like Matveev, the great "Westerniser", had already grasped that there was a more influential way to manipulate public opinion about Russia abroad, that is, by making use of the foreign correspondents living in Muscovy itself. This chapter has shown that Muscovite authorities handed over official statements to Koch at several instances, and we can be sure that Koch was not the only foreigner who was given such "favour". In his report of 6 June 1671, written immediately after Razin's execution, Koch mentions the communication—Razin's "wicked deed" and the verdict—that was publicly read aloud on Red Square, and we should recall his comment "I will try to get this [text] and send it over". Apparently, he knew that it would not be difficult to acquire this document. Although I have not yet seen it in the Swedish archives, it might well be there,[85] and in any event we have evidence that this "verdict" was handed over to foreigners, since it appeared in print, for instance, in *Kort waerachtigh verhael, van de bloedige rebellye in Moscovien* [...][86] and in similar German,

---

84 See, for instance, *Krest'ianskaia voina*, vol. 3. no. 236, pp. 285–86.
85 I would like to stress the fact that this document might indeed be somewhere else in the Swedish State Archives; of course, I have not looked through all possible files. Beyond the huge collections 'Livonica' and 'Muscovitica', such a document could also have ended up in another collection (e.g., 'Extranea').
86 *Kort waerachtigh Verhael, Van de bloedige Rebellye in Moscovien, Aen-gerecht door den grooten Verrader en Bedrieger Stenko Rasin, Donsche Cosack... Nevens sijne Sententie...*

English, and French printed versions of the years 1671–72.⁸⁷ It also appears that the Kremlin was disseminating other documents: in one case a coloured drawing—undoubtedly produced in a Muscovite chancery—ended up in at least three countries (Sweden, England, and Germany); I do not doubt that even more copies were produced, although it seems that only one is preserved today (and two have left indirect traces behind them). Spreading "pictorial proof" of the executed Razin's body parts was a means of fighting against rumours of his successes. In another case, as we have seen, the tsar's official declaration about Razin's rebellion, sent to Novgorod to be read aloud to the crowds, also ended up in Helmfelt's hands and was eventually forwarded to the Swedish government in Stockholm. While that statement probably had as its target first and foremost a Muscovite public, it is likely that the tsar would not have protested if such information had been handed over to foreigners in Novgorod; in this case there was always a chance that a specific report would end up in a newspaper. Undoubtedly, the Kremlin tried actively to squelch rumours it did not like and to portray events with a positive spin. The correspondence sent by Governor Helmfelt in Narva to the Swedish king contains many official Russian documents, which may have come into Helmfelt's hands in the first place through Koch,⁸⁸ and in the second place through Swedish merchants in Novgorod and Pskov. Of course, not all "official" Russian news that ended up in Koch's correspondence or in a printed newspaper was spread deliberately by the Kremlin; in some cases—for instance, when we talk about instructions given to Russian ambassadors—we have to suppose that the news had leaked out.

The Swedish diplomatic correspondence from Moscow and Novgorod also shows us something about the Muscovite postal system.

(Haerlem: Pieter Casteleyn, 1671). Royal Library The Hague, KB Pflt 9875, p. 12–16 (with thanks to Arthur der Weduwen for a copy of this pamphlet, which is not freely accessible online).

87 The titles in all four languages are in *Zapiski inostrantsev*, p. 84n3–4; for the complete text of the English version and its translation into Russian see *ibid.*, pp. 91–119. According to A. L. Goldberg (*ibid.*, p. 158), the protograph was probably a Dutch version—however not exactly the version printed in the *Kort waerachtigh verhael*; see A. L. Gol'dberg, 'K istorii soobshcheniia o vosstanii Stepana Razina', in *Zapiski inostrantsev*, p. 158. For the English version see note 70.

88 A qualified guess is that the mediator usually was Artamon Matveev.

Koch usually wrote one newsletter every week (every Tuesday[89]), and Helmfelt also would send one letter every week to his king. The Muscovite "international" postal line went through Riga (at certain periods there was also another line, through Vilna, today's Vilnius), but no *official* Russian postal line connected Novgorod with Narva. However, as Philipp Kilburger writes in his report from 1674, although there is no ordinary postal line between Novgorod and Narva, "almost every week during the whole year there are opportunities to send letters from one place to the other".[90] The mailbag for Narva seems to have left Moscow with the Riga post, which was running once a week; it would be taken out in Novgorod to be put into the Narva post from there.[91] So usually Helmfelt would receive weekly reports from Moscow and/or Novgorod, but sometimes the connection in Novgorod missed its departure, which explains the fact that occasionally Helmfelt included Koch's dispatches from two subsequent weeks into his own report to the Swedish government.[92] An interesting example in this connection is Helmfelt's letter of 30 June 1671, which was sewn together with the two "relations" and the drawing about Razin's execution: apparently both relations, dated 6 June and 13 June, arrived at Narva on the same day, since Helmfelt mentions both reports in his own communication (and includes copies of both).

This chapter has also shown that the German newspapers — especially the Hamburg *Nordischer Mercurius*, on which I have focussed in the first place (mostly due to the fact that the complete run for the year 1671 has been preserved) — were not, after all, so bad. During the Razin uprising not even the tsar and his closest advisers were always well-informed about, for instance, the numbers of people killed on each side in a battle, or about Razin's whereabouts, and when the Muscovite government itself created confusion by stating that the rebel had been captured, long before he was actually seized, we cannot really blame the newspapers for publishing information that later on would prove

---

89 The mail to Novgorod left Moscow every Tuesday evening; see Kurts, *Sochinenie Kil'burgera*, p. 160.
90 Ibid.
91 See Daniel C. Waugh, 'Istoki sozdaniia mezhdunarodnoi pochtovoi sluzhby Moskovskogo gosudarstva v evropeiskom kontekste', in *Ocherki feodal'noi Rossii*, vol. 19 (2017), 394-442.
92 Ibid.

to be false. As we can still see today, confusing political situations lead to confusing reports in the press; this was all the more true during the seventeenth century, the first century of the printed newspaper. Both Christoff Koch and the publisher of the *Nordischer Mercurius* constantly stressed the fact that the latest news had not yet been confirmed. Only when it had been verified, from two or more independent sources, did they make it clear to their readers that the news now could be trusted.

III.
NEWS AND POST IN RUSSIA

5. Communication and Obligation: The Postal System of the Russian Empire, 1700–1850

John Randolph

In 1854, the Imperial Russian Historical Society published a portrait, in numbers, of Russia's postal system. 3,950 relay stations, the Society reported, formed the system's spine. Mail couriers, imperial officials, and even private travellers could find at these "posts" all manner of travel necessities—above all, fresh drivers and draft animals. The stations were spaced at intervals, along some 85,000 *versts* (roughly 90,500 kilometres) of relay roads.[1] 16,510 mail couriers rode these routes with bags of correspondence; tens of thousands more labourers (men, women, and children) served the stations and drove wagons and sledges between them. Finally there were the horses, the prime motors of the post. The Division calculated that the empire harnessed 50,534 horses for its relays, alongside 432 reindeer and 1,800 dogs. On their backs, or in the vehicles they drew, some 733 Russian towns received deliveries of packages and letters. Most towns got mail twice a week, though 63 cities received mail 6 times a week—and Kamchatka twice a year.[2]

---

1 This figure excluded Poland and Finland.
2 I. A. Gan, 'O pochtakh v Rossii', in *Sbornik statisticheskikh svedenii o Rossii, izdavaemyi Statisticheskim otdeleniem Imperatorskogo Russkogo istoricheskogo obshchestva* (St Petersburg: Tipografiia Imperatorskoi Akademii nauk, 1854), p. 37, pp. 44–46. These counts align with others from the early nineteenth century.

The historian John Hyslop once called the postal roads of the Inca Empire—at least 23,000 kilometres in length—"South America's largest contiguous archaeological remain".[3] While the material culture of Russia's postal system is mostly buried—a good part of it under modern Russian roads—the whole must be regarded as a similarly massive monument of the Russian Empire. By the end of the eighteenth century, this relay network traversed the realm as few other official institutions did. Close studies of rural Russia in the pre-industrial period often describe it as under-governed, or even "ungoverned".[4] Yet the relays gave the Russian Empire a localised expression in both urban and rural areas, on the frontier as well as in the centre: indeed, quite often in the middle of nowhere.[5] And the presence of relay stations mattered not only because of the things they moved—most famously, people and mail—but because of the mandatory contributions the state demanded from local populations to move them.

Organisations "so stupendous and so costly that it baffles speech and writing" (as Marco Polo described the Mongol posts), imperial relay systems did not appear spontaneously.[6] Rather, empires created their posts by requisitioning the necessary resources from local people, a technique of power employed from ancient history well into the nineteenth century. Animals, food, fodder, shelter, labour, harness, and wagons: everything essential to support the relays might be demanded, on terms that were variously exploitative—and sometimes paired with ameliorating privileges—but never voluntary. For this reason, imperial communications exerted a noticeable and usually unwanted pressure on local societies. Thomas Allsen calls the Mongol Empire's system of relay obligation "one of the most widespread and distasteful of labor

---

3   John Hyslop, *The Inka Road System* (Orlando: Academic Press, 1984), p. xii, p. 3.
4   On the lack of official institutions in rural life, see Steven L. Hoch, *Serfdom and Social Control in Russia: Petrovskoe, A Village in Tambov* (Chicago: University of Chicago Press, 1986), p. 1.
5   For a thoughtful discussion of the post's role as a 'Grundbedingung staatlicher Machtpräsenz', Roland Cvetkovski, *Modernisierung durch Beschleunigung: Raum und Mobilität im Zarenreich* (Frankfurt am Main: Campus Verlag, 2006), p. 114, *passim*.
6   Marco Polo, *The Travels of Marco Polo*, trans. by Ronald Latham (London: Penguin Classics, 1958), p. 151.

duties".⁷ The sentiment is common across the experience of empire, providing one of history's few constants.⁸ "Of all the burdens which lie upon a subject", the Swedish King Gustavus Adolphus conceded to his people in 1613, "there is none greater, none more irritating, and none more troublesome".⁹

Calculated by governments according to a variety of formulae, and used to bear varying amounts of traffic, such obligations might be a marginal "irritation" in some areas and the central fact of life in others. Russian provincial governors in the early nineteenth century, for example, counted relay obligations by the "soul" (that is, per adult local man registered on the census). The merchants of Astrakhan were required to provide one horse for every eighty "souls" in their community in 1801; local Tatars, one for every twenty-five or thirty-five. Some particularly obligated villages bore relay burdens as high as three horses for every twenty-eight souls.¹⁰ And with these horses came other demands: not only for each animal itself, but also for the fodder, shelter, labour and vehicles necessary to serve it at the stations. Such impositions remained the foundation of both mail and official

---

7   Thomas T. Allsen, *Mongol Imperialism: The Policies of the Grand Qan Möngke in China, Russia and the Islamic Lands, 1251–1259* (Berkeley: University of California Press, 1987), p. 212.
8   Adam J. Silverstein, *Postal Systems in the Pre-Modern Islamic World* (Cambridge: Cambridge University Press, 2007); Anne Kolb, *Transport und Nachrichtentransfer im Römischen Reich* (Berlin: Akademie Verlag, 2000); Peter Olbricht, *Das Postwesen in China unter der Mongolenherrschaft im 13. und 14. Jahrhundert* (Wiesbaden: O. Harrassowitz, 1954); Didier Gazagnadou, *La poste à relais: La diffusion d'une technique de pouvoir à travers de l'Eurasie. Chine-Islam-Europe* (Paris: Editions Kimé, 1992); Colin J. Heywood, 'The Ottoman Menzilhane and Ulak System in Rumeli in the Eighteenth Century', in *Turkiye'nin Sosyal ve Ekonomik Tarihi (1071–1920)/Social and Economic History of Turkey (1071–1920): Papers Presented to the First International Congress on the Social and Economic History of Turkey*, ed. by Osman Okyar and Halil Inalcik (Ankara: Hacettepe University, 1980), pp. 179–86.
9   Michael Roberts, *Gustavus Adolphus: A History of Sweden, 1611–1632*, vol. 1 (London: Longman, Green & Co., 1953), p. 117. On the evolution of Swedish obligations thereafter, see Magnus Linnarsson, 'The Development of the Swedish Post Office, c. 1600–1721', in *Connecting the Baltic Area: The Swedish Postal System in the Seventeenth Century*, ed. by Heiko Droste (Huddinge: Södertörns högskola, 2011), pp. 25–47.
10 RGIA, coll. 1289, descr. 1, file 118 ('O soobshchenii Gosudarstvennomu Sovetu svedenii ob"iasniaiushchikh ustroistvo pocht' [1801]), ll 220–21. The communities in question here were the specially obligated "relay suburbs" (*iamskie slobody*), about which more below.

transportation throughout Russia until the mid-nineteenth century (and in some places stayed in force until the early Soviet period).[11]

Communication and obligation thus go hand in hand in the history of imperial postal systems, in Russia as elsewhere. Since relay roads were generally supported through direct (if variable) demands on local societies rather than through monies paid out by central treasuries, the growth of the posts meant a corresponding expansion in the inherently unequal, and differentiating, geography of relay obligations. Yet scholarship about relay posts tends to foreground only one of these themes at a time, letting the other drop. This is true in Russian history, as well.

Before 1700, scholars focus on how the princes of Moscow used relay obligations to build official communications for their nascent Russian Empire. The Russian name for such duties—*iamskaia povinnost'*—takes its root from a Turkic word (*jam*, meaning "relay" or "post"), employed by the Mongol Empire to describe its relay system.[12] This, and other similarities, caused sharp historical debate in the nineteenth century over the degree to which Russia's relays were inherited from Mongol Imperial practice. Most today would see it as a transformation, under Chinggisid inspiration, of a still older duty to support travelling royalty, called *podvoda* in Kievan Rus.[13] Regardless of origin, relays and the obligations that supported them were crucial to Moscow's rapid early

---

[11] F. I. Bunina provides the best overview of the evolution of relay obligations in the nineteenth century in F. I. Bunina et al., *Materialy po istorii sviazi v Rossii. XVIII-nachalo XX vv.*, ed. by N. A. Mal'tseva (Leningrad: Ministerstvo sviazi SSSR, 1966), pp. 23–29. She portrays the system as gradually being transferred onto a commercial, rather than obligatory basis: that said, the late imperial and early Soviet systems still had recourse to transport obligations, see Yanni Kotsonis, *States of Obligation: Taxes and Citizenship in the Russian Empire and Early Soviet Republic* (Toronto: University of Toronto Press, 2014).

[12] Maks Fasmer, *Etimologicheskii slovar' russkogo iazyka*, trans. by O. N. Trubachev, vol. 4 (Moscow: Progress, 1973), p. 555; Allsen, *Mongol Imperialism*, p. 114.

[13] See I. P. Khrushchov, *Ocherk iamskikh i pochtovykh uchrezhdenii ot drevnikh vremen do tsarstvovaniia Ekateriny II* (St Petersburg: A. S. Suvorin, 1884), pp. 3–5; I. Ia. Gurliand, *Iamskaia gon'ba v moskovskom gosudarstve do kontsa XVII veka* (Iaroslavl: Tipografiia Gubernskogo Pravleniia, 1900), pp. 29–50; P. Miliukov, *Spornye voprosy finansovoi istorii Moskovskogo gosudarstva. Retsentsiia na sochinenie A. S. Lappo Danilevskogo, 'Organizatsiia priamogo oblozheniia v Moskovskom gosudarstve'* (St Petersburg: Tipografiia Akademii nauk, 1892), pp. 21–22; A. N. Vigilev, *Istoriia otechestvennoi pochty*, 2nd ed. (Moscow: Radio i sviaz', 1990), pp. 44–45; Donald Ostrowski, *Muscovy and the Mongols: Cross-Cultural Influences on the Steppe Frontier* (Cambridge: Cambridge University Press, 1998), p. 47, pp. 119–21; Gustave Alef, 'The Origin

modern extension to new conquests and frontiers, such as the White Sea, Kazan, Siberia, Ukraine, and the Baltic. "With each step further into new territory, relay institutions penetrated deeper into the country", Ilia Gurliand argues in his foundational study of the early development of Russian relay transport.[14]

So the story goes until 1650. Histories of communication thereafter, however, typically concentrate on relay functions, rather than on relay obligations. In particular, scholars explore how kinds of postal services that developed across early modern Europe began to appear in Russia, and to what effect. Thus, for example, the organisation of the first regularly scheduled mail route (weekly between Moscow and Riga, in 1665) is often presented as marking the advent of "European", "modern", or "proper" posts in Russia.[15] Previously couriers had been dispatched by the court only when needed. The reign of Peter the Great (1689–1725) is generally seen as accelerating this break, just as it supposedly energised other modernising currents of Russian life. Histories thereafter focus on charting the functional parameters of these new postal services: the growth of mail routes, for example, or their reliability or speed.[16] The labour system supporting these innovations, meanwhile, recedes to the background of this history, if it is mentioned at all.

The following survey of Imperial Russian postal communications between 1700 and 1850 will try to strike a better balance. I will explore both the development of relay services during this period and the

---

and Early Development of the Muscovite Postal Service', *Jahrbücher für Geschichte Osteuropas*, New Series, 15. 1 (March 1967), 1–15.

14 Gurliand, *Iamskaia gon'ba*, p. 54.

15 This tradition goes back to the nineteenth century: see A. Brückner, *Die Europäisierung Russlands : Land und Volk* (Gotha: Friedrich Andreas Berthes, 1888), pp. 67–94; I. P. Kozlovskii, *Pervye pochty i pervye pochtmeistery v Moskovskom gosudarstve*, vol. 1 (Warsaw: Tipografiia Varshavskogo uchebnogo okruga, 1913); Vigilev, *Istoriia otechestvennoi pochty*, p. 96.

16 Vigilev, *Istoriia otechestvennoi pochty*; Cvetkovski, *Modernisierung durch Beschleunigung*; D. A. Redin, *Administrativnye struktury i biurokratiia Urala v epokhu petrovskikh reform (zapadnye uezdy Sibirskoi gubernii v 1711–1727 gg.)* (Ekaterinburg: Volot, 2007). The best general histories of posts—including both obligation and service in its brief—are provided in Oleg Kationov's studies of Siberia: O. N. Kationov, *Moskovsko-Sibirskii trakt i ego zhiteli v XVII–XIX vv.* (Novosibirsk: NGPU, 2004); O. N. Kationov, *Moskovsko-Sibirskii trakt kak osnovnaia sukhoputnaia transportnaia kommunikatsiia Sibiri XVIII–XX vv.*, 2nd ed. (Novosibirsk: NGPU, 2008).

concurrent evolution of relay obligations to support them. Keeping both sides of the story in mind seems important, for it will allow us to create a more expansive history of the meanings produced by this old imperial technique as it entered the modern empire. As Georg Simmel observes in 'Bridge and Door', the creation of a connection across space does not merely allow packets of information to be transferred between two points. It also reshapes the landscape between them — thereby creating a new arena for the production of meaning. When people build a bridge, they make waters easier to cross, but they also reshape the rivers' banks to connect and support the new structure. The bridge focusses the interest of human community and polity to this spot, and not another, marking it on maps and devoting to it resources brought from elsewhere. In the same way, we might imagine that not only the people and things circulated by Russia's posts, but also the vast infrastructure of relay obligation that made their movements possible, gave meaning to the landscape of Russian empire.[17]

Or, at least, we might engage in such a line of interpretation if we had histories of communicative practices that accounted for both sides of the coin. The following reconstruction of the development of the Imperial Russian relay across the long eighteenth century is meant to help make such research possible. We may begin by stepping a little further back.

The first concrete testimonies to the existence of a postal system at the court of Moscow date to the fifteenth century. In particular, Prince Ivan III, "the Great" (1462–1505), whose conquest of Novgorod and its hinterlands laid the foundation for Muscovy's expansion into an empire, relied on horse relays extensively. Ivan III was so convinced of his post's importance that in his last will and testament he told his heirs to "keep relays and horses on the roads in those places, where relays and horses were kept in my time".[18] He need not have worried: between his death in 1505 and 1650, Moscow's relay system grew with Muscovy itself, by leaps and bounds. The seventeenth-century tsardom developed nine main relay routes, radiating outward from Moscow in all directions,

---

17   Georg Simmel, 'Bridge and Door', in *Simmel on Culture: Selected Writings*, ed. by David Frisby and Mike Featherstone (London: Sage, 1997), pp. 170–74.
18   'Dukhovnaia gramota velikogo kniazia Ivana III Vasil'evicha', in *Dukhovnye i dogovornye gramoty velikikh i udel'nykh kniazei XIV–XVI vv.*, ed. by L. V. Cherepnin (Moscow and Leningrad: Izdatel'stvo Akademii Nauk SSSR, 1950), p. 362.

like spokes of a wagon wheel.[19] (This architecture remained constant throughout the imperial period, and indeed can be seen from Google's "God's eye" view of Russian highways to this day.) A central chancery, the "Relay Chancery" (*Iamskoi prikaz*), planned the relay roads and organised stations along them. It also issued authorising documents, called "route letters" (*podorozhnye gramoty*), which governed the use of relay resources. These "letters", or requisitions, specified such things as the travellers' names and titles, their origin and destination, and the number of horses to which they were entitled.

Administered by the Relay Chancery, the local forms of relay obligation supporting the system varied. In some places, populations were asked to work the relays themselves, detaching their horses from the plough to hook them to official wagons or sledges. (The chaos caused in everyday labour by such interruptions was one of the major irritations of relay duty.) Other communities—either unofficially, or by charter—pooled resources to hire permanent teams of designated "volunteers" (*okhotniki*) to do this relay driving for them. Still elsewhere, by the late sixteenth century, the Grand Principality began to organise special societies of the road, called "relay suburbs" (*iamskie slobody*). These communities bore higher levels of relay obligation, harnessing more horses to ferry more traffic. To make these burdens more bearable—and also to distinguish their particular place in Muscovite life—the suburbs were granted a changing (and locally variable) set of privileges: such as the use of arable land, the right to trade in towns, and a yearly allowance from the treasury. Over time, Gurliand argues in his classic study, this created the foundation for the emergence of the so-called *iamshchiki* (literally "relay men", though women as well as children also lived in these communities) as a special social caste within the growing empire.[20]

Muscovy's posts supported the rapid but irregular transportation of royal couriers, and with them royal mail. Riders—or teams of officials and cargo in wagons—were only dispatched according to the sovereign's needs. The middle of the seventeenth century saw the introduction

---

19 V. Z. Drobizhev, *Istoricheskaia geografiia SSSR* (Moscow: Vysshaia shkola, 1973), pp. 160–66; A. S. Kudriavtsev, *Ocherki istorii dorozhnogo stroitel'stva v SSSR: Dooktiabr'skii period*, vol. 1 (Moscow: Dorizdat, 1951), pp. 78–104.

20 Gurliand, *Iamskaia gon'ba*, pp. 206–70, esp. pp. 220–23.

of new kinds of postal services to Russia, however. In particular, increasing commercial as well as diplomatic contacts with Western states encouraged the establishment of regular mail routes. These included lines to Riga (established 1665), Vilna (1667) and Archangel (1693). This "German" or "foreign post" (*nemetskaia pochta*), as the routes came to be called, possessed several novel features. It operated according to timed schedules (such as bi-weekly or weekly). It usually relied on sealed mail pouches that were relayed from station to station, rather than on couriers riding the whole route. Lastly, the "foreign post" transported merchants' letters and other personal mail on a for-profit basis. In effect, all three lines—which were run by Dutch and Baltic immigrants to Moscow—were limited commercial concessions, granted to individuals by the tsars. Earning their own money from civilian use of the mail routes, these men promised to deliver the tsars' own correspondence on a regular basis, in return.[21]

As Daniel Waugh and Ingrid Maier demonstrate in their chapter in this book, the information carried by the "foreign post" had great importance for the politics, culture and commerce of late seventeenth-century Muscovy. Yet the new routes did not have an equally transformative effect on Moscow's existing system of relay communication. The "foreign post" did not, for instance, change the shape or size of Russia's relay roads. The basic, wagon-wheel structure of routes from Moscow, including those through which the Riga, Vilna, and Archangel posts would run, had existed since Ivan III's time.[22] Nor did the "foreign post" disrupt the Muscovite practice of supporting postal relays through obligation. Quite the contrary: the tsars allowed the families organising these new routes to exploit the horses and riders provided by obligated communities. In effect, they privatised the profit from an imperial duty into the hands of a series of entrepreneurs.[23]

---

21 Kozlovskii, *Pervye pochty*, vol. 1, pp. 99-111, pp. 145-55, pp. 299-312; Vigilev, *Istoriia otechestvennoi pochty*, pp. 98–118, pp. 147–62.

22 Kudriavtsev, *Ocherki istorii dorozhnogo stroitel'stva*, vol. 1, pp. 72–80; Vigilev, *Istoriia otechestvennoi pochty*, p. 147.

23 N. I. Sokolov, *Sankt-Peterburgskaia pochta pri Petre Velikom* (St Petersburg: Tipografiia Ministerstva Vnutrennikh Del, 1903), p. 9; Kozlovskii, *Pervye pochty*, vol. 1, pp. 102-11, p. 164; I. P. Kozlovskii, *Pervye pochty i pervye pochtmeistery v Moskovskom gosudarstve*, vol. 2 (Warsaw: Tipografiia Varshavskogo uchebnogo okruga, 1913), pp. 3–39; Vigilev, *Istoriia otechestvennoi pochty*, pp. 102–18, pp. 130–40. The best detailed examination of the Riga services' initial functioning is Daniel C. Waugh's

As it happened, even this organisational outsourcing was only temporary. In 1701, the Vinius family—the last of the original concessionaires—was forced to relinquish control of the Riga, Archangel, and Vilna posts.[24] Peter transferred control of the "foreign post" into the hands of his powerful favourite and diplomat Petr Shafirov. Shafirov was later to claim that the routes and the profits they generated were a personal reward for his services; perhaps not coincidentally, he fell into disgrace for corruption in the early 1720s.[25] For a brief moment, it seemed that the "foreign post" might be combined, in its management, with the old relay system, still managed by the Relay Chancery.[26] Yet in the end, this "overseas post" (as the routes were also known) remained in the hands of powerful favourites who operated on the international stage (such as Heinrich Johann Friedrich Ostermann, in the 1730s). Its management was handled by the College of Foreign Affairs—through whose coffers its earnings also flowed—rather than the Relay Chancery.

Rather than transforming the geography, social underpinnings, or even the functions of Russia's imperial postal system, the "foreign post" thus spun off as a specially-managed, profit-seeking enterprise. Ceasing by 1703 to be a commercial concession, its portfolio of regularised relay routes was attached to one particular branch of the state and the grandees in charge of it. This division of Russia's postal services, old and new, remained in place for several decades to come.[27] To find the beginnings of more profound break in the history of Imperial Russian

---

unpublished 2015 manuscript, 'The Beginnings of the Muscovite Foreign Post in its European Context', pp. 10–22. I am grateful to Professor Waugh for letting me consult this essay.

24 Vigilev, *Istoriia otechestvennoi pochty*, pp. 133–34.
25 See his remarks to that effect in a report attached to RGADA, coll. 248, descr. 16, bk. 1065, fol. 43 ('O soderzhanii pochty v Rossiiskom gosudarstve'.)
26 In 1722, the Petrine government imagined fusing the whole of postal administration—including the "foreign post" and the Relay Chancery—in the hands of a Post-Director-General; but though the decree survives this merger did not, and the Relay Chancery and the "foreign post" existed side by side until the 1780s, when a central postal administration was finally created. See *Polnoe sobranie zakonov Rossiiskoi imperii*, Series 1 (1649–1825) (hereafter *PSZ* 1), no. 4073. As a result, the organisation of local post offices long remained a responsibility unclearly divided between the Relay Chancery and local governors. See Vigilev, *Istoriia otechestvennoi pochty*, pp. 260–64, pp. 294–301.
27 Sokolov, *Sankt-Peterburgskaia pochta pri Petre Velikom*, pp. 137–50; Vigilev, *Istoriia otechestvennoi pochty*, pp. 134–35, pp. 263–67.

relay practice, meanwhile, we need to look to the 1710s, and to deep changes in the organisational structure of the empire itself.[28]

In 1712, Tsar Petr Alekseevich (later crowned Peter I) shifted the seat of his government to St Petersburg and his empire's newly-conquered Northwestern frontier on the Baltic. The move to St Petersburg signaled Russia's rise as a power in Europe, displacing Swedish authority in the North. But it also raised the problem of how to connect the new but peripheral capital to the empire's main body. These concerns became even more pressing when Peter and his advisers sought to reform imperial governance, as well. In 1711, the tsar created a central Senate, to coordinate in St Petersburg the activities of Moscow's old chanceries; in 1717, he started to eliminate many of the latter altogether, in favour of a smaller number of Petersburg-based colleges. To make improved local partners for these new central institutions, meanwhile, Peter reworked the system of territorially-based "governments" (or provinces) he had established a decade earlier. Entrusting the management of these territories to hand-picked intendants and military commanders, he expected them to be responsible to the new central bureaucracy in St Petersburg.[29]

The result, however, was still a two-legged stool. The new central and provincial administrations were perceived to be inefficient, without better communications to support them. As Heinrich Fick (one of Peter's closest advisers) observed in 1718,

> The Colleges cannot manage their affairs, unless a proper saddle-post is started at least once a week between the chief towns and governments of the State.

Both the geography and the timetable of imperial relay communications had to change, Fick argued, "if Your Highness's enlightened and most caring intentions for the State Colleges are to be fulfilled". Nor was Fick

---

[28] In support of this periodisation, see Sokolov, *Sankt-Peterburgskaia pochta pri Petre Velikom*, p. 22.

[29] On the Collegial and Provincial reforms in general, see Claes Peterson, *Peter the Great's Administrative and Judicial Reforms: Swedish Antecedents and the Process of Reception*, trans. Michael F. Metcalf (Stockholm: A.-B. Nordska, 1979), pp. 52–67, pp. 242–49; A. B. Kamenskii, *Ot Petra I do Pavla I. Reformy v Rossii XVIII veka. Opyt tselostnogo analiza* (Moscow: Rossiiskii gosudarstvennyi gumanitarnyi universitet, 1999), pp. 116–17.

the first to make this observation: five years earlier, when the Senate was created, Shafirov had said much the same thing.[30]

Already in 1712, designated mail routes (for on-demand use) had been planned between St Petersburg and the provinces. In response to Fick's 1718 memorandum, Peter declared that these new internal "posts" (*pochty*) should be multiplied and operated on a timed, regular basis.

> Posts should be arranged first between St Petersburg and all the chief towns where Governors now reside; then the master of the post, consulting with the Governors, should designate routes from those towns to others further away, as needed.[31]

It should be observed that these new provincial mail routes altered not only the timetable but also the geography of relay communications in the empire. No longer a wagon-wheel set of main highways meant to connect Moscow with its borders, the relay system of the eighteenth century was envisaged as a finely branching network for internal communication, a web that extended inward and between the main lines. Its chief purpose was not the conduct of diplomatic relations with rival powers—or commercial ties with foreign interests, which as before ran through the "foreign post"—but rather the coordination of "central" and "provincial" institutions within Russia. Implicit in this conception was a great expansion in the network of relay stations, and with them relay obligation, in the century to come.[32]

In this respect, the name chosen for this new system—the "relay post", or *iamskaia pochta*—was significant. It reflected both the fact that the mail rode on relay horses and that local communities would continue to provide them (along with labour and other travel resources), through the *iamskaia povinnost'*. Spurning the entrepreneurial experiment of the "foreign post", Peter and his advisers thus planned for a continuation of the imperial relay technique they inherited. That is not to say that the

---

30 *PSZ* 1, no. 3208.
31 'Vysochaishie rezoliutsii na memorial inozemtsa Fika', pp. 574–75; the construction of these new, "ordinary" (that is, regular) posts was confirmed in 1720: *PSZ* 1, nos. 3591 and 3691, discussed below.
32 One of the first actions the government took in response to the decree on provincial posts was to conduct a survey of the existing relay network and "how it is maintained". This fascinating document is RGADA, coll. 248, bk. 1065, fols. 42–115, 'O soderzhanii pochty v Rossiiskom gosudarstve'. Quotation, fol. 43.

relays were placed entirely outside of markets in transportation services. Quite the contrary, to reinforce the existing system for the additional burdens of the eighteenth century, the St Petersburg government sought to stabilise relay communities by giving them a special status within roadside markets.

Peter established this principle in 1713, in a decree entitled "On the Settlement of *Iamshchiki* in St Petersburg Province".[33] The primary aim of this decree was to shore up the society of the Petersburg road, by commanding that hundreds of *iamshchik* households be resettled, from other provinces, to the stations between Moscow and St Petersburg. Though families from as far away as Kiev, Azov, and Kazan were indeed sent, the settlements seem not to have taken hold.[34] The agricultural lands near St Petersburg were difficult to work, the demands of relay obligation high, and no matter how often they were replanted relay villages did not thrive there in the early part of the eighteenth century. By 1720, nearly two thirds of the 150 *iamshchik* households settled at Tosna (near St Petersburg) had fled or "died out"; as late as 1740, the government was still trying to get officials around Russia to find and return fugitive coachmen from the Petersburg road.[35]

Yet if Peter's 1713 *ukaz* failed in its stated purpose, it nonetheless contained clauses codifying the economy of relay obligation, in a manner that stuck for the century to follow. Henceforth, Peter decreed, no one should use relay horses for free (*darom*), "neither for State nor for particular needs". Instead, people travelling on requisitioned horses were to pay specified, per-*verst* fees (*progony*) directly *"into the hands of the coachmen, and not to the Chancery or to Commissars"*. (These payments were to be based on a new formula Peter included: 1 kopek per *verst* from Petersburg to Novgorod, ½ a kopek per *verst* elsewhere.[36]) Relay horses and wagons, it was further specified, should only be used for travel (*proezd*), and not for freight (*klad'*). This latter clause not only limited the literal weight of relay obligations, it also stood at the centre of the licit

---

33 *PSZ* 1, no. 2741.
34 See also *PSZ* 1, no. 2833.
35 See *PSZ* 1, no. 3600; and *PSZ* 1, no. 8031.
36 This differential pricing scheme — whereby the Petersburg road charged higher rates, while the mileage fees in the provinces were smaller — would continue into the nineteenth century. Indeed, for much of the eighteenth century, the fees remained exactly these.

market for transport services Peter wished to develop around the relay stations. Outlawing the transport of freight via relay obligations, he authorised all travellers to "hire peasants or relay coachmen not under their normal obligation, but for a free price".[37]

In this way, Peter's 1713 decree became a kind of a charter, explicitly defining the intersection of imperial obligations, postal services, and transportation markets on which the relay system stood. Peter himself seems to have assigned its provisions broad significance, declaring it should apply "not only along that road, but throughout the entire State".[38] More importantly, and regardless of his intentions, this 1713 decree took on a life of its own after his death. In court cases and petitions filed by obligated communities throughout the century that followed, the 1713 decree is cited as the foundation of the society of the road's rights; it has the same role in an official guide to the post published in 1803.[39]

Some of the decree's provisions, it should be said, were not novel. Mileage fees (*progony*) had been paid to someone — if not necessarily directly "into the hands of coachmen" — on a per-*verst* charge since the sixteenth century.[40] In the absence of clear evidence to the contrary, we must presume that relay communities had long been in the informal business of transporting "particular" travellers and goods, for a price. Their concentrations of valuable human and horse power were surely too valuable to lay idle.

By codifying this practice for "the entire State", however, Peter's 1713 decree set the old relay system on a novel path. Unofficial, "particular" travel was now an explicitly licenced function of the system, rather than an informal local arrangement; people bearing relay obligations were likewise ubiquitously chartered to sell passenger and freight services

---

37 *PSZ* 1, no. 2741.
38 Ibid.
39 *Noveishii Rossiiskii dorozhnik, verno pokazuiushchii vse pochtovye puti Rossiiskoi Imperii i novoprisoedinennykh ot Porty Osmanskoi i Respubliki Pol'skoi oblastei* (St Petersburg: Imperatorskaia Tipografiia, 1803), p. 279. See also Sokolov, *Sankt-Peterburgskaia pochta pri Petre Velikom*, p. 22.
40 The Muscovite government had tried to quantify the monies needed to travel across the realm, so that they could be paid (by petitioners seeking official action) in the fifteenth century, as in the 'Decree on Travel' in the famous judicial code of 1497: S. I. Shtamm, *Sudebnik 1497 goda* (Moscow: Gosudarstvennoe izdatel'stvo iuridicheskoi literatury, 1955), pp. 83–86.

at the stations. Civil and commercial on a state-wide scale, no longer restricted to the Sovereign's use, the relay was becoming, in effect, a public institution of the Russian Empire. Yet this institution was being built within an old imperial framework, extending back centuries (and indeed millennia in other contexts). The "particular" market in relay travel the 1713 decree imagined was meant to make the old practice of relay obligation more bearable, and to prevent the communities it touched from breaking down, rather than to replace this system altogether.

Two types of services lay at the heart of Peter's ambition for the posts: regular mail delivery (*pochta*) and relay transportation (*proezd*). Both were meant, first and foremost, to support official communication, in particular the circulation of decrees and personnel throughout the empire. This priority found expression in basic decisions about how these functions were organised, which remained in force deep into the nineteenth century. After some hesitation, for example, Peter's government decided that official mail would be carried by the system "without payment". One hundred years later, a member of Alexander I's Permanent Council blamed this privilege—which fully externalised the cost of official mail—for "the excessive correspondence, that so greatly burdens all branches of government today".[41] Notions of rank (*chin*) had been used to codify the number of horses a man could demand in the seventeenth century; Peter maintained this practice in his newly reformed Russia as well. Thus, according to a schedule published in 1721 but still cited as normative in 1824, a general or Senator could demand up to fifteen horses for his official use at a station, while a privy councillor could expect seven and a travelling translator one.[42]

How did these services work? The relay-driven "regular mail"— *ordinarnaia* or *obyknovennaia pochta*, imagined in 1718 and further elaborated in 1720—was essentially an inter-urban service, connecting St Petersburg to the empire at large.[43] Regular mail delivery within towns began to be organised only in the second quarter of the nineteenth

---

41 *Arkhiv Gosudarstvennogo soveta*, vol. 3, pt. 2 (St Petersburg: Tipografiia Vtorogo Otdeleniia sobstvennogo Ego Imperatorskogo Velichestva Kantseliarii, 1878), p. 848.
42 *PSZ* 1, no. 3855.
43 *PSZ* 1, no. 3691.

century.⁴⁴ Though this service was initially designed to deliver "letters and decrees from all the Colleges and Chanceries to Moscow, and thence where needed", in October 1720 the Relay Chancery received instructions to "accept and deliver all manner of personal letters, except merchants' letters (which are accepted and delivered, upon scheduled payment, at the special post established at the Foreign College)".⁴⁵

To handle this mail, the following regulations were established in the 1720s. (Though details varied over time, and a special "heavy post" was added for large parcels in the 1780s, the same basic procedures guided the operation of the posts until the mid-nineteenth century.)⁴⁶ First, correspondence was to be brought, wrapped and addressed, to one of the new post offices set up in major towns. The postmaster then was supposed to log the origin and destination of the parcel in a ledger, and collect a fee for its delivery. (For much of the eighteenth century, postage rates depended upon both destination and weight, with deliveries on some routes costing more than others. In 1785, however, a universal tariff based on weight and distance was announced.)⁴⁷ Adhesive stamps, marking payment of postage, were not adopted until the mid-nineteenth century. Even so, starting in the mid-eighteenth century, post offices possessed postmarks, used to mark each letter or package once the proper fees had been collected and it had been accepted for delivery by the post.⁴⁸

At some regular interval — twice a week in the capitals and weekly elsewhere, to start, though with greater frequency as the system developed — all the mail so collected was placed into a special pouch. The postmaster then added a contents list or "register" (*reestr*) to

---

44 See *Bol'shoi filatelisticheskii slovar'*, ed. by N. I. Vladinets, et. al. (Moscow: Radio i sviaz', 1988), p. 66.
45 *PSZ* 1, no. 3691; *PSZ* 1, no. 6987; and *PSZ* 1, no. 3591. See also Sokolov, *Sankt-Peterburgskaia pochta pri Petre Velikom*, pp. 133–37.
46 See *PSZ* 1, no. 3691 and compare it with, e.g., *PSZ* 1, no. 13400; *Pochtovyi dorozhnik (1824)*, pp. 436–40. On the division of the regular mail into "light" and "heavy" deliveries, see *PSZ* 1, no. 15330.
47 For an initial schedule of fees, see *PSZ* 1, no. 4814; numerous subsequent decrees specify the weight charges for further provincial lines, as they are built (see nos. 6376, 6987, 8911, 9929, 12961, 13861, etc.) across the eighteenth century. Finally, in 1785, a general tariff by distance and weight was ordered, as became practice in the nineteenth century. See *PSZ* 1, no. 15875.
48 M. A. Dobin, *Pochtovye shtempelia Rossiiskoi Imperii: domarochnyi period*, 3rd ed. (St. Petersburg: Standart Kollektsiia, 2009), 9–15.

the bag, noting all the parcels the pouch contained as well as their destinations. The bag was then sealed, and entrusted to the first of the many postillions (*pochtaliony*), who relayed it from station to station. Although these riders might travel on a single saddle horse, the Relay Chancery was instructed to authorise up to three horses, with accompanying harness, for each mail delivery.[49] Keeping ready a constant supply of these special "postal" horses—in addition to relay horses for transportation use—became an additional burden on relay communities. The arrival of postal deliveries was scheduled according to an estimate of how long it would take to travel from the previous station; only one, or at the most two hours, was to pass between the arrival and departure of any given delivery.[50] In Petrine times, mail riders were expected to travel at an average speed of eight *versts* an hour. Target speeds were later adjusted seasonally, according to regulations of the late eighteenth and early nineteenth century, with eight *versts* per hour being expected in the muddy months of spring and fall, and ten or even twelve *versts* per hour being the norm for summer or winter.[51]

All along the way, at each intervening post office, the pouch was to be opened and its register inspected. Letters arriving to their destination— or that had to be transferred to side-routes—were removed; new mail was likewise added, with the list adjusted accordingly. The time and day logged, the pouch was then re-sealed, and dispatched to its final destination. When it arrived there, and its last contents were finally removed, a copy of the completed register was prepared and sent back to the original post office. At this point, so the 1720 instructions direct, mail was to be "given out" to its recipients. Though there was no regular delivery of mail within towns, messengers were evidently sent from post offices to official institutions and important people; both officials and "particular" recipients, meanwhile, could also send servants or come themselves to collect their parcels.[52]

---

49 *PSZ* 1, no. 3691; Sokolov, *Sankt-Peterburgskaia pochta pri Petre Velikom*, pp. 19–20.
50 'Ob uchrezhdenii pochty v raznykh gorodakh', p. 276.
51 Sokolov, *Sankt-Peterburgskaia pochta pri Petre Velikom*, p. 126. See also *PSZ* 1, no. 13435; *Pochtovyi dorozhnik (1824)*, p. 432.
52 *PSZ* 1, no. 3691.

Travel by "relay" or "postal" horses was the other service supported by Russia's postal system. It was governed by its own set of official procedures, as well as by informal practices (both legal and illegal) that developed around the relays' transportation markets. Travellers who were issued official requisitions had the right to demand fresh horses, in set quantities and at set mileage rates.[53] At each new station, they were required to present their "route letters" to a local stationmaster (*upravitel'*), who was typically a retired soldier. After inspecting the document and recording its data in his own logbook, the stationmaster calculated the mileage charges due for the next link, demanding payment in advance. A station elder (*starosta*) was then in charge of rallying the required horses and drivers, upon the signal of the stationmaster. These horses were harnessed to the traveller's carriage, and local relay men seated on the box or the front horse as drivers and guides, and the traveller was once again en route.[54]

Unfortunately, few of the local log books documenting the use of travel requisitions survive. The ones that do, however, testify to the requisitioning of thousands of horses for relay travel in central Russian cities. In Vladimir in 1741, horses were requisitioned 3,915 times for relay duty; in Murom, 2,713; in Moscow in 1737, by another official count, 7,607 horses were demanded for relay transport, alongside nearly 3,200 more for mail and packet service. In these central Russian towns, at least, the dispatch of horses provided by obligated communities was a daily occurrence.[55]

In 1717, the Senate decreed that such requisitioned transports could be used by people travelling for "their own needs", but only if they paid twice the official mileage fees.[56] Though literature of the late eighteenth

---

53 Periodically, the government needed to crack down on the range of institutions issuing such requisitions, to prevent their overuse. In 1742, for example, the government sought to forbid the use of pre-printed requisition "blanks", claiming that they were too freely distributed and contributed to the immiseration of relay communities. *PSZ* 1, no. 8509.

54 For Petrine era practices — which again held true, with variants, for the century that followed — see *PSZ* 1, no. 4073; *Pochtovyi dorozhnik (1824)*, pp. 425–32.

55 The logbooks for Vladimir and Murom are preserved in the archive of the Relay Chancery: see RGADA, coll. 290, descr. 16, file 337, fol. 195 and RGADA, coll. 290, descr. 16, file 336, fol. 147. A corruption case from the Senate archives, meanwhile, provides the Moscow figures: see RGADA, coll. 248, descr. 1071, fol. 399.

56 *PSZ* 1, no. 3075.

and nineteenth centuries abounds with references to such a practice, it is not clear how quickly it began to be used. In the Vladimir and Murom logbooks from the 1740s, for example, there are only a few elusive entries that suggest use of the system for a personal purpose; the vast majority of entries document travel by ranked servitors, as authorised by the Relay Chancery or provincial governors for some official purpose. As in other empires, the practice of charging lower rates for official travel created a strong incentive for elites to claim this status even when travelling for "particular" ends. Quite often, it seems, men of stature travelling for "their own needs" simply demanded the cheaper, official rate; the few women mentioned in the logbooks are listed as the wives and daughters of servitors (and not as independent travellers themselves). Numerous petitions from local communities, alongside central decrees, bemoan private use of official rates as a disruptive "abuse". Yet, though banned legally and protested (sometimes violently) at the stations, the practice seems to have been quite difficult to curb.[57]

Just as importantly, however, the existence of the official relay network encouraged modes of civilian travel that drew on resources provided by the system, but did not engage its formal system for requisitioning labour. The regularly spaced markets for food, shelter, horses, and labour the routes provided were key. In addition to licensing these markets, the imperial government advertised their existence. As early as 1733, the yearly official almanac published in St Petersburg began to include information about Russia's posts. In 1762, this section spun off into a separately published series of itineraries (*dorozhniki*) that listed routes, stations, and the distances between them. These guides allowed travellers to chart and calculate the stages of their journeys, and to imagine the rest stops that might be available to them.[58] Building

---

57 For "individuals trying to pass themselves off" as officials to use the Mongol post, see Allsen, *Mongol Imperialism*, p. 213. Senate cases protesting personal abuse of obligated transports include RGADA, coll. 248, descr. 16, bk. 1069, no. 36, fol. 174; RGADA, coll. 248, descr. 16, bk. 1069, no. 30, fol. 147–147v. Both are from the 1730s; decrees across the eighteenth century sought to clamp down on the practice, evidently unsuccessfully. See, e.g., *PSZ* 1, nos. 2491, 3045, 3488, 8035, 8166, 8836.

58 *Dorozhnoi kalendar' na 1762 god, s opisaniem pochtovykh stanov v Rossiiskom gosudarstve* (St Petersburg: Imperatorskaia Akademiia nauk, 1762); V. G. Ruban, *Dorozhnik chuzhezemnyi i rossiiskii i poverstnaia kniga rossiiskogo gosudarstva* (St Petersburg: Tipografiia Veitbrakhta i Shnoora, 1777); *Rossiiskii pocht-kalendar', s pokazaniem razstoianiia vsekh gorodov Rossiiskoi Imperii* (St Petersburg: Gubernskoe Pravlenie,

from this infrastructure, various alternative civilian travel practices developed, at least for those permitted, in general, to travel. Although internal controls limiting the movement of women, serfs, royal peasants, and other categories of the population lie beyond the scope of this chapter, it should not be forgotten that they existed.[59]

Most simply, people owning draft animals could and did travel postal roads "on their own [horses]" (*na svoikh*). This required frequent rest stops for the animals, and thus was inevitably slower; by the same token, it was cheaper, requiring the purchase of labour and supplies only as needed. It was also possible to travel by hiring fresh teams of horses locally, at each stage. This practice was known as travelling "on free horses" (*na vol'nykh*). The expense involved was unpredictable, being subject to constant haggling and negotiation. Yet according to many accounts it seems to have been tolerable within central Russia. Foreign travel writers, for example, often praise the cheapness of this arrangement, by comparison with the European posts with which they were familiar. With time this practice seems to have become more organised, with drivers from separate villages working in combination. According to the famed statistician Heinrich Storch writing in 1803, peasants organised their own stable relay networks along important highways, complete with "Kommissars" in the major towns to promote and represent these long-distance services.[60] Unfortunately, unlike the state system, such businesses seem to have left no archives behind them. Last, but not least, it was not unknown to hire teams of horses and drivers for entire journeys.[61]

How reliably, how comfortably, did these relay practices work? Better than one might suppose. Today, Russian roads are legendarily

---

1800); I. P. Kondakov, ed., *Svodnyi katalog russkoi knigi grazhdanskoi pechati XVIII veka, 1725–1800*, vol. 4 (Moscow: Kniga, 1966), p. 216, p. 227.

59 V. G. Chernukha, *Pasport v Rossii, 1719–1917* (St Petersburg: Liki Rossii, 2007); John Randolph and Eugene M. Avrutin, 'Introduction', in *Russia in Motion: Cultures of Human Mobility since 1850*, ed. by Randolph and Avrutin (Urbana: University of Illinois Press, 2012), p. 14, n. 25.

60 Heinrich Storch, *Historisch-statistisches Gemälde des Russischen Reichs am Ende des achtzehnten Jahrhunderts*, vol. 7 (Leipzig: Johann Friedrich Hartknoch, 1803), pp. 254–55.

61 Iu. M. Lotman, *Roman A. S. Pushkina 'Evgenii Onegin': Kommentarii* (Leningrad: Prosveshchenie, 1983), pp. 106–09; Cvetkovski, *Modernisierung durch Beschleunigung*, 109–10; Kationov, *Moskovsko-Sibirskii trakt* (2004), pp. 299–327.

awful; in the early eighteenth century they were largely non-existent. The first paved highways, or *chaussées*, did not appear in Russia until 1817; before that, apart from a few experiments, road building consisted of "choosing a direction, clearing a way and arranging temporary fords across rivers and marshy places", using axes and saws.[62] Though the labour involved could be colossal—one late seventeenth-century embassy from Moscow to Smolensk counted 533 such crossings, made out of logs—nature remained the master of these surfaces, which could be washed out or made impassable by flood and mud alike. That said, the same was true of Europe and the world at large in the eighteenth century, where (as one scholar has written) "most roads were little more than unmaintained mud tracks or bridlepaths".[63] In such conditions, Ferdinand Braudel argues, differences in speed were dependent not on travelling surfaces, but on regular "services provided by other people", food, shelter, labour, and above all draft animals chief among them.[64] Only in the late eighteenth and early nineteenth centuries did combinations of new road-making technologies (such as McAdam's famous method), horse breeding, and improved postal organisation begin to allow a noticeable breakthrough in speed, as compared to ancient times.[65]

In an extensive archival analysis of the speeds attained by official transport in the Urals in the 1740s, the historian Dmitrii Redin has estimated that a courier travelling the system could reliably average fifty-five kilometres a day in Western Siberia (Tobolsk), and between fifty and seventy kilometres a day elsewhere. While short of the targets announced by official decrees, these averages correspond to similarly mountainous provincial regions in Europe, such as the Pyrenees, he claims.[66] Indeed, speeds of forty to fifty miles (or sixty to eighty kilometres) a day were typical for central Britain and much of Europe

---

62 Kudriavtsev, *Ocherki istorii dorozhnogo stroitel'stva*, vol. 1, p. 67, pp. 75–76, p. 80; Drobizhev, *Istoricheskaia geografiia*, pp. 251–57.
63 Simon Ville, *Transport and the Development of the European Economy, 1750–1918* (New York: St Martin's Press, 1990), p. 13.
64 Fernand Braudel, *Civilization and Capitalism, 15th-18th Century* (New York: Harper & Row, 1982), pp. 415–29.
65 See also Philip S. Bagwell, *The Transport Revolution* (London: Routledge, 1988); Theo Barker and Dorian Gerhold, *The Rise and Rise of Road Transport, 1700–1900* (Cambridge: Cambridge University Press, 1993).
66 Redin, *Administrativnye struktury*, pp. 363–87, pp. 585–90.

in the eighteenth century, as well as Rome two thousand years before.[67] In the central corridors between St Petersburg, Moscow, and Kazan, European observers from Herberstein (early sixteenth century) to Storch (early nineteenth century) were usually favourably impressed by the constant availability of horses—and with them, the speed and reliability of travel in Russia—even as they bemoaned the bumpy roads. (Winter was even better, when snow and ice created astonishingly fast roads for sleighs, "whose transport is agreeable and convenient" (*dont la voiture est douce et commode*), as Jean Struys rhapsodised about the Smolensk road in winter, in the late 1680s).[68] The greatest difference noted was the lack of private inns in Russia—forcing travellers to sleep and eat in the common rooms of relay courtyards, or their own wagons—and the voraciousness of summer mosquitoes.[69]

None of this meant, of course, that Imperial Russian communications were up to the task Fick and other central planners set for them. As Redin observes, being able to achieve European speeds for horse travel did not shrink the size of a state that dwarfed its European contemporaries.[70] Though travel times between Moscow and St Petersburg slowly dropped across the eighteenth century, Tobolsk was still two months from Moscow even under ideal conditions, and on any given journey these could be disrupted by "capricious weather, the condition of the horses, and, in the end, the personal qualities of the courier".[71] Delivered by postmen selected from locally obligated people, correspondence could easily go astray at any point, creating mysteries not easily resolved from

---

67 Barker and Gerhold, *Rise and Rise*, pp. 26–27; Dorian Gerhold, *Carriers and Coachmasters: Trade and Travel before the Turnpikes* (Chichester, UK: Phillimore & Co., 2005); Braudel, *Civilization and Capitalism*, p. 424; W. R. Mead, *An Historical Geography of Scandinavia* (London: Academic Press, 1981), p. 91; Silverstein, *Postal Systems*, p. 31, p. 191.

68 Jean Struys, *Les voyages de Jean Struys, en Moscovie, en Tartare, en Perse, aux Indes, et en plusieurs autres Païs étrangers*, vol. 1 (Lyon: C. Rey and L. Plaigniard, 1682), pp. 310–12

69 Sigizmund Gerbershtein, *Zapiski o Moskovii*, ed. A. L. Khoroshkevich, vol. 1 (Moskva: Pamiatniki istoricheskoi mysli, 2008), pp. 266–69; Friedrich Christian Weber, *The Present State of Russia* (London: Frank Cass & Co., 1968), pp. 115–16; Phillip Johann von Strahlenberg, *Historie der Reisen in Russland, Sibirien, und der Grossen Tartarey* (Leipzig, n.d.), pp. 183–85; John W. Randolph, 'The Singing Coachman Or, The Road and Russia's Ethnographic Invention in Early Modern Times', *Journal of Early Modern History*, 11. 1–2 (February 2007), 33–61.

70 See Redin, pp. 385–87, pp. 585–90.

71 Redin, p. 382.

the centre. "Letters disappeared en route", the historian A. N. Vigilev observes,

> A relay-man might forget to give the bundle of letters to his comrade, might drive past the town, to which they were addressed. If there were no pouches in which to drive the mail, the relay headman, if he thought it necessary, might keep correspondence at the station during bad weather, and letters might stay there for a long time.[72]

Although it achieved quite a lot by sustaining a workable system of relay communications across a vast early modern empire, the Russian posts of the eighteenth century could not coordinate the actions of a vast empire as fully as Russia's rulers desired. It is doubtful that any animal-powered system could have.

By the 1760s, it was the spatial and social footprint of its postal system—more than its speed or technology—that distinguished Russia's relay network from those of its European contemporaries. First there was the matter of network size and density, which made gigantic Russia seem suddenly small. By the middle of the eighteenth century, according to various modern estimates, Russia had between eleven and fifteen thousand kilometres of relay roads.[73] Using published itineraries, E. G. Istomina estimates this number rose to roughly seventeen thousand by the end of the century.[74] Yet, in 1776 France, whose overall territory was only a fraction of Russia's, had a nearly equivalent 14,000 kilometres of relay roads (after which the French posts went on to experience a period of explosive growth).[75] More generally, by comparison with mail and transport systems throughout Europe, Russia's postal system remained a thin and lacy structure, stretching in single lines across great distances to connect the empire's "chief towns and cities", even as the postal networks of

---

72 Vigilev, *Istoriia otechestvennoi pochty*, p. 261.
73 Cvetkovski, *Modernisierung durch Beschleunigung*, p. 108, n. 79.
74 See L. M. Marasinova, 'Puti i sredstva soobshcheniia', in *Ocherki russkoi kul'tury XVIII veka*, Part 1, ed. by B. A. Rybakov (Moscow: Izdatel'stvo Moskovskogo universiteta, 1985), 270; E. G. Istomina, *Vodnye puti Rossii vo vtoroi polovine XVIII-nachale XIX veka* (Moscow: Nauka, 1982), 25–26.
75 Muriel Le Roux, 'Expanding the Network of Postal Routes in France 1708–1833 (Histoire des réseaux postaux en Europe du XVIIIe au XXIe siècle)', trans. by Nicolas Verdier and Anne Bretagnolle, *HAL archives-ouvertes.fr/Comite pour l'histoire de la Poste*, May 2007, p. 6, https://halshs.archives-ouvertes.fr/halshs-00144669/document

its smaller European contemporaries extended into the everyday life of hamlets and villages.[76] Somewhat more dense on Russia's Western frontiers—where the empire had many trading partners and interacted with other postal systems—the system of relay communications grew ever sparser East of the Moscow-Tula line.[77]

Yet if the density of the Russian postal network was relatively low, its footprint in imperial society was both larger than this would suggest, and distinctively shaped. Instead of clinging close to the roads and towns the post served, the social supports anchoring Russia's relays stretched sporadically in various directions. This was because—in contrast to most of its contemporaries—Russia continued to rely on direct obligations on individual communities to support its posts. Most generally, in states throughout Europe, relay services were run as farmed monopolies. Local notables (such as the ubiquitous French *maître de poste*) contracted to provide for official communications in exchange for the right to run postal services for profit. These postal "entrepreneurs", as Daniel Roche has called them, hired their workers and horses from their own purses and conducted their relays as a business, on a local, regional, or even national scale.[78] This was, of course, the same general model that had been used to establish the first "foreign post" in Russia, in the mid-seventeenth century.

---

76 See Wolfgang Behringer, 'Communications Revolutions: A Historiographical Concept', *German History*, 24. 3 (1 July 2006), 333–74; Wolfgang Behringer, *Im Zeichen des Merkur: Reichspost und Kommunikationsrevolution in der Frühen Neuzeit* (Göttingen: Vandenhoeck & Ruprecht, 2003); Philip S. Bagwell, *The Transport Revolution* (London: Routledge, 1988); Barker and Gerhold, *Rise and Rise*.

77 See Istomina, *Vodnye puti*, 23.

78 Daniel Roche, *La culture équestre de l'Occident XVIe-XIXe siècle: L'ombre du cheval*, vol. 1 (n.p.: Fayard, 2008), p. 307. The Thurn-und-Taxis dynasty operated such a concession on an empire-wide scale, while in England not only mail and transport, but the actual construction of roads, was outsourced through the turnpike trusts. See Patrick Marchand, *Le maître de poste et le messager, les transports publics en France au temps du cheval, 1700–1850* (Paris: Belin, 2006); Wolfgang Behringer, *Thurn und Taxis: Die Geschichte ihrer Post und ihrer Unternehmen* (Munich: Piper, 1990); Gerhold, *Carriers and Coachmasters*; Barker and Gerhold, *Rise and Rise*; Bagwell, *The Transport Revolution*; John Copeland, *Roads and Their Traffic 1750–1850* (New York: August M. Kelley, 1968); Magnus Linnarsson, 'Postal Service on a Lease Contract: The Privatization and Outsourcing of the Swedish Postal Service, 1662–1668', *Scandinavian Journal of History*, 37. 3 (2012), 296–316; Linnarsson, 'The Development of the Swedish Post Office, c. 1600–1721'.

Yet, during his reign, Peter repudiated this model in favour of the older imperial practice of relay obligation. As a result, the 574 stations that (by official count) comprised the Russian relay system in 1762 possessed a distinctive social footprint. They were connected to communities not simply through licenced markets, but through the reach of relay obligations.[79] And this reach varied wildly, as Russia's postal roads developed across the century, in some cases much faster than the structures of obligation that supported them. Even in Peter's time, it will be recalled, "relay suburbs" provided only a portion of the horses needed by the system, with serfs, tribute-paying Muslims, Ukrainian Cossacks, town magistracies and "district people" (*uezdnye liudi*), among others, providing the rest. In 1767, meanwhile, the Relay Chancery observed that shifting routes had resulted in a situation where it was not uncommon for communities "two or three hundred *versts* or more" away from a station to be obligated to supply it with horses and drivers.[80]

Catherine II (r. 1762–96) took vigorous action to push Imperial Russian communications down to the district level. Inheriting the territorial order created under her predecessors, in the 1770s she radically renovated it, increasing the number, responsibilities, and local subdivisions of Russia's provinces; as in Peter's time, this implied an internal refinement of Russia's relay network.[81] In 1782, Catherine ordered her provincial governors to draw up plans for creating three distinct levels of postal roads: 1) central arteries between Petersburg, Moscow, and the provinces; 2) roads between provincial capitals; and 3) roads from provincial capitals to the administrative centres of districts.[82]

---

79 For count, see August Ludwig Schlözer, 'Vom Postwesen im Russischen Reiche', in *M. Johann Joseph Haigold's Beylagen zum Neuveränderten Russland*, vol. 1 (Riga and Mietau: Johann Friedrich Hartknoch, 1769), p. 303.

80 'Nakaz, otpravlennomu iz Iamskoi kantseliarii v Moskvu, v stolitsu eia Imperatorskogo Velichestva, deputatu byvshemu v Iamskoi kantseliarii nadvornym sovetnikom, kotoryi nyne glavnogo kommissariata prokuror, gospodinu Nelidovu', in *Sbornik Imperatorskogo russkogo istoricheskogo obshchestva*, vol. 43 (Nelden, Liechtenstein: Kraus Reprint, 1971), p. 363.

81 On Catherine's provincial reforms in general, see Robert E. Jones, *Provincial Development in Russia: Catherine II and Jakob Sievers* (New Brunswick: Rutgers University Press, 1984); A. B. Kamenskii, 'Administrativnoe upravlenie v Rossii XVIII v.', in *Administrativnye reformy v Rossii: istoriia i sovremennost'* (Moscow: ROSSPEN, 2006).

82 *PSZ* 1, no. 15323; this followed an order of the previous year to begin building district posts: *PSZ* 1, no. 15127.

Though tracking the process by which these plans were implemented is difficult, early nineteenth-century maps and centrally collected statistics both document the rapid local expansion of Russia's relays that followed.

Thus, in 1769, according to Schlözer, the empire's 574 stations harnessed 3,866 postal horses in their service; by 1775, according to Vasilii Ruban, there were 4,895 horses provided for the relays, with 1,417 of those (or about 29%) being located on the vital Petersburg-Moscow road. (Ruban also counts 101 relay routes by this time.)[83] By 1801, the Chief Postal Directory informed the Ministry of Internal Affairs that there were 3,222 relay stations in the empire, commanding 37,840 horses, a six-fold and nine-fold increase, respectively, in a little over two decades. Whereas in 1781 there had been 73 post offices in the empire—regional depots for the collection and circulation of letter and packet mail—by 1801 there were 450.[84] This growth continued into the next quarter of the nineteenth century, as Kelly O'Neill's digitisation of V. P. Piadyshev's 1827 *Geographical Atlas of the Russian Empire* has shown. By this count, there were 3,567 post stations in the empire (as well as 576 "post houses", concentrated largely in Finland and Ukraine).[85]

Between 1775 and 1825, in other words, Russia's horse relay networks were placed on the path that would lead to their mid-nineteenth-century apogee. The network of 1854 is visible only in outline in the itineraries of the 1760s, but it exists in detail on the provincial postal maps of the first quarter of the nineteenth century (allowing, of course, for some subsequent growth).[86] By comparison with this development, other innovations in postal services during Catherine's reign seem minor. In 1781, a "heavy" post (for bulk official mail and larger parcels) was established twice a week between Petersburg and Moscow, alongside the

---

83   Schlözer, 'Vom Postwesen', p. 303; Ruban, *Dorozhnik*, pp. xi–xv, pp. 223–24.
84   Cvetkovski, *Modernisierung durch Beschleunigung*, p. 114. See also RGIA, coll. 1289, descr. 1, file 118, 1801 g. ('O soobshchenii Gosudarstvennomu sovetu svedenii ob"iasniaiushchikh ustroistvo pocht v Rossii'), fols. 37, 47v.
85   See 'Post Stations', *The Imperiia Project*, http://dighist.fas.harvard.edu/projects/imperiia/document/676
86   See, for example, *Karmannyi pochtovyi atlas vsei Rossiiskoi Imperii, razdelennoi na Gubernii s pokazaniem glavnykh pochtovykh dorog* (St Petersburg: Sobstvennyi Ego Imperatorskogo Velichestva Departament Kart, 1808).

established "light" post (for correspondence).[87] Deliveries continued to be added to the mail routes of major towns. In 1770, Procurator General Aleksandr Viazemskii designed a stagecoach system to run between St Petersburg and Narva. The first public coach in Russia, it was meant to carry up to six passengers with their luggage in a carriage drawn by four relay horses, with scheduled times of arrival and departure. Despite this Northern experiment, however, public coaching did not become common in Russia until the 1820s and 1830s, when private companies were licenced for this purpose.[88]

Indeed, in retrospect, the most ambitious postal reform imagined in the Catherinean era failed outright. Both Viazemskii (in his plans for the Narva posts) and Prince Aleksandr Bezborodko (a favourite deeply involved in postal affairs in the 1780s) believed it might be possible to shift the support of the postal service onto some form of commercial- or tax-based footing. Catherine was sympathetic to these plans, and in 1784 issued a personal decree "On the Emancipation of the Residents of St Petersburg and Olonetsk Provinces from Postal Obligation". According to this plan, the "relay suburbs" in these regions were disbanded, and a tax was to be imposed on the whole provincial population. With this money, the plan was to hire relay servitors and organise relay stations directly from the treasury.[89]

In the mid-1790s, however, Nikolai Arkharov, Governor-General of St Petersburg, pronounced this reform unworkable. In a memorandum, he urged Paul I to reorganise the "relay suburbs", and reinstate relay obligation more generally as the foundation of the province's postal service. Paul approved this proposal, and went even further. In 1798, in a general decree on the proper organisation of the posts, Paul instructed his governors that support of the posts was a general "societal obligation" (*obshchestvennaia povinnost'*), to be born as needed by communities under their authority, whenever "relay suburbs" were not available.[90] The effect was to urge governors to freely employ relay

---

87   *PSZ* 1, no. 15330.
88   Alexandra Bekasova, 'The Making of Passengers in the Russian Empire: Coach-Transport Companies, Guidebooks, and National Identity in Russia, 1820–1860', in *Russia in Motion*, ed. by Randolph and Avrutin, pp. 199–217.
89   *PSZ* 1, no. 16012; see also similar provisions in Viazemskii's plans for the Narva post.
90   *PSZ* 1, no. 17582; *PSZ* 1, no. 17721; *PSZ* 1, no. 17744.

obligations as they continued to extend imperial communications down to the district level.[91]

In point of fact, to meet the demands posed by Catherine's order to expand the network, they had already been doing so. The population of the "relay suburbs" had stagnated in the second half of the eighteenth century, growing by a mere 26% even as the demands made of them, in terms of stations and horses served, grew by leaps and bounds, 461% and 673% respectively.[92] As a result, when asked in 1801 to describe how relays were supported in the provinces, Russia's governors painted a spectacularly mixed picture. In Kaluga, local *iamshchiki* provided 48 horses, the rest of the population 184; in Tambov, *iamshchiki* drove 72 horses along 248 *versts* of roads, while "local district residents" maintained nearly 2,000 additional horses along 1,715 *versts* of roads (!). In Perm, 9,970 "souls" in towns were somehow made to pay for 19 horses; Pskov taxed merchants at a rate of 1 horse for every 200 "souls", and townspeople at a rate of 1 horse for every 337. The only pattern that emerges from this detailed report on relay obligations is that the maintenance of the relays was rarely confined to the estate of *iamshchiki*. Instead, as the system developed, it was spilling over into ever-broader categories of the population, often assuming the character of a local or even province-wide tax, whereby specific communities would pool resources to send a horse and driver to fulfill their obligation.[93] Ever more ubiquitous, the society of the road was less and less a caste, and more and more a finely differentiated web obligating variable contributions from a range of Russian societies, and staffed using hired labour.

As an evolving spectacle in daily life, this broad performance of relay duty attracted concentrated attention, from politics, commerce, and art

---

91   The central Relay Chancery was eliminated in 1781, and administrative power over local relay obligations transferred to the provincial governors: see *PSZ1*, no. 15178.

92   *Arkhiv Gosudarstvennogo soveta*, vol. 3, pt. 2, p. 874. For "soul" counts of *iamshchiki*, see See V. M. Kabuzan and N. M. Shepukova, 'Tabel' Pervoi Revizii Narodonaseleniia Rossii (1718–27)', *Istoricheskii arkhiv*, 3 (June 1959), 129, 165, as well as the overall population calculation made by Ia. E. Vodarskii, *Naselenie Rossii v kontse XVII-nachale XVIII veka (chislennost', soslovno-klassovyi sostav, razmeshchenie)* (Moscow, 1977), Table 44, p. 192; *Arkhiv Gosudarstvennogo soveta*, vol. 3, pt. 2, p. 874; 'Nakaz iz Iamskoi Kantseliarii', p. 363.

93   'O soobshchenii', fols. 99v., 104b, 188, 153, 158–158ob, 162–162v. The figures for Smolensk, for example, seem to line up exactly with the census count of the population as a whole, but elsewhere the pattern is more local, see fols. 88–97v.

alike. On the one hand, between 1802 and 1825, the social conditions underlying the posts attracted the attention of no fewer than five high-level government committees, most of which focussed on the question of whether and how to end the system of relay obligation.[94] Some felt that Russia's posts would never operate efficiently and equitably until they stood on a more universal footing: either a fully commercial system that placed the costs on the users of the post (including the government), or a nationalised one, where all of Russia's subjects, through a common, empire-wide tax, subsidised this public good. Others, including Tsar Alexander I, regretted the inequitable distribution of postal obligations, but nonetheless believed in sustaining, and perhaps even expanding, the practice of organising communities specially obligated to serve the roads (the network of *iamskie slobody*).[95]

Nicholas I finally cut the Gordian knot in the late 1830s. Upset by what he perceived to be the chronic instability of relay stations on the Moscow-Petersburg highway, he was impressed by stations on the Dünaburg road, which connected Smolensk to Riga. Part of partitioned Poland, these routes had been organised on a commercial basis for decades, according to a project devised in the 1770s. After four years of planning, Nicholas ordered the transition of Russia's system onto much the same foundation, in 1843. From then on a contract system would fund Russia's postal stations, with prospective operators agreeing to run the relays on a for profit basis on terms set by the state. Using hired rather than obligated workers, such commercial posts gradually replaced relay duty as the basis of postal communications in the empire. Nicholas also ordered his Minister of State Domains, Pavel Kisilev, to oversee the conversion of Russia's special estate of *iamshchiki* into the ordinary status of state peasants.[96]

This process took decades. In his autobiographical story 'The Sovereign's Coachmen', Vladimir Korolenko would recall seeing remnants of the old relay order in the Siberia of the 1880s, left behind (as

---

[94] This complex official history is summarised in 'Zhurnal i polozhenie komiteta o novom ustroistve pochtovoi gon'by mezhdu stolits', RGIA, coll. 1289, descr. 1, file 621, fols. 16–26v., from the early 1840s. See also Bunina et al., *Materialy po istorii sviazi*.

[95] See the discussion in *Arkhiv Gosudarstvennogo Soveta*, 3, part 2, pp. 843–96.

[96] 'Zhurnal i polozhenie', fol. 2v., 65–102, 135. The invention of the postal system of partitioned Poland dates to the 1770s, see *PSZ* 1, no. 13911.

he put it) like a primordial glacier in a deep valley.[97] Meanwhile, as its social underpinnings were being transformed, the imperial postal system became the object of a growing consumer and artistic cult, providing a set of objects and symbols imperial subjects could use to perform and represent their relationship to Russia. Already in the early nineteenth century, for example, merchants and rich peasants eagerly bought official-style "relay bells" (*iamskie kolokol'chiki*) to decorate their own troikas, despite official decrees forbidding the practice.[98] In the 1820s, Russia's first lithographers created quick-selling images of dashing mail troikas, even as poets and composers wrote widely popular songs about them.[99] In this way, the culture of relay obligation in the Russian Empire not only served to shuttle people and things across points in space, but also helped generate cultural commonplaces to populate and unite the spaces between them.

---

[97] V. G. Korolenko, '"Gosudarevy iamshchiki"', in *Sobranie sochinenii*, ed. by S. V. Korolenko and N. V. Korolenko-Liakhovich, vol. 1 (Moscow: Khudozhestvennaia literatura, 1953), pp. 414–20.

[98] *Lit" v Kasimove: katalog-spravochnik duzhnykh i podsheinykh kolokol'chikov Kasimovskogo kolokololiteinogo tsentra XIX-nachala XX v.*, ed. by A. A. Glushetskii (n.p.: Collector's Book, 2005); A. Glushetskii, *Rossii bronzovoe slovo: o chem govorit duzhnyi kolokol'chik* (Moscow: Tsentr delovoi informatsii ezhenedel'nika "Ekonomika i zhizn'", 2007), p. 25.

[99] A. F. Korostin, *Russkaia litografiia XIX veka* (Moscow: Gosudarstvennoe izdatel'stvo "Iskusstvo", 1953), pp. 8–14, 25–26; Thomas P. Hodge, *A Double Garland: Poetry and Art-Song in Early-Nineteenth-Century Russia* (Evanston: Northwestern University Press, 2000), pp. 81, 143–44; L. I. Sazonova, 'Literaturnaia rodoslovnaia gogolevskoi ptitsy-troiki', *Izvestiia Akademii Nauk*, Seriia literatury i iazyka, 59. 2 (2000), 23–30.

6. Information and Efficiency: Russian Newspapers, *ca*.1700–1850

Alison K. Smith

At the end of 1702, while he was engaged in war with Sweden, Peter the Great decreed that a newspaper be established to spread information about "military and every sort of affairs" to "the people of Muscovy and of neighbouring states". The newspaper (the word used was *kuranty*, a seventeenth-century holdover soon to be replaced by the word *gazeta*) was to be compiled from reports from the state's various chanceries, all sent to the Monastery Chancery, and printed there in the state printing house.[1] Within a month, the first issue of this state-sponsored *Vedomosti* (*The News*) was published, marking the beginnings of Russia's history of newspapers.[2] Over the next century, imperial decrees founded other newspapers (and a few independent newspapers appeared, as well), nearly all based in Moscow or St Petersburg institutions. Then, in the 1830s, the number and scope of official newspapers in the empire was expanded significantly when a series of provincial newspapers (*gubernskie vedomosti*) was established, again by official decree.

---

1   *Polnoe sobranie zakonov Rossiiskoi imperii*, Series 1 (1649–1825) (hereafter *PSZ* 1), no. 1921.
2   Historians of Russian journalism usually take this event as their starting point, reifying its status as Russia's first newspaper, though others find its erratic publication a "disqualification" from that status, as in Louise McReynolds, *The News Under Russia's Old Regime: The Development of a Mass-Circulation Press* (Princeton: Princeton University Press, 1991), p. 19.

Newspapers in Imperial Russia have most often been interrogated as part of a world of print culture, as sites where something like a civil or civic society might develop. This practice comes largely out of a focus on the later nineteenth century, when a "mass-circulation" press developed, bringing with it a space for the development of a public sphere.[3] Earlier newspapers, however, are difficult to discuss in these terms. It is in part due to this kind of focus that Peter the Great's *Vedomosti* has played an awkward role in the history of newspapers. It came first, but, as Lindsey Hughes put it, "controls from above and lack of initiative and expertise from below meant that a Russian free press was still in the distant future".[4] The general desire to focus on newspapers and their role in developing a civil or civic society may also explain why historians of journalism in Russia have generally skimmed over newspapers in favour of thick journals, where figures like Catherine the Great, Nikolai Novikov, and the first generation of the Russian intelligentsia appear as publishers and regular authors.[5]

Less discussed in histories of the Russian press has been the role of newspapers in Imperial Russian governance. In many ways, however, particularly in the eighteenth and early nineteenth centuries, newspapers were perhaps above all intended to play roles in policing information: in spreading it from the imperial state, in collecting it from the population, and in allowing a certain degree of information sharing between lower-ranking administrative bodies and even between individuals. Gary Marker argued that during the eighteenth century in particular, "Russia's rulers aggressively attempted to use the printing press to convey their own absolutist vision of politics and society to the entire populace".[6] Although he tempers this claim with a description of the ways that individual authors and publishers had a rather different set of interests in the wider world of print, newspapers viewed narrowly do in may ways fit this vision of print as a tool. In particular,

---

[3] McReynolds, *The News Under Russia's Old Regime*, pp. 1–2, pp. 11–13.

[4] Lindsey Hughes, *Peter the Great: A Biography* (New Haven: Yale University Press, 2002), p. 66.

[5] P. N. Berkov, *Istoriia russkoi zhurnalistiki XVIII veka* (Moscow: Izdatel'stvo Akademii nauk SSSR, 1952), p. 21; B. I. Esin and I. V. Kuznetsov, *Trista let otechestvennoi zhurnalistiki (1702–2002)* (Moscow: Izdatel'stvo Moskovskogo universiteta, 2002), pp. 8–25, p. 30.

[6] Gary Marker, *Publishing, Printing, and the Origins of Intellectual Life in Russia, 1700–1800* (Princeton: Princeton University Press, 1985), p. 10

newspapers in eighteenth- and early-nineteenth-century Russia become a kind of information technology, one of "those mechanisms that are used to organise, present, store, and retrieve information".[7] This could be information about international relations, about domestic reform, about crop and weather conditions, about prices and financial affairs, or about social control. All of these elements are reflected in the laws governing newspapers and their publishing.

From the time Peter the Great established the *Vedomosti* as the first civil newspaper in Imperial Russia through the middle of the nineteenth century, laws set out the parameters under which the Russian Empire's newspapers operated.[8] The intent behind those many laws focussed on a series of issues, all to do with controlling the distribution of information. They set out rules for who could publish newspapers. They set out rules for the sorts of information about the imperial state the newspapers should disseminate. They set out rules for notices that ought to be published in newspapers. They set out parameters for oversight and censorship. And they set out a financial structure that emphasised certain of these elements as particularly important. In so doing, they traced out a network of information to be sent initially out of Moscow and St Petersburg. This network disseminated information from the imperial state and from local administrations, and eventually allowed information to move back and forth between individuals, as well. In the second third of the nineteenth century this system expanded dramatically with the introduction of provincial newspapers meant to ease the circulation of information to an ever-wider audience. However, all through this period, as newspapers were consistently legislated as methods of information transfer, they were also evolving into rather less controllable sites, where other kinds of information created other visions of the Russian world. The laws imagined a perfectly efficient

---

7 David R. Maines, 'Varieties of Information Technology: An Editorial Introduction', *Qualitative Sociology*, 21. 3 (1998), 221–24 (p. 221).

8 The discussion below draws primarily on the *Polnoe sobranie zakonov Rossiiskoi imperii*, the "complete" collection of the laws that first, does not always include the discussions that led to individual decrees, and second, is not actually complete. Despite these issues, it still acts as an entry into the desires of the state, although the results of those desires were far more complicated than the decrees themselves envisioned.

information technology; the newspapers themselves were far more unruly.

The first newspaper, Peter's *Vedomosti*, was compiled from information sent to the state printing house, then under the control of the Monastery Chancery and based in Moscow. Gradually, responsibility for the newspaper moved to St Petersburg, a move codified in 1728 when a Senate decree gave responsibility for publishing to the Academy of Sciences. Founded only in 1724, the Academy of Sciences had a printing press and the ability to print "in Latin, German, and Russian dialects" (which meant that it had all three typefaces) and was starting to transmit news gleaned from foreign newspapers within Russia itself. Now the Senate decreed that the Academy of Sciences press ought to publish domestic news, as well.[9] As a result, by the middle of the eighteenth century, Russia had two newspapers, one based in St Petersburg and printed by the Academy of Sciences (usually referred to as the *St Petersburg Vedomosti*), and one in Moscow eventually printed by the new Moscow University (the *Moscow Vedomosti*).[10]

According to official decrees, the clear goal of these official newspapers was to disseminate information from the state to the general public. Practically, this led to *Vedomosti* that were quite short, and which featured a mix of news from abroad and closer to home. One issue reported on military news from Warsaw and England, on the travails of the Genevan ambassador in Constantinople, and on news of ships carrying gold and silver from the Americas sunk in the Atlantic (to the dismay of merchants everywhere). Domestic news was limited to a report on the status of the ice on the river Neva in St Petersburg (it was now traversable on foot).[11] Other editions contained only a single report on a battle of particular importance.[12] Richard Pipes saw Peter the Great's establishment of his *Vedomosti* as marking "a dramatic constitutional innovation", part of Peter's turn from secrecy toward "tak[ing] the people into his confidence".[13] Looking at the way news

---

9   *PSZ* 1, no. 5267.
10 For an overview, L. P. Gromova, ed., *Istoriia russkoi zhurnalistiki XVIII–XIX vekov* (St Petersburg: Izdatel'stvo Sankt-Peterburgskogo universiteta, 2003), pp. 14–27.
11 *Vedomosti* (St Petersburg), 8 December 1715.
12 *Vedomosti* (St Petersburg), 28 November 1715.
13 Richard Pipes, *Russia Under the Old Regime*, 2nd ed. (London: Penguin Books, 1995), p. 129.

was reported during his reign, it seems that, above all, the tsar wanted his people to know more about the world around them—the *Vedomosti* of his era feature foreign news almost to the exclusion of everything else. This is fully in keeping with Peter's mania for all things foreign; knowledge of the world would make Russian subjects citizens of the world.

In 1725, in the early months of the reign of Catherine I, a decree reiterated that "all important matters other than secret news" should be shared in print with the public by the colleges and chanceries of the state.[14] When news-gathering responsibility was transferred to St Petersburg and the Academy of Sciences, the terms of the 1725 decree stayed in force. All colleges and chanceries were to send important information to the Academy for publication. The laws did not clearly define "all important matters", but the contents of the newspapers that resulted seem much the same as what had appeared in the reign of Peter. A single issue might contain news of the King of Sweden's success at the hunt, earthquakes in Italy, military and diplomatic developments in Constantinople, and the report of a celebration at the Russian court.[15] Later laws rarely address this kind of news explicitly, but do occasionally mention it, as when a 1769 Senate decree noted that information about the empire's successes against the Turks in its current war were being regularly published in the St Petersburg newspapers.[16]

Later in the eighteenth century, laws most often focussed on newspapers as methods of disseminating not news from abroad, but basic information from inside the empire. As laws laid out responsibilities for various new bureaucratic offices, they often also included demands that certain kinds of transactions or activities be published in the newspapers. Catherine the Great's Provincial Reform of 1775 laid out extensive rules for the administration of her lands. New local institutions were to publish certain kinds of transactions in St Petersburg and Moscow newspapers. Purchases of real estate, in particular, were to be made public in the central newspapers. Anyone who wished to contest such a purchase had two years from the time of publication to make his or her

---

14   *PSZ* 1, no. 4694.
15   *Rossiiskie vedomosti* (St Petersburg), 11 December 1725.
16   *PSZ* 1, no. 13304.

case.¹⁷ Provincial offices were also to publish all sorts of other news that the state wanted the larger population to know. They were to advertise public auctions, particularly of state lands. They were to give notice of outstanding wages owed to state servitors. They were to place notices of undecided legal affairs. They were to inform the public of bureaucrats appointed to new positions.[18]

Newspapers were also brought to bear on a particular concern of eighteenth-century governance: fugitives and vagrants. From at least the era of Peter the Great, the imperial state had sought to control its population through requiring passports, initially hand-written, and, later on printed forms. The goal was to wipe out fugitives and vagrants and thereby make the entire population productive.[19] The reality was that vagrancy continued to be a real problem, as local police arrested many travellers who were either without documents, or who had expired or otherwise doubtful documents. In 1765, a Senate decree on fugitives and vagrants told local police officials to question such criminals carefully, and then, "so that owners may know of them", to publish accounts of those they had detained in the newspaper of the Academy of Sciences.[20]

Two decades later, a request from local officials in the Caucasus flipped this responsibility for publishing. By this time, Catherine the Great had instituted a new policy of granting amnesty to fugitives, but officials in the Caucasus found this an additional burden on their resources.[21] There were so many fugitives living in the region, and transportation was so challenging, that returning those fugitives to their proper places was too big a task. As a result, they asked first for more support, and second that serf owners place notices of their fugitive serfs in newspapers for ease of identification (and so that those serf owners could be approached to pay for the return of their serfs, or, instead, to let them transform themselves

---

17   *PSZ* 1, no. 14392, st. 205, 487. A few months later, a second decree clarified these instructions: all such notices had to include the price paid for a piece of land. *PSZ* 1, no. 15109.
18   *PSZ* 1, no. 15212; no. 15794; no. 18184; no. 18637.
19   Simon Franklin, 'Printing and Social Control in Russia 1: Passports', *Russian History*, 37 (2010), 208–37, esp. pp. 214–24.
20   *PSZ* 1, no. 12506.
21   On the amnesties, see Alison K. Smith, '"The Freedom to Choose a Way of Life": Fugitives, Borders, and Imperial Amnesties in Russia', *Journal of Modern History*, 83. 2 (2011), 243–71.

into state peasants and receive a credit toward the next military draft in return).[22] The Senate approved this proposal, though the language is unclear—was this a demand, or a voluntary measure for those who wished to have fugitives returned to them? Was it to apply only in this particular case, or to set new precedent?

Already by the 1740s, newspapers were also seen as places to spread more general information about the state of the Russian Empire. In 1744, Empress Elizabeth decreed that the Academy of Sciences' newspaper should publish accounts of new converts to Orthodoxy; the decree was sparked by two members of her court, one Catholic, one Lutheran, who had recently converted and taken new baptismal names.[23] The demand that such conversions be made public served two purposes. The first was practical: people needed to know the new names. The second spoke to Elizabeth's own strong evangelical Orthodox streak, and served to publicise a kind of activity she herself wished to encourage.

Catherine II expanded the kind of information that should be shared by means of newspapers. Early in her reign, a decree demanded both that population statistics be collected, and that certain of them be sent to the Academy of Sciences for printing in its *News*. The decree particularly focussed on mortality statistics in St Petersburg—all priests were to report on deaths in their parishes, with information on age and cause of death.[24] A few years later, another Senate decree ordered that population statistics for Lifland province be published in both Moscow and St Petersburg newspapers "for popular information".[25] Later in her reign, in reaction to inflation in Moscow, Catherine ordered that newspapers publish weekly notices of current prices for grain and other comestibles.[26] The first decrees spoke to an interest in spreading knowledge about the state of the empire. The last spoke to a more practical desire, to let people know current costs for their own well-being (and perhaps also to shame publicly any merchants caught demanding higher than average prices).

---

22 *PSZ* 1, no. 16715.
23 *PSZ* 1, no. 8945.
24 *PSZ* 1, no. 12061.
25 *PSZ* 1, no. 12895.
26 *PSZ* 1, no. 16143.

In part in order to control these many sources of information, laws also set out parameters for oversight and, eventually, censorship. By granting only a limited number of presses the authority to publish official statements, imperial decrees were already controlling the flow of information. That control quite quickly turned out to be insufficient in the eyes of the imperial state. As a result, already during the reign of Elizabeth, several laws set out additional restrictions on what could be printed. First, in reaction to "many untruths" published in the *Russian News* of the Academy of Sciences, and in particular to its statement that the empress had awarded Mikhail Bestuzhev a particular honour "which Her Imperial Majesty did not do", a decree gave the Senate oversight over what was printed in the newspaper. All news now needed the approval of the Senate before publishing.[27] A later decree was even more specific: no news about the imperial family could be published without proper approval (in this case, the decree was in response to an article about the empress going out of the capital to hunt).[28]

In 1780, another limit was placed on what newspapers ought to publish. The Senate heard cases on many topics, and the newspapers had been publishing most of them—a Senate decision was a Senate decision, whatever its subject. Now, however, a restriction was imposed: they were to publish only those meant for "general information" or with a specific notation that they were to be published.[29] The rationale behind this law is unclear from its text. It might have been an effort to control information, so that if a decision only affected a few people, or was intended to guide administrative practices rather than set general precedents, it could be sent only to those who needed to know of it. But it may also have been a kindness to the newspapers themselves, seeking to free them from the responsibility to publish pages and pages of information with limited utility.

While this sort of information was limited, in other cases decrees reduced the amount of oversight on publication. In 1781, a Senate decree declared that future advertisement of public auctions of state lands could be sent directly to the Moscow and St Petersburg newspapers,

---

27 *PSZ* 1, no. 8529.
28 *PSZ* 1, no. 9903.
29 *PSZ* 1, no. 15001.

bypassing Senate approval.[30] The reason for this was a purely practical one: to get advertisements placed in time for more people to take part in the auction, thereby hopefully increasing the returns on the auctions (and therefore the state's income). Not all such advertisements were made freer, however. Half a year later, another Senate decree affirmed that the Senate itself was to receive notice of land transactions between non-state actors—direct publishing was not acceptable in these cases.[31] Several years later, two additional decrees clarified the variety of land transactions that needed to be sent to the Senate, and also created a form for such notices.[32] This last provision is an important one in the context of viewing newspapers as a type of information technology. It standardised information, giving a list of exactly what needed to be included in notices regarding this kind of transaction. Eighteenth century laws also began to address an important question: who was to pay for putting information into newspapers? In 1766 the press of Moscow University, which had been publishing the *Moscow News*, asked that local government offices that wished to print reports of their actions should bear the cost of publication. The Senate agreed, and sent out decrees to that effect.[33] This was not always a simple matter, however. Later that same year, both the St Petersburg Academy of Sciences press and the Moscow University press asked local bank offices (*bankovaia kontora*) to pay the costs associated with printing information they were required to publish. The costs, however, were large (the Academy of Sciences estimated the paper costs alone as two hundred and seventy rubles) and the bank offices were themselves confined by statute as to their expenses. The Senate decreed that they be allowed to use interest income hitherto kept in reserve to pay the costs of publication.[34]

In these cases, the Senate believed that the dissemination of particular information to wider audiences was worth the cost to

---

30   *PSZ* 1, no. 15212.
31   *PSZ* 1, no. 15413.
32   *PSZ* 1, no. 16460, no. 16506. Nor was this the end; more decrees repeating the need to send out this kind of information continued to appear, including *PSZ* 1, no. 16885.
33   *PSZ* 1, no. 12767.
34   *PSZ* 1, no. 12783. Later laws also touched on questions of payment. In 1811 the Academy of Sciences approached the Synod for help in collecting outstanding fees for notices placed by Consistories. The Synod told all its consistories to pay up promptly. *PSZ* 1, no. 24749.

public administrations. In other cases, however, decrees ordered other methods of payment. A 1765 decree requiring police departments to publish information about arrested fugitives did not lay out responsibility for bearing the costs of such publication. In 1770, another Senate decree clarified the issue: those who placed the notice (i.e. the police departments that arrested fugitives) were to pay for publication. However, if the notice resulted in sending a fugitive serf back to his or her owner, the police department could recover publication costs from that serf owner.[35]

By the time Alexander I came to the throne in 1801, newspapers were well established as a means of circulating information, and decrees from his reign only emphasise that fact. Newspapers already not only transmitted information that the state wanted transmitted but also made the larger legal system work efficiently. Several decrees from the reign of Alexander I reaffirmed the use of newspapers to circulate information about runaways.[36] Other decrees focussed on property disputes. A decree of 1803 stated that Senate decisions on property deemed "worthy of attention" should be published "through the newspapers so that petitioners or heirs or their delegates" should know of them and take proper, prompt action.[37] Over the next several years, a number of Senate decrees also focussed on the Surveying Chancery — the results of its investigations were to be published as of a decree of 1805 (though matters involving court peasants were exempted from the duty to publish in 1810).[38] That process of publication was intended to make decisions about property more efficient. As a result, when the notices placed by the Surveying Chancery turned out to be inexact, and therefore to cause the Senate "difficulties and excessive correspondence about matters", the Senate sent it a "severe correction" to be more exact and more complete in its notices.[39]

---

35 *PSZ* 1, no. 13507. Later, after rules on publishing notices changed, so too did the rules on payments; *Polnoe sobranie zakonov Rossiiskoi imperii*, Series 2 (1825–1881) (hereafter *PSZ* 2), no. 1021.
36 *PSZ* 1, no. 21939; no. 28263.
37 *PSZ* 1, no. 21048.
38 *PSZ* 1, no. 21735; expanded in no. 22029. Matters concerning court peasants were exempted in 1810. *PSZ* 1, no. 24371.
39 *PSZ* 1, no. 26332; no. 26654.

As in the eighteenth century, these demands for publication created a problem of funding. In 1808 the Senate decided a question of who was responsible for paying for the notices of purchases required by law. Now, every provincial administration sending such notices to St Petersburg or Moscow for publication was to include one ruble fifty kopeks to cover the cost of printing the notice three times.[40] The provincial administration could collect the money from those involved in the purchase or other matter requiring official notice.

There was also something very new in the decrees of Alexander's reign: a new kind of language that emphasised a broader vision of information that could bring benefit to the Russian state. Eighteenth-century news encompassed foreign affairs, military matters, and internal governmental decisions. Now, in several early decrees, Alexander began to emphasise the importance of developments in industry and technology to the state, asking the Academy of Sciences to find "useful" information, translate it into Russian, and publish it in its newspaper.[41] In 1809 he went further. In a personal decree sent to the Minister of Internal Affairs, Alexander appointed a new editor within the Ministry to begin publishing a new newspaper, *The Northern Post, or New St Petersburg Gazette*.[42] It was not only "useful that information from [...] the provinces be brought to the attention of the public", but even "all the more necessary because much of this information concerns not only the police, but agriculture, factories, and other elements of the state economy". In other words, the goal was not just that newspapers be brought to bear on a narrow vision of governance, but also that they should communicate information that would support other goals of the state.

That new newspaper was only one of several founded at the turn of the eighteenth century. Alexander's father Paul had granted a Riga printer permission to begin publishing a German-language newspaper that would have the status of a state publication in return for its printing, without charge, all of the Riga provincial government's decrees.[43] Two years later, under Alexander, another decree approved the founding of a *Commercial News* to be published by the recently-created Ministry

---

40 *PSZ* 1, no. 22793; a further clarification appeared in *PSZ* 1, no. 23266.
41 *PSZ* 1, no. 20144; no. 20153.
42 *PSZ* 1, no. 23768.
43 *PSZ* 1, no. 19496.

of Commerce.[44] Now faced with competition from other options for news, the newspaper of the Academy of Sciences soon asked for and received exclusive rights to publish central state information.[45] Only a few years later, in 1808, the Minister of Justice asked permission to reorganise the Senate press; it had developed haphazardly and was now overburdened and stuck with failing equipment. In addition, he asked that the press be given a monopoly on printing and selling laws. It would, in return, publish a weekly newsletter about current legal matters (to which readers could subscribe for a fee).[46] In other words, it would gain a monopoly on one kind of state information in order to increase its revenue. Quite quickly, however, this limit on other presses was relaxed in the name of information transfer. In July 1809 the Minister of Commerce asked that the *Commercial Gazette* be allowed to publish legal decisions of particular interest to merchants.[47] They needed to know this information, and their *Gazette* was clearly the best option for getting it to them. Alexander agreed. Proper dissemination of information to those who needed it was more important than the financial status of any one institution.

The reign of Nicholas I saw another significant shift in the role that newspapers were to play in the Russian Empire. Nicholas is a difficult figure for historians, who see his reign as both the "apogee of autocracy" and as the time of the flowering of the Russian intelligentsia, a time of public conservatism and private discussions of reform.[48] Both these sides of his personality and his reign are apparent in his attitude towards the use of print. At base, Nicholas's decrees regulating newspapers went back and forth between an emphasis on control and an emphasis on their utility as an information technology.

First, Nicholas's reign brought in new regulations limiting what newspapers might print. Certain topics came to require special oversight for security reasons. Any publications about medicines or medical affairs

---

44 *PSZ* 1, no. 20565. After the Napoleonic wars, Alexander founded another newspaper, the military paper *Russkii invalid*, to focus on issues of particular interest to veterans and serving forces. *PSZ* 1, no. 27663.
45 *PSZ* 1, no. 20863, §§ 115, 124.
46 *PSZ* 1, no. 23390.
47 *PSZ* 1, no. 23747.
48 A. E. Presniakov, *Apogei samoderzhaviia: Nikolai I* (Leningrad: Brokgauz-Efron, 1925).

had to be approved by the medical faculty of whichever university was closest to the place of publication,[49] since inaccurate news about health could have potentially harmful outcomes. No news about the imperial family or events at court was to be published without approval by the Ministry of the Imperial Court.[50] This had less to do with a concern for security than it reflected a growing desire to project the proper image of the imperial family, in order to promote the empire itself.[51]

Nicholas's reign also saw an attempt to create an overarching censorship structure for the empire. Newspapers (and other periodical publications) were singled out in the new censorship regulations released in the first year of Nicholas's reign (and then replaced a few years later by a second set of regulations that unified censorship of Russian and foreign-language materials, until then under the jurisdiction of separate ministries).[52] As the first set of regulations put it, such censorship was absolutely necessary for Russia: "The goal of the establishment of Censorship is so that works of Literature, the Sciences and the Arts, when they are published for the World by means of printing, engraving, and lithography, give useful, or at least not harmful, guidance for the well-being of the State". Censorship allowed for the useful, and avoided the harmful.

Second, Nicholas's reign recognised the many uses of newspapers. Nicholaevan decrees added to earlier decrees that used print as a method of spreading official information, sometimes simplifying, sometimes adding layers of complexity to these existing laws. Therefore, one decree of 1828 continued to demand that property transactions, whether sales between two individuals or auctions to pay off someone's debts, be advertised in newspapers so that any challengers were properly informed.[53] Later laws regulating different kinds of property transactions and documents often included clauses that required

---

49 *PSZ 2*, no. 3994.
50 *PSZ 2*, nos. 4236 and 4237. At nearly the end of Nicholas's reign, some information about the imperial family—their travels—no longer needed special permission. *PSZ 2*, no. 24979.
51 Richard S. Wortman, *Scenarios of Power: Myth and Ceremony in Russian Monarchy from Peter the Great to the Abdication of Nicholas II* (Princeton: Princeton University Press, 2006).
52 *PSZ 2*, no. 403; no. 1979.
53 *PSZ 2*, no. 2139. *PSZ 2*, no. 4237 similarly reaffirmed earlier practices involving publishing in newspapers as a method of confirming property transfers.

the advertisement of changes in ownership or lost documents in newspapers.[54] Decrees continued to order that news of vagrants be published in order to find their owners or proper place of registry.[55] Other forms of advertisement were also mandated in law. Schools were to publicise openings for students.[56] Spouses seeking a divorce on the grounds of abandonment were to advertise in newspapers to provide evidence of that abandonment.[57]

The many different kinds of notices that were to appear in newspapers, and the many different decrees that had established that fact, soon required new fee structures. In 1831 the Senate released overarching guidelines for how such notices were to be handled when it came to payments.[58] These included notices from the Senate about appeals; elections to Noble Assemblies; reports of dead bodies, fugitive peasants and townspeople, prisoners, and draftees; of lost and found passports and documents; of missing state stamps; of lost and found property (and also stray livestock); notices seeking inheritors of estates or creditors, and many others. In general, if there was an obvious profit to someone as the result of a notice, such as the return of property (including serfs), that profit paid for the advertisement. If the benefit was to the proper and efficient functioning of some state apparatus, then the notice was to be printed without charge.

There were larger statements made about the role of newspapers, as well. In 1828, the Committee of Ministers heard a project presented by the Minister of Education "to improve the St Petersburg Academy Newspaper".[59] It spoke of a need to "make it as worthy of attention as possible", and listed a number of kinds of news it would print in order to meet that goal. Not only would it publish "domestic and foreign news", but also "notices from the police" as well as "other news, curious for the public". In return for receiving things like "police notices that up to now have been in part in print, in part in manuscript, distributed by police servitors to houses", the Academy promised to publish the

---

54 *PSZ* 2, no. 3262, §§ 16, 42; no. 3693; no. 4255; *PSZ* 2, no. 5360, § 361; no. 5462, § 99; no. 5463, §§ 21, 48, 110, 127; no. 5464, §§ 167–69; no. 8545.
55 *PSZ* 2, no. 1893, §§ 14–15; no. 8536, §§ 2–5.
56 *PSZ* 2, no. 5470, § 9.
57 *PSZ* 2, no. 5870, § 123.
58 *PSZ* 2, no. 4402.
59 *PSZ* 2, no. 2516.

newspaper faithfully every day, and to include any such notices sent to it at least a few hours before the newspaper was to appear in print. It would also publish news of those entering and exiting St Petersburg, weekly bulletins on prices, and reports on imports, health statistics, and the current population of the capital "by calling and sex, after every Police census". Furthermore, the proposal gave a rationale for using the newspaper in this matter: it was "the most simple and convenient method for informing the public in a timely fashion of various police actions and orders".

This was certainly the main goal of many of the decrees about newspapers: making the state, the bureaucracy, and the economy function more efficiently.[60] One Senate decree ordering that the Surveying Chancery give proper attention to the publication of its notices explicitly observed that such publication was an effort to "fend off the endless correspondence" that otherwise resulted.[61] This suggests that newspapers played a role as a form of information technology used by the state. Other decrees, however, blur the line between that interpretation and the idea that newspapers were a space for the development of a civic culture. Several decrees from the reign of Nicholas I focussed on a very different kind of notice—notices giving thanks. In one case, a noble assembly wished to publish a notice in a regional newspaper praising a particularly good bureaucrat for his service. There were, however, no rules that allowed such a notice. The Ministry of Internal Affairs asked the Committee of Ministers, and the Committee decided that such notices should be authorised and did not henceforth need special permission.[62]

On the one hand, this is an example of the desire to have the regulations spelled out clearly. It is hard to imagine why thanking a bureaucrat publicly might be a problem, and yet the local society was not certain it was acceptable. On the other hand, it set out a new way of thinking about the kind of information that should be included in newspapers. Regulations built on the idea that newspapers were places to thank individuals for particular services, be they in the bureaucracy, or

---

60 *PSZ 2*, no. 11109, § 109 founded a new St Petersburg police newspaper, in order to make its ordinances better and more easily known.
61 *PSZ 2*, no. 5439.
62 *PSZ 2*, no. 4218.

in philanthropic activities. Regulations regarding a school, for example, included a notice that any particularly large charitable contributions to the school could and should be reported in local newspapers.[63] These sorts of notices could be read as examples of a kind of civil or civic consciousness on the part of individuals or societies. The fact that they were mandated by law emphasises their role in supporting the aims of the imperial state, by rewarding effective bureaucrats and those who supported education.

Nicholas's reign also saw the biggest expansion of newspaper publishing Russia had yet seen via decrees that established a network of *Gubernskie vedomosti*, or *Provincial News*, through much of the empire.[64] This was an attempt to solve a consistent problem that plagued the regulation of newspapers: the problem of the provinces. Many of the decrees envisioned a world in which newspapers were used to transmit information from St Petersburg and Moscow to a wider readership. There was a problem, however. St Petersburg and Moscow were well served, but already by the 1760s, decrees began to mention the question of how to get important information out beyond them. So, for example, a 1765 decree that ordered police to publish reports on arrested fugitives in the St Petersburg newspaper also included a method to disseminate information even further: "send such information to Provincial and Town Chanceries".[65] What those chanceries were to do with the information, however, was unclear.

A more specific response to the problem of the provinces first appeared in a 1769 decree to communicate information about Russia's successes against the Ottoman Empire. As the decree put it, although St Petersburg and Moscow newspapers were publishing reports on such victories, "these newspapers are not received in all towns of the Russian Empire, and so not everywhere has received news of [our] military successes". In this case, the solution was to place responsibility onto the Senate printing press itself. News would be extracted from the St Petersburg newspapers and reprinted by the Senate press for circulation

---

[63] *PSZ* 2, no. 6788, § 38.
[64] There is a recent extensive Russian-language literature on individual or regional provincial newspapers, summarised in V. V. Shevtsov, '*Tomskie gubernskie vedomosti*' *(1857–1917 gg.) v sotsiokul'turnom i informatsionnom prostranstve sibiri* (Tomsk: Tomskii gosudarstvennyi universitet, 2012), pp. 13–16.
[65] *PSZ* 1, no. 12506.

in the wider Russian world.⁶⁶ Similarly, in the early nineteenth century, a number of decrees focussed on how best to disseminate information about fugitives and the passportless. Local authorities were supposed to "publicise" such information, but through what means? Decrees came to describe "public notices (*vedomosti*)" in provincial towns, but these were themselves undefined and poorly regulated.⁶⁷

Finally in 1830, Nicholas promulgated a charter founding *gubernskie vedomosti*.⁶⁸ There had been a few newspapers based in provincial towns before, but none had lasted very long.⁶⁹ The first, a shortlived *Tambov News*, had been established in 1788 by the region's then governor, the poet Gavril Derzhavin. Derzhavin explicitly tied his desire to establish such a publication to the need to simplify government work.⁷⁰ According to the decree listed in the *Complete Collection of the Laws*, the proposal to found a wider network of newspapers came from the Ministry of Internal Affairs and was approved by the Committee of Ministers and by Nicholas I. According to Susan Smith-Peter, however, the Minister of Finance, E. F. Kankrin, had actually originated the idea several years before.⁷¹ She furthermore points to continued tension between the two ministries (or the two ministers) about the content of the newspapers, with the Minister of Internal Affairs emphasising their role in governance, and the Minister of Finance more interested in their broader role in developing provincial economies.

The new decree set out an ambitious plan for a great network of newspapers "in every one of the provinces [*guberniia*]" under the authority of provincial governors and their staffs. According to the proposal, "the goal of publishing *gubernskie vedomosti* is to aid Chanceries in their affairs by decreasing paperwork, and in addition to give a means for state offices, and also for private individuals, to get information that pertains to them". In other words, it was a culmination of the idea that

---

66   *PSZ* 1, no. 13304.
67   *PSZ* 1, no. 21939; no. 24516; no. 25516; no. 25746.
68   *PSZ* 2, no. 4036.
69   B. I. Esin, *Russkaia dorevoliutsionnaia gazeta, 1702–1917 gg.* (Moscow: Moskovskogo universiteta, 1971), pp. 17, 20.
70   Susan Smith-Peter, 'The Russian Provincial Newspaper and Its Public, 1788–1864', *Carl Beck Papers in Russian and East-European Studies*, 1908 (2008), 6–7, https://carlbeckpapers.pitt.edu/ojs/index.php/cbp/article/view/145
71   Smith-Peter, 'Russian Provincial Newspaper', pp. 7–8, also Shevtsov, *Tomskie gubernskie vedomosti*, p. 26.

newspapers had a practical role in circulating information necessary for the proper functioning of the state apparatus and for the proper participation of citizens in society.

This was a general statement of goals; the proposal also included more specific guidance "on the subjects that should be covered in the *gubernskie vedomosti*". All such newspapers should include four major sections. The first was to include "decrees and regulations", including imperial manifestos, notices about the imperial family, "about peace, war, taxes", and decisions by the Senate or Committee of Ministers. These were primarily new legal decisions that might change some aspect of administration or of everyday life. In addition, this section could include news from an individual province's administration, either from the governor and his staff, or from the provincial treasury. To help decide on "the choice of topics" that ought to appear in the newspapers, the proposal went on to list twenty-two separate kinds of information that might be produced by provincial authorities and were deemed worthy of inclusion. They include news about comings and goings in the provincial bureaucracy, about taxes and tolls, about the draft, about diseases in the province, and about opportunities for charitable contributions.

The second section of the *gubernskie vedomosti* was allocated to notices of matters pertaining to the treasury. In the context of Imperial Russia, where provincial treasury departments (*kazennye palaty*) served both fiscal and census functions, this was a broad category. Here were notices of property transactions of various sorts, and of opportunities for tax farming. Postal matters appeared in this section, as did reports of bankrupts, of fugitives, of vagrants, and of found dead bodies.

The third section was simply labelled "news" and included a whole series of different topics. First, it meant "important events", like the travels of significant people or the deaths of local notables, whether first-guild merchants or artists and scholars. Second, it meant news about the economy. New factories and inventions, reports on markets, trade, and prices were supposed to appear in this section. So too were "subjects helping to improve agriculture", ranging from "methods of fertilising fields", to specific reports on successes in animal husbandry or agriculture in the province. "Various statistical and historical news" meant anything from information about current building projects in towns, to archaeological finds, to vital statistics. This listing of appropriate sources of news also included a note giving additional information about what this section was intended to promote: "all these news relate to that Province in which the *vedomosti* are printed". News from neighbouring provinces was allowed, if it was particularly important to residents of the paper's home province.

Finally, the fourth section gave space to "private advertisements". In many ways, these advertisements complemented the second section, which included notices of found property, including documents, physical objects or, in its notices about vagrants, runaway serfs, that had been brought to the attention of provincial authorities. Here in the fourth section, private individuals could likewise place notices about their lost property or runaway serfs. They could also advertise property for sale or for rent, or place notices seeking servants. In addition, any other advertisements "that cause no harm to anyone" and which were allowed in the St Petersburg and Moscow newspapers were allowed here, as well. Owners of shops or restaurants could and did place advertisements here.

Only one topic was outright banned from inclusion. The very first point made under the broad topic of subjects to be included in the news was, in fact, the subject to be excluded: "in the *gubernskie vedomosti* the printing of political articles, as they do not correspond to their goals, is not allowed". If the goal was to streamline administration and transmit useful knowledge, politics would, it seems, only muddle things.

Not only did the proposal legislate the topics appropriate to provincial newspapers, it also legislated, at least in part, their readership. The plan gave instructions for how to subscribe to the newspapers (in provincial capitals, turn to the newspaper offices; in district towns, look to the postal service) and what its cost should be (no more than ten rubles a year). It also noted that all state servitors in the province were required to receive a copy of the newspaper. So too were bureaucrats of the Ministry of Internal Affairs who dealt with issues pertaining to agriculture, of the Main Administration of Transportation who dealt with provincial transportation issues, and of local offices of the Ministry of Finance and Ministry of Education. In addition, township-level boards of both court and state peasants were to receive their appropriate provincial newspapers.

Finally, the proposal for the new newspapers emphasised the practical role they would play in streamlining administrative processes in the provinces. The first two sections—"decrees and regulations" and notices from the treasury—were the focus here. The plan was clear: those two sections "have in their own province official strength". That is, they were to serve as official notice from the government of new regulations and laws. No one was to await further instructions once these were placed in the newspapers. Local administration even received explicit guidelines on how to read and use the newspapers: they were to read through them carefully, make a note in their own records of any applicable new decrees, and from that point on, follow them. Local authorities were also to pay attention to all the issues they received, and to make note of their numbers—if any went missing in the post, local authorities were responsible for turning to the post office to replace them. At the end of the year, authorities were to bind all issues, and place them in archives.

There were several immediate refinements to the plan. When the proposal for the new *gubernskie vedomosti* was publicised, it included a preface from the Senate. It announced a scaled down version of this new scheme—*vedomosti* were initially only to be founded in six provinces (in Astrakhan, Kazan, Kiev, Nizhnii Novgorod, Slobodo-Ukrainsk, and Iaroslavl provinces), and if they proved to be a success there, they would gradually be rolled out elsewhere. In addition, the preface gave a number of Nicholas's personal additions to the proposal. The *vedomosti* should be printed "on the best paper possible, with a good typeface and in a proper form". At the same time, Nicholas recognised that "due to the current insufficiency" of printing facilities in the provinces, state aid would be given to their development.

Only in 1837 did Nicholas I's regime follow up on its initial establishment of six provincial newspapers and realise the plan for a wider network of *gubernskie vedomosti*. In a long new set of instructions for provincial administrations (which was itself in the middle of a series of new instructions for provincial governors and other provincial offices) appeared a second, more forceful, and slightly altered statement of the need for *gubernskie vedomosti* in all provinces of the empire. Again, the stated goal of the *vedomosti* was to make the spread of information more efficient—for "ease" of access, for "a most convenient method of getting news in proper time".⁷²

The plan had shifted somewhat since the initial 1830 decree. Now, *gubernskie vedomosti* were to consist of two major sections: Official and Unofficial. The Official section included all notices and reports pertaining to circulars and decrees from central and provincial authorities; notices of town and noble assembly elections; notices of newly appointed bureaucrats (or of those leaving their posts or receiving awards); notices of lost passports or other documents; notices of found property, and of public auctions; of infectious diseases in the province, or of dangers to crops or livestock. The section was also to include reports of fugitives, of arrested vagrants, and of dead bodies discovered (all with descriptions of their physical characteristics).

For all that most of these subjects were intended to circulate information outward, the list of possible topics also framed a broader network of information transfer. Official sections might include notices of what police departments were doing in one district, "which may serve as guidance in similar situations for the police departments of other districts".⁷³ Similarly, Official sections were to be shared beyond provincial limits—a copy was to be sent to the Ministry of Internal Affairs and to other provincial administrations. The reason was similar—they were to republish useful information, including news of infectious diseases and cattle plague and reports of fugitives, vagrants, lost and found objects, and auctions.

There was also a limit, but this time an odd one: "In the provincial newspapers not in any circumstance should decrees, laws, and announcements published in the news printed by the Governing Senate be republished". The persistent importance of the Senate news was also addressed in terms of circulating knowledge. Any information that provincial governments believed needed to be shared with the entire empire was to be sent to the Senate for publishing in its newspaper (along with the proper fees, of course).

---

72 *PSZ* 2, no. 10304, § 86. In 1838, St Petersburg got its own version for local affairs (the existing St Petersburg *Vedomosti* had an empire-wide focus, leaving St Petersburg as a town and as a province without the same local source of information). *PSZ* 2, no. 11109, § 109 and no. 11849, §§ 7–31; Moscow followed almost a decade later. *PSZ* 2, no. 20997.

73 *PSZ* 2, no. 10304, § 88, no. 3.

The Unofficial section might include all sorts of other subjects. Here was a general "news" section, to include "unusual events in the province", information about the provincial economy, agriculture, weather, new schools, and local history. The Unofficial section was also the place for private advertisements—buying, selling, and renting property, seeking servants or employees, private notices of runaway servants or serfs, lost documents or objects. Such advertisements were priced "by the line and letter".

This decree did something quite different from the 1830 plan. Now the two sections were to be printed separately, an act that more fully disentangled the functions of the press. The Official section continued to serve as a mechanism of governance, as a way of regularly publishing important official information. Decrees or instructions that required some specific action from local authorities were to be printed there with space left for notes by those local authorities. The Official section also had an official audience—all provincial, district, town, and township authorities; the Marshals of the Nobility; church leaders, both Orthodox and non-Orthodox. District level marshals of the nobility received three copies of the Official section. One stayed with the marshal, and the other two copies could be circulated around the district, shared with "nobles or estate managers". The Unofficial section now became something rather different, and presaged a shift towards a more civically engaged press in the later nineteenth century.

At the end of 1838, the Committee of Ministers released a decision that emphasised the specific ways that the *gubernskie vedomosti* were intended to function.[74] A question arose over the cost of a subscription to the *gubernskie vedomosti* after the governors of Olonets and Podolsk had raised local prices. The committee drew on the 1830 and 1837 instructions in their deliberations. According to the Committee, the first instructions had ordered that *gubernskie vedomosti* bear a "moderate price" in order that "people of all *sosloviia* be given the possibility of receiving them". It therefore found that increasing the cost to private subscribers would oppose this goal. Raising the cost of subscription to official subscribers, who were forced by law to take in the newspaper, was only allowable if the raise was "not burdensome". As a result, the

---

74 *PSZ* 2, no. 11889.

committee decided to set a maximum cost for a year's subscription to the *gubernskie vedomosti* in any province at 10 rubles for a private subscriber, and 20 rubles for an official one.

Although most *gubernskie vedomosti* did not appear until the very end of the 1830s, decrees began to refer to them much earlier. An 1831 Manifesto gave new rules for elections to noble assemblies. All such elections were to be announced in advance, and to be advertised "throughout the Rural and Town Police, or through the *Gubernskie vedomosti* (where they are published), and in their absence through public notices".[75] As more and more laws included provisions for publishing in newspapers over the next several years, that phrase or a variation kept appearing: "through the *gubernskie vedomosti* where they exist".[76] Not all did — in a few cases, statutes continued to refer only to "the newspapers of both capitals".[77] That was, at the time, the more sensible way to refer to things, for there were few provincial newspapers actually in print.

As more provincial newspapers began to appear, decrees continued to reference them, both to disseminate information and to make clear official positions. A decree instructed all *gubernskie vedomosti* to publish monthly reports of what was going on in their regional administrative offices.[78] In this case, the governor of Tula province had started the practice, and Nicholas, upon reading of this action in a yearly report, wrote next to it "good idea, it wouldn't be bad to order it done everywhere". Another stated that reports on fraud published in the capitals ought also to appear in the provinces.[79] In 1838, a decree laid out rules for how to know that a given published announcement had official weight. The answer was mostly simple: if it came from the Senate, it had official weight. If it came from a ministry, it had official weight. So too did the *gubernskie vedomosti*: they were, in essence, "an extension of Senate publications".[80]

Of course, there was a real problem with using newspapers as a major part of governance, as the laws that treated them as a form of information technology tended to do. It was a problem based in the

---

75   PSZ 2, no. 4989.
76   PSZ 2, no. 5360, § 361; no. 5464, § 168.
77   PSZ 2, no. 5463, §§ 21, 48, 110, 127; no. 6588, §§ 20, 26.
78   PSZ 2, no. 16886.
79   PSZ 2, no. 23686.
80   PSZ 2, no. 10978.

difference between the laws regulating newspapers in principle and the actual newspapers as they existed in practice. In law, newspapers were almost imagined as a pure method of transferring the information deemed important by some level of the imperial state. Property, fugitives, official decrees, local decisions—newspapers were a way to keep track of the population and to make sure that population knew how it related to the imperial state. Even more abstract information served a purpose: introducing newly Europeanised Russians to the world; making their empire familiar to them; improving agriculture. Even here, newspapers were to be purely efficient.

But none of the newspapers were ever that pure. Even the very first publications at the beginning of the 1700s were compendiums of foreign news that brought in all sorts of novel ideas. As such, they not only give historians a glimpse of a long-ago Russia but also gave Russians of the time an insight into far-away worlds. How else to understand news reports like the very first one from Madrid in an issue from June 1725: "The prophecy of a nun about which something was written earlier has turned out to be false and baseless"?[81] It might be a warning against anti-modern superstition, but given that it implies the prophecy had been reported as news earlier, that message was blurred at best. As a result, for all that one Soviet historian of newspapers referred to the *Vedomosti* of Peter the Great's era as having a strong pro-Petrine reformist propaganda role, they are in reality much harder to define so neatly.[82] From a very early period, newspapers aimed to be "not only useful but also entertaining".[83]

By the end of the eighteenth century, and after nearly a century of laws that viewed them as methods of transmitting official or semi-official information, *Vedomosti* played roles that were obviously more complicated. The St Petersburg *Vedomosti* included official reports as well as news from St Petersburg and military reports from around Western Europe. Then came advertisements, first "news" of books for sale at the Academy of Sciences bookshop—an example of the publisher of the newspaper advertising its other wares. Then followed private advertisements offering firewood for sale, seeking purchasers of

---

81 *Vedomosti* (St Petersburg), 2 June 1725.
82 Esin, *Russkaia dorevoliutsionnaia gazeta*, pp. 10–11.
83 *Istoriia russkoi zhurnalistiki*, p. 25.

property ranging from settled estates to horses and ducks to individual serfs. Shopkeepers invited people to look over their imported goods, like coffee and tea and "cured beef from Hamburg". Advertisements sought people to do particular jobs, like translating a "not too big notebook" from English into Russian. At the end, an official notice about debt was followed by a table naming all the debtors and enumerating their debts.[84] In another issue, much the same mixture appeared, plus notices of people leaving St Petersburg, and a report on the weather for the past three days.[85]

Already, newspapers in their practice challenged any effort to conceive of them as a pure tool of the state. Pages devoted to advertisements easily outnumbered those devoted to official news. In part this was due to the legislated demands that they publicise certain things, like debts and property transactions. As a result, however, newspapers created an image of an official world that existed largely outside Russia, and then an everyday world that consisted primarily of debts and secondarily of trade in goods and people. This divergence was even more true in Moscow, where Nikolai Novikov, often lauded as a progenitor of the intelligentsia, took over publishing the Moscow *Vedomosti* for a time during the 1780s.[86] It is only because newspapers had taken on this role that they were able to play a major role in Alexander I's first small steps toward ameliorating the condition of serfdom. Alexander did not ban outright the sale of serfs without land—a practice seen as particularly demeaning to the personhood of the serf—but instead forbade advertising the sale of serfs without land in newspapers.[87] This law only had meaning in a context in which publicity via newspapers made things known and real.

Over the first half of the nineteenth century, newspapers diversified significantly in their content. In part this diversification reflected sheer growth in numbers. Many new newspapers came to be. Those based in particular ministries or administrations had particular focusses, whether

---

84 *Sanktpeterburgskie vedomosti*, 2 January 1795.
85 *Sanktpeterburgskie vedomosti*, 5 January 1795.
86 Berkov, *Istoriia russkoi zhurlalistiki*, pp. 112–13.
87 *PSZ* 1, no. 19892. Of course, he had to repeat the law several times, including in *PSZ* 1, nos. 25775 and 29525.

military or agricultural,[88] while those founded in the provinces existed to develop a richer sense of provincial life. All of this, though, had the potential to expand the goals of the state to unrecognisable ends.[89] Publishing news about the provinces, even when "political" news was explicitly excluded, could not but bring to light a vision of society that might not entirely match up with state goals. The experience of a decade of their development apparently led to concern that things were not properly controlled. As a result, at the beginning of 1851, during the most repressive years of Nicholas's reign, a new decree stated that the Unofficial sections of provincial newspapers henceforth had to undergo a new level of censorship. Either a censorship committee within the provincial government, or a single professor or high-ranking bureaucrat, was to read and approve all materials published.[90]

It is in this context, too, that the provincial newspapers, particularly their Unofficial sections in which local editors published articles of local interest, seem to represent a dramatic shift in the development of something approaching a "free press" (despite being founded by decree). The Soviet historian B. I. Esin described the *gubernskie vedomosti* as "shabby", and claimed that even figures like Alexander Herzen were "powerless to change them, to enliven them".[91] More recent historians have been kinder to them, however. Now *gubernskie vedomosti* are more often interpreted as a major part of the provincial print culture of early nineteenth century Russia.[92]

This problem with newspapers in reality, as opposed to newspapers in principle, places the specific case of Russia before 1850 within larger discourses current in the study of information technologies. Studies of modern information technologies have come to focus on both state

---

88 *Istoriia russkoi zhurnalistiki*, pp. 201–04. On the *Farming Gazette*, founded to improve agriculture, see Alison K. Smith, *Recipes for Russia: Food and Nationhood under the Tsars* (DeKalb: Northern Illinois University Press, 2008), pp. 128–31.
89 This is also part of the argument of L. P. Burmistrova, *Provintsial'naia gazeta v epokhu russkikh prosvetitelei (Gubernskie vedomosti Povolzh'ia i Urala 1840–1850 gg.)* (Kazan': Izdatel'stvo Kazanskogo universiteta, 1985).
90 *PSZ* 2, no. 24979; it was soon followed by another decree stating that the unofficial section of the Moscow Police news also needed special censorship: no. 25370.
91 Esin, *Russkaia dorevoliutsionnaia gazeta*, p. 22.
92 For a discussion of the *Vedomosti* in the contexts of print culture, regionalism, and emerging civil society, see Smith-Peter, 'The Russian Provincial Newspaper', Katherine Pickering Antonova, *An Ordinary Marriage: The World of a Gentry Family in Provincial Russia* (New York: Oxford University Press, 2013).

regulation and its efforts to create efficient "information societies" on the one hand, and a much more unruly use of technologies that emphasise publicity and create spaces for civil societies on the other. Periods of growth in those technologies create increased spaces for freer interactions, and are as a result at times followed by periods of increased regulation focussed on eliminating that space for civil society in the name of efficiency.[93] Early newspapers in Russia, then, become emblematic of an information technology conceived as a method of governance and efficiency, transformed by practice into something with the possibility of unsettling, if not actively undermining, the goals of the imperial state.

---

93   Byoung Won Min, 'Biting Back Against Civil Society: Information Technologies and Media Regulations in South Korea', *Journal of International and Area Studies*, 20. 1 (2013), 111–24.

7. What Was News and How Was It Communicated in Pre-Modern Russia?

Daniel C. Waugh[1]

Increasingly those who study the mechanisms for the spread of news in Europe are moving away from an emphasis on what, it has been argued, was a principal "modernising" medium in the pre-modern era, the printed newspaper with its ostensibly secular emphasis and focus primarily on political and economic news.[2] There is a huge, largely uncharted territory of manuscript news. Some of the most widespread conveyers of news were the brochures and pamphlet separates, whose focus often was the paranormal and the sensational, and underlying even the sober printed newspaper reports was a great deal that had first been transmitted orally and might well be categorised as unverified rumour. Public display—festivals, religious and political ceremonies, theatrical events—are among the means by which even the illiterate could be informed. A critical component in the shaping and transmission of

---

1   This chapter was written with support provided by The Swedish Foundation for Humanities and Social Sciences (Riksbankens jubileumsfond, project no. RFP12–0055:1) and the National Endowment for the Humanities (grant RZ-1635–13), the latter for work in the National Archives (London). Any views, findings, or conclusions expressed in this chapter do not necessarily represent those of the National Endowment for the Humanities.

2   For a recent and balanced treatment of the development of news media in Europe, see Andrew Pettegree, *The Invention of News: How the World Came to Know About Itself* (New Haven and London: Yale University Press, 2014).

news was oral communication, and it seems very likely that, even over centuries in the pre-modern era, the way that operated changed little.

My goal here is thus to look beyond the *kuranty*, the Muscovite compilations of translated news from foreign sources (much of it from printed newspapers) about which Ingrid Maier and I write in Chapter 3. With rare exceptions, the information the *kuranty* contained was not deliberately circulated to the public, and, one might suggest, that public (however we might define it) probably would have shown little interest in what were largely accounts of foreign places and events whose relevance for domestic concerns would have been difficult to ascertain. What other kinds of news were there in Muscovy, and how was it transmitted? If the *kuranty* were for the privileged few of the court elite, was that same elite interested in other kinds of news, and what was news for broader segments of the population? My *a priori* assumption here is that "news" is information presumably of potential or actual current interest for its recipients either because it was new to them and/or because it related to matters that they might have perceived affected their daily lives or professional activity. That is, news is something that may relate to ordinary experience, but has some element of novelty, and possibly would have some consequence requiring action. As the evidence discussed here suggests, specifically with regard to this last point, we may wish to classify a lot of news as "transactional" in that it pertained to the immediate personal or economic concerns of individuals.

If some news is thus highly personal and relevant mainly for its immediate consumer and perhaps his close associates, is it also possible to distinguish different categories of news, which might have had broader relevance for a community or social group? As an astute anonymous reviewer of this essay wondered, is there not some danger that my approach might produce "an undifferentiated notion of 'news' that is so broad and all-inclusive as to risk obscuring, rather than illuminating the issue at hand"? That is, should we not need to distinguish clearly between various kinds of "information", including but not limited to rumour and intelligence gathering, and determine how the relationships between them changed over time? The discussion that follows will demonstrate that indeed there are differences in the way "news" was acquired, the purposes to which it was put, and the degree to which what was "news" may not fit any formal analytical category but rather may be a moving target reflecting the changing perceptions of its consumers and creators. We are confronted with a picture of complexity in which the boundaries between one type of news and another are permeable. This will be evident especially in the final section here, when we shall see how oral testimony, some of it easily characterised as rumour, passes through institutionalised mechanisms of intelligence gathering and verification, and enters the written record. When this material ceases to have current relevance, it arguably might cease to be "news". But short of that, the information may continue to operate as news, communicated in part orally, in part in writing, in part in public performance and symbol. If ideally news should be factual, in our own times we have ample evidence that this may not necessarily be the case. News may still contain rumour, may be based on contrafactual invention, be communicated (and in the process distorted) for purposes of propaganda, and so on.

I can, then, only offer a very preliminary inquiry to determine where we might locate information about "news" in its many manifestations in Muscovy. Much more study will be needed to clarify distinctions and trace transformations. I have deliberately not attempted to provide a review of the methodological literature on studying news, a task for which I have limited enthusiasm even though I recognise it will be necessary if the questions raised here are to be pursued in greater depth. Perhaps most importantly, there is an increasingly significant body of analysis on rumour which I have not yet explored in order to deal as fully as I would have wished with that aspect of my topic.

The road to uncovering evidence about oral transmission of news lies through the written record, several genres of which are treated here: certain kinds of missives (*poslaniia, gramotki*), reports and orders (*otpiski, ukazy*) communicated by or to government officials, chronicles (*letopisi*), and accounts about miracle-working icons. For communication networks, customs records (*tamozhennye knigi*) are invaluable, since they closely track frequent merchant travel, even if they are silent on what news those travellers may have carried. Some of the written record is disappointingly opaque on the subject of news. To some degree, then, we may have to relax normal rules for source-based historical argument and indulge in a certain amount of imaginative reconstruction of the scenarios in which news spread. While the focus here will be on the seventeenth century, some of my examples are earlier. And my use of the term "Russia" (instead of Muscovy) in part reflects the inclusion of evidence from Novgorod when it still was independent, and from border regions that may have been in the process of being incorporated into Muscovy but were hardly Russian in any ethnic or linguistic sense.

Private Letters

There is still a great deal to learn about literacy in Russia, even though we have some idea of the varied levels for different social groups.[3] Even those with no formal literacy could ask someone to write for them or read to them a written message. Keeping this in mind, the substantial amount of private communication in seventeenth-century Russia is a logical place to start if we wish to learn what might have been news. Most letters follow a standard format with a salutation and an exchange of sentiments about the health of both the writer and the addressee. Sometimes the writer merely asks that he or she be kept informed of the addressee's well-being. Letters often include concern for relatives, information about deaths and funerals or about marriages. A certain Ganka Iakovlevich Tukhachevskii wrote to his (rich?) brother about his ill son's disappointment at not being able to see his uncle when the latter's servant informed the family after a church service that the uncle would be visiting in a neighbouring village.[4] It seems that such short personal messages were mainly a way to maintain family communication. Even highly placed members of the Russian elite (e.g. Prince Vasilii Vasilevich Golitsyn) engaged in such correspondence.[5] In an expansive moment, presumably to impress his father, Golitsyn's son Aleksei wrote on 1 September 1677, "You should know, my lord

---

3 See, for example, Gary Marker, 'Literacy and Literacy Texts in Muscovy: A Reconsideration', *Slavic Review*, 49. 1 (1990), 74–89.

4 *Gramotki XVII-nachala XVIII veka*, ed. by N. I. Tarabasova, N. P. Pankratova and S. I. Kotkov (Moscow: Nauka, 1969), no. 140, p. 79.

5 For a summary on Golitsyn's correspondence, see Lindsey A. J. Hughes, *Russia and the West, the Life of a Seventeenth-Century Westernizer, Prince Vasily Vasil'evich Golitsyn (1643–1714)* (Newtonville, MA: Oriental Research Partners, 1984), pp. 12–13; for a selection of his personal letters, see *Moskovskaia delovaia i bytovaia pis'mennost' XVII veka*, ed. by S. I. Kotkov, A. S. Oreshnikov and I. S. Filippova (Moscow: Nauka, 1968), Section 1, pp. 16–35.

father, that I was in attendance on the procession to Kolomenskoe with the sovereign and on the name day of Tsarevich Ioann Alekseevich met his majesty face to face and attended the feast, whereas there were few (other) gentlemen of the bedchamber present".[6] News, then, in the first instance might be narrowly personal, conveyed for the most part by private messengers, though individuals in government service took advantage of opportunities to use official networks. In one unusual case of correspondence between Fedka Zinovev and Fedot Tikhanovich Vyndomskii in 1697, an annotation indicates that one letter had arrived "through the post at the post court", where it was picked up and then delivered.[7] The instructions were that the delivery was to be via the Novgorod residency (*podvor'e*) in Moscow.

A great deal of correspondence was what I term "transactional", in that, following the opening sentiments, the letters would shift to some specific business between the correspondents.[8] This might involve asking someone for financial assistance or intercession on behalf of the writer or someone connected with him. A missive might introduce an agent travelling on behalf of the writer, for whom accommodation was being sought. Letters could involve specific economic interests — peasant villages owned by one of the parties, the shipment of goods, the management of resources. A husband sends his wife instructions about brewing beer, an archbishop writes from Vologda to order bells for a newly constructed church since none are to be had locally.[9] At the very end of the seventeenth century, there is a remarkable set of long letters between Klement Prokofevich Kalmykov, a member of the *gostinnaia sotnia* (one of the privileged corporations of merchants), and his agents on the Volga concerning very substantial business operations.[10] So here too we have a kind of news, specific to the individuals involved.

---

6 *Moskovskaia delovaia i bytovaia pis'mennost'*, Section 1, no. 9d, p. 26.
7 *Gramotki*, no. 172, p. 99. The following letter, no. 173, was also delivered by the post.
8 Note, here I am not including petitions (*chelobitnye*) and a number of other formal genres of documents submitted to or generated by the bureaucracy, even though the issues they raise undoubtedly could have been "newsworthy" to the circles of those who generated or read them. For military governors' reports (*otpiski*) and the instructions sent to them though, see the final section below.
9 *Moskovskaia delovaia i bytovaia pis'mennost'*, Section 1, no. 17v, p. 39; *Gramotki*, no. 462, p. 285.
10 *Gramotki*, pp. 176–248.

It is rare to find in such correspondence other kinds of news such as a report on the taking of Azov in July 1641 and the decision to release the Turkish captives to go home. Some 500 Arians and a certain foreigner Iakushka, described as a traitor, who was with them, were turned over to the Don Cossacks; the traitor was then crucified.[11] In autumn 1696, a Petrushka Lvov, writing to Gavriil, the Archbishop of Vologda and Beloozero, prefaced the substance of his letter, which dealt with attacks on Lvov's peasants by those under Church jurisdiction, with the following news:

> In addition, lord, you should know that the pious sovereign Tsar Peter Alekseevich arrived in Moscow on 27 October. And the infantry and Don Cossacks were left at Azov and the *voevoda* (commandant) left there was Akim Iakovlev syn Rzhevskoi from among the *stol'niki*. And my friends write from Moscow that they expect instructions to all about their service and a campaign to be mounted beginning on 1 March or earlier.[12]

Two letters by Gavrilko Ivanovich Snarskii to his parents include some details of the campaign in which he was participating in the border region near Pechory not far from Pskov.[13] A distinctive feature of these letters is that in part they are written in Polish, and the parents' home address is in the Belsk *uezd* of Dneprovskaia *volost'*—that is, presumably somewhere on the Western frontier where the family may well be Belorussian. The father Ivan Aleksandrovich was a high-ranking court official (a *stol'nik*).

In one instance, the bulk of a message from Mishka Prokofev, writing from Moscow to his employer, the *stol'nik* Andrei Ilich Bezobrazov, describes a major fire:

> I inform you, my patron, that on 13 October in the fourth hour of the end of the night a fire began in the *Belyi gorod* [one of the central areas of Moscow—DW] behind the sovereign's large stable in the parish of the Church of the Miracle Worker Antipii. It broke out in the courtyard of

---

11   The letter, written from Moscow on 1 August by one Nikishko (Nikita) Druzhinin, is to an addressee whose name has not been preserved, which makes it difficult to explain the possible context for the inclusion of the news about Azov; see *ibid.*, no. 47, pp. 37–38.
12   *Ibid.*, no. 476, p. 292.
13   *Ibid.*, nos. 224, 225, pp. 120–22, written on 21 September and 15 October but the year not specified. There are several additional letters in this series, apparently from the father's personal archive.

> *dumnyi dvorianin* (conciliar lesser noble) Semen Fedorovich Tolochanov, and from that fire the roofs of seventeen churches began to burn, and among them in two churches people of various strata burned. Five hundred and four homes burned and twenty-six courtyards were destroyed, fifteen monastic cells on church grounds, two hundred and thirty-eight shops in the marketplace and in the same market area eight trading houses, and bathhouses burned. It was impossible, lord, to put out the fire by any means due to a great storm, and had the wind not subsided, I expect it would have been a lot worse.[14]

As we shall see, the frequent fires which devastated the largely wooden Russian towns were certainly a subject of news that must have been of great concern for all social strata. One might assume that this particular fire affected the economic interests of Bezobrazov.

In examining such correspondence, so far I have not come across any communication of news about unusual weather (unless the subject is merely when the first shipping can move after the ice on the river melts), paranormal events, or supposed miracles connected with a local cult. Some letters by supplicants mention that the writer's circle is starving, but that is not an indication of some larger famine affecting a region and may simply be a rhetorical device to elicit sympathy.

Correspondence, then, in the first instance seems to have been for practical purposes focussed on immediate concerns. If this were our only source, it would be tempting to suggest that news in any broader sense simply was of very little interest to most writers. Indeed, what we know about Patrick Gordon's correspondence suggests that a lot of it stuck closely to personal and family matters.[15] Yet in his case there is ample evidence that he was a voracious consumer (and active disseminator) of news, notably in his correspondence with the important state secretary and postmaster Andrei Vinius.[16] Gordon's personal letters on private and family matters seem by and large simply not to have been the

---

14 *Pamiatniki russkogo narodno-razgovornogo iazyka XVII stoletii (Iz fonda A. I. Bezobrazova)*, ed. by S. I. Kotkov and N. I. Tarabasova (Moscow: Nauka, 1965), no. 147, p. 84.
15 A Scottish mercenary in Russian service, Gordon compiled a distinguished record of military service, undertook diplomatic missions, and advised the young Tsar Peter I. For more information about Gordon, see Chapter 3 of the present volume.
16 See my 'The Best Connected Man in Muscovy? Patrick Gordon's Evidence Regarding Communications in Muscovy in the 17th Century', *Journal of Irish and Scottish Studies*, 7. 2 (2014 [2015]), 61–124. On his interaction with Vinius, see esp. pp. 106–09.

occasion for conveying other kinds of information, which perhaps should not surprise us.

Amongst the Russian elite in pre-modern Russia, personal family letters might be only part of the correspondence carried on by an individual who had official or business obligations. Of course it can be difficult to draw a line between the private and family- or clan-oriented concerns on the one hand, and that which related to public or official function on the other. A lot might depend on a particular individual's education and outlook. Vasilii Golitsyn's correspondence is a case in point. Posted to the South in the campaigns of the mid-1670s, he corresponded about family matters but also received and acted on a request from A. I. Bezobrazov that he use his position to help retrieve the latter's peasants who had fled to territories under the jurisdiction of Cossack Hetman Ivan Samoilovich.[17]

Golitsyn, well known as a prominent "Westerniser" in late seventeenth-century Muscovy and ambitious for his own career, was certainly interested in all kinds of news. Not only his family but also his stewards or other employees in Moscow clearly had instructions to keep him informed of the latest business at court when he was off on campaign. There are several long letters from Matiushka Boev to Golitsyn, which passed on details about events in Moscow and about what the Russian commander in the Chyhyryn campaign of 1677, Grigorii Grigorevich Romodanovskii, had reported to the tsar.[18] Since his role in that campaign had been eclipsed by Romodanovskii's, Golitsyn felt that he had been slighted when the rewards were handed out. Reports transmitted in this fashion were not official, such as the formal dispatches that military commanders and governors were expected to submit with some regularity to a central office in Moscow, even if some of the content might be similar. Later, in the 1680s, when on a mission in Western Europe, Patrick Gordon was formally instructed to send regular reports to Golitsyn. Was Golitsyn a special case? Based on the isolated examples quoted above, we might at least hypothesise that many others would have been receiving in their correspondence news that was not merely "transactional". We might hypothesise that important merchants in Northern Russia, like the Fuggers (the German

---

17 *Pamiatniki*, no. 22, pp. 19–20; no. 88, p. 54.
18 *Gramotki*, pp. 128–133.

merchant and banking family) in the West, had an active interest in international news which might affect their business. Since some of the news translated for the *kuranty* arrived in Moscow via the White Sea and the commercial highway that ran South through Velikii Ustiug, Vologda and Iaroslavl, it is easy to imagine how the foreigners who brought it might have communicated it to the Russian merchants with whom they interacted.

Evidence from Chronicles

To broaden our perspective on what might have been news, let us now examine evidence from what may at first seem an unlikely source, the chronicles. Chronicles, after all, were often compiled well after the events they record, and there is a somewhat mistaken impression that their regular compilation died out before the end of the seventeenth century.[19] If our interest is the concerns of ordinary people, not just a small literate elite, the chronicles may seem to be a rather imperfect window through which to find evidence of news. Their focus often is on princely politics, births and deaths in the ruling families, high-level ecclesiastical affairs (but also the building of churches), invasions or military campaigns. It is not as though such information would have been deemed totally irrelevant to the daily well being of ordinary people, but one has to imagine that the news of very specific local consequence may have been deemed more important. The chronicles of Novgorod and some other places in the Russian North are known for the abundance of such local reporting. Of course, one challenge in assessing chronicle entries is to determine when and how the information they contain became known in the place where the chronicle was compiled or how current it was when recorded. Even though my main focus in this chapter is the seventeenth century, by stepping back to a specific example from a much earlier source, we can see the potential for locating information about what was news and how it was transmitted. Later and better

---

19 Taking note of this, Malte Griesse dismisses the chronicles as a useful source for the kind of analysis about revolts highlighted in several essays in the stimulating volume *From Mutual Observation to Propaganda War. Premodern Revolts in Their Transnational Representations*, ed. by Malte Griesse (Bielefeld: Transcript Verlag, 2014), p. 14.

documented examples may help us to interpret the earlier evidence and may also suggest that in important ways the subject of the news and mechanisms for its transmission changed little between the periods we artificially label as "medieval" or "modern".

My example is from the so-called Novgorod First Chronicle, where the entry for the year 6898 (1389–90) opens with political and local church news and then reads:

> The same autumn there was a great plague in Novgorod; all this came upon us because of our sins; a great many Christians died in all the streets. And this was the symptom in people: as death approached, a swelling would appear, and death came within three days. Then they erected a church to St. Afanasii in a single day, and Bishop Ioann, Archbishop of Novgorod, consecrated it, with all the abbots and priests and with the synod of the Cathedral of St Sophia; so by God's mercy, the intercession of St Sophia, and the blessing of the bishop, the plague ceased.
>
> The same winter the Church of St Dmitrii in Danislav Street burned down, and all the icons, and books and all the church stores, and a great many goods burned, for the fire took hold rapidly.
>
> In the year 6899 [1390–91]. There was a fire, which burned from Borkova Street up to Gzen [Brook], and on the other side from Mikitin Street to Rodokovichi: eight wooden churches burned down and three stone churches were partially burnt, and fourteen men, women and children perished, on 5 June, the day of the holy Martyr Dorofei. On the 21st of the same month, the day of the holy Martyr Ulian, a fire broke out in Prussian Street at the Church of the Presentation of the Holy Mother of God, and the whole of the Liudin Quarter burned up to St Alexei. Seven wooden churches burned down, and four stone churches were partially burnt.[20]

Surely much of this is eye-witness reportage, either directly by the writer or recorded from someone else's testimony, even if transmitted through a later manuscript. There is little here to distinguish the descriptions of the fires from that in Mishka Prokofev's letter quoted earlier, a report that clearly must have been written down very soon after the fire in Moscow. Nor do the Novgorod reports on the plague and fires

---

20 *Novgorodskaia pervaia letopis' starshego i mladshego izvodov*, ed. by A. N. Nasonov (Moscow-Leningrad: Izdatel'stvo Akademii nauk SSSR, 1950), pp. 383–84. The translation is largely mine, though some parts follow *The Chronicle of Novgorod 1016–1471*, tr. by Robert Michell and Nevill Forbes. Camden Third Series, vol. XXV (London: Camden Society, 1914), pp. 163–64.

7. *What Was News and How Was It Communicated in Pre-Modern Russia?* 223

differ significantly from what one might find in European manuscript newsletters or in a printed seventeenth-century German newspaper whose priority was to publish news as quickly as possible about a recent occurrence. Sir Peter Wyche, the English resident in Hamburg, was the regular informant for Sir Lionell Jenkins, the Foreign Secretary in London. In June 1680, Wyche included information about plague in Eastern Europe in more than one dispatch, and in his letter of 15 June, news of a fire that had gutted the centre of Stralsund. While he himself apparently did not subscribe to such beliefs, he passed on information about "superstitious feares" that such events engendered.[21] Fires in Russia did make the news in the West, especially if they occurred in locations where foreign interests were affected. One such report, about a fire in Arkhangelsk in 1695, was translated or at least summarised in the *kuranty* in Moscow, the news having originated in Muscovy, been printed in a yet unspecified Western newspaper, and then come back to Russia.[22]

It does not take much imagination to place oneself in Novgorod in those two years the chronicle covers and reconstruct how the news might have spread quickly throughout the city about the threats to life and property, or how the construction and consecration of churches would have involved a lot of people who would walk away from the consecration ceremony and perhaps later say something about it to those not present whom they might meet at the market. These are specific reports on the fires and plague, life-threatening events which surely would have been of great concern to Novgorodians.

Ideally we would be able to find documentation clearly labeled as eyewitness testimony for analogous events of such crucial local interest. In fact, there is at least one unusually revealing source about what happened when a fire broke out on 17 May 1646 in an area of Moscow called Kulishki in the house of Uliana, the widow of an under-secretary Ivan Eremeev Fustov.[23] The district administrative office (*Zemskii dvor*) investigated to determine whether or not Uliana was responsible by

---

21 NA (National Archives, London), State Papers 82/16, fols. (printed numbering) 128v, 130v, 135v.
22 S. M. Shamin, *Kuranty XVII stoletiia. Evropeiskaia pressa v Rossii i vozniknovenie russkoi periodicheskoi pechati* (Moscow-St Petersburg: Al'ians-Arkheo, 2011), p. 192, no. 130.
23 *Moskovskaia delovaia i bytovaia pis'mennost'*, Section 3, no. 1, pp. 125–27.

having left unattended a lighted stove in the living quarters of the home. The sworn testimony of several individuals was taken ("[name] said, having sworn an oath by kissing the cross"), most of them government clerks in various departments, as Kulishki seems to have been their home. As professional scribes, most submitted their testimony in their own hand. Interestingly, the surviving record includes no testimony from Uliana herself. The assembled depositions (*perechnevaia vypiska*) were then submitted under the signature of a state secretary and sent to the *Zemskii dvor* on 26 May, only nine days after the fire.

Under-secretary Ramashko Protopopov of the Great Revenue Chancery (*Bol'shoi prikhod*) recorded that he was at home asleep, and "when the fire began on Kulishki and I heard the bell of St Nicholas the Miracle Worker, I raced over to it". He could not say whether Uliana had lit the fire but knew that she was out visiting. A *zhilets* (the designation for a lower service rank) Ivan Samoilov syn Savin, who also wrote down his own testimony, indicated simply that he saw the fire but had no idea whether she had started it. An under-secretary of the *Zemskii* chancery, Mikiforko Vyrshin, confirmed that Uliana had been visiting at the home of the secretary Timofei Golosov. Vyrshin was at his office at the time, whence he rushed home to find his barn afire. "And at that moment Semen Stepanov, the son of the sexton of St Nicholas Podkopaev, told me, Mikiforka, that the fire had broken out atop the upper story under the roof of the home of Uliana, the widow of under-secretary Ivan Eremeev, and when he, Semen, had run up to her home, at that moment the roof took fire, and he Semen poured water on the fire and broke the lock of the upper chamber". The Siberian Chancery under-secretaries Eufimka and Vikulka Panov reported: "I, Eufimka, was at that moment attending evening vespers in the Church of the Miracle Worker St Nicholas Podkopaev, and just then a man on a horse raced up and yelled out that there was a fire in Kulishki, and in an instant I leapt out of the church and ran up to her house where already the entire upper story was aflame. I, Vikula, had gone into town and had almost reached the Frolov Gate when the alarm was rung. Seeing that there was a fire in Kulishki, I raced over [to it]".

Under-secretary Petrushka Koludarov of the *Novgorodskaia chet'* (an office with fiscal responsibilities) was at work. On his way home, he stopped at the home of the secretary Timofei Golosov, since his mother was visiting there, and they had left in their own home their neighbour Arinka. He did not recall exactly when they got home but went to bed only to be awakened when the neighbour Arinka "cried out that next to our house, the home of Uliana, widow of Ivan Eremeev, was burning, and I, Petrushka, jumped up…and I, Petrushka, splashed water [on the fire], and I do not know what caused the fire, but on that day the widow Uliana was home in the morning and then went to visit at Timofei Golosov's in the afternoon". However, he could not say whether she had lit the stove before going. Two other clerks testified simply that they knew nothing about the cause of the fire. Under-secretary Smirnoi Bogdanov of the Foreigners' Chancery (*Inozemskii prikaz*) explained his ignorance by the fact that he was not at home but at work where "I heard from people" about the fire. Finally, the icon painter Senka Stepanov reported that he had been at the home of Prince Semen Pozharskii, and as he was leaving "he heard a racket and saw smoke and ran up just as his widow's [place] went up…and the chamber was locked, and having raced up, they broke the lock and poured water on the fire. But at that moment the widow Uliana was not home and was over at the secretary Timofei Golosov's".

All in all, this is a remarkable record of how news spread, unique perhaps in that it is largely the reports of witnesses who wrote down their accounts within days of the actual event (most of the reports seem to have been written on 20 May). Although populated with literate officials, Kulishki otherwise probably was typical of almost any neighbourhood in Moscow or any small town in Russia, where everyone seems to have known everyone else, and many people interacted socially. In such a neighbourhood, oral transmission of news, rumour and gossip might have been quite normal even if not in moments of crisis. The first knowledge of the fire for some was from their direct observation, but in other cases because they heard the alarm or someone told them. The written documentation came soon after, preserving a directness and immediacy that the report in the Novgorod chronicle fails to convey, even if it may have likewise been recorded from eyewitness testimony when the event was still news. True, the requirements for bureaucratic paperwork in mid-seventeenth-century Moscow likely had advanced considerably over those in fourteenth-century Novgorod, but what was newsworthy, and the role of oral transmission at the moment it happened, surely must be similar in both cases.

What I have seen of the still largely unpublished later seventeenth- and eighteenth-century Novgorodian chronicles indicates that analogous reportage of local events was an ongoing preoccupation of the compilers, as many of the manuscripts evidence a continual process of record-keeping by different scribes, marginal additions, and the like.[24] Possibly our analogies here would be with some of the larger printed compendia of news published in the West, starting with the volumes sold at fairs in the late sixteenth century,[25] and then in the era of the periodical press, evident in the consecutively paginated numbers of newspapers which might be bound into annual volumes. Some publishers would also bring together at the end of a year a large volume containing such reports, which are generally included in any analysis of news in early modern Europe.

If Novgorod even in its decline after its incorporation into Muscovy continued to be well connected to news networks and retained a remarkably vibrant tradition of chronicle-writing well into the era when, so we are told, the genre was dying, what about a more remote location? My main example here will be Khlynov (re-named Viatka in the late eighteenth century; now Kirov), North of Kazan as one heads up river into the Urals, the town which in later perceptions was the quintessential provincial backwater of Russia. As near as we can tell, regular recording in writing of news and historical information in Khlynov began only around the middle of the seventeenth century.

As in Novgorod, churchmen in Khlynov were the primary recorders of the news in the local chronicles.[26] Key roles in the development of chronicle writing in Khlynov were played by the town's first bishop,

---

24 See S. N. Azbelev, *Novgorodskie letopisi XVII veka* (Novgorod, 1960), some of whose observations I have confirmed in a (granted, cursory) examination of one or two of the manuscripts in the collection of the Russian National Library in St Petersburg.

25 See Esther-Beate Körber, *Messrelationen. Geschichte der deutsch- und lateinischsprachigen "messentlichen" Periodika von 1588 bis 1805* (Presse und Geschichte—Neue Beiträge, Bd. 92) (Bremen: Edition lumière, 2016).

26 For details of the rather complicated history of the compilation and interrelationship of those texts, readers are referred to my book, Daniel C. Waugh [D. K. Uo], *Istoriia odnoi knigi. Viatka i 'ne-sovremennost'' v russkoi kul'ture Petrovskogo vremeni* (St Petersburg: Dmitrii Bulanin, 2003).

Aleksandr, appointed in 1657, and by a sacristan Semen Popov, whose father had also served as a sacristan in the main cathedral. Popov was obviously well connected in the community, with access to libraries and to the local chancery; he served for a time as one of the newly created Petrine *burmistry*, the officials in charge of local tax collection. Events of "all Russian" significance were the context for and background to his inclusion of events of local interest, one of them involving the history of the venerated miracle-working icon of St Nicholas Velikoretskii (about which more below). That Popov may have viewed the chronicle information, or at least some part of it, as "news" would seem to be confirmed by the fact that over a period of more than a decade at the beginning of the eighteenth century, he assiduously collected and preserved in chronological sequence copies made from the published Petrine newspapers (*Vedomosti*) and other reports about the ongoing events of the Northern War. The boundaries between keeping a historical record and keeping a record of current events surely were permeable.

For the late seventeenth century, there was a particular focus in the Khlynov chronicles on the Romanov succession and births, deaths, and marriages in the royal family. There is good reason to think that at least some of the information in such entries derived either from the writer having witnessed the celebration of the events in the local cathedral and/or from having accessed the decrees sent from Moscow with the news and the indication that it was to be celebrated locally. Such official commemorations surely would have served to disseminate the news to a broader public. Apart from news of the royal family, another item of "national" significance was an entry encapsulating the history of Stepan Razin, from his rise to his execution by quartering in Moscow. One might imagine that the ultimate source for this compact (single paragraph) treatment was some official communication circulated from Moscow.

Local reportage understandably included the installation of a new bishop. When Iona was appointed bishop in August 1674, a musketeer arrived ahead of him in town with a missive from the new appointee conveying the news, and then a service was celebrated on its receipt. Apart from such items, as in the Novgorod case, the local chronicles included information about natural or manmade disasters:

> In the year [6]175 [1667] on the twelfth day of the month of July there was in the town of Khlynov frightful thunder and lightning, and on account of the lightning the monastery stable and all the horse tack burned.
>
> In the year [6]179 [1671] on the sixteenth day of June the Dormition Cathedral of the monastery took fire from lightning and on account of that, the entire monastery burned on 16 June at the thirteenth hour in daytime, and the bells melted.[27]

It is likely that the source for these two entries was a record kept in the monastery, though of course the events would have been witnessed by many and undoubtedly not readily forgotten.

Destruction caused by storms was also news elsewhere in Europe. One of Peter Wyche's reports to London in 1680 from Hamburg told of the damage caused by an unusually severe hailstorm in a nearby town:

> The memory of Men cannot second it, it hath scarce left a Tile on the roofe of any house, or a paine of Glasse in any Window in the Towne, which looks as desolate, as if it had past through the hands of an unruley Army. The Corne thereabouts is soe platted, that it lyes as if t' had beene mowed. The Poultrey, some Sheepe and Young Cattell were struck dead, and one relation saith, there were Haile Stones of a Pound and a halfe.[28]

Even though chronicle entries about newsworthy events such as bad weather or disastrous fires are quite common, we should not necessarily expect that a chronicle account would retain the immediacy of an eyewitness report. For example, in the Ustiug chronicles of the late seventeenth and early eighteenth centuries, entries about fires, which sometimes include a long list of villages and even precise numbers of houses burned, may but transmit a dry bureaucratic assessment by some junior clerk who walked through the ruins.[29] It is difficult to tell how accurate such reporting was, especially if, in some cases, such accounts of disasters keep company with entries about unnatural occurrences and sentiments about divine dispensation. In context then, what we might have is less the keeping of the news and more the combination of entries that reflect a particular providential stance

---

27 *Ibid.*, p. 329.
28 NA, SP 82/16, fol. 148v, Wyche to Jenkins 23 July 1680.
29 *Polnoe sobranie russkikh letopisei*, vol. 37, *Ustiuzhskie i vologodskie letopisi XVI–XVIII vv.* (Leningrad: Nauka, 1982), pp, 124–25.

of the writer/compiler. Typically, the other local entries would concern the appointments of prelates or building of churches, but in the case of the appointments as reported in the Ustiug chronicles, it seems we are not dealing with an immediate record but rather a retrospective entry which would also summarise how long the bishop served, where he went if he left and when he died.

The chronicle notes, which Semen Popov was keeping in the beginning of the eighteenth century, included an entry for 1637 about a particularly warm spring when the planting was done early; later in that year, the river froze only four days after Christmas. He brought together the information about the appointment of the first three bishops of Viatka, Aleksandr, Iona and Dionisii. While he recorded few entries on local events other than those pertaining to the Church, an event in the neighbouring town of Slobodskoi clearly must have been in the news: "In [6]204 [1695] on 21 December in Slobodskoi while on the way to the monastery, seven people were bitten by a wolf, and two of them died". Now that surely was news to make the local population sit up and take notice!

Paranormal Events

Despite the common perception that, on the cusp of the modern era, rational and scientific thought was taking hold in Europe, the line between a natural phenomenon and the paranormal or possibly divinely inspired occurrence was blurred in popular belief in the seventeenth century. Unusual natural events—whether simply bad weather, an outbreak of infectious disease, or astronomical phenomena such as an eclipse, a meteor shower or the appearance of a comet—were newsworthy in part precisely because they inspired awe and speculation about divine intervention in human affairs. In the Russian tradition, as is well known, heavenly signs had long been recorded in the chronicles, often, it seems, retrospectively inserted (and sometimes thus misdated) as portents of some coming disaster which might be attributed to human sin and divine retribution.

Stepan Shamin has effectively summarised Russian responses to direct sightings of, or news about, comets in the last third of the seventeenth century, all of which in one way or another interpreted them as portents of some impending catastrophe.[30] The comet that appeared in 1680 was news everywhere in Europe. Sir Peter Wyche in Hamburg wrote about it in some detail in his reports to London. As a corresponding member of the Royal Society he recorded serious observations, and even though he clearly did not believe popular superstition as to what it meant, he reported on the widespread speculation that the comet inspired.[31] Reports about it apparently continued to appear in the West well after it had come and gone. The news of this particularly brilliant comet made it into Semen Popov's Khlynov chronicle and the translated *kuranty*, and was invoked in verses by Evfimii Chudovskii as foretelling the death of Tsar Fedor Alekseevich.

Popular belief in miracles continued to be widespread throughout Europe, with miraculous cures occupying a prominent place. Within Russia, news of miraculous healing most commonly was associated with some holy relic. Particularly venerated was the object understood to be the robe of Christ, sent as a gift to Moscow from the Shah of Persia in 1625, and then "tested" for its efficacy. When it produced the anticipated miracles, it was installed with great ceremony in the Cathedral of the Dormition in the Moscow Kremlin and a service for its annual commemoration printed.[32] Its acquisition and installation surely were newsworthy events, in the same way that the bringing to Moscow a few years ago of the relic believed to be the right hand of John the Baptist was newsworthy and inspired Muscovites to queue for its veneration.[33] Among the holy objects most commonly associated with miraculous cures were particular icons and the relics of saints.

An example is the miracle-working icon of St Nicholas Velikoretskii (so named for having been found in a village near Khlynov on the

---

30 Shamin, *Kuranty*, pp. 216–25.
31 NA, SP 82/16, Wyche to Jenkins, 23 November; 10, 28, 31 December; 7, 4, 21 January.
32 See Daniel C. Waugh, 'The Writings about the Translation of the Savior's Robe to Moscow in 1625: Materials for Further Study', Appendix I B in Edward L. Keenan, *The Kurbskii-Groznyi Apocrypha: The Seventeenth-Century Genesis of the 'Correspondence' Attributed to Prince A. M. Kurbskii and Tsar Ivan IV* (Cambridge, MA: Harvard University Press, 1971), pp. 142–47, 226–29; S. N. Gukhman, '"Dokumental'noe" skazanie o dare shakha Abbasa Rossii', *Trudy Otdela drevnerusskoi literatury*, 28 (1974), 254–70.
33 Nick Paton Walsh, 'Hand of John the Baptist in Russia', *The Guardian*, 9 June 2006, http://www.theguardian.com/world/2006/jun/10/russia.religion. As I saw from a tour bus that drove by the Cathedral of Christ the Saviour in Moscow, the line of those wishing to worship at the relic extended around the block.

Velikaia river, whose history provides some insights into the ways news spread in Russia.[34] Its discovery, veneration and the miracles attributed to it were items of news that undoubtedly would have had great significance both for the Church hierarchy and ordinary believers. A peasant reported its miraculous appearance to the church authorities, who removed it to the provincial capital. On two occasions the icon was taken off to Moscow, where it received national recognition before returning to become the local palladium in Khlynov. Those who prayed before it reported miraculous cures; it was the focal point of an annual procession around the lands of Viatka. Some 220 healings were attributed to the icon prior to the beginning of the eighteenth century.[35] There are analogies here with the accounts about the miraculous healings reported at the North German Protestant spa of Hornhausen, published accounts of which were translated for the Muscovite *kuranty*.[36] Of course there is an important difference too, in that the fame of Hornhausen, while undoubtedly spread by word of mouth, was also disseminated in published brochures and leaflets. As a result, many of the European elite patronised its healing waters. In the case of the icon of St Nicholas, there are relatively few manuscripts about its history, and the record of these healings, appended to the tale of its founding and installation, is even more rare.

Clearly the local authorities, ecclesiastical and secular, played a role in spreading the fame of the icon, presumably both because of religious conviction and because of the economic benefits the icon could bring to

---

34 For details of its history, see Daniel C. Waugh, 'K voprosu o datirovke Velikoretskogo krestnogo khoda', *Gertsenka: Viatskie zapiski*, 6 (2004), 129–36; Waugh, 'Religion and Regional Identities: The Case of Viatka and the Miracle-Working Icon of St. Nicholas Velikoretskii', in *Die Geschichte Russlands im 16. und 17. Jahrhundert aus der Perspektive seiner Regionen*, ed. by Andreas Kappeler, Forschungen zur osteuropäischen Geschichte, 63 (Wiesbaden: Harrassowitz, 2004), pp. 259–78; Waugh, 'Mestnoe samosoznanie, religiia i "izobretenie" regional'nogo proshlogo', *Trudy Otdela drevnerusskoi literatury*, 57 (2006), 350–58.

35 In the absence of a full critical edition of the text that includes all the miracles, my observations are based on the rendering (some is quotation, some is rephrasing) in Stefan Kashmenskii, 'O chudotvornoi Velikoretskoi ikone Sviatitelia i Chudotvortsa Nikolaia', *Viatskie eparkhial'nye vedomosti*, Otdel dukhovno-literaturnyi, 1875, no. 9, 286–94, no. 10, 311–27, no. 11, 359–71, no. 12, 379–93, no. 16, 495–510, no. 17, 523–38; 1876, no. 9, 256–62; and on A. S. Vereshchagin's sometimes indecipherable notes from the manuscript in GAKO (Gosudarstvennyi arkhiv Kirovskoi oblasti), coll. 170, descr. 1, no. 270.

36 See Waugh and Maier's chapter in this volume, esp. the references in note 30.

those who promoted it. The earliest itinerary of the annual procession of the icon in the Viatka lands was a relatively short one, but then over time, the routes were expanded, with every iteration then generating news and expectations along its path. Reports about miraculous cures surely have to have spread in the first instance by word of mouth, although with the bureaucratisation under the Synod in the eighteenth century, church authorities began to issue explicit instructions to prepare for the icon's arrival on its route.

The written record occasionally describes the reception of the icon with great public ceremony and the witnessing of the miraculous cure, not only by a priest, but also by local secular officials or members of the elite and in some cases by a large crowd. The visual and performative would have contributed to the spread of news. On 28 September 1614, the icon was welcomed in Kazan by the citizens of that town and the church hierarchs in a public ceremony, when it was placed (temporarily) in the main cathedral. When a miraculous cure occurred there the next day "archpriest Iakov began to pray to the assembled […] and offered up praise". Before it left the city, another miracle occurred

> before the assembled clergy and the boyar Prince I. M. Vorotynskii, before the commandants and a great multitude of people. And the boyar and all the people having witnessed this… offered up praise… and thus they accompanied the icon from the city of Kazan to the imperial city of Moscow.

It arrived in Cheboksary, where it was met by "all the people". When it finally arrived back in Khlynov at the end of August 1615, it was met by the church hierarchs, commandants F. A. Zvenigorodskii and V. T. Zhemchuzhinov, secretary M. Ordintsov, and a large crowd. A few years later, one of the recorded miracles occurred during the public reception of the icon back in Khlynov on its return from the annual procession to Velikoretskaia.[37]

For the most part we can but speculate how those not resident in Khlynov would have heard about it and come to the town to seek a cure. As discussed below, the towns of the Russian North were well connected. Moreover, some copies of the Khlynov icon were deposited

---

37 Kashmenskii, 'O chudotvornoi Velikoretskoi ikone', 1875, no. 16, 501–02.

in churches in other locations, one in the Cathedral of the Intercession on the Moat, popularly known as St Basil's, in Moscow's Red Square. One can envisage a "catchment area" centred on the location of the icon at any given moment. Its central point would be Khlynov, soon expanded into the area adjoining the route of the annual procession to Velikoretskaia and back. As the route of that procession grew, the catchment area would eventually include much of the Viatka region. Certainly the history of this one icon is not unique in Muscovy. In all such cases, oral testimony must have been the first method to communicate the news about the miracles, even if then entered in a written record.

In the seventeenth and especially in the early decades of the eighteenth century, the Church authorities tried to control such manifestations of popular piety. It seems to have been a losing battle, however. An entry dated 24 February 1714 near the end of one of the late Novgorod chronicles relates how a widow in Kargopol witnessed that an icon of the Kazan Mother of God in her home began to weep.[38] She told the local priest, who took it off to his church, installed it, and performed the appropriate prayers. At the hour when, according to the Gospels, Christ had breathed the last on the Cross, the icon began to weep again "in the presence of all the people". Over the next days, further such incidents occurred, "and this miracle was witnessed by many citizens". The icon then was sent to Novgorod, where it was responsible for many miraculous cures. Somewhat less than a year after its miracles had first been reported, it was returned to Kargopol.

Analogous examples can be found in accounts about locally venerated saints, whose cults became embedded and who attracted widening circles of devotees. Certainly the local parish or a regional centre of a bishopric or important monastery provided a focal point where people gathered on a regular basis and shared all kinds of news or rumour about events, near and far, and gossip (another kind of news) about their neighbours. Another opportunity for the exchange of news could have been the ongoing interactions amongst merchants or the annual fairs which were so important for bringing together people from distant towns.

---

38 RNB (Russian National Library), Collection of M. P. Pogodin, no. 1411, fols. 314(315)-315(316).

Connectivity in Northern Russia

It is important to remember that despite the low density of population in the Russian North, the region was well connected via the river routes and in certain instances by roads. The seventeenth-century customs registers (*tamozhennye knigi*) kept in the major towns such as Velikii Ustiug and Solvychegodsk testify to the regularity and rapidity of communication involving merchants from distant locations. Beyond the official horse relays and foreign post then, there were networks that communicated news that merit further study.[39] Each entry in the registers identifies the traveller by his town or region of origin. To take one year (September 1, 1634–August 31, 1635), of a grand total of 433 individuals, the merchants who bought and sold in Velikii Ustiug registered as living in other towns or regions, included 66 from Solvychegodsk, 31 from Totma, 13 from Vaga, 9 from Kholmogory, 8 from Viatka, 30 from Vologda, 147 from Galich, 29 from Moscow, 18 from Iaroslavl, 8 from Kazan.[40] In 1642 P. D. Gogunin, from Solvychegodsk, came to Ustiug four times, a high number, whereas the most normal pattern might be a single annual visit. A second type of evidence is the indication of whence came the individual arriving in Ustiug (irrespective of his home town). As far as I know, this evidence has yet to be systematised. The impression is that the most common routes were those connecting Ustiug with Vologda, Kholmogory and Solvychegodsk. Lalsk, to the North of Khlynov, was an important stopping point on the way to the Urals. Vaga is on the list too, as the location of an important annual trade fair. Since the registers tell

---

39 In particular, I have drawn on *Tamozhennye knigi Sukhono-Dvinskogo puti XVII v.*, comp. by S. N. Kisterev and L. A. Timoshina, Vyp. 1 (St Petersburg: Kontrast, 2013); and *Tamozhennye knigi Moskovskogo gosudarstva XVII veka. Tom 1. Severnyi rechnoi put': Ustiug Velikii, Sol'vychegodsk, Tot'ma v 1633–1636 gg.*, ed. by A. I. Iakovlev (Moscow-Leningrad: Izdatel'stvo Akademii nauk SSSR, 1950). For details about their contents and observations about the challenges in studying them, see A. Ts. Merzon, 'Ustiuzhskie tamozhennye knigi XVII v.', *Problemy istochnikovedeniia*, 6 (1958), 67–129.

40 A. Ts. Merzon and Iu. A. Tikhonov, *Rynok Ustiuga Velikogo v period skladyvaniia vserossiiskogo rynka (XVII vek)* (Moscow: Izdatel'stvo Akademii nauk SSSR, 1960), pp. 224–31. They also tabulate percentages for a later period, pp. 635–39. Ideally one might map the "connectivity" of Velikii Ustiug by plotting the locations from which the visitors came. One should note that the dramatic map Merzon and Tikhonov provide (foldout, following p. 240) illustrates not the human connections but rather the source of the products which came to the market in Ustiug.

us of both arrivals and departures (recording payment of a departure or arrival tax and duties on goods that were being carried), it is possible to determine in some cases the travel time, or, if a merchant arrived and stayed on for a few days, the duration of the round trip that would have brought him back to his departure point.

In the very small sample I have tested, for December 1634 there were fourteen departures or arrivals in Ustiug, eight on the route to Solvychegodsk, three on the route to Vologda, two the route to Iaroslavl and one from Sysola. The *iaroslavtsy* Roman and his brother Petr Oglodaev were involved in several of these trips, Roman having arrived in Ustiug from Vologda apparently at the beginning of September. He went to Solvychegodsk on 5 December, while there (on 12 December) sent goods back to Ustiug, paid for other goods on 19 December and arrived back with them in Ustiug in what would appear to have been a very fast trip over the distance of seventy-seven versts (approximately eighty-two kilometres) on 21 December. When his brother Petr arrived in Ustiug from Iaroslavl on 30 December, he immediately packed up and went on to Solvychegodsk. Two days later on 1 January, Roman shipped off to Iaroslavl the goods obtained in Ustiug. On 6 January in Solvychegodsk, Petr Oglodaev was in a group which paid for a large convoy of goods being sent on some forty-five sledges (these probably belonged to several different merchant houses), though he himself stayed on. One of Roman's agents came from Solvychegodsk to Ustiug on 17 January. On 19 January, Roman reported in Ustiug that he had received a shipment from his brother on two sledges, and the following day Petr himself returned. Two days after that Roman left for Iaroslavl with three sledges, and on 10 February, Petr followed on seven of them.

The evidence from the customs registers would seem to suggest some seasonal patterns of greater or less communication. Clearly there was a navigation season before the rivers froze. Once they were solidly frozen, they provided highways for most of the sledge traffic (in a few instances, roads through the woods and swamps were used).[41] In the seasons between the two best suited for travel, there might be

---

41 In 2003 I was with a group that drove from Lalsk to the ferry landing where one then took the boat to Ustiug. In one or two places in this now sparsely populated area with its decaying villages, the dirt road showed stone paving that we were told by our local historian-guide dated back even as far as the seventeenth century.

less traffic, since boats might not risk the remains or the onset of the winter ice, and a good hard freeze or two would be needed to firm up the surface for safe travel. My sampling shows relatively few entries for September-November, substantially more for December-March, but fewer again after spring arrived. Possibly, of course, other registers would fill gaps here, as little of what I have seen so far relates to major boat traffic even in the season when it was possible. Other factors in the frequency of travel might include the nature of the goods to be moved — products were seasonal and may have had limits on the time they could be stored. Yet another consideration was the nature of the market, since there was, for example, a focus on travel to seasonal fairs. So one should not expect here a kind of predictably regular schedule of departures or arrivals such as became the feature of the Western postal networks. Communication would be opportunistic.

Granted, what we learn for Velikii Ustiug, a major node, cannot necessarily be generalised for the smaller, less frequented or less accessible towns. However, we see how the communication of news without significant delay would have been possible quite apart from any government-sponsored initiatives or institutions such as the official horse relay system. Of course the registers tell us about goods carried, not stories told or packets of letters. Even if we may never be able to correlate particular arrivals with the receipt of certain news, we should at least consider systematising the evidence of the registers to develop a much more concrete idea than we have had previously regarding the actual communications networks. Where people travelled, they brought with them more than the customs registers record: as our next section will demonstrate, those who travelled on private business in Muscovy might in fact have important news to communicate.

Oral Testimony and Written Reports

For my concluding example I have chosen to focus on reporting about the rebellion of Stepan Razin, who is the subject, with a different emphasis, of Maier's Chapter 4 in this volume.[42] As is well known, the rebellion

---

42 See also her article co-authored with Stepan Shamin '"Revolts" in the *Kuranty* of March-July 1671', and André Berelowitch, 'Stenka Razin's Rebellion: The

had major implications not only for the stability of the Muscovite state but for all of those who lived in the areas directly involved or in the path of the rebels and the government forces sent to defeat them. What seemed initially to be but another example of Cossack piracy on the lower Volga and Caspian Sea exploded with the seizure by the rebels of Tsaritsyn (now Volgograd) in mid-May 1670, the taking of Astrakhan near the mouth of the river on 22 June, and further successes. The turning point came when they failed to take Simbirsk. While the analysis which follows here includes some material from the reporting about Razin prior to his taking of Tsaritsyn and later into autumn, the focus will be on the news about his movements and successes between about mid-May and mid-July.

The rebellion was indeed a news sensation and as such has left a much richer body of documentation than have other examples examined above. In fact, it is possible here to probe deeply into the way the different "categories" of news appeared, intersected and spread—in short, to appreciate the complexity of what we may hope eventually to unravel if we are to gain a full understanding of what news was in Muscovy. My emphasis will be on information in the dispatches sent to Moscow by its military governors and others in the South and in the responses sent back from the central government.[43] On the face of it, this was just government-sponsored intelligence gathering, hugely informative about the processes by which news was collected, communicated and checked for accuracy. Importantly, the evidence documents the role of ordinary individuals in the reporting of news and the relationship between their oral testimony and written communication. The way in which the news then was manipulated and in specific instances publicly broadcast is an

---

Eyewitnesses and their Blind Spot', both in *From Mutual Observation to Propaganda War*, ed. by Malte Griesse, pp. 181–203, and pp. 94–124 respectively. Berelowitch, pp. 99–106, provides a good compact summary of the rebellion's history, and, *passim*, offers some astute observations about the domestic accounts.

43 I am relying on the extensive collection of documents in *Krest'ianskaia voina pod predvoditel'stvom Stepana Razina. Sbornik dokumentov*, comp. by E. A. Shvetsova, ed. by A. A. Novosel'skii *et al.*, 4 vols in 5 (Moscow: Izdatel'stvo Akademii nauk SSSR, 1954–1976), esp. vols 1, 2. 1 and 2. 2. The editors' notes make clear that the collection does not include all of the relevant material; they have selected from among many documents which may simply repeat what is in the ones they publish, or contain information they deemed peripheral. To a certain degree, the selection undoubtedly was influenced by the prevailing Marxist interpretations of the rebellion.

essential part of this history. It was difficult enough to separate truth from unverified and in many instances inaccurate rumour, but even when some accurate understanding of events had been achieved, that in turn might be deliberately distorted and communicated as "news".

Several government departments were involved in news acquisition: the Chancery of the Kazan Court (*Prikaz Kazanskogo dvortsa*), which had under its purview the middle Volga region; the Military Service Chancery (*Razriadnyi prikaz*), to which Muscovite military governors reported and from which they received their instructions; the Ambassadorial Chancery (*Posol'skii prikaz*), charged with foreign affairs and involved here especially because of its concerns about relations with Persia, the Crimea and the Turks as well as the Cossacks of the lower Don; rarely, the tsar's Privy Affairs Chancery (*Tainyi prikaz*), which was responsible for bringing important matters directly to the attention of Aleksei Mikhailovich. Within the Military Service Chancery were separate desks for the affairs of various commands, for example, that at Belgorod, on one of the primary defensive lines in the South. Coordination of the various departments occurred in meetings of the tsar with his boyars and key departmental secretaries.

The seriousness of the Razin rebellion is underscored by the regular annotations on the news reports coming to Moscow that they had been read to the tsar and the boyars. Often those annotations then indicate an immediate decision taken in response to the latest news (e.g.: "Order that the Voronezhian and Nizhnii Novgorodian be interrogated in the Military Service Chancery").[44] Orders sent from Moscow frequently summarised the news about Razin (to underscore the importance of the order now being issued), with a specific citation of the date and source of a report, and might include the phrase "on the basis of that news".

The annotations also regularly include the indication of when a particular report was received and who had brought it. The messengers were varied—musketeers (*strel'tsy*), horsemen (most frequently called *striapchei koniukh*), townsmen (*posadskie liudi*), sometimes accompanied by the individual who had first brought the news in order that he be interrogated again in Moscow. The urgency of rapid reporting from the military governors was constantly stressed.[45] The institutionalised

---

44 *Krest'ianskaia voina*, vol. 1, no. 154, p. 217.
45 Ibid., no. 116, p. 170.

service of the horse relays (*iamskaia gon'ba*) seems to have been largely irrelevant, since it was slow. For the express couriers, horses were provided by emergency transport (*zavodnye podvody*), obtained in the first instance on demand from small Cossack detachments posted in various places. One order sent back from Moscow to Korotoiak, a key border town in the Don region, travelled as follows: "This was sent with a boyar son with Ivan Shatskii on 1 August to the village of Moloda, and from that village, horsemen posted to the [Cossack] detachment were ordered to speed to Korotoiak".[46] There is no indication that the absence of any more formally organised communications network caused delays. Messages from any of the major military outposts in the South might take a week or less to reach Moscow, though the news they contained often was much older.

While the Muscovite bureaucracy required written communication, the ultimate source of the news about Razin was oral testimony. Once the seriousness of the rebellion became apparent, Moscow issued strict orders to interdict any and all passage into territories under the control of or potentially loyal to the rebels. Anyone coming from the rebel areas was to be closely interrogated and the results sent on immediately to Moscow. A typical report might include only the results of a single interrogation of an informant, though there also could be several interrogations of individuals who had arrived in a group. The informants thus included a lot of townsmen or those engaged in economic activity for some noble or the church who had gone down the Volga or Don for legitimate business (the fisheries on the Don frequently are mentioned). Some individuals had arrived at Tsaritsyn unaware that it was in rebel hands, to be greeted by confiscation of their goods, abuse, imprisonment or execution. While there, they conversed with their captors, from whom they learned details of the recent events and speculation about what Razin's next moves might be. Typically,

---

46 *Ibid.*, no. 165, p. 229. An instruction from the Ambassadorial Chancery to the military governor in Voronezh on 8 July 1670 specified that any news be sent to Moscow by express courier (*ibid.*, no. 38, p. 194). In his message to Moscow of 29 July, the commandant in Voronezh reported the results of an interrogation, and indicated he was sending the informants on to Moscow by the horse relays, whereas his report was being taken separately (and presumably much more rapidly) by a horseman first to Elets. The annotation made in Moscow on its arrival on 3 August indicates that from there it had been carried by *striapchii koniukh* Ievko Voronin (*ibid.*, no. 166, p. 231).

one or more of these captives then managed to escape across the steppe to the Don, where often they were met with suspicion by the Don Cossacks, some of whom were reported as being sympathetic to Razin, others loyal to the tsar. In the Cossack communities, they then heard more talk about the news, at least some of which probably derived from missives Razin was sending in order to recruit adherents. Eventually the informants made their way North, where they were immediately interrogated at the nearest Russian outpost. Captured rebels and their sympathisers were subject to brutal interrogation, presumably under the assumption that they had insider information. Once tortured and interrogated, they were summarily executed, hanged after their limbs had been cut off.[47]

The local officials conducting the interrogations had often quite specific instructions.[48] A standard list of questions about Razin's whereabouts and the disposition of various forces had the potential, of course, to skew or ignore the information provided by the informants. Informants identified themselves, and explained why they had gone where they did, how long they were there, and under what circumstances. The testimony specifies who told them (*skazal*; *skazyvaiut*) a particular item of news or, somewhat more vaguely (there seems to have been a clear distinction), who said what (*govoril*) or what they heard (*slyshali*). Sometimes the particle *de*, indicating reported speech, is added. Occasionally there is an indication of particular confidence in something the informant heard (*a slyshno de podlinno*); occasionally too the informant indicates he actually saw something (*videl*). Where an informant did not know the answer to a question that had been posed, generally the response was what we assume was a quite honest: "I had no genuine information"; "and we do not know that [...] they did not hear that either"; "they had no knowledge of that". In a few instances, we learn specifics about deliberate efforts to obtain information by sending an agent who might have personal connections (*po druzhbe taino*) among the Cossacks, friends who then could elicit the intelligence in the enemy camp.[49] One of the longer reports was obtained from merchants who found themselves trapped in Tsaritsyn with the rebel Cossacks and there

---

47   For examples, see *Krest'ianskaia voina*, vol. 2. 2, nos. 19, 20, 33, 35, pp. 24–29, 42–47.
48   E.g., *Krest'ianskaia voina*, vol. 1, no. 129, p. 181; no. 109, p. 161.
49   Ibid., no. 179, pp. 244–46.

had repeated conversations with them, learning, among other things, about the missives Razin had sent them with news of his successes and instructing his forces in Tsaritsyn to set out up river to Kamyshenka. Of course by the time that information was recorded in Tambov on 13 July, it would have already been too late to save Kamyshenka, to which the rebels had set out nearly a month earlier.[50]

Assessing the accuracy and value of the news so reported was a major concern of the Muscovite officials; even for modern historians, it can be difficult to determine where the informants out of ignorance or through deliberate deception may have garbled some part of the news. The frequency with which news began to arrive in from the South is impressive. However, since informants often arrived back in a Muscovite town only after a rather long peregrination, reports might be substantially dated and might keep coming in long after the events had occurred and perhaps had been well documented in other sources. On 13 August, a Cossack from Voronezh, Timoshka Savostianov, who had previously been interrogated on 7 August in Voronezh, reported at the Military Service Chancery in Moscow how he had been fishing on the Don and arrived at the town of Piat Izb ("Five Huts").[51] Some twenty of Razin's followers showed up there, having left Astrakhan four weeks earlier following its seizure by Razin. By the time of his interrogation in Voronezh, Timoshka's memory of his conversation with the rebels was three weeks old. It had taken him some two weeks travelling secretly at night from the Don just to reach the Russian border post. The news of Astrakhan's fall on the night of 21 June thus was was nearly two months old by the time it arrived in the Kremlin, delivered there by Timoshka himself. As it turned out, Timoshka's was one of the first reports Moscow received on the event. Curiously, when the government was issuing important new commands in response to receiving this news, it cited not Timoshka's report, but one received eleven days later on 24 August from a minor noble (*syn boiarskii*) and resident of Astrakhan who somehow had escaped the city after, apparently, having witnessed the

---

50   *Ibid.*, no. 150, pp. 209–12.
51   *Krest'ianskaia voina*, vol. 2. 1, no. 8, pp. 15–16; for the Voronezh commmandant's report, no. 7, pp. 14–15.

events first-hand.⁵² This may have been a matter of wishing to present only reliable eyewitness testimony (though the two accounts seem to have differed little in their essentials), but perhaps, too, the government was reluctant to cite a report that might have been doubted, coming from an *ataman*'s son and ultimately originating in what the rebellious Cossacks told him, however accurate it may have been.

The consistency of many of the reports regarding the details of Razin's successes is striking. Yet one cannot simply assume mutually supporting accounts are independent confirmation of accuracy, since the informants may well have heard the same stories from the same individuals with whom they had talked, and it is possible, given the way in which news was being manipulated by both the rebels and the Muscovite authorities, that certain standard accounts that were widely distributed then became part of a master narrative. How well this fact came to be understood in Moscow can be seen in an instruction sent from the Military Service Chancery to the important regimental commander in Belgorod, Grigorii Grigorevich Romodanovskii, on 24 September 1670.⁵³ He was to send on to Moscow "only the most believable individuals, who would relate concerning any news only the truth, with no embroidery, and who were eyewitnesses to it. And people who had not themselves seen it, and who undertake to tell re-told tales should not be sent to Moscow", because, "as you yourself know […] much that is bad comes from news that has been embroidered or is false".

Oral transmission, of course, is fraught with other problems, in that memories may be flawed both on the part of those talking and on the part of those later reporting the conversations. One remarkable string of reports would have to give us pause about news that then arrived in Moscow on 21 July in a report from the *dumnyi dvorianin* (conciliar lesser noble) Iakov Timofeevich Khitrovo, commandant of the important post of Tambov.⁵⁴ Agents (loyal Cossacks, *stanichniki*) he had sent off to Penza to gather information returned to Tambov on 17 July (probably the day he wrote to Moscow), bringing with them a written report from another commandant in the town of Lomov. In it, this commandant

---

52 Ibid., no. 17, pp. 23–24; also, for a subsequent citation of the same report a few days later, Ibid., no. 19, p. 26.
53 *Krest'ianskaia voina*, vol. 2. 2, no. 36, pp. 47–48.
54 *Krest'ianskaia voina*, vol. 1, no. 156, p. 219. An analogous but shorter string of "nested" reports is in no. 178, pp. 243–44.

related how he had received a report on 5 July from a commandant in another town, Insar, basing his information on a report from Saransk, which in turn related the arrival there on 29 June of people who were fleeing Saratov. They had reported in their interrogation having gone to Saratov to buy horses, encountering there fishermen who had come up the Volga, whence they had met musketeers who told them about how the Razin forces had taken the town of Komyshenka and burned it, killing its commandant. The musketeers had fled the disaster. Now the Razin forces, they indicated, were heading up the Volga to Saratov. So here we have a chain of information relayed in part through accidental encounters: musketeers on the Volga → fishermen on the Volga → fugitives from Saratov on the Volga → report from Saransk → report from Insar → report from Lomov → report to Moscow from Tambov. This is not news once or twice removed, but seven times removed from its source some weeks earlier. It is not as though Khitrovo was lax in his attempts to learn the news. He quizzed his agents on their return from Lomov, who reported that in the market there the local residents told everything about Razin—in other words, probably rumour, guesswork, market gossip—how he was heading to Saratov, how he had in fact not been at Astrakhan but instead after his victory at Chernyi Iar had headed toward Saratov. On hearing this, Khitrovo sent the same agents to Penza and Saratov to obtain more news, and he was now awaiting their return. Moreover, Khitrovo had sent some twenty of his loyal Cossacks off to Tsaritsyn to gather intelligence, but they had been captured by Razin's men and were being held in Tsaritsyn. The Russian military authorities were not just waiting for information to come their way but were actively engaged in intelligence missions into rebel-held territory.

By 30 July 1670, Moscow had been deluged with reports about Tsaritsyn and Chernyi Iar; on that single day several more arrived, three from the diligent commandant Mikhail Oznobishin in Korotoiak. That tested the patience of the tsar, despite the fact that he had made it clear he was to be kept informed. In the annotation to one of Oznobishin's reports is the remarkable indication Aleksei Mikhailovich had heard quite enough and knew the basic facts:

The great sovereign listened to this report and it was read to the boyars. And the great sovereign disposed and the boyars confirmed [the order]:

write to Korotoiak to Mikhail Oznobishin and to Voronezh to Boris Bukhvostov, that in the future concerning the treason of the bandit Stenka Razin and his robber Cossacks, how they went from the Don to Tsaritsyn, and concerning the surrender of the town of Tsaritsyn, and how he went from Tsaritsyn to Chornyi Iar, they should not write to the great sovereign on such matters, inasmuch as the great sovereign has been informed by many reports regarding the one and all. Rather, having strenuously undertaken by all means to obtain news, they should write to the sovereign what other news in the future is obtained concerning this bandit and continue to exercise great vigilance in those towns. Also when news is obtained about the arrival of military men, they should write the sovereign about it immediately.[55]

This instruction notwithstanding, similar reports continued to arrive over the next month and more.

Care was taken to check the stories of those who were suspected of having willingly collaborated with the rebels. Of particular interest was a priest from Kursk, Nikifor Kolesnikov, who had arrived on the Don after spending some time with the rebels in Tsaritsyn.[56] He then fell into the company of some musketeers who had managed to escape after the debacle at Tsaritsyn. The group made its way to the important frontier post of Belgorod, where they were interrogated, the musketeers accusing Kolesnikov of having collaborated with the rebels. When the report of the interrogation reached the Kremlin, it ordered Prince Grigorii Romodanovskii to send on to Moscow as quickly as possible the musketeers and the priest, the latter "chained and under guard". The priority given to the case may well be explained by the fact that in his earlier career, Kolesnikov had ministered to some of the tsar's regiments. Two of his sons had for some eight years worked as clerks in the Service Estates Chancery (*Pomestnyi prikaz*), the older, Naum, having been sent off with an embassy to Persia in 1669 which Razin's troops had then detained in Astrakhan on its return. Naum therefore had his own account to tell about the rebels, independently of his father. Kolesnikov's interrogation in Moscow on 4 August provided one of the

---

55 *Krest'ianskaia voina*, vol. 1, no. 157, p. 220.
56 Ibid., nos. 130, 134, 171, 182, 183, pp. 182–84, 187–90, 234–38, 240–52; notes pp. 276–77, 281–82. As the editors note, on p. 276, Kolesnikov is referred to in the documents as Mikifor (Nikifor) Ivanov; his surname Kolesnikov was established on the basis of records concerning his sons.

most detailed eyewitness accounts about what was going on inside the Razin camp, including the discussions at the Cossacks' council (*krug*) in which they were deciding on their next movements.

The documents about the Razin rebellion suggest that in response to the crisis, the Muscovite government very quickly was able to improve its intelligence network by tightening border controls and by issuing to all its provincial commanders the strictest instructions about the gathering of information and instructing all those under their jurisdiction to do the same. Typical was the order sent on 13 July 1670 to Grigorii Romodanovskii, who was only one of several dozen recipients of the same instruction.[57] There were but few incidents where violations of the border blockade and/or failure to broadcast locally the tsar's order were reported.[58] Most of the commanders, recognising the urgency of the situation, seem to have been zealous in carrying out their orders.

As the reports accumulated, the officials in Moscow then were tasked with collecting the dispatches into single documents. In one of the earliest such examples (February 1670), the assignment was given to the Ambassadorial Chancery, which was to solicit a set of reports that had been sent to the Chancery of the Kazan Court.[59] The resulting document was a veritable chronicle quoting reports beginning with 1667 and ending in early 1670. The stated purpose of the collection was for it to be sent on by the Ambassadorial Chancery to the loyal Don Cossacks to warn them about Razin and (presumably) to call for their continued loyalty to Moscow in the face of this threat. Another factor here seems to have been the petition by Persian merchants who had been robbed by Razin that the tsar reimburse them for their losses. Presumably a compendium of information was needed to check their claim. That the compilation of such summaries was in the first instance somehow connected with foreign policy concerns seems to be confirmed when another summary was drawn up in the autumn of 1670, apparently with the intention that it be communicated widely in Novgorod (a significant centre for foreign merchant activity and the dissemination of news that

---

57 *Ibid.*, no. 149, pp. 208–09.
58 *Ibid.*, nos. 117, 126, 175, pp. 170–71, 177–79, 240–41.
59 The instruction is *ibid.*, no. 105, pp. 133–34; the compendium from the Office of the Kazan Court is no. 106, pp. 134–56.

might go abroad).⁶⁰ As Maier and Shamin have suggested, something like that latter compendium could have been a source for a report that made its way into a Dutch newspaper and which was very dated by the time it appeared.⁶¹

Mere compilation of what were supposed to be accurate and carefully vetted intelligence reports was one thing, but there the matter did not rest. As is well known, the Muscovite government was very concerned to control the news about Razin for foreign consumption, wishing to undercut any idea, such as that being spread in certain foreign news accounts, that he was a serious problem and a major threat to the state. For internal consumption, the goal in manipulating the news may have been more complex. On the one hand, there would have been every reason to reinforce the impression that the tsar's divinely sanctioned government was in control. On the other hand, it was essential to undercut any possible sympathy for Razin by portraying him and his actions as quintessentially evil and out of control.

In issuing orders about vigilance, intelligence gathering, recruitment, and the assembling of supplies and transport, the government followed its usual procedure of explaining in a preamble why the particular order was being given. There is a certain progression in such preambles, with some of the earlier instructions citing more than one report. As events unfolded, the tendency was to focus specifically on the most recent news, an indication of the urgency now felt in the Kremlin and the rapidity with which decisions were being made in response to new information. Thus, once the taking of Tsaritsyn was history, the taking of Astrakhan might be cited; as events moved on in 1670 and some of Razin's followers were captured and interrogated, what they related might be cited.⁶² As the news became more alarming in 1670, the Kremlin was not content simply to quote the reports but began to re-write them, adding horrific details and rhetoric to convince those who would read or hear the reports that Razin was truly godless and an instrument of the

---

60 *Krest'ianskaia voina*, vol. 2. 1, no. 277, pp. 339–42.
61 Maier and Shamin, '"Revolts" in the *Kuranty*', p. 198.
62 *Ibid.*, no. 1, pp. 7–8. The orders to Grigorii Romodanovskii sent from Moscow on 26 August cite a report received in Moscow on 24 August about the fall of Astrakhan'. A change in Romodanovskii's previous orders regarding the disposition of his troops was a response to some of the new information obtained from captive Cossack rebels: *Ibid.*, no. 53, pp. 66–68, dated after 10 October 1670.

Devil, a threat to both the state and the Church. What had originated as news, necessary for the government to formulate an effective response to a growing crisis, morphed into ideologically charged propaganda. There is some reason to think that the news, so transformed into propaganda, then may have come full circle, when those providing testimony adopted some of the same rhetoric in describing the rebels. The tsar's admonitions to Grigorii Romodanovskii cited earlier testify to a recognition that recycled "news" might feed upon itself and prove to be worthless (which would be true even if the message was one the government had tried to shape).

As we know, Razin too was engaged in the same kind of propaganda war, sending messages to potential supporters about his victories and trying to induce them to join in what he alleged would be an attempt to end the injustices inflicted by the boyars in Moscow. Among the rumours was one that Razin intended to restore Patriarch Nikon as head of the Russian Orthodox Church, an idea that probably originated in the fact that Razin does seem to have contacted the deposed Patriarch (who, however, refused to be drawn in).[63] Once afoot, such rumours could escalate: a peasant testified on 7 September that Nikon was already on his way down the Don to join the rebels.[64] We have to imagine that a good deal of what various Cossacks told the individuals who then were interrogated as they came across the border back into government-controlled territory was simply repetition of what Razin had summarised in his own missives.

The Razin materials thus provide vivid evidence of how both sides attempted to influence public opinion, and in the process engaged actively in the dissemination of "news", however distorted some of it may have been. It was not merely a matter of sending letters or commands, but involved the often explicit instruction that they be read aloud to audiences assembled specifically for that purpose. Such occasions were orchestrated performances, from which there was every reason to think the listeners would take away and spread the information to those who had not been present. There were several

---

63 *Ibid.*, no. 22, p. 31; note on p. 552. A similar report is in no. 29, pp. 43–44, which, however, relates some apprehension among Razin's followers as to what the future may hold.
64 *Krest'ianskaia voina*, vol. 2. 2, no. 19, p. 25.

kinds of situations where such public proclamation could occur. One of the earliest examples, composed in Moscow on 28 May 1670, was sent to Grigorii Romodanovskii, indicating that on its receipt, he was to inform the Belgorod administrator, a *stol'nik* Petr Skuratov, and that he in turn was immediately to distribute to "all towns, to the military commanders and government officials" copies of this decree certified by scribal signatures. All those officials were in their turn to call together all of the military and ordinary residents of their respective towns and read to them aloud the sovereign's decree.[65] The annotations indicate that copies of the document were to be distributed to several Moscow offices.

The regional commandants who received such orders dutifully responded about how they had carried them out. At some point in the first two weeks of June (the exact date has not been preserved; the report was received in Moscow 13 June), the commandant in Kozlov, Stepan Ivanovich Khrushchev, reported:

> And in accordance with, lord, thy great sovereign's order and thy great sovereign's missives, I, thy servant, in Kozlov, having gathered the people of Kozlov, thy great sovereign's military and civilian inhabitants of all ranks, read to them thy great sovereign's beneficent word and thy great lord's missive about the bandit and about the apostate and traitor about the Don Cossack Stenka Razin and about all of his banditry. I ordered that all this be read aloud. And in Kozlov district, lord, I sent to all of the detachments and villages and hamlets verbatim copies of thy great sovereign's missive. And I ordered, lord, that in the villages and hamlets copies of thy great sovereign's missive be read aloud to all the people, in order that they, the people of Kozlov, the people of all ranks, know about his, Stenka's, banditry and treachery and, keeping in mind the holy conciliar and apostolic Church and thy great sovereign's sworn oath on the cross, and their nature and service and blood, and for thy great sovereign's reward for their service, and the eternal honour of their ancestors, so that no one join in his banditry.[66]

Some commandants went one step farther and had the tsar's orders read aloud on more than one occasion.[67]

---

65 *Krest'ianskaia voina*, vol. 1, no. 111, p. 162.
66 Ibid., no. 114, p. 167.
67 Ibid., no. 142, p. 200.

The public reading of decrees seems to have been a common phenomenon and would have served to disseminate news even if only of the kind I have termed "transactional".[68] A recruitment order issued in Moscow on 22 August was read aloud from the porch of one of the chambers in the Kremlin palace to an audience that included both palace and court officials, lesser nobles and various ranks of the army.

It was not enough merely to paint the rebels in dark colours by rhetorical excesses. Also important was to demonstrate to the public the inevitable and grisly fate of those who would question royal authority. Of course there was a long history of this in Muscovy, well before the *Sobornoe Ulozhenie* (law code) of 1649 elaborated on the seriousness of impugning the authority and honour of State and Church. If we believe all the lurid accounts passed down mainly through foreign sources, Tsar Ivan IV did not hesitate to orchestrate the most horrific public executions. As Nancy Kollmann has stressed in her recent book, though, we should not generalise from such examples that justice in Muscovy was uniformly arbitrary and harsh.[69] Traitors, pretenders, and others who seemed to threaten the ordained political order were a special case that justified summary justice. And yet there were procedures to be followed: formal interrogation, even if under torture; for many, review of the testimony and evidence in Moscow even if it had first come to the attention of provincial authorities. The tendency seems to have been not to believe professions of innocence by those who claimed to have "served" the rebels under duress.[70] Once the decision came down, at least nominally from the highest secular authority, the tsar himself, punishment was swift. The government clearly wished to have a crowd attend the public dismemberment and/or hanging of the rebels, and

---

68 Concerning the public reading and posting of decrees, see Simon Franklin, 'Printing and Social Control in Russia 2: Decrees', *Russian History*, 38 (2011), 467–92 (esp. pp. 473–75).

69 Nancy Shields Kollmann, *Crime and Punishment in Early Modern Russia* (Cambridge: Cambridge University Press, 2012).

70 There was a progression in the level of suspicion as the rebellion took a more serious turn. An annotation to a document of June 1668 indicated: "And if they say that they are good people and have not participated in banditry, release them under collective guarantee" (*Krest'ianskaia voina*, vol. 1, no. 75, p. 110). However, by July 1670, orders ran: "And as for those who undertake to say that they were with the bandit Cossacks unwillingly, after they have been tortured, hold them closely guarded and in prisons under strong guard" (*ibid.*, no. 144, p. 203).

prior to their execution, a formal, rhetorically-charged document listing the charges against them was read.[71] The remains then were displayed in a prominent place (e.g. those of the Cossack Fedka Ageev hung on the Iauza Gate in Moscow through which ran the road to Vladimir). Razin's execution then, the descriptions of which circulated outside of Muscovy and presumably with the encouragement of Muscovite officials, was certainly not the first or last of such spectacles.[72]

If ritualised public executions were intended as a moral lesson and deterrent to keep the population at large from straying in their loyalty, there also were ceremonies intending to convey a more positive message that successful service in suppressing the rebellion brought its rewards. In September 1670, the security of the upper Don region came under threat, with some of the local population throwing their lot in with the rebels. Quick action, in part by loyal local forces and backed up by a detachment sent by the Belgorod regiment's commander Grigorii Romodanovskii, saved the threatened towns. In recognition of this, the Military Service Chancery sent a commendation to Romodanovskii, his troops, and the others who had been involved.[73] The Tsar's emissary, Mikhail Bogdanovich Prikonskii, was to travel to Romodanovskii's regiment without delay, and having arrived, to send a message to Romodanovskii to assemble his "comrades" and soldiers in the tent which had been erected for the occasion. Once they were all there, he was to read aloud the citation, first of all to Romodanovskii, then in a separate speech to all the ranks of the infantry and cavalry. After addressing them, he was to commend aloud Gerasim Kondratiev, a colonel from Suma, and lastly, in yet another address, to commend a colonel from Ostrogozhskii for his having rejected the overtures of the rebels and having captured a number of them. These final two received material rewards from the tsar, since they apparently had not previously been in government service and on the state payroll. For the rest, the reward was just the recognition and praise from the ruler, not a trivial reward of itself.

---

71 For examples, *Krest'ianskaia voina*, vol. 2. 2, no. 33 (esp. pp. 44–45), and nos. 42, 43 pp. 53–56.
72 See Kollmann, *Crime and Punishment*, pp. 289–302.
73 *Krest'ianskaia voina*, vol. 2. 2, no. 51, pp. 63–65.

Conclusion

The Razin materials underscore how news in Russia in the seventeenth century was not a commodity only of the elite, and how, along with the government, the broader public (however we might wish to define it) played an active role in the reporting, consumption and transmission of news. While we presented earlier a somewhat speculative scenario about how the normal interactions along the Northern river routes could have contributed to the dissemination of news, in the South during the Razin rebellion we have very explicit evidence concerning the way in which those who travelled on personal business could and did acquire information and passed it on. Granted, its transmission there, both stimulated and hindered by the crisis, was often considerably delayed. There is no reason to think that what individuals reported in interrogations was in any way confidential: not only had they learned of it from others' oral reports (whether or not the information was accurate, of course, is another matter), but they surely then passed on what they knew to others with whom they interacted. Much of the news seems to have derived from what was "common knowledge" amongst both the adherents of Razin and those in the communities that felt threatened by him. Of course, in an atmosphere of fear and uncertainty, any amount of distortion and rumour might spread. Certainly, before the rebellion reached crisis proportions, people were still travelling on their daily business. The Volga and the Don were busy thoroughfares, connected in various directions; not the least of those connections was that between the two river basins. Even when the events triggered by the rebellion interdicted many of the normal routes of travel and commerce, in the process creating shortages of food and other goods, individuals could find their way across the steppe, make contacts in the communities that they encountered, obtain transport, and eventually arrive at a border post if they chose to go North. A great deal of other evidence from the files of the Military Service Chancery concerning other regions and times reinforces this picture of the role ordinary people played as reporters of and consumers of the news. Moreover, the Military Service Chancery was by no means the only department which collected the news in Moscow. To assess all the evidence effectively is going to take a lot more work.[74]

Possibly a good starting point for a broader overview would be to examine the way news spread during the Time of Troubles at the beginning of the seventeenth century.[75] In the various efforts to restore control over the central government and drive out the occupying Poles, the leaders of the Russian forces circulated letters outlining the history of the troubles to date and calling for people to join in the movement to re-take control of the country. Once it became possible to elect a new ruler, the call went out to all the provinces to send their representatives to the Assembly of the Land. Even before the Troubles had ended, various accounts representing different positions on what was happening were compiled and circulated. Rumour was rife.

To conclude then, when we look beyond the *kuranty*, we discover a whole new world of news in Muscovy, of news consumers and news purveyors. In the foregoing review I have selected but a few of the ways we might learn more about how well connected and well informed Russians were. In saying this, I am not suggesting that information which would interest a broad spectrum of Muscovite society is necessarily analogous to what might have interested a similarly broad segment of society in Western Europe. However, it may well be that broadening the perspective on what was news in the West will reveal closer analogies than we so far have imagined.

---

74 The potential value of analysing the reports of military governors was first underscored in the nineteenth century by N. Ogloblin, 'Voevodskie vestovye otpiski XVII v. kak material po istorii Malorossii', *Kievskaia starina*, 12 (1885), 365–416. For some observations about the processes of news acquisition and transmission through Kiev, see Waugh, 'The Best Connected Man in Muscovy?', esp. pp. 114–21. Of particular importance for learning about the acquisition of foreign news and the ways in which it was used by the government is evidence about intelligence operations, where the Muscovite government had agents embedded at other courts. There is some very interesting information about one such agent in K. A. Kochegarov, *Rech' Pospolitaia i Rossiia v 1680–1686 godakh. Zakliuchenie dogovora o Vechnom mire* (Moscow: Indrik, 2008).

75 On the Time of Troubles, one can consult Chester S. L. Dunning, *Russia's First Civil War: The Time of Troubles and the Founding of the Romanov Dynasty* (University Park: Pennsylvania State University Press, 2001); Maureen Perrie, *Pretenders and Popular Monarchism in Early Modern Russia: The False Tsar of the Time of Troubles* (Cambridge: Cambridge University Press, 1995). A useful documentary collection is *Pamiatniki istorii Smutnago Vremeni*, ed. by A. I. Iakovlev (Moscow: N. N. Klochkov, 1909).

IV.
INSTITUTIONAL KNOWLEDGE AND COMMUNICATION

8. Bureaucracy and Knowledge Creation: The Apothecary Chancery

Clare Griffin[1]

In 1628, physicians in the Russian palace's medical department were presented with a root, and ordered to give their opinion on it.[2] The root in question had been taken as evidence in a witchcraft case, as possession of herbs and roots was commonly seen as evidence of malefic magic

---

1 This chapter started life as a part of my Ph.D. dissertation, before undergoing a number of transformations, aided at every stage by the kindness and generosity of funders and colleagues, into its present state. I would like to thank the Arts and Humanities Research Council, who funded my graduate work, the Wellcome Trust and the Max Planck Institute for the History of Science, Berlin, who have funded my postdoctoral work, for their financial support. Endless comments, criticisms, suggestions, revisions, and improvements to this chapter—and its previous incarnations—were suggested by a great number of colleagues during my Ph.D. work, the workshop from which this volume emerged, and the *Pre-Modern Conversation* Seminar Series at the Max Planck Institute for the History of Science, and in particular by Sergei Bogatyrev, Harold J. Cook, Simon Dixon, Sebastian Felten, Lauren Kassell, Elaine Leong, Martyn Rady, and Faith Wigzell, as well as the three anonymous peer reviewers of the present volume. My thanks also go, as ever, to the staff of the Russian State Archive of Ancient Documents (RGADA), Moscow, for the use of their materials, and for the wonderful work they do. Finally, thanks also to our tireless editors, Simon and Katia, without whom this chapter would have been much less than it is. All remaining mistakes and deficiencies are entirely my own.

2 N. Ia. Novombergskii, *Materialy po istorii meditsiny v Rossii*, 5 vols (St Petersburg: M. M. Stasiulevich, 1905), 3. 1, pp. 9–12. This case is discussed in Eve Levin, 'Healers and Witches in Early Modern Russia', in *Saluting Aron Gurevich: Essays in History, Literature, and Other Related Subjects*, ed. by Yelena Mazour-Matusevich and Alexandra S. Korros (Leiden: Brill, 2010), pp. 105–33 (pp. 117–18). For an analysis of how the documentary process worked in Russian witchcraft trials in general, see Valerie Kivelson, *Desperate Magic: The Moral Economy of Witchcraft in Seventeenth-Century Russia* (Ithaca and London: Cornell University Press, 2013), pp. 38–51.

in seventeenth-century Russia. So the medical experts—foreigners, and graduates of prestigious Western European universities—spoke in Latin on the medical and magical properties of this root, a response that was translated and taken down in Russian, and then sent from the medical department to the Military Service Chancery (*Razriadnyi prikaz*), the department handling the case, and from whom the order for the report had been received. This was by no means an unusual event: the medical experts of the Apothecary Chancery, as the seventeenth-century Russian palace medical department was called, were commonly called upon to compose learned reports for their own department, the tsar, and other parts of the Muscovite administration. Reports covered a range of subjects: autopsies to establish cause of death, "physicals" of servitors to see if they were still fit to serve, investigations into the private trade in medical drugs, proposed courses of treatments, notes regarding unsuccessful treatments, and considerations of illnesses, medicines, and medical practices. In every case, Russian bureaucrats posed a specific, practical question; medical experts answered orally or in writing in Latin, drawing on their expertise and their books; the answer was translated into Russian and circulated to the relevant bureaucrats in writing, but often read aloud; the further progress of the case at hand was decided in part on the basis of that expert knowledge; and the report was then stored within the relevant case-file. Such a process can be seen as an information technology. This term, widely used yet rarely explicitly defined, is most commonly used to refer to modern devices such as computers, but it has also been applied to early modern technologies such as printing.[3] Discussions of the nature of information technologies revolve around a device or system's capacity not only to communicate a concept, but to reify it, making it storable.[4] We can thus see information technology as a device or system which allows the encoding, recording, communication, storage, and retrieval of information, a definition which applies to computers, the printing press, paper technologies more generally, and, most significantly

---

[3] See for example Jeremiah E. Dittmar, 'Information Technology and Economic Change: The Impact of the Printing Press', *The Quarterly Journal of Economics*, 126 (2011), 1133–72.

[4] See Michael E. Hobart, and Zachary S. Schiffman, *Information Ages: Literacy, Numeracy, and the Computer Revolution* (Baltimore: Johns Hopkins University Press, 2000), especially pp. 4 and 212.

here, the Apothecary Chancery's reporting system. The Apothecary Chancery's reports thus allows us to investigate knowledge circulation and information technologies in the context of seventeenth-century Russian administration, and in turn to see what the Russian case can reveal about information technologies in the early modern context.

The Apothecary Chancery, the Chancery System, and Knowledge for the State

The 1628 case concerning the potentially magical root involved documents being passed between the regional governor in Rzhev — where the accused witch, Andrei Loptunov, had first been arrested — the regional governor in Toropets, Loptunov's home town, the Moscow jail in which Loptunov was being held, the Military Service Chancery, who were investigating the case, and the Apothecary Chancery, who were providing expert testimony on the properties of said root. Such a circulation of documents was a feature of Muscovite administration. This administrative network, known as the chancery system, was composed of around sixty departments, or chanceries. Not all these departments were permanent fixtures, with some only lasting a matter of years, and yet the number of departments remained relatively constant across the century.[5] Departments were created to deal with all significant areas of Muscovite life: finances and tax-collection; military affairs; administration of regions, especially those recently acquired; court life; and the Church. Where chanceries shared similar duties, close collaboration was necessary. For example, there were different chanceries responsible for general military and service activities, new formation regiments, and foreign mercenaries, all of whom had to cooperate to allow the Muscovite armed forces to function effectively. Alongside these central chanceries, Muscovy was also administered through the use of provincial governors, who communicated with the central chanceries on a number of issues. Chancery directors played a key role in this system, as conducting correspondence with other branches of the Muscovite governmental system was a vital part of their duties.

---

5   Peter B. Brown, 'How Muscovy Governed. Seventeenth-Century Russian Administration', *Russian History*, 36 (2009), 459–529 (p. 476).

Figure 1. The Apothecary Chancery today.

The chancery directors were helped in their duties by the secretaries, another key group who undertook much of the day-to-day record-keeping. Across the course of the seventeenth century there were significant changes in chancery staffing. N. F. Demidova has shown that the overall number of secretaries rose dramatically across the seventeenth century: in the 1640s, there were 837 secretaries and under-secretaries in central chanceries; by the 1680s, this number had risen to 2,739.[6] The growth in secretary numbers identified by Demidova is consistent with the figures provided by Grigorii Karpovich Kotoshikhin (*ca.* 1630–67), a former chancery secretary who defected to Poland and, later, Sweden, and author of the only contemporary Russian account of the chancery system. During the 1660s, Kotoshikhin puts the numbers of secretaries and governors at 100, and the number of undersecretaries at 1000; consideration of his numbers would suggest that the numbers of secretaries rose most precipitously between the 1660s and the 1680s.[7] Some departments were more reliant upon specialist staff than

---

6   N. F. Demidova, *Sluzhilaia biurokratiia v Rossii XVII v. i ee rol' v formirovanii absoliutizma* (Moscow: Nauka, 1987), p. 37.

7   G. K. Kotoshikhin, *O Rossii v tsarstvovanie Alekseia Mikhailovicha* (Moscow: ROSSPEN, 2000), p. 141.

secretaries. The Apothecary Chancery only employed 2–3 secretaries at a time, with the vast majority of its staff consisting of medical practitioners. Like the secretaries, the numbers of medical practitioners employed at the Russian court rose dramatically across the seventeenth century. Figures compiled by Sabine Dumschat give the overall number of Apothecary Chancery medical staff in the period 1600–20 as 17; by 1680–96 there were 112.[8] This rise in staff numbers of both medical practitioners and secretaries is indicative of a general expansion of the chancery system across the seventeenth century.

The expansion of the chancery system necessitated and drove an institutionalised form of literacy. Literacy in seventeenth-century Russia was commonly seen as a specialised skill, and was largely (although by no means exclusively) restricted to those who read and wrote professionally, such as the administrators and monastic copyists.[9] The chancery system, as it required the transmission of orders and information, relied heavily upon written documentation to perform its duties, leading to a proliferation of administrative documents. As departments communicated with one another, or with other government agents in Russia or abroad, written documents were used to ensure accurate transmission and to record those communications.

The chancery system produced and circulated a great variety of documents, each with its own name: petitions (*chelobitnye gramoty* pl., *chelobitnaia gramota* sg.); orders from the tsar (pl. *ukazy*, sg. *ukaz*), his counsellors (*prigovory* pl., *prigovor* sg.), and from department heads; communications between department heads (*pamiati* pl., *pamiat'* sg.); responses from underlings to their superiors confirming that they had fulfilled an order (*otpiski* pl., *otpiska* sg.); interrogation records (*rassprossnye rechi* pl., *rassprosnaia rech'* sng.); torture records (*pytochnye rechi* pl., *pytochnaia rech'* sng.); and reports such as those created by the Apothecary Chancery medical experts (*skazki* pl., *skazka* sg.).[10]

---

8   Sabine Dumschat, *Ausländischer Mediziner im Moskauer Russland* (Stuttgart: Franz Steiner Verlag, 2006), p. 104.
9   Clare Griffin, 'In Search of an Audience: Popular Pharmacies and the Limits of Literate Medicine in Late Seventeenth- and Early Eighteenth-Century Russia', *Bulletin for the History of Medicine*, 89 (2015), 705–32.
10 On the different kinds of document, see S. O. Shmidt and S. E. Kniaz'kov, *Dokumenty deloproizvodstva pravitel'stvennykh uchrezhdenii Rossii XVI–XVII vv. Uchebnoe posobie* (Moscow: MGIAI, 1985); O. F. Kozlov et al. *Gosudarstvennost' Rossii: gosudarstvennye i tserkovnye uchrezhdeniia, soslovnye organy i organy mestnogo samoupravleniia, edinitsy administrativno-territorial'nogo, tserkovnogo i vedomstvennogo deleniia (konets XV veka*

Some departments produced special kinds of document, like the *Vesti-Kuranty*, a modern term for Russian translations of foreign newspapers produced by the Ambassadorial Chancery, and discussed elsewhere in this volume by Ingrid Maier and Daniel C. Waugh. A number of chanceries owned or produced books. The Ambassadorial Chancery produced a large number of translations, like Maciej Stryjkowski's Polish Chronicle.[11] Simeon Ushakov, who worked in the Armoury (*Oruzheinyi prikaz*), proposed (although never completed) a manual on icon painting.[12] Nikolai Diletskii produced a textbook of music theory to help musicians at the Russian court understand and compose music.[13] The Apothecary Chancery owned a library of medical, natural historical and other miscellaneous books.[14] A number of those medical works were translated, and in the later seventeenth century Apothecary Chancery employees also composed their own texts.[15] A central feature of the chancery system was thus its production, storage and circulation of documents.

In the historiography of the chancery system as a whole, and in the historiography of individual chanceries, the issue of function has always been seen as important. Attempts have been made to classify the

---

    –fevral' 1917 goda): slovar'-spravochnik, 6 vols (Moscow: Nauka, 1996–2009); Peter B. Brown, 'Early Modern Russian Bureaucracy: The Evolution of the Chancellery System From Ivan III to Peter the Great' (Ph.D. dissertation, University of Chicago, 1978), pp. 147–58; M. N. Tikhomirov, *Rossiiskoe gosudarstvo XV–XVII vekov* (Moscow: Nauka, 1973), pp. 364–69.

11 Christine Watson, *Tradition and Translation: Maciej Stryjkowski's Polish Chronicle in Seventeenth-Century Russian Manuscripts*, Studia Slavica Upsaliensia XXXXVI (Uppsala: Acta Universitatis Upsaliensis, 2012).

12 Lindsey Hughes, 'The Moscow Armory and Innovations in Seventeenth-Century Muscovite Art', *Canadian-American Slavic Studies*, 13 (1979), 204–23.

13 Claudia R. Jensen, *Musical Cultures in Seventeenth-Century Russia* (Bloomington and Indianapolis: Indiana University Press, 2009), pp. 122–23, p. 277, n. 54.

14 *Katalog knig iz sobraniia Aptekarskogo prikaza*, ed. by E. A. Savel'eva (St Petersburg: Al'faret, 2006), pp. 19–25. See also M. I. Slukhovskii, *Bibliotechnoe delo v Rossii do XVII veka. Iz istorii knizhnogo prosveshcheniia* (Moscow: Kniga, 1968), pp. 87–89; S. P. Luppov, *Kniga v Rossii v XVII veke* (Leningrad: Nauka, 1970), pp. 203–08.

15 On the translation of medical texts by the Apothecary Chancery, see 1672 translation of a German medical book, L. F. Zmeev, *Russkie vrachebniki. Issledovanie v oblasti nashei drevnei vrachebnoi pis'mennosti*, Pamiatniki drevnei pis'mennosti i iskusstva, no. 112 (St Petersburg: [n. pub.], 1896), pp. 72–73. In 1679 ten medical books were ordered to be translated, RGADA, coll. 143, descr. 2, file 1290. On the lack of a translator hampering translation work in the Apothecary Chancery: Mamonov, *Materialy*, 4, pp. 989–94. On the compilation of medical texts by the Apothecary Chancery staff see Griffin, 'In Search of an Audience'.

chanceries, by dividing them up into their relative spheres.[16] Eve Levin, Maria Unkovskaya, and a number of historians of the chancery system have all proposed that the Apothecary Chancery was either exclusively or primarily a court institution.[17] This view is particularly dependent upon the treatment of patients undertaken by the Apothecary Chancery: a substantial proportion of patients were members of court, therefore the Apothecary Chancery was a court institution. It should be noted, however, that the department also provided medical services for the army from at least 1632.[18] Other scholars of the Apothecary Chancery have seen it as having a somewhat wider purview: M. B. Mirskii highlighted the fact that the Apothecary Chancery had some responsibility for the health of Muscovites outside of court circles and the army; M. K. Sokolovskii described the department as acting in several capacities, including as an Academy of Sciences, referring to both its library and its production of reports.[19] Such approaches are in line with the views of K. A. Nevolin, who suggested that the Apothecary Chancery was defined by its function, medicine, not by its relationship to the court.[20] In such a schema, then, the Apothecary Chancery is commonly seen as a court department, concerned primarily or exclusively with the medical needs

---

16   For a detailed analysis of this historiographical trend, see Peter B. Brown, 'Muscovite Government Bureaus', *Russian History*, 10 (1983), 269–330.

17   D. V. Liseitsev, N. M. Rogozhin and Iu. M. Eskin, *Prikazy Moskovskogo gosudarstva XVI–XVII vv. Slovar'-spravochnik* (Moscow and St Petersburg: Tsentr gumanitarnikh initsiativ, 2015), pp. 33–35; Eve Levin, 'The Administration of Western Medicine in Seventeenth-Century Russia', in *Modernizing Muscovy: Reform and Social Change in Seventeenth Century Russia*, ed. by Jarmo Kotilaine and Marshall Poe (London and New York: Routledge Curzon, 2004), pp. 363–89 (pp. 366–67); Maria Unkovskaya, 'Learning Foreign Mysteries: Russian Pupils of the Aptekarskii Prikaz, 1650–1700', *Oxford Slavonic Papers*, 30 (1997), 1–20 (p. 2); N. V. Ustiugov, 'Evoliutsiia prikaznogo stroia russkogo gosudarstva v XVII v.', in *Absoliutizm v Rossii XVII–XVIII vv: Sbornik statei k semidesiatiletiiu so dnia rozhdeniia i sorokapiatiletiiu nauchnoi i pedagogicheskoi deiatel'nosti B. B. Kafengauza*, ed. by N. M. Druzhinin (Moscow: Nauka, 1964), 134–67 (p. 146); Brown, 'Muscovite Government Bureaus', pp. 292, 94.

18   1632 provision of medicines and field surgeons to the army: RGADA, coll. 143, descr. 1, file 114.

19   M. B. Mirskii, 'Aptekarskii prikaz (k 410-letiiu gosudarstvennogo upravleniia meditsinskimi delami v Rossii)', *Sovetskoe zdravookhranenie*, 11 (1991), 72–77 (pp. 74–76); M. K. Sokolovskii, 'Kharakter i znachenie deiatel'nosti Aptekarskogo prikaza', *Vestnik arkheologii i istorii*, 16 (1904), 60–89 (pp. 60–61).

20   K. A. Nevolin, *Polnoe sobranie sochinenii K. A. Nevolina*, 6 vols (St Petersburg: Tip. Eduarda Pratsa, 1857–59), 6 (1859), pp. 143–44, 168.

of the palace, with little or no competencies outside of those duties.[21] However, such an analysis excludes or undervalues certain aspects of the Apothecary Chancery's work. Most importantly for our purposes here, the Apothecary Chancery was frequently called upon to provide reports to various institutions.[22] What, then, does this reporting work tell us about the function of the Apothecary Chancery, and about the functioning of the chancery system as a whole?

Work on information technologies, information management, paper technologies, and paperwork provide useful models here. The study of information in early modern Western Europe has focussed on the idea of an 'information overload', that early modern Europeans had access to an impossibly large amount of information, hence much intellectual work of the period was directed towards sorting, categorising, preserving and managing that information. This problem was particularly acute for two groups: experts and bureaucrats, the same groups involved in the Apothecary Chancery reporting system. This literature reveals the great variety of ways in which early modern Europeans sought to organise information: Ann Blair has written about manuscript notes and printed reference books; Anke Te Heesen has emphasised the influence and various utilities of double-entry book-keeping; various medical historians have looked at case-books; and Staffan Müller-Wille and Isabelle Charmantier have looked at the great Swedish botanist Carl Linnaeus's use of index cards.[23] All these historians focus on the issue

---

21 N. P. Zagoskin, *Vrachi i vrachebnoe delo v starinnoi Rossii* (Kazan: Tip. Imperatorskogo Universiteta, 1891), p. 5; F. L. German, *Kak lechilis' Moskovskie tsari? (mediko-istoricheskii ocherk)* (Kiev and Kharkov: F. A. Iorganson, 1895), p. 79; N. Ia. Novombergskii, *Cherty vrachebnoi praktiki v Moskovskoi Rusi (kul'turno-istoricheskii ocherk)* (St Petersburg: Tip. Ministerstva vnutrennikh del, 1904), pp. 53–54; N. V. Ustiugov, 'Evoliutsiia', p. 146; Brown, 'Muscovite Government Bureaus', pp. 292, 94; John Appleby, 'Ivan the Terrible to Peter the Great: British Formative Influence on Russia's Medico-Apothecary System', *Medical History*, 27 (1983), 289–304 (p. 290); Mirskii, 'Aptekarskii prikaz', p. 74–76; Unkovskaya, 'Learning Foreign Mysteries', p. 2; Levin, 'Administration', pp. 366–67; N. V. Rybalko, *Rossiiskaia prikaznaia biurokratiia v smutnoe vremia nachala XVII v.* (Moscow: Kvadriga, 2011), p. 12.

22 Sokolovskii, 'Kharakter i znachenie', pp. 60–61. Nevolin, *Polnoe sobranie sochinenii*, 6, pp. 143–44, 168.

23 Ann M. Blair, *Too Much to Know: Managing Scholarly Information Before The Modern Age* (New Haven: Yale University Press, 2010); Staffan Müller-Wille, and Isabelle Charmantier, 'Natural History and Information Overload: The Case of Linnaeus', *Studies in History and Philosophy of Science Part C: Studies in History and Philosophy of Biological and Biomedical Sciences*, 43 (2012), 4–15; Anke Te Heesen, 'Accounting for the Natural World: Double-Entry Bookkeeping in the Field', in *Colonial Botany:*

of paper, manuscript and print, either singularly or in interaction. Paper was also vital to the Apothecary Chancery, and indeed the chancery system as a whole. Yet following the path of Apothecary Chancery reports highlights another issue: the spoken word as a meaningful part of how knowledge was created and circulated.[24] Orders for reports to be made were given orally; reports were either written down immediately, or spoken out loud and then transcribed; they were conveyed to bureaucrats in speech. Oral communication was a fundamental, inalienable part of the system. This is an aspect of knowledge exchange the focus on *paper* tends to obscure: although orality has been discussed as a part of early modern scientific exchange, it is not seen as an integral part of early modern scientific information technologies.[25] Here, then, we will use the term information technology, rather than paper technology, to highlight that it is the information—the reports—that we choose to follow and to highlight, and not the paper. The concept of information technology gives us a new way to approach the chancery system, one which focuses on how departments worked together, rather than what divided them; conversely, the Russian case highlights the interactions of paper with speech as a fundamental part of knowledge circulation.

Ordering Knowledge

Before the questionable root found on Loptunov in 1628 was sent to the Apothecary Chancery, Loptunov himself had been interrogated regarding his possession, where he stated

> the root he had wrapped around a crucifix was given to him by a passer-by on the road, and from which town [this man came] he does

---

Science, Commerce, And Politics in the Early Modern World, ed. by Londa Schiebinger, and Claudia Swan (Philadelphia: University of Pennsylvania Press, 2005), pp. 237–51.

24 The utility of orality in Muscovy has been discussed by Christoph Witzenrath. See Witzenrath, 'Literacy and Orality in the Eurasian Frontier: Imperial Culture and Space in Seventeenth-Century Siberia and Russia', *Slavonic and East European Review*, 87. 1 (2009), 53–77.

25 See for example Eileen Adair Reeves, 'Speaking of Sunspots: Oral Culture in an Early Modern Scientific Exchange', *Configurations*, 13 (2007), 185–210; Walter J. Ong, 'Orality, Literacy, and Medieval Textualization', *New Literary History*, 16 (1984), 1–12.

not know, and [the man] gave him that root because Andrei suffers from epilepsy [lit. black illness].[26]

It was Loptunov's claim that the root was medical, and not magical, that led to the involvement of the Apothecary Chancery, but it was not Loptunov's decision. Counsellor Secretary Fedor Fedorovich Likhachev, head of the Military Service Chancery and so the man ultimately responsible for Loptunov's trial, was the person who ordered the report, sending both root and order to the Apothecary Chancery. At the Apothecary Chancery, Likhachev's order was then affirmed and reiterated by the director, boyar prince Ivan Borisovich Cherkasskii. Such a process was typical for the creation of Apothecary Chancery reports: their writing was ordered by a senior Russian bureaucrat, who was commonly a noble.

The role of a noble official in ordering reports relates to the issue of boyar involvement in chancery affairs, a topic that has been controversial. One substantial issue is the education of Russian nobles: not all of them were functionally literate, and certainly none of the Apothecary Chancery directors had any medical training. How, then, could they have contributed to the administration of a literate bureaucracy, especially when it dealt with expert knowledge? Borivoj Plavsic has proposed that the boyars did little in the chanceries, with the real work being done by the secretaries, who worked as their assistants.[27] Robert O. Crummey has a more positive view of the boyars' contribution, proposing that they would have used their long tradition of military service to bring much needed leadership to chancery affairs.[28] Crummey, however, does not think that the boyars made a practical contribution based on skill. Peter B. Brown has proposed a third view: looking at the organisation and work of the Military Service Chancery, he notes that this institution

---

26 Novombergskii, *Materialy*, 3. 1, pp. 9–12; V. B. Kolosova, 'Name—Text—Ritual: The Role of Plant Characteristics in Slavic Folk Medicine', *Folklorica*, 10 (2005), 44–61 (p. 52).

27 Borivoj Plavsic, 'Seventeenth-Century Chanceries and Their Staffs', in *Russian Officialdom: The Bureaucratization of Russian Society from the Seventeenth to the Twentieth Century*, ed. by Walter McKenzie Pintner and Don Karl Rowney (London: Macmillan, 1980), pp. 19–45 (pp. 25–26).

28 Robert O. Crummey, 'The Origins of the Noble Official: The Boyar Elite, 1613–1689', in *Russian Officialdom*, ed. by Pintner and Rowney, pp. 46–75 (p. 75).

fulfilled its duties competently, which reflects well on the boyars.[29] Similarly, George G. Weickhardt has argued that, judging by their successes and failures during the seventeenth century, there was no clear difference in the competence of the boyars and the secretaries.[30] Apothecary Chancery directors, who before 1696 were all boyars, always had substantial administrative experience in other departments before taking up that post.[31] It thus seems that boyar directors were expected to take active part in the administration of their departments, which, in the case of the Apothecary Chancery, included ordering reports. Indeed, as such an order could be conveyed orally, there is no reason that functional illiteracy would have been an issue. Russian boyars formed a vital, initial stage in the information technology of Apothecary Chancery reports.

Not all extant Apothecary Chancery reports have retained their initial pages, meaning it is not always known exactly which Russian official ordered the report. Such preliminary pages survive in enough reports to show that very commonly such orders came from the Apothecary Chancery director. Such was the case in 1643, when head of the Apothecary Chancery, Fedor Ivanovich Sheremetev, asked the German physician Belau for a report explaining his treatment of Grigorii Gorikhvostov for worms.[32] When Sheremetev asked for the report, Gorikhvostov had been under Belau's care for a month; apparently, this was considered to be too long, and Belau was called upon to explain why his treatment had failed to produce results. Here Sheremetev was evidently concerned with the efficiency and efficacy of patient treatment in the department, a problem he sought to resolve partly through the production of knowledge. Similar reports ordered by the Apothecary Chancery director concern cooling

---

29   Peter B. Brown, 'Military Planning and High-Level Decision-Making in Seventeenth-Century Russia: The Roles of the Military Chancellery (Razriad) and the Boyar Duma', *Forschungen zur osteuropäischen Geschichte*, 58 (2002), 33–43.

30   George G. Weickhardt, 'Bureaucrats and Boiars in the Muscovite Tsardom', *Russian History*, 10 (1983), 342–49 (pp. 347–49).

31   For an overview of the careers of Apothecary Chancery directors, see Clare Griffin, 'The Production and Consumption of Medical Knowledge in Seventeenth-Century Russia: The Apothecary Chancery' (Ph.D. dissertation, University College London, 2013), pp. 221–23, http://discovery.ucl.ac.uk/1388075/

32   Unusually for an Apothecary Chancery document, we are not given any further information about Gorikhvostov other than his name. Mamonov, *Materialy*, 1, pp. 39–40.

medicines (1643), and autopsies (1677, and 1679).[33] Orders from the Apothecary Chancery head commonly dealt with strictly medical matters.

Orders for reports could come directly from the ruler. Between 1619 and 1633, Patriarch Filaret was co-ruler with his son, Tsar Mikhail Fedorovich, and Filaret himself commissioned certain reports. In 1623 Filaret launched an investigation into Mikhail Fedorovich's former fiancée, Mariia Ivanovna Khlopova, in particular concerning her sudden sickness that had ended the engagment in 1616; the investigation included an Apothecary Chancery report on her health.[34] In 1644 a member of the retinue of Count Valdemar (son of King Christian IV of Denmark by morganatic marriage) was killed when Valdemar attempted to flee Moscow to escape the stalled negotiations to marry Tsarevna Irina. As a result, Tsar Mikhail Fedorovich ordered an official autopsy be conducted on the luckless Danish servitor.[35] An order from Tsar Aleksei Mikhailovich in 1679 calls for an autopsy of boyar prince Ivan Alekseevich Vorotynskii, who had died suddenly shortly after a meeting with the tsar, raising the possibility that the tsar had been infected with a deadly disease.[36] Orders from the tsar or his co-rulers also concerned medicine, but as a way to solve political problems.

Even when the order came from the Apothecary Chancery director, there is often direct or indirect evidence that the tsar was involved in the process. In 1645 Count Valdemar again came to the attention of the Apothecary Chancery, as he had requested some medicines from the department; Apothecary Chancery director Fedor Ivanovich Sheremetev ordered a report on which illnesses such medicines could be used to treat.[37] Given the tsar's interest in his potential son-in-law and heir (Mikhail only had one son, the future Tsar Alexei Mikhailovich, not a sure dynastic bet, and Valdemar's parents' morganatic marriage meant he could not claim the Danish throne), it is likely he was involved in this case. Another significant group of reports involving the tsar concern negotiations

---

33 1643 report on cooling medicines: Mamonov, *Materialy*, 1, pp. 45–46. 1677 report on Blumentrost's wife and daughter: Mamonov, *Materialy*, 4, pp. 908. 1679 report on the Patriarch's groom: Mamonov, *Materialy*, 4, pp. 1161–62.

34 *Sobranie gosudarstvennykh gramot i dogovorov, khraniashchikhsia v gosudarstvennoi kollegii inostrannykh del*, 4 vols (Moscow: N. S. Vsevolozhskii, 1813–28), 3, pp. 257–66.

35 Mamonov, *Materialy*, 1, pp. 62–63.

36 Mamonov, *Materialy*, 4, pp. 1304, 1198–99.

37 Mamonov, *Materialy*, 1, p. 125.

over the purchase of unicorn horns.[38] Unicorn horns, most of which were actually narwhal tusks, were a prized—and hugely expensive—commodity, sought after both as ornaments and as medicaments in early modern Europe.[39] During the course of purchase negotiations in 1657, the Apothecary Chancery head relayed the tsar's order that reports be produced, on the specific horn in question, and on unicorn horn and its medical properties in general.[40] Orders relayed from the tsar via the Apothecary Chancery director thus also commonly focus on politics, but sometimes also concerned expensive medicines.

The Apothecary Chancery also received orders to produce reports from other sections of the Muscovite administrative system. One of the largest groups of such documents is the examinations of soldiers and other servitors to assess their fitness to serve. In such cases, Apothecary Chancery physicians were tasked with three questions: was the servitor genuinely sick, injured, or otherwise incapacitated; could the ailment be treated; and, once treatment was completed, could the service person in question return to his duties. For example, in 1666 the Musketeers' Chancery had a group of their servitors examined, with the Apothecary Chancery report detailing the bodily state of each man and how it related to their ability to serve.[41] Notably, the document does not record any actual treatments, only information on the necessity and possible outcomes of any future treatments. The military departments thus were involved in ordering reports relating to the usefulness of servitors' bodies.

As in the case with which we began, the 1628 witchcraft investigation, reports were also requested as a part of judicial proceedings conducted by various chanceries. Such reports always explicitly state the limits of the report, posing a specific question for the experts to answer. In 1657, the Apothecary Chancery was sent a herb and asked "what is

---

38   These reports are discussed in Robert Collis, 'Magic, Medicine and Authority in Mid-Seventeenth-Century Muscovy: Andreas Engelhardt (d. 1683) and the Role of the Western Physician at the Court of Tsar Aleksei Mikhailovich, 1656–1666', *Russian History*, 40 (2013), 399–427.

39   On the use of unicorn horn as an *objet d'art*, see Aleksandr Plukowski, 'Narwhals or Unicorns? Exotic Animals as Material Culture in Medieval Europe', *European Journal of Archaeology*, 7 (2004), 291–313. On the use of the horn in medicine, see Brian Fotheringham, 'The Unicorn and its Influence on Pharmacy and Medicine', *Pharmacy History Australia*, 10 (2000), 3–7.

40   Mamonov, *Materialy*, 2, p. 160.

41   *Ibid.*, pp. 311–12.

that herb and is it criminal (*vorovskoe*)?"—criminal being a common synonym for *maleficia*, or magic intended to cause harm.[42] In a case from 1703, the physicians were asked "whether that root is evil, or good, or good for the aforementioned illness, and is useful for medicine".[43] A similar set of orders concern illicit medical practice. In 1685 the head of the Musketeers' Chancery, Counsellor Secretary Fedor Leontevich Shaklovityi, requested a report from the Apothecary Chancery on the herb *p'ianoe zelie* (lit. heady herb), which was being sold on the market stalls (*zelenyi riad*, herb row) as a medicine.[44] As with the orders relating to witchcraft cases, Shaklovityi wanted to know if this herb had been licenced for sale (*i poskolko ego veleno prodavat i s porukoiu l' ili bes poruk*), and if this herb was appropriate for use as an internal medicine. Reports ordered for inclusion in trials thus focus on the physical evidence upon which the decision of the case rested.

Non-expert, noble officials from across the Muscovite administration played a central role in both initiating, and determining the limits, of Apothecary Chancery report production. They set the questions upon which the reports were to be focussed and initiated the exchange of documents around the administration, which was also an essential part of the process. The limits of expert medical reports, and the nature of the chancery system as an information technology, was determined by Russian bureaucrats, not by medical experts.

Compiling Knowledge

Returning again to 1628, the Military Service Chancery, having heard the testimony of both Loptunov and his master, decided on further tests of Andrei's story, and his characterisation of the root as medicinal, by sending the root to the Apothecary Chancery for examination. The resulting report states,

> Doctor Valentine [Bills] and his colleagues, having looked at the root, said that this root [is called] Goose-flesh, and is used in medicines, and has nothing evil in it, and [people] put that root in the mouth. And if someone wished to commit a crime, and [if] he used the good herb

---

42 1657 witchcraft case against Andrei Durbenev: Mamonov, *Materialy*, 3, 676–77.
43 RGADA, coll. 143, descr. 2, file 1618.
44 1685 investigation into the sale of *p'ianoe zelie*: RGADA, coll. 143, descr. 3, file 172.

badly, for criminality or witchcraft, that they do not know, [and they do not know] if there is a curse on that root.[45]

In this case, the report was created in part by an examination of a natural object. That examination was informed by the expertise of the physicians, and their ability to identify a root and to know and recount its properties, based on the training in botany and natural history that Western European university-trained physicians possessed. This process of selecting brief snippets of information from a much larger corpus of knowledge in order to give a focussed answer to a specific question was central to the Apothecary Chancery reporting system.

Reports created from a combination of experience and expert knowledge made up a substantial proportion of such texts, with particular emphasis on natural objects and human bodies. All of the reports produced for witchcraft and medical malpractice trials involved such examinations, usually of herbs and roots. Interestingly, these were the only cases in which Russians played a role as experts rather than patrons. Until 1654, all medical practitioners were foreigners from Western Europe. After that date, the Apothecary Chancery began to train medical practitioners for the first time: field surgeons, to serve the army; and apothecaries, to prepare medicines.[46] The department also employed Russians as herb collectors (*travniki*) who were expected to be knowledgeable in the properties of local plants. These Russian medical practitioners occasionally took part in report creation. In the 1685 *p'ianoe zelie* case all the examiners were foreign medical practitioners.[47] With one exception (1703), all of the medical experts who composed testimony for witchcraft trials were foreign.[48] In contrast, in a 1679 medical malpractice case two separate groups of experts were consulted, the first group being led by foreigners, and the second group entirely consisting of Russians.[49] Examination of a natural object was often a central part of the report-creation process, and in cases involving herbs and roots, Russians played a role in creating knowledge, as well as ordering it.

---

45 Novombergskii, *Materialy*, 3, part 1, pp. 9–12.
46 Unkovskaya, 'Foreign Mysteries', p. 12; Zmeev, *Vrachebniki*, p. 266; V. F. Gruzdev, *Russkie rukopisnye travniki* (Leningrad: Voenno-morskaia meditsinskaia akademiia, 1946), p. 25.
47 1685 malpractice case: RGADA, coll. 143, descr. 3, file 172.
48 1703 witchcraft cases: RGADA, coll. 143, descr. 2, file 1618.
49 1679 malpractice case: Mamonov, *Materialy*, 4, pp. 1110–11.

A second substantial group of examination-based reports involved human bodies. Such was the case with post-mortems, for example that of the unfortunate Danish servitor killed in 1644. The report on his cause of death stated "that cupbearer is wounded by a harquebus [and] the wound is just under the right eye".[50] Unusually for post-mortems in Muscovy, the doctors then went on to attempt to remove the bullet by cutting into the body: such incisions were rarely made. In this case the incision was unproductive, as the bullet failed to materialise, with the doctors proposing that it likely had gone too deep into the skull to be easily retrieved. Whether a post-mortem included an internal probe, as in this case, or was only external, close examination of the body was key to creating the report.

As well as examining natural objects and human bodies whose state was in question, Apothecary Chancery medical experts also referred to books in making their reports. In such cases, the only experts involved were foreigners, although the Apothecary Chancery did own Russian-language texts. The use of books was made explicit in the 1685 report on the questionable herb *p'ianoe zelie*, as the Apothecary Chancery experts declared it unfit for use in internal medicine after an examination of texts in the Apothecary Chancery library revealed that it was not listed as medicinal.[51] The report further added that *p'ianoe zelie* was a dangerous herb, capable of causing amnesia (*zabvenie uma*) and even death; such information may well also have been taken from a book.[52] In this case, multiple works from the Apothecary Chancery library were apparently used to construct the report.

Many reports mention individual authors and authorities. Samuel Collins's 1664 report on obesity cites Hippocrates.[53] Andreas Lichifinus's 1657 report on the Indian unicorn references both Marco Polo and Andrea Bacci, a sixteenth-century papal physician.[54] In Laurentius Blumentrost's 1690 report on the education of medical graduates from Padua (one of whom was then seeking a position in the department), he praised their knowledge of Galen and humoural medicine, but railed

---

50 Mamonov, *Materialy*, 1, pp. 62–63.
51 'v optekarskom prikaze v optekarskikh kn[i]gakh nigde ne napisana chtob ivo vnutr ch[e]l[o]v[e]komu upotrebliat', RGADA, coll. 143, descr. 3, file 172.
52 RGADA, coll. 143, descr. 3, file 172.
53 Mamonov, *Materialy*, 3, pp. 787–89.
54 Mamonov, *Materialy*, 2, p. 160.

against their ignorance of chemical medicine, a practice he ascribed not only to Paracelsus and Jan Baptist von Helmont (two of the most important chemical medical thinkers of early modern Europe), but also Hippocrates, Plato, and "other most ancient teachers, who are now and from ancient [times] accepted and respected".[55] In this case, like Collins and Lichifinus before him, Blumentrost only makes mention of specific elements of a huge corpus of writing and ideas, selecting only the parts which make sense in the context of his report. Books and their authoritative and expert authors were important to Apothecary Chancery reports, but only small pieces of information were chosen from a vast amount of available and relevant medical and natural historical thought in order to craft a direct, expert answer to a particular question.

On rare occasions, Apothecary Chancery reports even delved into the Bible as a form of textual authority. The Latin version of Samuel Collins's report on venesection, written in 1664, contains several Biblical references.[56] In creating an *apologia* for astrology as both medically useful and acceptable to Christianity, Collins included three Biblical quotations: Daniel 5. 27, Job 38. 31, and Judges 5. 20. All these quotations deal with God as an interventionist force in the universe, manipulating it according to his will and leaving signs for Christians to interpret. A marginal comment by Collins references the first century Roman-Jewish scholar Flavius Josephus, on Seth, the third son of Adam and Eve, to whom Josephus attributes the discovery of many of the secrets of astronomy.[57] Here Collins took on two enormous corpora—the Bible, and Biblical scholarship—and, like his colleagues using other learned authorities, selected specific elements to support his argument. In this he was apparently unsuccessful: the Russian version of Collins's report excludes all these references, an issue dealt with below. Nevertheless, Collins's attempt to include in his report quotations from the most authoritative of all authorities in early modern Europe, the Bible, demonstrates the fundamental importance of brief, selective use of major textual authorities to create the Apothecary Chancery reports.

---

55   RGADA, coll. 143, descr. 3, file 322.
56   RGADA, coll. 143, descr. 2, file 738.
57   Flavius Josephus, *The Antiquities of the Jews*, trans. by William Whiston (Cirencester: The Echo Library, 2005), p. 444.

In all of these cases the Apothecary Chancery reports took one, short, aspect of a larger textual authority, and re-contextualised it. Such an approach was by no means typical for early modern experts when dealing with information; they produced and reproduced information, and textual authority, in a variety of fashions. In perhaps the shortest format, Linnaeus placed individual words on index cards.[58] At the other end of the scale, many intellectuals produced critical editions of ancient world texts in their entirety, often accompanied by substantial glosses, which could rival the length of the original work. Florilegia, miscellanies, botanical works, medical recipe books and natural histories all reproduced shorter textual elements, ranging from a paragraph to several pages of a chapter.[59] The Apothecary Chancery's methods of dealing with textual authorities thus sat within a variety of approaches to such in the early modern world, which ranged from wholesale reproduction and even extension of the original, to the use of individual words. Considered in this context, Apothecary Chancery reports are notable for their selection of sentence-long pieces of information from textual authorities to be contextualised within longer prose compositions.

The creation of expert reports by the Apothecary Chancery was conducted on two bases, which often overlapped: examination of a natural object, and reference to established textual authorities. Interestingly, the only cases in which Russians worked as experts who created knowledge, rather than bureaucrats who ordered that knowledge be created, are those cases concerning examinations. It was the Western European, university-trained physicians who produced reports using textual authorities. The use of those authorities is hugely significant: the Hippocratic corpus, which comes up multiple times, is massive. Apothecary Chancery reports select only one or two elements from within this, and other extensive collections of writing, to create a selective, direct answer to a specific question.

---

58   Müller-Wille and Charmantier, 'Natural History and Information Overload'.
59   Blair, *Too Much to Know*.

Figure 2. An illuminated page from Josephus's *Antiquities of the Jews* (1466).

Translating Knowledge

A particular feature of knowledge circulation in the Apothecary Chancery was the central role of translation. The medical staff members were commonly native speakers of English, German or Dutch, although there were also occasionally French, Italian and Greek speakers present as well. Those trained in universities, such as the physicians, would have known Latin; those trained in guilds, such as apothecaries and surgeons, may not have done. Bureaucrats, both department heads and secretaries, were Russian speakers, only a few of whom knew foreign languages. This situation necessitated translation as a key part of knowledge exchange. This could take place as written translation, with the medical practitioners providing a Latin text, in which case the documents use the phrase "translated from a Latin document" (*perevod s Latinskogo pis'ma*). It could also take place as an oral interpretation, with the Latin being spoken aloud, interpreted into Russian, and then taken down. In such cases, the verb "to say" (*skazat'* inf.) is used. Such was the case in Loptunov's 1628 witchcraft trial, in which the document records: "And Doctor Valentine [Bills] and his colleagues, having looked at the root, *said* [my emphasis]…".[60]

This was common, both within the Apothecary Chancery, and within the chancery system more widely: the same formulation is used in reports on cooling medicines[61] and on worms[62] in 1643, a report on the uses of animal parts in medicine in 1664,[63] and autopsies in 1677[64] and 1679.[65] It is notable that all of these reports were particularly brief, even by the standards of the Apothecary Chancery: the autopsies, and the 1628 report on Loptunov's root, each run to only a few sentences; the other reports a couple of paragraphs. It thus seems that orally translated reports were made for particularly brief answers, when perhaps the process of composing a text and then translating it would have been unnecessarily time-consuming.

---

60 Novombergskii, *Materialy*, 3, part 1, pp. 9–12.
61 Mamonov, *Materialy*, 1, pp. 45–46.
62 *Ibid.*, pp. 39–40.
63 Novombergskii, *Materialy*, 1, pp. 54–55.
64 1677 report on Blumentrost's wife and daughter: Mamonov, *Materialy*, 4, pp. 908.
65 1679 report on Patriarch's groom: Mamonov, *Materialy*, 4, pp. 1161–62.

Transcription of oral reports could significantly shape the final form of the report. On 1 January 1658 a priest's wife was found dead, and three Apothecary Chancery physicians—Lichifinus, Engelhardt and Graman—examined the body for signs of plague. Engelhardt said: "That woman had scrofula of the stomach... and that [scrofula] does not cause the plague".[66] Graman agreed, stating that: "That woman had scrofula of the stomach... and that [scrofula] does not cause the plague".[67] A significant feature of these two statements is the high level of similarity between them; they are almost identical. It likely indicates that these were not the exact words of Engelhardt and Graman, as the sole difference between them is orthographical: variant spellings of the word for scrofula (*zolotukha* and *zolotik*). It is probable that the scribe reproducing Engelhardt's and Graman's statements paraphrased their words; as noted by Daniel E. Collins, such minor adjustments are common in other Muscovite documents that transcribe speech.[68] Despite the lack of an original for comparison, we can nevertheless see that oral reports do seem to have been subject to adjustments by scribes.

The process of translation can be traced in greater detail when both an original and a translation are extant, as is the case in a number of the written reports. Significantly, although Apothecary Chancery medical staff spoke many languages, and even wrote some documents in other languages during their time in Russia (letters relating to their delays by officious border guards are typically written in German), all extant originals of the reports are in Latin. This was likely simply a practical consideration: reports were most commonly composed by the physicians, who all knew Latin; restricting the reporting to one language limited the numbers of translators the department required, which staff group was always in high demand across the chancery system.

The translation process was used to edit reports. As noted above, although Samuel Collins attempted to marshall Biblical authority in his defence of astrology as a useful and Christian activity, the sentences in which Collins references the Bible in his Latin original

---

66 Mamonov, *Materialy*, 3, pp. 694–95.
67 Ibid.
68 Daniel E. Collins, 'Speech Reporting and the Suppression of Orality in Seventeenth-Century Russian Trial Dossiers', *Journal of Historical Pragmatics*, 7 (2006), 265–92 (p. 283). See also Collins, *Reanimated Voices. Speech Reporting in a Historical-Pragmatic Perspective* (Amsterdam and Philadelphia: John Benjamins, 2001).

were redacted in the Russian translation.⁶⁹ A. P. Bogdanov, who first noted that parts of the Latin original of this text were not preserved in the Russian translation, calls the removed sections insignificant (*maloznachitel'nye*).⁷⁰ Alternatively, Maria Unkovskaya argues that the edited sentences were concerned with cosmology, and were not translated due to the ban she proposes existed in the Apothecary Chancery on the discussion of medical theory or natural philosophy.⁷¹ However, as shown in examples above, various other Apothecary Chancery reports do mention medical theorists, medical theories, and natural philosophy, often relying on works owned by the department. Moreover, sentences present in Collins's original Latin that are absent from the Russian are all Biblical, and not cosmological or natural philosophical. For example, Collins wrote

> There is an ancient custom among the Persians, to which the Prophecy of Daniel in the presence of King Belshazzar may have referred with the word 'Tekel': *You have been weighed on the scales and found wanting.* [Emphasis my own]

The reference to Daniel's conversation with Belshazzar remains in the final Russian version, but Daniel's interpretation of the Word of God has been removed: you have been weighed, and found wanting (see Daniel 5. 13–28). In each case where sentences are removed, they were extracted from different parts of the text, in a way which leaves the remaining text comprehensible, but removes direct quotations from the Bible. This is likely due to concerns over heresy. In contrast to the highly adaptive approach to text and translation found in the Apothecary Chancery reports, and for that matter the *Vesti-Kuranty*, the text of the Bible and other religious works were approached entirely differently: the word, and the words, of God, were sacrosanct, and changing them was fundamentally problematic.⁷² This was evidenced by the problems of

---

69 RGADA, coll. 143, descr. 2, file 738.
70 A. P. Bogdanov, 'O rassuzhdenii Samuila Kollinsa', in *Estestvennonauchnye predstavleniia Drevnei Rusi* ed. by R. A. Simonov (Moscow: Nauka, 1988), pp. 204–08. Bogdanov's edition of the Russian text is published here pp. 206–08.
71 Unkovskaya, 'Foreign Mysteries', p. 9.
72 On adaptive translation in the *Vesti-Kuranty*, see Ingrid Maier, 'Newspaper Translations in Seventeenth-Century Muscovy. About the Sources, Topics and Periodicity of *Kuranty* "Made in Stockholm" (1649)', in *Explorare necesse est. Hyllningsskrift till Barbro Nilsson*, ed. by Per Ambrosiani, Elisabeth Löfstrand,

Patriarch Nikon's Church reforms of the 1660s, which revolved around proposed changes to the service books. According to David Frick, many of those involved in the Muscovite religious debates were using Polish Bibles, but went to great lengths to conceal that fact.[73] The Book of the Bible that Collins was citing here—Daniel—was in the Slavonic Bible, but Collins was not citing the Slavonic Bible; he was citing a Western European Bible. For Muscovites, this difference was substantial. The Slavonic Book of Daniel was canonical; a Western European Book of Daniel was heretical. Collins's text was familiar to Russian scribes, but nevertheless sufficiently alien and problematic to necessitate excision. In this case, then, the translation process led to the deliberate removal of whole sentences deemed inappropriate for religious reasons.

The translation process was also used to add information to a report. In the 1665 text on valerian root Collins covers the physical appearance, properties, methods of preparation and modes of consumption of the plant.[74] In the Russian version of the document there is an additional section, introduced in the report as excerpts from the herbal with 520 chapters, an as-yet unidentified Russian-language herbal. As the text specifies that the origin of the additional articles is a Russian-language herbal, it is unlikely that Collins, who knew very little Russian, could have chosen those excerpts to accompany his report; they are more likely to have been chosen by a Russian-speaking member of the Apothecary Chancery staff, perhaps the scribe who prepared the final, Russian version of Collins's report. The articles from the herbal complement Collins's abstract description of the properties of the root by providing specific recipes for its use. Here, Russian scribes used their ability to change the text of a report to include extra material relevant to the topic.

Close examination of the translation stage in the Apothecary Chancery's reporting information technology reveals two significant points: the impact of translation upon the content of a report, and the respective roles of the spoken and written word. The Russian text of a report could substantially differ from the Latin original, often because

---

Laila Nordquist, and Ewa Teodorowicz-Hellman (Stockholm: Acta Universitatis Stockholmiensis, 2002), pp. 181–90.

73 David A. Frick, 'Sailing to Byzantium: Greek Texts and the Establishment of Authority in Early Modern Muscovy', *Harvard Ukrainian Studies*, 19 (1995), 138–57.

74 Mamonov, *Materialy*, 3, pp. 791–94.

of deliberate changes to the text undertaken by the translator, who either added or removed elements. Translation was thus a form of editing, which could have a major influence on the final content of a report. Alongside these written reports, reports were also spoken aloud, then translated and transcribed, which process also affected the final form of the report. In the chancery system, the spoken word was a fundamental part of report creation, and so of the chancery system's form of information technology. The chancery system was a literate bureaucracy, but it also relied heavily upon the spoken word.

Figure 3. A herbal page (*ca.* seventeenth century).

Circulating Knowledge

Once an Apothecary Chancery report had been written and translated, it was then circulated. In the case of the 1628 witchcraft trial with which we began, it was sent back to the Military Service Chancery bureaucrats overseeing the case, and possibly forwarded to the governor of Rzhev, under whose authority the arrest was initially made, and, for that matter, the governor of Toropets, the accused's home town, and the Archangel monastery in Ustiug Velikii, to which he was then sent. That report thus circulated not just within the Apothecary Chancery, or even between that department and the palace, but within the wider Muscovite administrative system. It is even possible that the accused himself, Loptunov, a peasant from a rural noble estate, and his master, Mikhail Polibin, who was losing a peasant, were also made aware of the contents of the report affecting Loptunov's fate. That would again expand the circulation of this report of expert Western European medical knowledge, out into Muscovite society. Following the further progress of Apothecary Chancery expert reports thus tells us about how these reports circulated, and whom in Muscovite society was the end user of this information technology.

Commonly, the end user of a report was the man who had ordered it: the Apothecary Chancery head, the head of the Military Service Chancery or other section of the administration, or indeed the tsar himself. In all the cases for which such information is available, the orderer was at least part of the circle to whom the report was distributed. The head of the Apothecary Chancery was a particularly vital part of this distribution system. As well as receiving his own reports, reports written by his department for others were sent to him first and, in the case of reports to be passed on to the tsar, he then personally delivered them. Such was the case in 1655, with the report on unicorn horn, and the 1679 autopsy of the boyar Vorotynskii.[75] Similarly, when reports requested by other departments were completed, they were always first sent to the Apothecary Chancery director before being delivered

---

[75] 1655 report on purchase of unicorn horn: RGADA, coll. 143, descr. 2, file 147; Mamonov, *Materialy*, 2, p. 157; Mamonov, *Materialy*, 3, pp. 636–39. 1679 autopsy of Vorotynskii: Mamonov, *Materialy*, 4, p. 1304, pp. 1198–99.

to the relevant chancery. Such was the case in 1679, for the autopsy of one of the Patriarch's grooms on behalf of the Land Chancery (*Zemskii prikaz*).[76] The head of the Apothecary Chancery was thus a vital figure in circulating reports created by his department to a relevant audience.

Consuming a report did not necessarily mean reading it. We know from other sources that reports were commonly read to the tsar and his advisers.[77] Far from all Russian nobles were functionally literate, so this was an efficient system for transmitting information. Leaving aside the literacy issue, there are reasons that the spoken word is particularly helpful in exchanging information. As pointed out by more than one colleague during the workshop from which this chapter emerged, academics regularly fly around the world to speak face-to-face, even though we could rather more easily send a text to each other to read. This circumstance is (hopefully) not a statement on the literacy of the academics involved, but rather reflects the special role the spoken word can play in knowledge exchange (the opportunity to exchange that knowledge in chic local restaurants is merely a pleasant by-product). There were also good reasons to use the spoken word to convey certain reports at the seventeenth-century Russian palace. The number of people holding a counsellor rank, and so who could advise the tsar, went from around thirty before 1645, to approximately seventy in the latter part of the century.[78] In reality, the tsar's council was often rather smaller, but he could still be in discussion with perhaps fifteen people.[79] Reading the report aloud to such a group would be a rather more efficient way of conveying the information than making and circulating anything from sixteen to seventy-one manuscript copies, or alternatively circulating a

---

76 Mamonov, *Materialy*, 4, pp. 1161–62.
77 Ingrid Maier and Wouter Pilger, 'Second-hand Translation for Tsar Aleksej Mixajovich—a Glimpse into the "Newspaper Workshop" at Posol'skij Prikaz', *Russian Linguistics*, 25 (2001), 209–42 (p. 215).
78 Marshall Poe, *The Russian Elite in the Seventeenth Century*, 2 vols (Helsinki: Finnish Academy of Sciences and Letters, 2004), 1, pp. 13–15; Poe, 'Tsar Aleksei Mikhailovich and the End of the Romanov Political Settlement', *Russian Review*, 62 (2003), 537–64; Robert O. Crummey, *Aristocrats and Servitors: The Boyar Elite in Russia, 1613–89* (Princeton and Guildford: Princeton University Press, 1983), p. 88. See also Hans-Joachim Torke, 'Oligarchie in der Autocratie—Der Machtverfall Der Bojarenduma Im 17. Jahrhundert', *Forschungen zur osteuropäischen Geschichte*, 24 (1978), 179–201.
79 See P. V. Sedov, *Zakat Moskovskogo tsarstva. Tsarskii dvor kontsa XVII veka* (St Petersburg: Dmitrii Bulanin, 2008), pp. 13–19.

smaller number of copies among that many people. In such situations, the spoken word was a more efficient way to communicate reports.

Apothecary Chancery reports were also made available to people outside the chancery system. When the department produced reports for witchcraft and medical malpractice trials, that report may well have been shown to the defendant, a person who often came from outside the chancery system. Indeed, in 1690, one of the defendants in a witchcraft and blasphemy case, Perfilii Rokhmaninov, a townsman (*posadskii chelovek*) from Galich, petitioned for the herbs found in his possession to examined by the Apothecary Chancery, asking that "those herbs be examined in the Apothecary [Chancery], and those herbs are not magical".[80] The date of Rokhmaninov's request is significant: in the late seventeenth century, former and current Apothecary Chancery staff members were compiling self-help medical texts aimed at literate Russian audiences.[81] This circumstance likely raised the profile of the Apothecary Chancery as a centre for medical expertise in Russian society, and this possibly motivated Rokhmaninov's request. Rokhmaninov knew that having an expert Apothecary Chancery report written for his case was a possibility, suggesting a significant knowledge of that department's reporting activities even outside the chancery system.

There is also some evidence that Apothecary Chancery reports may have been made available to foreign governments. We return here to the 1644 autopsy of Count Valdemar's retainer.[82] The servitor in question died from a gunshot wound to the face, which wound he received in front of numerous witnesses. An autopsy would then seem to serve little purpose here, unless it was to send on to the Danes as part of an official response to the incident. In 1715 an autopsy report was written on the death of Charlotte Christine of Brunswick-Lüneburg, Tsarevich Alexei's wife. In this case, it is the language of the report that is odd: the file appears to be complete and undamaged, and yet it contains only a German and a Latin version of the autopsy, and no Russian text.[83] Charlotte Christine was the sister-in-law of the Holy Roman Emperor

---

80 N. Ia. Novombergskii, *Vrachebnoe stroenie v do-Petrovskoi Rusi* (Tomsk: Parovaia tipolitografiia Sibirskogo tovarishchestva pechatnogo dela, 1907), p. 93.
81 See Griffin, 'In Search of an Audience'.
82 Mamonov, *Materialy*, 1, pp. 62–63.
83 RGADA, coll. 143, descr. 2, file 1635.

Charles VI, whom Russia hoped to count as an ally in an expected war against the Ottomans. It is thus very possible that the report on her death was prepared primarily to send to Charles VI, in which case the languages of the report would make perfect sense. These two cases thus show that the chancery system's form of information technology could communicate information not only outside the chancery system, but potentially even outside of Russia.

The readership of Apothecary Chancery reports highlights vital aspects of knowledge circulation in the Russian context. Firstly, it speaks to the role of the Apothecary Chancery within the chancery system, and indeed our ideas of how the chanceries worked as a system, rather than merely a group of institutions. The Apothecary Chancery is commonly viewed as a palace instrument, as indeed it often functioned. But devoting attention to the flow of reports reveals the broader networks in which the Apothecary Chancery was involved, linking together the wider Muscovite administration beyond the walls of the Kremlin, some parts of Russian society, and even, potentially, other governments. Secondly, looking at circulation shows us *how* things circulated: the spoken word was as important here as the written word. Muscovites were as likely to find out the contents of a report by having it read to them as by reading it themselves. The Apothecary Chancery's reporting system shows substantial circulation of medical knowledge, circulation that was achieved by the purposeful use of both manuscript and the spoken word.

Storing Knowledge

The final stage of all Apothecary Chancery documents was storage. In a sense though, this was a stage long in preparation through the very processes of creating the document. As the orders, reports, and responses circulated through the system, they gained a manuscript form of metadata, data about data. When the order for a report on Loptunov's root reached the Apothecary Chancery in 1628, it did not arrive merely as an order, but was accompanied by a précis of the case up until the moment the order arrived at the department. That précis was then used to form a file in the Apothecary Chancery, along with a copy of the report; similarly, a copy of the report was also sent back to the Military

Service Chancery to be included in their file. In many cases, we have both draft versions of a document (*chernovik*) and the final, clean version (*belovik*). The existence of drafts and clean copies reflects the great care taken in creating these documents. In the seventeenth century Russia still imported much of its paper. Nevertheless, even the most mundane of documents was drafted and redrafted before a final version of the document could be approved, showing the meticulous construction of Muscovite files.

These files were *stolbtsy*, scrolls, which were used for the majority of Russian administrative documents until around the 1690s.[84] This was a security measure: as each document was added to a file, it would be glued to its predecessor and an elaborate signature made across the back of the join, so that original documents could not be removed, nor fakes introduced, without someone noticing. One reason for such care was to ensure that one could refer back to the documents accurately. We have evidence that the Apothecary Chancery did just that on a number of occasions: several prescriptions contain a note that either they were created on the basis of an earlier prescription, or that a prescription was repeated later.[85] I have not come across any such notations in the reports discussed here, but the careful recording and storage of these documents indicates that reports, like the Apothecary Chancery prescriptions, were kept for the possibility of such reference.

The knowledge created by the Apothecary Chancery was directed towards particular, limited, problems and questions, but it was not transitory. On the contrary, like all chancery documents, it was created in a secure and traceable manner, both to aid its real-time use and to help its storage for potential later reference. Direct evidence of such references only exists for prescriptions, not reports. Nevertheless, it is important that this was a possibility that was anticipated and allowed for by the system itself. The Apothecary Chancery information technology ensured that data, once created, could be retrieved.

---

[84] Shmidt and Kniaz'kov, *Dokumenty*, pp. 21–27.
[85] See for example the 1674 order to repeat a previous prescription: RGADA, coll. 143, descr. 2, file 1093, fol. 45. 1666 prescription for I. D. Miloslavskii from earlier prescription by Dr Engelhardt: RGADA, coll. 143, descr. 2, file 743, fol. 46.

Conclusion

We began this chapter in 1628, when the arrest of a man possessing a peculiar root set in action the massive bureaucracy of the Muscovite administration, allowing us to follow the process by which expert reports were ordered, created, translated, circulated, and stored. Examining these processes reveals the nature and role of information technology and knowledge exchange in seventeenth-century Russia, and also gives us a specific case of an early modern information technology to help us to examine that concept more closely. The Apothecary Chancery reporting system allowed the creation of orders for specific pieces of knowledge, the creation of knowledge to that particular end, the transformation (translation) of that knowledge into a form fit for usage in context, the circulation of that knowledge around a system, and the storage of that knowledge for potential later retrieval. This was an information technology.

Looking at the Apothecary Chancery reporting system as a form of information technology gives us a new view on that department, the chancery system as a whole, and indeed the running of the seventeenth-century Russian state. The chancery system has often been studied by dividing it up, with the Apothecary Chancery seen as limited to palace medicine. Looking at the report circulation, it is clear that, while the Apothecary Chancery did indeed serve the court, it fulfilled a number of functions beyond merely treating the sick, and also regularly provided expert knowledge to a number of other departments. Tracing such interactions shows the chancery system to be dynamic and interactive, with the Apothecary Chancery being far more than simply a dispensary for the Muscovite elite.

Most interesting is how this information technology functioned. The chancery system was a bastion of literacy in a culture where literacy was not always highly valued. Literacy and documentation played a substantial role in the encoding and storage of Apothecary Chancery knowledge. Printed texts likely played a part as reference texts in the Apothecary Chancery library, but it was the chancery manuscript scrolls which took centre stage. Orality was also a major element in this system. Orders were given orally; some reports were produced, and translated, orally before being written down; and reports were consumed orally.

Here, the spoken word was not subordinate to the written word, nor used when one could not read or write. It was used alongside writing, and even in preference to it, because orality has its own utility. In the Apothecary Chancery's early modern information technology, manuscripts and the spoken word were the key mediums; this argues for the inclusion of oral communication in interaction with written, and printed, communication in histories of early modern information technologies.

9. What Could the Empress Know About Her Money? Russian Poll Tax Revenues in the Eighteenth Century

Elena Korchmina[1]

Given the inadequate size and training of Russia's provincial bureaucracy, one might ask how it managed to govern so many people and so much territory. The simple answer is that for the most part it could not and did not govern them.[2]

Governments have always faced the need to get sufficient operational information about current affairs at all social and political levels. As John P. Le Donne has articulated, "Without adequate revenue, properly accounted for, a government's freedom of action is severely circumscribed, both in the conduct of foreign policy and in building the foundations of a civilized society".[3] The subject under discussion—how thoroughly the Russian government in the eighteenth century was informed about the situation in its provinces—is often overlooked. But within the last few decades the concept that Russia was "undergoverned"

---

1. The study was completed in the framework of the Basic Research Program at the National Research University Higher School of Economics (HSE) in 2016. I thank the Prokhorov Foundation for supporting my research through the Karamzin Fellowship. I am also grateful to Vera Dubina, Nataliia Malysh and Ilya Voskoboynikov for invaluable research assistance and comments.
2. Robert E. Jones, *Provincial Development in Russia: Catherine II and Jacob Sievers* (New Brunswick: Rutgers University Press, 1984), p. 14.
3. John P. Le Donne, *Absolutism and Ruling Class. The Formation of the Russian Political Order, 1700–1825* (Oxford: Oxford University Press, 1991), p. 239.

has become more and more popular, and scholars have examined various aspects of the empire's institutional development through this prism.[4] Stephen Velychenko observes, "Although undefined in the specialist literature, and untranslatable into Russian, this term [undergoverned] includes the idea that a government which has successfully monopolized the use of physical violence does not have enough administrators per capita to carry out policies effectively and efficiently. From this perspective a unique attribute of the tsarist bureaucracy was not its bigness or pathologies but its smallness".[5] Thus, the number of state officials per capita is assumed to be a key indicator of the Russian Empire's "undergoverning".

Some information does exist about the size of Russian officialdom at the end of the seventeenth and the beginning of eighteenth centuries. Calculations by Ludmila Pisarkova show that in 1698 the ratio between officialdom and the general population was 1:2250, and in 1726 it was 1:3400.[6] Velychenko has suggested that, until 1795, the proportion of state clerks in relation to the civil population in Russia and European countries (Austria, Britain and Prussia) was close in number (1:1375 and 1:1833, on average, respectively).[7] Nevertheless Velychenko does not make it clear whether the Russian Empire was "well-governed" in the beginning and middle of the eighteenth century,[8] or what number of state clerks was supposed to be sufficient to let the government make so-called effective and sound decisions. Most historians agree that Russia was undergoverned in the nineteenth century.[9] The present chapter focuses on the question of whether the Russian government

---

4   Jones, *Provincial Development*, p. 13, Stephen Velychenko, 'The Size of the Imperial Russian Bureaucracy and Army in Comparative Perspective', *Jahrbücher für Geschichte Osteuropas*, Neue Folge, 49. 3 (2001), 346–62 (p. 347), Boris N. Mironov, *Rossiiskaia imperiia: ot traditsii k modern*, vol. 2 (St Petersburg: Dmitrii Bulanin, 2014).
5   Velychenko, pp. 347–48.
6   Ludmila F. Pisar'kova, 'Rossiiskaia biurokratiia v epokhu Petra I', *Otechestvennaia istoriia*, 1 (2004), 18–41.
7   Velychenko, p. 352.
8   "Great Russia did not seem to have been undergoverned relative to its western neighbors": Velychenko, p. 357.
9   Peter Gatrell, 'Economic Culture, Economic Policy and Economic Growth in Russia, 1861–1914', *Cahiers du Monde Russe*, 1 (1995), 37–52 (p. 42); The review of the latest historiography appears in Sergei V. Lyubichankovski, 'The State of Power in the Late Russian Empire: The English-American Historiography of the Second Half of the XXth-early XXIst centuries', *Proceedings of the Samara Scientific Center of the Russian Academy of Sciences*, 2 (2007), 342–47 (p. 343).

in the middle of the eighteenth century had enough informational resources to conduct a sensible financial policy, and whether there were enough officials to collect taxes and report on the revenue (in this case, the poll tax): that is, whether or not Russia was undergoverned.

I chose the poll tax as a case study because it was a key direct tax in Russia, the revenue of which supplied military forces in peacetime. When Peter the Great introduced the new tax, he tried to organise it for ease of calculation and collection. The taxable base did not change for decades. Money collection and distribution were decentralised, so the cash flows never accumulated in the centre; instead they were directed according to the authorities' orders right to their destination points. This configuration solved the most important logistical problem: money delivery to the consumer. The government obtained information on tax revenues and expenditures only from reports. The poll tax collection chain may therefore be split into two relatively connected procedures: the first, money gathering, distribution and delivery (the *material layer*); and the second, making reports on cash inflows and outflows (the *information layer*). The same officialdom—provincial, regional and local clerks—was in charge of both layers.[10]

Was There a Required Number of Civil Servants for Tax Collection?

Starting from the 1730s, poll tax collection was undertaken in provincial clerical offices where the taxpayers (landlords, countermen, delegated representatives, etc.) arrived twice a year (originally three times a year) and handed cash to a clerk (e.g. a copyist) who made an entry on the tax payment in one or several accounting books; within three days a taxpayer had to receive a receipt from the clerk confirming his payment. Other officials, enumerators (*shchetchiki*), under the supervision of a poll

---

10 The idea of a distinct informational part of poll tax collection has been expressed before; see Le Donne, *Absolutism and the Ruling Class*, p. 243: "Fiscal management consists of three distinct operations: collecting revenue, depositing it in a treasury from which it can be disbursed, and auditing both the revenue and the expenditures. This third operation was the most difficult and the most sensitive because it required reliable statistical information, which collecting agencies were for long both unable and unwilling to supply, and because it threatened to expose the fraudulent practices that everyone had an interest in concealing".

tax officer (*ofitser pri podushnom sbore*) counted the money, packed it into sacks and barrels, sealed them, and transported them on carts to their destinations, escorted by a convoy. Upon handing the money over to the recipients they were given delivery receipts and returned to their offices. In addition to the main tax, taxpayers paid a service tax of two kopeks per ruble for clerks' salaries (*zhalovanie*) and transportation costs. If the individuals failed to meet payments on time and accrued arrears, a crew of retired soldiers was sent from the local provincial office to the village and stayed there for some time fully at the debtors' expense; such an order was legislated.[11] In cases of long-term indebtedness, peasants or even landlords might be imprisoned and detained on their own account (*na svoem koshte*).[12]

The number of officials engaged in poll tax collection was not large: one or a few clerks (*podkantseliarist* or *kopiist*) received the money and kept records, and one or two officials (the poll tax officer, the local commissar, etc.) supervised tax collection and signed documents (*u shcheta denezhnoi kazny*). For instance, in 1741 the Smolensk clerical office included forty-six "secretaries, clerks, junior clerks and copyists", only three of whom were directly involved in the collection of poll tax money.[13] The other forty-three employees compiled and distributed other payments, filled in, and kept other registries. In 1738 the population of the Smolensk region comprised about 214,000 males listed as poll tax payers.[14] Examining the correlation between the number of civil servants and the regional population, two ratios come to light: 1:4652 (the correlation between the total number of regional officials and the adult male population), and 1:71,000 (the ratio of dedicated poll tax officials to the adult male population). Neither of these is relevant, however, as a certain number of officials were not considered: the detachment of soldiers tasked with money transportation and debt collection. Table 1 represents the number of civil servants in different Russian regions in 1739.

---

11 *Polnoe sobranie zakonov Rossiiskoi imperii*, Series 1 (1649–1825) (hereafter *PSZ* 1), no. 6674.
12 V. N. Zakharov, Y. A. Petrov, M. K. Shatsillo, *Istoriia nalogov v Rossii. IX–nachalo XX v.* (Moscow: ROSSPEN, 2006), p. 97.
13 RGADA, coll. 278, descr. 1, file 6692.
14 RGADA, coll. 248, descr. 7.

Table 1. Required Staff for poll tax collection in the Russian Empire in 1739 estimated by the General War Commissariat (*General-kriegs-komissariat*).[15]

Rank	Provinces (*gubernii*)								
	Moscow	Siberia	Novgorod	Arkhangelsk	Belgorod	Smolensk	Kazan	Voronezh	Nizhniy
				The first group					
colonel	1								
lieutenant colonel (*podpolkovnik*)		1	1		1	1	1		
major (*prem'er-maior*)	4		1	2	1		4	2	2
second major	3	1	2	2	1		1	2	1
captain	5		2			1		1	
lieutenant (*poruchick*)	16	2	4	4	7	1	4	6	4

15 RGADA, coll. 248, descr. 7. file 412, fol. 117v. This document's origin lies in the trend of sorting out questions of regional management. See *Oblastnye praviteli Rossii, 1719–1739*, ed. by I. Babich and M. Babich (Moscow: ROSSPEN, 2008), pp. 8–12.

ensign (*praporshchik*)	34	6	8	8	11	3	14	9	3
subtotal	63	10	18	16	21	6	24	20	10
The second group									
sergeant	20	3	7	7	12	2	10	9	2
quartermaster (*kaptenarmus*)	37	1	10	6	12	1	12	8	6
corporal	53	7	18	15	22	5	23	21	9
soldier	886	96	280	203	290	117	390	279	194
subtotal	996	107	315	231	336	125	435	317	211
The third group									
clerk (*kantseliarist*)	24	2	8	5	6	2	11	7	6
junior office clerk (*podkantseliarist*)	29	4	8	6	11	4	5	5	4

copying clerk (kopiist)	121	12	34	24	38	12	47	29	31
subtotal	174	18	50	35	55	18	63	41	41
total*	1233	135	383	282	412	149	522	378	262
male population**	2,066,000	132,000	551,000	386,000	565,000	217,000	799,000	512,000	440,000

* The latest consolidated data are in Mironov, Rossiiskaia imperiia: ot traditsii k riodernu, vol. 2, p. 431, table 8.1.

** "Generalitetskaia perepis'" 1738 goda', in Perepisi naseleniia Rossii: itogonye materialy podvornykh perepisei i revizii naseleniia Rossii, 1646–1858, vols 2–3, ed. by L. G. Beskrovnyi, Ia. Ie. Vodarskii, V. M. Kabuzar (Moscow: Institut istorii AN SSSR, 1972).

Table 2. The number of officials per 1000 men in Russia, by region, in 1738.

Officials	Moscow	Siberia	Novgorod	Arkhangelsk	Belgorod	Smolensk	Kazan	Voronezh	Nizhniy	Total
The 1st group	0.03	0.08	0.03	0.04	0.04	0.03	0.03	0.04	0.02	0.03
the 2rd group	0.48	0.81	0.57	0.60	0.59	0.58	0.54	0.62	0.48	0.54
The 3rd group	0.08	0.14	0.09	0.09	0.10	0.08	0.08	0.08	0.09	0.09
All	0.60	1.02	0.70	0.73	0.73	0.69	0.65	0.74	0.60	0.66

The first group of officials—from a colonel down to an ensign—was in charge of poll tax collection supervision. Alongside them, governors (*voevody*), who acted as poll tax officers during the receipt of tax payments, might have had responsibility for control over the whole process if administrative resources were insufficient in a particular region. As such, governors had the right to sign all papers issued to record the amount of tax collected, and were responsible for shortfalls. The second group, estimated to be more than 80% of the whole, included errand crews consisting primarily of retired enlisted soldiers whose duties were logistical: to convey and deliver money, correspondence, etc. This group of clerks was responsible for the *material layer* of tax collection. The third group, about 13%, undertook the receipt of money and bookkeeping. This group of clerks was responsible for the *information layer* of tax collection.

Comparing the number of taxpayers with the number of clerks gives an estimate of 1:1509[16] (or 0.66, Table 2),[17] which in general corresponds to the ratio in European countries (Austria, Britain and Prussia).[18] But the ratios of officials belonging to the various groups differ greatly. More bureaucrats of the second group were in charge of money transportation, but the officials of the third group, whose number was not sufficient, were responsible for money collection in provincial offices and, more importantly, for all poll tax documentary circulation.

We can consider the data used for the estimates presented above as trustworthy due to the fact that, in the second quarter of the eighteenth century, the provincial clerical staff list was defined and approved by the Senate, and the process of equipping all the provincial offices with personnel had just begun. It is important to stress here that in practice a significant number of provincial clerical positions remained vacant. The

---

16 This study takes into account only the male population because women were not on audit lists and were not subject to tax payments, or, at least, I have not found statements to the contrary in the sources at my disposal. Women did not participate in the delivery of money to the local offices, etc. At the same time, women along with men produced the goods, products, and materials which formed the taxable base.

17 But our estimation is almost three times higher than Mironov's; this discrepancy could be caused by the problems of defining a "bureaucrat" in the Russian context. These figures are derived from the primary source. See Mironov, *Rossiiskaia imperiia: ot traditsii k modernu*, vol. 2, p. 435, Table 8.2.

18 Velychenko, 'The Size', p. 93.

following is an example of a typical situation. In 1731 the local clerkdom in the Nizhnii provincial office reported on the reasons why they had failed to follow the Senate's directive, even though their office in 1722–23 was staffed with 167 clerks as per the schedule requirements. By 1732 the number of their personnel had dramatically changed. According to the clerks' report, thirty-seven officials had died and sixty-two either were transferred to other places, had run away or had been fined; consequently there were only sixty-seven employees left, several of whom were old, sick, or mentally ill.[19] The report especially noted that Nizhnii local authorities had previously reported to the government about the severe deficiency of their civil servants, but neither a resolution nor even a response had been received. Within ten years the number of clerks had decreased by almost 60%.

The calculations of the central authorities, concerning the costs of maintaining such state bodies as regional clerical offices, proved to be quite moderate, and, as mentioned above, these costs were reimbursed by an additional two-kopek levy to which taxpayers were subjected. According to the General War Commissariat's estimates, civil servants' allowances and additional expenses should have been covered by the amount of the levy, presumably 75,000 rubles, gathered from 5.5 million male taxpayers. According to the staff schedule, about 50,000 rubles per a year were spent on clerks' wages, another 5,000 rubles were to be spent on administration expenses, and finally the difference of 20,000 rubles should have stayed in the budget every year.[20]

In cases of tax arrears a fine was imposed on the whole of the local officialdom; moreover, until the mid-1730s, there was a common and widespread practice of punishment by estate distraint and further confiscation. The imposition and disbursement of fines was an obscure and ineffective process owing to the fact that the search for the guilty clerk or his estate across the entire empire took significant time and was burdened by red tape. For this reason, huge sums of fines remained unpaid for years.

The extent of poll tax payments demonstrates the efficiency of state bodies' performance. Researchers have proven that the level of tax

---

19   RGADA, coll. 248, descr. 7, file 391, fol. 236–38v. NB: these are the figures cited in the document; the mathematical discrepancy is present in the source.
20   RGADA, coll. 248, descr. 7, file 412, fol. 117v.

collected was over 90%.²¹ We can therefore safely conclude that the system of poll tax collection in the Russian Empire of the eighteenth century proved to be quite effective. At the same time, the level of tax acquisitions was dependent on many factors, such as the severity of the tax burden on taxpayers and the extent of state tax claims' compliance with the legislation. As for the contribution of bureaucratic staff it is not easy to extract and assess their influence on the whole process of tax gathering and distribution, but at least, from the beginning, the system was organised in such a way as to ensure its fruitful operation, using the staff at hand to keep the population from total insolvency. That aim was achieved, so we may regard the bureaucratic capacities of the Russian Empire in that aspect as satisfactory for enabling tax circulation and providing the state governing system with the assets necessary for its functioning.²²

The next example demonstrates a case in which the straightforward system of poll tax collection met insuperable obstacles. On 15 October 1736 in the Military College, a man called Stepanov faced interrogation. Stepanov testified that, in 1722, while serving as a junior clerk in the Kostroma provincial office, he was sent to the Moscow Treasury Office with a coffer containing 7,000 rubles. In the Moscow Treasury Office, local clerks did not take the money but directed him to an equipment office (*mundirnaia kantora*) where only part of the load was accepted—3,000 rubles. At the equipment office Stepanov received an additional 11,000 rubles, so the total sum that he was to deliver to the St Petersburg commissariat amounted to 15,000 rubles. Escorted by the ensign

---

21 See, for example: E. V. Anisimov, *Podatnaia reforma Petra I* (Leningrad: Nauka, 1982), p. 267; Arcadius Kahan, *The Plow, the Hammer and the Knout: An Economic History of Eighteenth-Century Russia* (Chicago: University of Chicago Press, 1985), p. 321; N. N. Petrukhintsev, 'Tsarstvovanie Anny Ioannovny: problemy formirovaniia vnutripoliticheskogo kursa (1730–1740)' (Dokt. dissertation, Moskovskii gosudarstvennyi universitet, 2001); Igor I. Fediukin, Elena S. Korchmina, 'Sobiraemost' podushnoi podati v seredine 18 veka: k voprosu ob effektivnosti gosudarstvennogo apparata v Rossii v istoricheskoi perspektive', *Ekonomicheskaia istoriia. Ezhegodnik 2013*, ed. by L. I. Borodkin, Iu. Petrov (Moscow: Rossiiskaia politicheskaia entsiklopediia, 2014), pp. 89–127.

22 For another example that uses the Urals as a case study for assessing the effectiveness of the local administration by analysing the tax burden, see Mikhail Kiselev, 'State Metallurgy Factories and Direct Taxes in the Urals, 1700–50: Paths to State Building in Early Modern Russia', *Kritika: Explorations in Russian and Eurasian History*, 16. 1 (Winter 2015), 7–36.

Kalashnikov, he set out for the Russian capital. In the commissariat, an expense-recorder, Akim Poletaev, received the money, but Stepanov did not get a delivery receipt because he had fallen ill. After recovering, he could not return to his service in the Kostroma office due to the absence of the receipt and his reasonable fear of possible imprisonment. Until all the circumstances were elucidated, Stepanov was taken into custody.[23] After a scrupulous investigation it was revealed that the revenue register kept by Poletaev did not contain a record of the 11,000 rubles received from Stepanov, but it did have a record dated February 1722 that Kalashnikov together with six enumerators (including Stepanov) delivered 128,000 rubles from the Moscow equipment office. Based on that evidence it was decided to let Stepanov return to the Kostroma provincial office.

This episode demonstrates that the reasons for financial "losses" could have been logistical problems and a crude system of accounting. Thus, on the one hand, the financial transactions were posted in ledgers thoroughly enough to enable outside users to reconstruct the cash flows in detail twelve years later; but, on the other hand, ordinary life incidents such as illness made it impossible to keep records correctly. In this situation, since a written confirmation (receipt) was never issued, and the province from which the payments had come was not posted in the ledger, 4,000 rubles were actually calculated as a shortfall from the Kostroma provincial office, despite the sum in question having been collected in Kostroma, sent, and delivered to its destination.

Officials as "*Schreibmaschine*"?[24]

A study of provincial clerical reports reveals a phrase which reoccurs in most of them stating that the poll tax was being collected and sent to the proper destinations on time—in accordance with instructions—but that the locals were not able to make and submit financial reports at

---

23 RGADA, coll. 248, descr. 7, file 412, fol. 757–757v.
24 I use this term metaphorically; for more on this metaphor, see Peter Becker, '"Kaiser Josephs Schreibmaschine": Ansätze zur Rationalisierung der Verwaltung im aufgeklärten Absolutismus', *Jahrbuch für europäische Verwaltungsgeschichte*, 12 (2000), 223–54.

the same time owing to the lack of clerks.²⁵ "According to the report of the Zaraisk provincial office the accounts about poll tax and the two-kopeck levy are being composed, but we cannot finish them on time and send them to their destinations because we do not have enough staff; at the moment there is only one scribe (*podkantseliarist*)".²⁶ Our ability to evaluate the truth of the proferred excuse requires knowledge of the volume of the turnover of financial documents in a provincial clerical office. They may be divided into two types: internal documentation of the office and external reporting.

Documentary Turnover in a Provincial Clerical Office

At the level of provincial offices, a significant number of financial documents must have been issued and kept. Moreover, from the imposition of the poll tax until 1736 (when an institute of poll tax collection officers and a unification of the reports on tax acquisition and distribution was implemented) the territory of a region might have been divided into several districts, and each district would have issued its own set of financial papers.

For instance, in January 1731 a governor, Dmitrii Mikhailovich Novokshchenov, delivered files from the Vladimir office to Captain Terentii Bogdanovich Mozovskii of the Estliandskii regiment.²⁷ The set of files included: a leather-bound alphabetical register sealed by Colonel Korobov; list registers sealed by Major General Chernyshov and Colonel Korobov; printed bills; the colonel's and the commissar's instructions; tables and sample accounting books; poll tax receipts issued in previous years sealed by a commissar; three capitation fee revenue registries from the current year sealed by the governor; one capitation fee expenditure registry also sealed by Novokshchenov; printed and written edicts received from senior authorities; orders and memos; inventories and notebooks; and finally, drawings and dispatches of the location of the headquarters by commissar Petr Mitkov.

---

25   M. Bogoslovskii, *Oblastnaia reforma Petra Velikago. Provintsiia 1719–27 gg* (Moscow: Universitetskaia tipografiia, 1902), p. 273.
26   RGADA, coll. 438, descr. 1, file 24, fol. 34.
27   RGADA, coll. 423, descr. 2, file 136, fol. 10–11.

A similar set of documentation was passed to an infantry captain of the Narvskii regiment,[28] Ivan Ivanovich Drozdov, in a district clerical office of Vladimir province. In addition it contained the following books: a register of forty-kopek fee revenues as of the current year (1731); and a register of forty-kopek fee distribution.

Starting from 1736, the list of books and registries it was compulsory to keep in a provincial office was standardised, as was the process of their completion. But the problems with record-keeping did not cease. Annually in the provincial offices on average seven ledgers were kept in which transactions were regularly posted, as we see in a typical situation drawn from the Oboian regional office in Belgorod province in 1753: there were seven accounting books kept on a permanent basis, and four of them as a rule lay on a clerk's desk.[29]

Ledger completion was allegedly not a problem in itself, but storing and finding archived files caused much inconvenience, as we see in the following episode which deals with the search for the proper poll tax office allocation in Moscow in 1754.[30] Due to the absence of a spare room in the Metal Mining and Manufacturing College, the poll tax collection was arranged in the basement of a provincial office where there was only one window and very little space, and which was stuffed with chests and boxes (in total amounting to thirty), placed on top of one another up to the ceiling, containing poll tax accounting audit books and expenditure receipts. The civil servants were supplied with only one desk because there was no room for another, and they worked with candles lit even in the summer, as the sunlight did not reach their basement office. It is no surprise that under those circumstances it was difficult for them to identify counterfeit coins. Another concern dealt with the storage of the collected money. On any given day up to a hundred sacks and barrels full of coins might have been delivered from different provinces simultaneously, so it was obviously difficult to find places to store this money and to find room for its conveyors. This last group might have amounted to more than fifty people who would have arrived at the same time. Officials frequently worried that

---

28   RGADA, coll. 423, descr. 2, file 136, fol. 12–13v.
29   RGADA, coll. 304, descr. 1, file 374, fol. 13v.
30   RGADA, coll. 248, bk. 2887, fol. 158–59.

documents might rot or be eaten by mice.[31] In such conditions, the main complexity was not in preparing financial documents, which demanded only the basic skills of reading, writing and counting, but in archiving and accessing the stored documentation.

Originally it was planned that all the basic documentation would be audited in the central state offices and, on this basis, central government clerks would make final financial reports. That scheme, however, did not last for long. Its implementation began with Peter the Great's Law (*Plakat*), which introduced a new rule of sending accounting books signed by staff- (*shtab*) and chief- (*ober*) officers directly to the Auditing Office for an annual audit and inspection. But soon, in 1728, it was reported to the Senate that the local financial document audit had failed. The reason, which transformed a well-intended idea into a fiasco, was banal: the audit could not be completed due to a lack of staff.[32] According to new rules introduced in 1728 the people who had to gather the tax money under the supervision of governors were *zemskii* commissars. They were to pass the collected imposts to governors who in turn sent revenues to the heads of the provincial authorities. The latter spread the poll tax that had been collected among staff officers to be delivered to the proper destinations as appointed in the Military College's edicts. The new rules also prescribed that regimental books and invoices should be inspected and audited in a commissariat first, and only afterwards sent to the Auditing Office where the reports totaling the figures for all Russian regions were prepared. But the very next year (1729) disclosed the weakness of the new arrangements: there were complaints sent to the Military College from a commissariat notifying them that the commissariat's staff was not sufficient for the audit of invoices, that they lacked the human resources to fulfill that task, and that at the same time the Auditing Office was reluctant to help, not wishing to take over someone else's duties. Obviously the point at issue was not the basic accounting books audit, but the precise invoices (annual and half-yearly). From that period onwards the completion of financial reports gradually developed into the main occupation of provincial clerical offices. Local clerks were to keep records of the basic documentation and compose reports.

---

31 *Ibid.*
32 RGADA, coll. 248, file 393, fol. 466–67.

Provincial Clerical Offices' Reports

A significant number of reports were supposed to be compiled at local clerical offices. Lists of poll tax shortfalls were prepared for annual, half-yearly, monthly or fortnightly periods. The most frequently encountered are the ones for annual, half-yearly and monthly intervals. By 1736 the format and the structure of compulsory financial statements had been established and passed down to the local offices, where provincial executives were in charge of filling in the necessary forms and sending them back to the higher authorities. The lists were arranged as handwritten tables presenting the information about the yearly arrears of poll tax payments of three types—seventy-kopek fees, forty-altyn fees, and forty-kopek fees—since the latest audit, i.e. within the five- to ten-year period before the current one. In practice the data on shortfalls referring to the same year, i.e. 1736, and the same territory, would differ in several lists, not only for the current year (1736), but for all the previous years as well. This difference occurred due to the fact that tax debts for any previous period might have been disbursed in the current year without adjustments being made; it took too much of a clerk's time to check all the documents dated later than the last audit each time a debt was paid out.

The process of report preparation was neither easy nor flawless. The first problem was the shortcomings of basic financial documentation. Originally, the tables in the documents did not have totals. Thus, I suggest that every time a reference to a document was needed its sums were recalculated. Moreover, instructions about the reports' format and content changed from time to time, so, in accordance with altering requirements, cumbersome tax books, registers and other documents had to be audited, recalculated, and their structure renovated. The government demanded scrupulous accounting of tax payment receipts and shortfall; the high level of detail required obviously slowed the whole system of reporting considerably. Simon Dixon notes that Ivan Pososhkov was critical of "unnecessarily complex accounts" as early as 1724 in his *Book of Poverty and Wealth*, one of the first Russian economics texts.[33]

---

[33] Simon Dixon, *The Modernisation of Russia, 1676–1825* (Cambridge: Cambridge University press, 1999), p. 67.

The second problem impacting the composition of the reports stemmed from the peculiarities of provincial state servants' modes of thinking. Though difficult to prove, it should nevertheless be considered. At first glance the task of filling in a form seems simple, In practice, reports which were sent to the central authorities were composed with a free hand and their comprehensive analysis reveals a wide variety of ways in which the data in report tables were presented. Governmental offices sent many complaints and directives to follow the standards for report structures, but all in vain.

In fact a note from the Military College to the Senate in 1738 stated that: "[…] accounts from the counting board (*shchetnaia kantora*) do not accord with the regulations of the Auditing Office; as a result there will be only pointless obstacles and correspondence, but we cannot audit the accounts […]".[34]

Officials of the central authorities, as well as some historians, regarded such behaviour by provincial clerks as sabotage. In 1768 Privy Counsellor Ivan Ivanovich Iushkov, governor of the Moscow province, received this dispatch from a Commissariat Head Office: "The Moscow provincial office did not do their best to compose and send accounts, and spent the whole time in useless writing".[35]

It was probably an excruciatingly difficult task for bureaucrats to compile the data on the various impost payments for different segments of the population. According to the first audit, the number of population groups amounted to forty, as stated in a list dated 1737 and adjusted to the tables' columns, but this was not observed everywhere. On the one hand, in the central part of the Russian Empire, where the process of the main social groups' (landlords, state and court peasants and merchants) self-identification had been almost completed, the task of arranging the information on shortfalls in correlation with each group's indebtedness did not cause much difficulty. On the other hand, in the outlying regions of the empire, that process had only just begun, so the task of over-detailed data presentation led to the incorrect allocation of figures in reports. It is no wonder that all the lists dated in the second and third quarters of the eighteenth century contained very long and elaborate

---

34 Rossiiskii gosudarstvennyi voenno-istoricheskii arkhiv, coll. 21, d. 12, sv. 14, d. 1, fol. 28–29v.
35 RGADA, coll. 400, descr. 11. file 295, fol. 100.

comments which interpreted and often altered the meaning of the data shown in the tables. The "local material" resisted easy adaptation and insertion into tables whose patterns had been worked out for central state bodies' usage. There remains, however, the unresolved issue of interpreting the local clerks' chosen method of allocating figures in lists. The government's position on that question was clear: information was to be presented in a precise and very detailed manner. Such an approach paradoxically contributed to the fact that provincial reports' tables were actually prepared arbitrarily.

The first two problems—the shortcomings of basic financial documentation and the peculiarities of provincial state servants' modes of thinking—could be summarised as follows: provincial officials genuinely wanted to fulfill their tasks, but were simply prevented from doing so. A third possible problem is, like the previous one, difficult to prove, but should not be disregarded: provincial officials may not have wanted to obey the wasteful requirements of the authorities.[36] The local clerks collected and distributed money in a proper manner, so their task was fulfilled completely, but they could have considered the government's desire to have scrupulous reports as just a whim. This was not sabotage in its direct meaning, but their knowledge of financial flows gave them a (false) sense of authority.

The three problems I have delineated reflect the statement that the bureaucratic processes were stalled "for want of people".[37] However, the reason for poor information acquisition by the state's central authorities was not only a lack of clerks, but also the fact that regional office workers were underqualified and could not satisfy the state's desire for updated, relevant financial data. Unfortunately for locals, a severe punishment was introduced in order to extract the necessary information from provincial offices: clerks were chained to their working places until the reports were completed.[38]

A further obstacle that inhibited the flow of information to the government was the delay in the delivery of reports. Summaries of tax collections regularly include marginal notes indicating which provinces had not yet submitted their reports. For instance, the Military College

---

36   I would like to thank Andrei Zorin for this suggestion.
37   RGADA, coll. 248, descr. 7. file 393, fol. 81.
38   See e.g. Petrukhintsev, 'Tsarstvovanie Anny Ioannovny', p. 461.

sent a dispatch to the Senate stating that within the last few years—1735, 1736 and 1737—they had sent many directives requiring information about the number of delivery workers (*rassyl'shchiki*). The required reports had not been delivered from the following areas, however: the Sviazhsk province of the Kazan region, Penza province, Viatka province, various towns of the Voronezh region, Eletsk, Tambov, Solikamsk, and Bakhmut provinces.[39] In fact the central official bodies' demands for timely fulfillment and delivery of local reports were numerous: "the first ones—on 2 December, 1735; the second—on 10 February, 1736; the third—on 24 February, 1736; the fourth—on 15 March, 1736; the fifth—on 20 April, 1736; the sixth—on 4 May, 1736; the seventh—on 13 May, 1736; the eighth—9 June, 1736; the ninth—on 14 September, 1736; the tenth—on 15 October, 1736; the eleventh—on 31 November, 1736; the twelfth—on 21 December, 1736; the thirteenth—on 11 January, 1736 [*sic*]".[40]

Consequently, the clerks of the central offices faced two contradictory problems: they were burdened with piles of local reports that had been filled in improperly, which were difficult to summarise and incorporate into cumulative lists, and simultaneously those office workers did not receive any registers at all from many regions. As Dixon observes, "[…] growing sophistication in bookkeeping methods was more often a barrier than an aid to understanding".[41]

The Constant Deficiency of Information in the Russian Government

Clearly the governmental bodies in the capital received irregular and hardly comparable information on the state's finances.[42] Thus, the government had to make decisions under the oppressive conditions of a constant lack of operable updated information, as described in the following episode.

Direct government regulation of poll tax collection had not been properly implemented across almost all of the Russian Empire until a

---

39 RGADA, coll. 248, descr. 7, file 387, fol. 522–23.
40 See, for example, RGADA, coll. 248, descr. 7, file 387, fol. 454.
41 Dixon, *The Modernisation of Russia, 1676–1825*, p. 67.
42 RGADA, coll. 248, descr. 7, file 387, fol. 1604.

new law was promulgated which reformed the whole system of poll tax fee gathering. On 16 February 1731, a new order was put into effect that prohibited enumerators who were soldiers from collecting the poll tax; thenceforth town scribes (*pod'iachie*) were in charge of it.[43] The story behind the appearance of such a directive was prosaic.[44] According to the *Plakat*, taxpayers were to give the fees to specially assigned soldiers, enumerators, who took the money under their own responsibility and packed it into sacks; the sealed sacks were then put into barrels and a colonel in charge fixed seals to the latter. Apparently the barrels were to be opened only in the presence of the enumerator, who held full responsibility for tax payments he had accepted. The performance and results of this scheme became evident within a few years and were described in a dispatch from the Military College to the Senate in October 1730 as follows: "[…] the work of the enumerators (*shchetchiki*) included a number of shortcomings so enumerators were condemned to the galleys […]".[45] In the meantime, while engaged in solving the problem mentioned above, state authorities bore in mind the edict of 1714, which stated that merchants were prohibited from engaging in the collection of imposts and levies, and that, instead, clerks were obliged to carry out that function. Finally, in February 1731, a new edict was published introducing a revised procedure for the gathering of tax fees, according to which provincial clerical offices had to begin conveying four representatives of their office staff to the appointed regiments for the purpose of counting the poll tax revenues. The directive was aimed at resolving the issue of the military forces' financing, and in general it was rational, but from the very beginning its implementation was impossible for basic logistical reasons. Moreover, the government had already been informed about the impossibility of the new order, but either neglected that data or did not realise its existence.

At almost the same moment that the new edict was announced to provincial offices, people began sending dispatches directly to the Senate explaining why it was impossible to follow the new instructions. A report dated 16 March from Vologda provincial office, as well as the next one dated 21 July, stated that, according to the February edict,

---

43 *PSZ* 1, no. 5697.
44 I wish to thank Maia Lavrinovich for noting this law.
45 RGADA, coll. 248, descr. 7, file 390, fol. 330.

their office was to send fourteen people to the regiments, but the whole office staff amounted to only twenty-seven clerks among whom "[...] clerk Iakov Sumorokov was a decrepit old man [...] Osip Mikhailov was severely ill so he often lost consciousness [...] *zemskii* scribe (*pisar'*) Ivan Goriachichnikov was not counted yet [...] junior office clerks (*podkantseliaristy*) Vasilii Savin, Vasilii Fedorov, Aleksei Galaktionov had been set fines [...] Stepan Stepanov was a decrepit old man, Ivan Sumorokov was in decline and deaf [...] young copyists could not be trusted because of their youth".[46] The governor's conclusion clearly stated that fulfillment of that edict would have led to all operations in the provincial office ceasing. Consequently, the edict's requirements had been left unfulfilled. The same happened in other provinces (Novgorod,[47] Archangelsk,[48] Simbirsk,[49] etc.) because the same situation existed in those clerical offices. In the Tver office, after sending a *zemskii* scribe, a *podiachii*, and two young clerks to the Koposr regiment, there remained only ten clerks, and among them three were drunkards.[50]

It is important to specify that dispatches reporting on an inability to perform as the directive demanded were sent repeatedly (for instance, from the Belozersk province on 20 May[51] and on 16 July[52]). In the Pereslavl Zalesskii local office's report it was stressed that they had already sent reports that they did not have enough clerks: twice to the Board of Revenue (*Kamer Kollegiia*) and three times to the Moscow provincial office.[53]

Obviously in the Russian Empire's provinces a controversial situation had been growing into a serious conflict. On the one hand, the local clerical offices proclaimed the edict's implementation to be beyond their capacities, but on the other hand, the regiments' headquarters, where the clerks who arrived were supposed to count the collected tax fees, found themselves in bizarre circumstances: while there were significant sums of taxes collected at the regiments' disposal, there were

---

46 RGADA, coll. 248, descr. 7, file 391, fol. 209–12, fol. 239–40.
47 RGADA, coll. 248, descr. 7, file 391, fol. 214–15.
48 RGADA, coll. 248, descr. 7, file 391, fol. 216–17.
49 RGADA, coll. 248, descr. 7, file 391, fol. 228–228v.
50 RGADA, coll. 248, descr. 7, file 391, fol. 213–213v.
51 RGADA, coll. 248, descr. 7, file 391, fol. 218–20.
52 RGADA, coll. 248, descr. 7, file 391, fol. 233.
53 RGADA, coll. 248, descr. 7, file 391, fol. 225–225v.

no enumerators to calculate and pack them. So the troops' authorities in their turn commenced reporting to the centre. Thus, the Iamburg Dragoon regiment's dispatch contained descriptions of the following misfortune: despite their repeated urgent demands that the Tambov and Voronezh provincial offices should send clerks to their headquarters, none had arrived, and, as a result, there were great arrears in the poll tax.[54] A similar situation occurred in the Nizhegorodskii regiment where an enumerator did not have time to take money from taxpayers.[55] As for the Russian government, it supported the regiments.[56] In fact the implementation of the edict would have inflicted either a breakdown in the local offices' routine activities or a compelled stoppage of the receipt of tax imposts in the regiments' headquarters. It is therefore no surprise that the nominal shortfall was posted simply because of the lack of clerical workers to count and register tax payments. The weak system was reformed within a couple of years and an institution of poll tax officers was introduced. Apparently this solution was successful, as clerical workers were moved from central state bodies out to provincial regiments' locations and regional clerical offices, instead of the local clerks shifting from local offices to central ones.

In sum, for most of this period, the main task of provincial clerks, to ensure that information flowed to the government by means of reports, statements, and other basic documentation, was not performed satisfactorily, either due to a lack of local staff or for deeper reasons. I want to stress that the local staff may have been the only people who were aware of the state of financial affairs at the provincial level.

What Could the "Higher Spheres" Really Know?

The short answer to this complicated question is "almost nothing". The difficulties mentioned above greatly impeded the government's ability to manage its finances — unless, of course, we agree with Dixon's statement that "the Russian old regime's problem was not that it governed harshly but that it scarcely governed at all".[57] The Russian

---

54 RGADA, coll. 248, descr. 7, file 391, fol. 229–229v.
55 RGADA, coll. 248, descr. 7, file 391, fol. 242–242v.
56 RGADA, coll. 248, descr. 7, file 391, fol. 244v.
57 Dixon, *The Modernisation of Russia*, p. 139.

government wanted to rule and it desperately needed information to do so.

The rank-and-file officials of central offices were very well aware that they did not have enough information and that they could not obtain it. Nikolai Chechulin notes, "From the very beginning there were many cases when the Board of Revenue thought that there should have been much more money than the Board of Expenditure, and neither Senate nor Supreme Privy Council could bring them into accord".[58]

The budgeting was almost blocked. There were too many reports. In the 1760s the Board of Expenditure complained that every year it received about 20,000 different reports, and most of the reports had been unsupervised for decades. It was impossible to match accounts from different provinces, because other central and provincial offices did not put their primary reports into a total account as they ought to have done according to the law; instead they sent the basic documentation to the main state financial offices.[59]

Top bureaucrats of the central government did not know the state of the empire's finances, so it is not surprising that the monarch also did not know how much money she had. Catherine II wrote that, after her accession to the throne, the Senate gave her a general account of empire revenues. Their total number reached 16 million rubles. After two years, she put Prince Aleksandr Viazemskii and Aleksei Melgunov, the president of the Board of Revenues, in charge of recalculating the revenues. It took them several years and they had to write to each provincial governor at least seven times. Finally they found an additional 28 million rubles,[60] but it remains unclear whether they discovered all the revenues.

Contemporary scholars knew very well that no available statistics could demonstrably be proved to be true. In the 1820s a famous statistician, Karl German, told the students of Petersburg University that "the government does not know even the most basic items. I do not know exactly even the number of cities in Russia. Nowhere is there

---

58 N. D. Chechulin, *Ocherki po istorii russkikh finansov v tsarstvovanie Ekateriny II* (St Petersburg: Senatskaia tipografiia 1906), p. 23.
59 Chechulin, *Ocherki po istorii russkikh finansov*, pp. 39, 38.
60 A. N. Kulomzin, 'Finansovye documenty tsarstvovaniia Imperatritsy Ekateriny II', *Sbornik Rossiiskogo Imperatorskogo Obshchestva*, vol. 28 (St Petersburg: tip. V. Bezobrazova i Komp., 1880), p. 22.

indicated a reliable number [...] The official statistical data, published by the Government, leave a great deal to be desired".⁶¹

Modern historians are unanimous in their opinion that the condition of Russian finances in the eighteenth century was a puzzle. Le Donne writes, "The state of auditing in the 1760s was such that one may safely assume that it had become a forgotten science".⁶² Janet Hartley observes, "The poor methods of accounting, the lack of a central treasury, the complexities of expenditure on the armed forces (divided into ordinary and extraordinary expenditure) meant that it is almost impossible to make sense of Russian financial records".⁶³ Peter Waldron states, "The Russian state did not have the bureaucratic capacity to maintain accurate records of its finances during this period and the budget-making process was still rudimentary".⁶⁴ As a result, as Dixon argues, "economic policy long relied more heavily on *a priori* social assumptions than on economic data, despite a dawning recognition that carefully digested information was a prerequisite of successful policy-making".⁶⁵

Finally, I would like to introduce a further suggestion, the proof and evidence for which is beyond the scope of the present chapter, but which is closely linked with its content. As I mentioned earlier, provincial clerks' activities can be divided into two levels: material (tax payment collection and distribution to the consumers) and informational (keeping records and preparing reports). In the present chapter, I have demonstrated that Russian local clerkdom succeeded at the first level, as poll tax collection resulted in high revenues; at the same time they failed to perform well at the second level—making and submitting the required reports in time. In dispatches and other reports the clerks divided their daily duties as I explained, and thus we may surmise that the office workers regarded these activities as different ones. Moreover, they treated tax collection as a more important obligation than composing reports. The government's attitude, however, differed from that of its subordinates. Seemingly the role of information collection was more important because the state

---

61 Mironov, '*Rossiiskaia imperiia: ot traditsii k modernu*', vol. 2, p. 437.
62 Le Donne, *Absolutism and Ruling Class*, p. 243.
63 Janet Hartley, *Russia, 1762-1825: Military Power, the State and the People* (Westport: Praeger, 2008), p. 69.
64 Peter Waldron, 'State Finances', in *The Cambridge History of Russia*, vol. 2 (Cambridge: Cambridge University Press, 2008), p. 484.
65 Dixon, *The Modernisation of Russia, 1676–1825*, p. 227.

budget was decentralised and the entire volume of gathered taxes was never accumulated in the centre, but instead was distributed from provinces directly to its appointed destinations. For the government, trustworthy and updated reports were therefore as valuable as the sums of the imposts collected.[66] The urge for organised and accurate financial information even led, as I mentioned earlier, to the legalisation of such cruel punishments as chaining a clerk to his desk until the work was completed.

To conclude, the Russian government lived in a chaos of paperwork, and the fact that it did not go bankrupt as a civil body in the eighteenth century was probably due to the decentralisation of the relationship between the capital and the provinces, which co-existed, to a certain extent, in parallel worlds. Now, we, as historians who have access to archives and, more importantly, to modern technologies, can calculate the level of tax collection in eighteenth-century Russia, but clerks from that period could not, because of internal problems of information flow. The task set them by the Russian government was beyond their means. The question remains: does this imply that Russian clerks were not effective?

---

66 It was even more noticeable at the end the eighteenth century and in the nineteenth century. See Galina Orlova, 'Biurokraticheskaia real'nost'', *Obshchestvennye nauki i sovremennost'*, 6 (1999), 96–106.

10. Communication and Official Enlightenment: The *Journal of the Ministry of Public Education*, 1834–1855

Ekaterina Basargina[1]

Government bureaucracies are institutional mechanisms of communication. They exist in part in order to gather, process, store and (perhaps less willingly) disseminate information. Some of the information that they gather consists of the hard administrative data required for core functions such as taxation or conscription. Some of the information that they disseminate consists of governmental pronouncements, laws, or decrees. However, some modes of communication can be less direct, more oblique. The Ministry of Public Education and its journal provide a case study in such institutional communication in the interests of the cultural policies of the state.

Russia's nineteenth century began with a palace coup. On the night of 11 March 1801, a group of conspirators brutally murdered the "mad tsar Paul".[2] The next morning, St Petersburg was overcome with riotous exaltation: people wept and embraced one another at home and in the street. The future was unclear, but for the moment the end to the terror

---

[1] This research was conducted with the support of the Russian Science Foundation (grant no. 14–18–00010 'The Interaction of Science and Power: Sketches of Institutional History of the Imperial Academy of Science, from the Eighteenth to the Early Twentieth Centuries'). The chapter was translated by Thomas Rowley.

[2] D. Davydov, *Sochineniia* (Moscow: Gosudarstvennoe izdatel'stvo khudozhestvennoi literatury, 1962), p. 471.

and stress of Paul's reign seemed an occasion for relief and celebration as the twenty-three-year-old Alexander I ascended the throne.[3] Liberally educated and an enthusiastic follower of French Enlightenment thought, Russia's young tsar quickly announced the new era of his rule with a series of decrees and manifestos. Among his first actions was an amnesty for those who had suffered exile and imprisonment without trial under Paul. The Secret Expedition, which carried out interrogations under torture, was destroyed. Thus Alexander I aimed to prove that he would not continue the harsh and unpredictable rule of his father. The new tsar made a grandiose promise to rule his people "according to the laws and the heart" of his grandmother Catherine the Great, declaring that he would "follow her most wise intentions".[4]

The new tsar's initial moves gave Russian society hope for future change. People expected a new form of governance, one that would replace arbitrary rule and violence with the rule of law and justice. Alexander's initial measures seemed to justify such expectations. The intense activity in the first part of his reign left a deep impression on many of his contemporaries. Aleksandr Pushkin would later call this period "the wondrous beginning of Alexander's days" (*Dnei Aleksandrovykh prekrasnoe nachalo*) in his "Epistle to the Censor" (1822).

Russia's new tsar was enthused by plans to reform the country from top to bottom and completely reorganise the state structure. He intended to put in place a series of measures that would eventually lead to the abolition of serfdom, and he dreamt of crowning his work with a new constitution modelled on the best examples of the period in Western Europe. However, before Russia could receive a constitution, Alexander had to educate and prepare the population for the coming reforms. Crucially, the tsar had to prepare those able to make his plans a reality—Russia's public officials. Thus, education was made the highest priority in this programme of wide-ranging transformations in order to guarantee Russia's successful Europeanisation; it was seen as the quickest means of distributing European ideals and values.

---

[3] See Allen McConnell, *Tsar Alexander I: Paternalistic Reformer* (New York: Crowell, 1970); Marie-Pierre Rey, *Alexander I: The Tsar Who Defeated Napoleon* (DeKalb: Northern Illinois University Press, 2012).

[4] *Polnoe sobranie zakonov Rossiiskoi imperii*, Series 1 (1649–1825) (hereafter *PSZ* 1), no. 19779.

Initially, Alexander put Catherine-era officials in charge of the government. He dismissed Count Petr Pahlen, who had led the conspiracy against Paul and who now aimed to guide the young tsar. However, Alexander managed quietly but firmly to avoid being thus guided, and selected advisers who shared his own outlook. He came to rely on a small circle of personal friends, his Private Committee, which had formed while he was still a prince. This group—which included Prince Adam Jerzy Czartoryski and Counts Viktor Kochubei, Nikolai Novosiltsev and Pavel Stroganov—had no official powers, but made decisions on all matters of state. Liberal to a man, this group dreamt of large-scale reforms to the operations of the Russian state, and the Private Committee was behind the highly important projects carried out during the first years of Alexander's reign. The tsar's "young friends" gathered privately in the imperial palace, discussing state business informally in lively and friendly conversation. The group's motto was "to stand above any personal interest and accept neither preferment, nor reward".[5] The tsar sometimes jokingly referred to this circle as the *Comité du salut public* (Committee of Public Health).

The Private Committee's most important works consisted of transforming Russia's central state institutions. The first project was to change the collegiate system of governance, which dated back to Peter I, into a ministerial one that would preside over all the state's administrative work, an important step in centralising Russia's governance.[6] On 8 September 1802, Alexander signed a decree "On the Institution of Ministries" to form eight ministries with remit over the army, navy, foreign affairs, judiciary, internal affairs, finance, commerce and public education, respectively.[7] A Committee of Ministers was also established to facilitate the joint discussion of state affairs; the tsar himself often attended this committee's meetings.

Russia's new system of rule placed the principle of personal authority and responsibility at its core. Each minister alone was responsible for all the actions of his ministry. Each minister had a deputy and chancery,

---

5 Adam Chartorizhskii, *Memuary* (Moscow: Terra, 1998), p. 184.
6 See N. P. Eroshkin, *Istoriia gosudarstvennykh uchrezhdenii dorevoliutsionnoi Rossii* (Moscow: Vysshaia shkola, 1968); *Vysshie i tsentral'nye gosudarstvennye uchrezhdeniia Rossii, 1801–1917*, 4 vols (St Petersburg: Nauka, 1998–2004), vol. 3; M. A. Prikhod'ko, *Podgotovka i razrabotka ministerskoi reform v Rossii* (Moscow: Sputnik, 2002).
7 *PSZ* 1, no. 20406.

and the ministries were subdivided into departments, which were headed by directors; departments were divided again into sections with section chiefs; and sections were divided into desks with individuals in charge of each desk. Ministers answered to the monarch and the Senate.

The establishment of a Ministry of Public Education was part of this grandiose reform of Russia's executive.[8] For the first time, the administration of Russia's public education was concentrated in a single independent ministry, which aimed at "the education of youth and the dissemination of learning". The new ministry was formed not only to bring order to the administrative sphere and establish a single system of education: it aimed to create an intellectual elite and a spiritual leadership within society.

In order to position this new education policy as a successor to Catherine's reforms, Alexander made Count Petr Zavadovskii (1739–1812) his first minister of public education, who had "once been famed for both his beauty and his intellect, and Catherine appreciated him not only for the latter".[9] The tsar's "young friends" were not particularly sympathetic to Zavadovskii, whom they regarded as intellectually crude. They derided him for what they claimed was "his inflexibility in both mind and body".[10] Nevertheless, they appreciated his kindness and his fair-mindedness. Alexander foresaw that "Catherine's old man" would not always be open to following progressive ideas.

The Ministry of Public Education, in contrast to other ministries, kept its collegiate features due to its inclusion of the Commission on Educational Institutions (from 1803, the Chief Directorate of Educational Institutions). Alexander counterbalanced the elderly Zavadovskii's indifference with the energy of his assistants. The members of the Chief Directorate of Educational Institutions were educated public officials: the trustees of Russia's education boards, members of the Academy of Sciences, or members of the church hierarchy. The Commission on Educational Institutions took up the task of developing a model for

---

8   S. V. Rozhdestvenskii, *Istoricheskii obzor deiatel'nosti Ministerstva narodnogo prosveshcheniia, 1802–1902* (St Petersburg: Ministerstvo narodnogo prosveshcheniia, 1902).
9   F. F. Vigel', *Zapiski* (Moscow: Zakharov, 2000), vol. 2, p. 108.
10 Chartorizhskii, *Memuary*, p. 230.

educational reform. Its main aim was to establish new universities that would form the core of a system to administer education in Russia.

In the course of this reform, Russia was divided into six regional education boards (Moscow, St Petersburg, Kazan, Kharkov, Vilnius and Dorpat (Tartu)), each of which had directors permanently based in Petersburg. The reform introduced a single system of education that encompassed primary school through to university. Thus, all the different stages of public school fitted together in a vertical system: each course of study provided complete training to a certain level and, at the same time, served as a preparatory stage for the next, higher level. The universities comprised the final link of the chain in the whole system and, beyond their traditional teaching and research functions ("the teaching of sciences to the highest degree"[11]), they also served as administrative centres for the regional education boards. All the education establishments of a given region—parish, district, and province-level gymnasiums—were subordinate to a university. This period saw the establishment of universities in Kazan (1805) and Kharkov (1805), and the reform of the universities in Dorpat (1802) and Vilnius (1803). In 1804, the universities in Dorpat and Vilnius received a charter granting them broad autonomy and freedom in teaching.

The general plan for education reform and its main principles were laid out in the "Preliminary Rules of Public Education", which became law on 24 January 1803.[12] Paragraph 41 of these rules read: "Under the authority of the Chief Directorate of Educational Institutions, a periodical publication will be issued so as to disseminate information about the successes of public education".[13] The *Journal of the Ministry of Public Education* was Russia's earliest ministerial periodical.[14] It was

---

11 'Ob ustroistve uchilishch', *PSZ* 1, no. 20597, p. 438.
12 'Ob ustroistve uchilishch', *PSZ* 1, no. 20597.
13 Ibid., p. 441.
14 Other ministries also established periodicals. For instance, during the period 1804–09, the Ministry of Internal Affairs published the *St Petersburg Journal* (*Sanktpeterburgskii zhurnal*), and, from 1829, *The Journal of the Ministry of Internal Affairs* (*Zhurnal ministerstva vnutrennikh del*). The Ministry of Transport published its own journal, initially under the title *The Journal of the Ministry of Transport* (*Zhurnal putei soobshcheniia*), which was then titled *The Journal of the Central Administration of Transport and Public Buildings* (*Zhurnal glavnogo upravleniia putei soobshcheniia i publichnykh zdanii*) from 1845, and later *The Journal of the Ministry of Transport* (*Zhurnal Ministerstva putei soobshcheniia*). See *Russkaia periodicheskaia pechat'* (1702–1894) (Moscow: Politicheskaia literatura, 1959).

issued under various titles: in 1803–17 it was called simply the *Periodic Publication of the Successes of Public Education*. The journal's first editor was the academician Nikolai Ozeretskovskii (1750–1827), who was a member of the Chief Directorate of Educational Institutions.[15]

Ozeretskovskii was a prominent figure in the reform of Russia's public education, and possessed an influential voice in the Chief Directorate of Educational Institutions. He was involved in creating charters for universities, gymnasiums, district and parish schools, as well as the draft of a censorship charter. Ozeretskovskii believed in judicious freedom of the press. "Restrictions on the press", Ozeretskovskii observed, "are hard to keep within their proper boundaries. When taken to excess they are frequently ineffectual and always harmful. It is unquestionable that excessive severity in such matters almost invariably has damaging consequences. It obliterates sincerity, weakens the intellect and, extinguishing the holy flame of love for truth, inhibits the spread of enlightenment".[16] In ambiguous cases where various interpretations might be possible, the censor should interpret the author's ideas and intentions "in the way most favourable to the author"; the censorship committee was instructed to respect works that included "modest and well-meaning pursuit of any truth".[17] The 1804 Charter on Censorship was Russia's most liberal such charter throughout the nineteenth century.

Ozeretskovskii carried the principles of academic freedom into the Ministry of Public Education. He edited the *Periodic Publication* from its inception in 1803 to its final issue in 1817. Aside from the journal's official section, useful information and translations were also published and a section of criticism and bibliography was also included.

From the very beginning of the journal's life as the *Periodic Publication*, Ivan Martynov (1771–1833), the director of the Department of Public Education and the head of the Chief Directorate of Educational Institutions, as well as a botanist and translator of ancient texts, had proposed that is should be transformed into the *Journal of the Ministry*

---

15 'Zhurnal Glavnogo uchilishch Pravleniia za mesiats aprel' 1803 goda', RGIA, coll. 732, descr. 1, file 1, fol. 39.
16 M. I. Sukhomlinov, *Istoriia Rossiiskoi akademii*, 8 vols (St Petersburg: Tip. Imp. Akad. nauk, 1874–1887), vol. 2 (1875), p. 373.
17 'Ustav o tsenzure', *PSZ* 1, no. 21388.

of Public Education.[18] According to Martynov's proposal this new incarnation was to take on the character of an official journal with an emphasis on scholarship. The journal was to include news of meetings held by the Chief Directorate of Educational Institutions, the Academy of Sciences, and the Russian State Academy. It would publish scholarly articles and the reflections of members of both academies, as well as regulatory decisions and other measures relating to the six regional education boards. Concurrently, Martynov presented a new publication proposal for a separate semi-official journal, *The Northern Messenger* (*Severnyi vestnik*).[19] The Chief Directorate of Educational Institutions approved the plan for *The Northern Messenger*, and Martynov published it during the course of 1804–05.

The Northern Messenger was closely linked to the reformist policies of Alexander I, and articles on issues of state and societal structure, on legislation and on education took a central place in the journal, alongside translations of classical and contemporary European authors. In 1806, Martynov's journal *Lyceum* (*Litsei*), with its expanded literary section, continued the work of *The Northern Messenger*.

The Chief Directorate of Educational Institutions did not reject Martynov's idea for a journal for the ministry, but also did not take any steps towards implementing it. In effect, then, the *Periodic Publication* remained on its former footing. The journal came out 4 times a year, and 44 issues were published from 1803 to 1817. The journal's print run of 1200 copies was subsidised by the Chief Directorate of Educational Institutions, and 605 copies were sent free of charge to universities, academies, gymnasiums and district schools.[20]

The production of *Periodic Publication* stopped in 1817. By the time the war with Napoleon had come to an end Alexander's views and domestic policy had undergone a significant shift—one that reflected the general crisis in the political and cultural life of Europe. In Russia, disillusion with European values set in, and the liberal innovations that had marked the beginning of Alexander's reign began to encounter intense criticism.

---

18 E. Ia. Kolbasin, *Literaturnye deiateli prezhnego vremeni: Martynov, Kurganov, Voeikov* (St Petersburg: Knizhnago magazina A. I. Davydova, 1859).
19 'Zhurnal Glavnogo uchilishch Pravleniia za mesiats oktiabr' 1803 g. Zasedanie 3 oktiabria 1803 g.', RGIA, coll. 732, descr. 1, file 2, fol. 135–135.
20 RGIA, coll. 732, descr. 1, file 1, fols. 64–65; file 2, fol. 164.

Barely established, the universities found themselves under attack, and piety was declared the basis of true education. This new ideology was reflected in the creation of a unified Ministry of Religious Affairs and Public Education in 1817, which Nikolai Karamzin called the "ministry of the eclipse".[21] Ozeretskovskii and Martynov were sacked from this new ministry.

At the same time, it was decided to continue publishing the ministry's journal under a new title, *The Journal of the Department of Public Education*. A plan for the new publication was drawn up in 1820, and its first issue was published in January 1821. To preserve continuity with the former publication, the first issue included all the imperial decrees issued after 1817. The new journal was published monthly, and contained ministry orders, news of research and teaching institutions, and academic, literary, and bibliographic sections. From 1820–24, the writer Nikolai Ostolopov (1783–1833) ran the journal, receiving a salary of 2500 rubles per year. Ostolopov had made a name for himself as the author of the 1821 *Dictionary of Ancient and New Poetry* (*Slovar' drevnei i novoi poezii*). In this new journal, Ostolopov published the essay "A Key to the Works of Derzhavin with a Short Description of the Life of this Famous Poet" (1822), which is considered one of the first attempts at literary commentary in Russia.

In 1824, Admiral Aleksandr Shishkov took over the direction of the ministry. Shishkov, a writer and critic, was known for using his philological essays as instruments to serve his nationalist agenda.[22] For many years, Shishkov had been president of the Russian Academy, the research institute dedicated to Russian language and culture set up by Catherine the Great in 1783, and had spared no efforts in transforming it into a centre of Russian spirituality and patriotism.

Under Shishkov, the united Ministry of Religious Affairs and Public Education was dissolved due to the significant replication of its functions by the Synod, and the Ministry of Public Education was restored. The ministry's journal also changed once again. It was renamed

---

21 N. M. Karamzin, *Neizdannye sochineniia i perepiska* (St Petersburg: Tipografiia N. Tiblena i Komp., 1862), vol. 1, pp. 11–12.

22 In 1812, moved to patriotic fervour, Shishkov wrote several manifestos; the most striking of them concerned the loss of Moscow. Dmitrii Bludov, an imperial official, commented that Moscow had to burn for Shishkov to write something beautiful. See N. I. Grech, *Zapiski o moei zhizni* (Moscow: Kniga, 1990), p. 210.

Notes of the Department of Public Education (*Zapiski Departmenta narodnogo prosveshcheniia*), lost its status as a periodical and instead was published only when enough material had been gathered to merit an issue. Editorial work was assigned to Petr Sokolov (1764–1835), a member of the Chief Directorate of Educational Institutions. The author of a work on Russian grammar, Sokolov was a diligent employee of the Russian Academy, and suited Shishkov, who made him his closest aide in both the Academy and in the Ministry.[23] Under Sokolov's direction, three large editions of *Notes of the Department of Public Education* were issued in 1825, 1827, and 1829, respectively. After Sokolov was dismissed in 1829, publication ceased.

The Ministry's official print organ was restored on the initiative of Minister of Public Education Count Sergei Uvarov (1786–1855).[24] Uvarov held broad views on the role of education in public life and defended the concept of education as a means of progress.[25] A godson of Catherine the Great, Uvarov was a favourite at aristocratic gatherings. He built his reputation as a leading autodidact of his time, and made a career even from an early age. He had been drawn to culture in his early years, and had the ability to find a common language with people of opposing views. Uvarov was acquainted with representatives of the

---

23   Sokolov had been actively incolved in the compilation of the Academy's dictionary (*Slovar' Akademii Rossiiskoi*), and was awarded a gold medal for his efforts. Sokolov's *Basics of Russian Grammar* (*Nachal'nye osnovaniia rossiiskoi grammatiki*) of 1788, a condensed version of Lomonosov's *Rossiiskaia grammatika*, was published in seven editions before 1829, with a combined print run of more than 200,000 copies. For more details, see Sukhomlinov, *Istoriia Rossiiskoi Akademii*, vol. 7 (1885), pp. 387–97; M. P. Lepekhin, 'P. I. Sokolov', *Slovar' russkikh pisatelei XVIII veka* (St Petersburg: Nauka, 2010), vol. 3, pp. 147–50.

24   'O vozobnovlenii izdaniia Zhurnala departmenta narodnogo prosveshcheniia', *Zhurnal ministerstva narodnogo prosveshcheniia* (hereafter ZhMNP) 1834, Ch. 1, viii–ix. For more details, see E. Basargina, 'Aus der Geschichte der Zeitschrift des Ministeriums für Volksaufklärung (Žurnal ministerstva narodnogo prosveščenija)', *Russische klassische Altertumswissenschaft in der Zeitschrift des Ministeriums für Volksaufklärung*, ed. by Anatolij Ruban and Ekaterina Basargina (St Petersburg: Bibliotheca Classica Petropolitana; Nestor-Verlag, 2012); idem, 'Iz istorii "Zhurnala Ministerstva narodnogo prosveshcheniia"', in *Klassicheskaia drevnost' v Zhurnale Ministerstva narodnogo prosveshcheniia (ZhMNP). Annotirovannyi ukazatel' statei 1834–1917 gg.*, ed. by A. Ruban (St Petersburg: Bibliotheca Classica Petropolitana, 2015), pp. 7–40.

25   For more on Uvarov, see C. H. Whittaker, *The Origins of Modern Russian Education: An Intellectual Biography of Count Sergei Uvarov, 1786–1855* (DeKalb: Northern Illinois University Press, 1984).

new trends in literary taste such as the poet Vasilii Zhukovskii and the writer and historian Nikolai Karamzin, yet simultaneously maintained friendly relations with the literary traditionalists from the society that called itself the "Colloquy of Lovers of the Russian Word" (*Beseda liubitelei russkogo slova*). Uvarov was among the co-founders of the Arzamas literary society and belonged to what Aleksandr Herzen later called the "Arzamas geese", those members who devoted themselves to state service rather than literary activity.[26]

Figure 1. Count Sergei Uvarov (1786–1855).

Uvarov was highly articulate and wrote with ease on historical and literary topics in French, German and, eventually, in Russian. His 1810 project to create an "Asiatic Academy" in Russia stimulated serious public discussion.[27] This project reflected the growing interest of the

---

26   A. I. Gertsen, *Byloe i dumy*, in *Sobranie sochinenii*, 30 vols (Moscow: Izdatel'stvo Akademii nauk SSSR, 1956), vol. 8, p. 304.
27   S. Ouvaroff, 'Projet d'une académie asiatique', *Études de philologie et de critique* (St Petersburg: L'Académie Impériale des Sciences, 1843); Sergei Semenovich Ouvaroff and Louis-Antoine Léouzon Leduc, *Esquisses politiques et littéraires* (Paris: Gide et Cie, 1848).

Russian state in its Eastern neighbours, as well as the need for academic study of the East. Uvarov's proposal made an impression in academic circles, particularly abroad. J. W. Goethe, having received a copy of the proposal from Uvarov, was intrigued by the broad conception of the research and wrote to him several times about the issue.[28] In 1811, Uvarov was elected an honourary member of the Academy of Sciences and of the Göttingen academic society.

Recognising the importance of the Orient in the history of civilisations, Uvarov nevertheless ascribed particular significance to Russia's cultural connection to Western Europe. He believed that Russia and Western Europe shared a common source of education and civilisation which could be traced back to antiquity, especially to the Hellenic world, and that this was important for the study of Russian history and literature. In his early years, Uvarov embraced the principles of neohumanism, which aimed to restore the lost ideal of *humanitas*. He assimilated the neohumanists' faith in the educational ideal of antiquity, and viewed classical philology as the path to a comprehensive knowledge of the ancient world. The neohumanists believed that only education in its classical form could lead to the complete and holistic realisation of man's spiritual potential. Learning ancient languages was an individual's best path to a rounded formation of personality, and the aim of such instruction was to encourage independent interpretation of the cultural achievements of the peoples of antiquity. The neohumanists tried to direct school education towards a creative perception of antiquity, not as a norm or as a model for blind imitation, but as the seed from which the principal cultural values of Western civilisation had emerged. Understanding ancient culture opened the way to asserting one's own national culture.

Uvarov enthusiastically accepted the call of the neohumanists, "Educate yourself in the Greek way" ("Bilde dich griechisch"), and was ready to learn to follow the spirit of the Greeks, to feel, think and act as a Greek. He respected Goethe, the recognised leader of neohumanism and romanticisim, and admired Friedrich Wolf, the pillar of classical

---

28 *Goethe und Uwarow, und ihr Briefwechsel*, ed. by G. Schmid, special off-print of *Russische Revue* 28. 2 (St Petersburg : R. Hammerschmidt, 1888); S. N. Durylin, 'Drug Gete', *Literaturnoe nasledstvo* (Moscow: Zhur.-gaz. ob"edinenie, 1932), vols 4–6, pp. 186–221.

philology. Uvarov was inspired by the ideas of Wilhelm von Humboldt, who reformed the Prussian education system by placing ancient languages at the centre of study.[29] Indeed, it was in no small part thanks to Uvarov that Nikolai Gnedich made the first attempt at a Russian translation of *The Iliad* into hexameter verse, as evidenced by the translator's letter to the minister in the foreword to the 1829 translation. In 1816, Uvarov was appointed an honourary member of the Institut de France.

Borrowed from German scholars, Uvarov's sense of Greek classicism's fundamental importance for Russia's cultural development formed the core of his entire educational policy. However, if in the 1810s Uvarov had slavishly followed Western models, then by the 1830s, under the influence of the revolutionary events spreading across Europe, he changed his views and began to doubt whether the Western model of societal development and education was universally applicable. On the whole, however, German philhellenism had a profound influence on Russian education, shaping the development of the humanities until 1917.

A large part of Uvarov's life was connected to the Ministry of Public Education. A turning point in his career came in 1810 when, at the age of 24, under the protection of his father-in-law, Minister of Public Education Count Aleksei Razumkovskii, Uvarov received the post of trustee of the Petersburg Regional Board of Education (1810–22). In 1818 he became the President of the Academy of Sciences. Towards the end of Alexander I's reign Uvarov found himself out of favour, and moved into the Ministry of Finances. However, with the accession of Nicholas I Uvarov re-entered the larger political arena.

When Nicholas I (1796–1855) came to the throne in December 1825, shooting broke out on Senate Square.[30] Although the Decembrist revolt was quickly suppressed and five of its leaders were executed, the uprising left a deep impression on the new tsar, fostering distrust and

---

29   John Edwin Sandys, *A History of Classical Scholarship*, 3 vols (Cambridge: Cambridge University Press, 1908), vol. 3, pp. 47–87.

30   A. E. Presniakov, *Emperor Nicholas I of Russia: The Apogee of Autocracy, 1825–1855*, ed. and trans. by J. C. Zacek (Gulf Breeze, FL: Academic International Press, 1974); W. Bruce Lincoln, *Nicholas I: Emperor and Autocrat of All the Russias* (Bloomington, IN: Indiana University Press, 1978); Richard S. Wortman, *Scenarios of Power: Myth and Ceremony in Russian Monarchy from Peter the Great to the Death of Nicholas I* (Princeton: Princeton University Press, 1995).

fear towards any manifestation of free thinking. Throughout the rest of his life, Nicholas wasted no effort in trying to eliminate "revolutionary infection". In the tsar's manifesto of 13 July 1826 informing Russia of the result of the Decembrists' trial, the spirit of rebellion was attributed "not to enlightenment, but to an idleness of mind" and "the destructive luxury of half-knowledge".[31] In this new age, Nicholas suggested, Russia needed to reform its now degraded educational system and foster an educated elite, loyal to the government. As part of this modernisation process, the government had to increase the number of educated people, and prepare a new generation of educated teachers, professors, doctors, and public officials.[32]

Uvarov was the kind of enlightened public servant who understood the breadth of his remit and was prepared to fulfil it. In 1832, he was appointed Deputy Minister of Public Education. In March 1833, Uvarov took on the duties of Minister of Public Education, and a year later his position was confirmed.[33] Uvarov carried out state educational and academic policies in Russia until 1849. As Russia's Third Department put it in their 1839 report: "No minister acts so autocratically as Uvarov. The name of the tsar is constantly on his lips".[34]

As Minister of Public Education, Uvarov saw his role as the promoter of the historical principles of Russian culture and statehood. In the name of maintaining the health and power of Russia, Uvarov tried to unite European Enlightenment with Russian national spirit (*narodnost'*) and to establish this on the basis of Russia's historic qualities of "autocracy, Orthodoxy, and *narodnost'*", which formed, according to him, the "anchor of our salvation". This triad became the core of official ideology, a "theory of official nationality".[35]

---

31   'O sovershenii prigovora nad gosudarstvennymi prestupnikami', *PSZ*, Series 2 (1825–1881), no. 465.
32   N. V. Riasanovsky, *A Parting of Ways: Government and the Educated Public in Russia, 1801–1855* (Oxford: Clarendon Press, 1977).
33   Nicholas A. Hans, *History of Russian Educational Policy, 1701–1917* (London: P. S. King and Son, 1931); Patrick L. Alston, *Education and the State in Tsarist Russia* (Stanford: Stanford University Press, 1969).
34   *Rossiia pod nadzorom. Otchety III otdeleniia, 1827–1869*, ed. by M. V. Sidorova and E. I. Shcherbakova (Moscow: Rossiiskii arkhiv, 2006), p. 211.
35   For more on the meaning of the triad, see Uvarov's five-year report on his work as Minister of Public Education in S. S. Uvarov, 'Obozrenie istekshego piatiletiia', *ZhMNP*, 1, 1839, Ch. 21, 7–8. See also Riasanovsky, *A Parting of Ways*.

Uvarov proposed this triad as a formulation for the core principles of public education for the first time in his 1832 report on the inspection of Moscow University. Here he defined two aspects of teaching in Russia's universities: first, the *scholarly* and *educational* aspect, and second, a *moral* and *political* aspect. Uvarov intended to give higher education in Russia a national character, combining the benefits of the European Enlightenment with the advantages of *narodnost'*. The requirement was, as he phrased it, "to be a Russian in spirit before attempting to be a European in education".[36]

Recognising the growing influence of the periodical press on society's consciousness, Uvarov was sharply critical of the state of contemporary journalism. He argued forcibly that "the path to the corruption of morals begins with the corruption of taste" and condemned the "brazen attempts" of journalists "to go beyond the limits of decorum", which brought serious harm to unformed minds and had a negative influence on the atmosphere of the university.[37]

In 1832, Uvarov took aim at Nikolai Polevoi, the publisher of the highly successful *Moscow Telegraph* (*Moskovskii telegraf*) for getting drawn into "journalistic polemics", for daring to print satirical sketches of high society, and for opining against Karamzin, whose scholarly authority had hitherto been reckoned unimpeachable. In 1834, Uvarov managed to shut down the *Moscow Telegraph*, and banned Polevoi from working in journalism.

Uvarov, who was responsible for censorship as Minister of Public Education, closed two other journals in addition to *Moscow Telegraph* during his ministerial duties, including *The Telescope* (*Teleskop*) in 1836 for publishing Petr Chaadaev's "First Philosophical Letter". Uvarov was outraged by Chaadaev's expression of bitter regret at the spiritual stagnation reigning in Russia, which was cut off from the "global education of the human race".[38] Chaadaev was accused of a lack of patriotism and officially declared insane; Nikolai Nadezhdin,

---

36 '4 dekabria 1832. S predstavleniem otcheta tainogo sovetnika Uvarova po obozreniiu im Moskovskogo universteta i gimnazii', *Sbornik postanovlenii po Ministerstvu narodnogo prosveshcheniia* (St Petersburg: Tip. V. S. Balasheva, 1875), vol. 2, column 512.

37 *Ibid.*, column 513.

38 Piotr Iakovlevitch Tchaadaiev, *Lettres philosophiques, adressées à une dame*, présentées par François Rouleau (Paris: Librairie des Cinq Continents, 1970).

the editor of *The Telescope*, was exiled. The severity of the punishment was explained with reference to the fact that Nadezhdin's position as a professor at Moscow University set the Ministry of Public Education in a poor light.

Uvarov clearly understood that restricting journalists by bans alone would not work. Thus, he proposed to the "educator class" (*soslovie obrazovatelei*), as he referred to the professors, that they publish their own journal, which would contain only serious articles "without political news and literary squabbles" and give the reading public (and particularly young people) "pure nourishment, mature and protective".[39]

When Uvarov became the Minister of Public Education in 1834, he had an ideological scheme already prepared. On the day of his appointment, Uvarov addressed his subordinates through a circular in which he repeated his tripartite formula, requesting that public education "be carried out in the united spirit of Orthodoxy, autocracy, and *narodnost*'".[40] Understanding the importance of state propaganda, Uvarov—without a hint of embarrassment—took on the role of ideologue of the Russian Empire. But in order to inculcate his cultural policies in society, he needed an official mouthpiece for his ministry, rather than an academic journal. With this in mind, Uvarov renewed the ministry's defunct journal, but with a broader remit and a more ambitious programme. The publication again received a new title, *Journal of the Ministry of Public Education*. In it Uvarov hoped to converse directly with educated society, manage culture, direct minds and shape public opinion in a direction supportive of the government.

The journal aimed not only to serve as the ministry's official mouthpiece—the "echo of the government", as Uvarov's put it—which would contain government instructions on teaching as well as reports from the ministry, but to become a kind of Russian equivalent of the French *Journal des savants*, allowing its readership to follow the progress of all branches of science and learning. In Uvarov's conception the journal was intended to reflect the status of academic life in the empire and, insofar as it was possible, become a replacement for foreign

---

39   *Sbornik postanovlenii po ministerstvu narodnogo prosveshcheniia*, vol. 2, column 516.
40   'Tsirkuliarnoe predlozhenie g. Upravliaiushchego MNP nachal'stvam uchebnym okrugov, o vstuplenii v upravlenie ministerstvom', *ZhMNP*, 1, 1834, xlix-l.

scholarly journals, which were inaccessible to a majority of the public. It was also meant to report news of academic life in Russia and abroad, and to cover the history of education and enlightenment in different countries.

As Uvarov was to write in his report of ministry activities for 1833–34, the journal's principal aim consisted of

> publicising the measures undertaken by the government in relation to the successful development of the sciences and of public education, reporting new useful methods to teachers, and disseminating information about the growth of Enlightenment in Russia in comparison with its development in other lands. In the past five years, twenty issues of this journal have been published. The teachers of young people who live close to the capital, as well as those who live in the remote steppe and in distant territories of the empire, are equipped with reading material, from which they can see what the government expects of them in the great work of public education: without being in Moscow, Petersburg, or Kiev, they can, as it were, attend the lectures of the universities there, become acquainted with all the fruits of our educated classes, and the lecturers at higher education institutions can compare their own thoughts and the observations of their fellow teachers in other towns. At the same time, teachers, knowing the direct intentions of the government in full, can bring their actions into line with it, without any need for direction from outside.[41]

Uvarov took on the general directorship of the journal, intending to turn it into the country's leading Russian-language academic journal. He personally developed a plan for the publication, defined its structure, and proposed rubrics that would guide the distribution of content.[42] The journal was organised as follows: 1) "Acts of government"; 2) "Literature, science, and the arts"; 3) "News of scholars and educational institutions in Russia"; 4) "News of foreign scholars and educational institutions"; 5) "The history of Enlightenment and public education" in different countries, particularly in Russia; 6) "News and miscellaneous".

The journal appeared monthly. Its publication required the joint efforts of many people, and Uvarov personally supervised the creation of an editorial board. This consisted of an editor, four staff members, and additional freelance employees. The board was located in St Petersburg,

---

41 S. S. Uvarov, 'Obozrenie istekshego piatiletiia', *ZhMNP*, 1, 1839, Ch. 21, 31–32.
42 RGIA, coll. 733, descr. 2, file 87, fol. 4.

where it occupied a single, dimly lit, low-ceilinged room with a semi-circular window—more like a kennel than a ministerial office—in the building of the Ministry of Public Education by Chernyshev bridge (today, Lomonosov bridge).[43]

Konstantin Serbinovich (1797–1874), who had previously worked as secretary to Karamzin, was the journal's first editor.[44] For Uvarov, a devotee of Karamzin's work, Serbinovich's previous employer was the best recommendation possible. Serbinovich was neither a scholar nor a writer, but he was an intelligent editor, and a good administrator.[45] Serbinovich diligently carried out all Uvarov's orders, who summoned him almost daily for various explanations and instructions.[46] Serbinovich read the third (i.e. the final) proofs of the journal and was supposed to make sure the dictates of the censor were followed, and that all the texts were in tune with the government's thinking. He gave Uvarov the final proofs to check, and after receiving his approval, the journal was published. Serbinovich made no serious errors in his work, and Uvarov valued his obliging editor, demanding of him little more. Serbinovich served as the journal's editor for twenty years, combining that position with duties as director of the Chancery of the Ober-Prosecutor of the Holy Synod, where he played a prominent role in attempts to re-unite the Uniate (Eastern-Rite Catholic) Church with the Orthodox Church.

The journal's editorial assistant role was demanding, and for many years Ivan Galanin (1817–73) occupied this position, managing the general work, an extensive correspondence with authors, the delivery of the journal to its subscribers, and other such administrative tasks. Galanin drew up the first, official section of the journal, covering the actions of the government. A ministry department, the Chancery of the Minister, and the Chancery of the Main Censorship Administration

---

43   A. V. Starchevskii, 'Vospominaniia starogo literatora', *Istoricheskii vestnik*, October 1888, vol. 34, 110.

44   'O naznachenii nadvornogo sovetnika Serbinovicha redaktorom zhurnala departmenta narodnogo prosveshcheniia, 8 aprelia 1833 g.' RGIA, coll. 733, descr. 2, file 87, fol. 2. For Serbinovich's views of editorial work, see 'Ob izdanii zhurnala pri Ministerstve narodnogo prosveshcheniia', RGIA, coll. 1661, descr. 1, file 245, fols. 16–17.

45   Compare the views of Serbinovich's background and beliefs in Starchevskii, 'Vospominaniia', 110 and the entry for 11 June 1843 in A. A. Nikitenko, *Dnevnik*, 3 vols (Moscow: Zakharov, 2005).

46   Starchevskii, 'Vospominaniia', 110.

presented the necessary information (decrees, decisions, instructions, and accounts of the ministry's work) to the editorial board. Aside from that, Galanin read the first and second proofs of the journal.

However, Uvarov considered that his main assistants in this work were Russian scholars, his subordinates: university and lyceum lecturers employed by the Ministry of Public Education, as well as members of the Academy of Sciences (Uvarov had served as President of the Academy since 1818). He counted on their assistance and hoped to receive the majority of the scholarly material for his journal from them. To facilitate a steady flow of articles, Uvarov used the administrative levers of influence he already had. For example, in a circular to the directors of regional education boards on 9 September 1833, Uvarov simply ordered the professors of universities to deliver one article a year to the journal.[47] The professors' texts were supposed to be "evidence of their talents and knowledge, and of the level to which they had raised the subject they taught".[48]

Thus, participation in the journal was seen as tantamount to a qualification required of the professors, while the journal itself became a means for control and oversight of the efficiency of academic work undertaken by employees of the Ministry of Public Education. When the council of the University of Dorpat refused to deliver articles at the minister's behest on the grounds that they were too busy, Uvarov modified his peremptory tone. He hastened to assure the Dorpat scholars that he was *inviting* them to write, but was not in any way *forcing* them to collaborate with the ministry's journal.[49] The professors of other universities, as well as members of the Academy of Sciences, readily agreed to take part in the journal. Before long, scholars had become the mainstay of the publication. Thanks to them, two of the journal's six sections, "Literature, science, and the arts" and "News of foreign scholars and educational institutions", were always saturated with scholarly material.

Uvarov supported the journal with an annual subscription of 2,000 to 3,000 rubles from the ministry's administrative funds. This went to pay the honoraria of the authors, which Uvarov set himself. The amount

---

47 RGIA, coll. 733, descr. 2, file 87, fols. 10–11.
48 *Ibid.*
49 *Ibid.*, fols. 25–28, fol. 33.

depended on the length of the composition, so the minister warned his authors against "superfluous productivity", requesting extreme clarity in exposition. For a composition of less than 1 "author's sheet" (i.e. around 40,000 characters), a contributor would receive 50 rubles; for between 1 and 2 "author's sheets"—100 rubles; for 2 "author's sheets"—150 rubles; for 3 or more—200 rubles.

The first issue of the *Journal of the Ministry of Public Education* was published in January 1834, and continued to appear once a month until 1917. In total, 434 volumes were published, each of which included several issues.[50] The first issue opened with the grand declaration that the "era of unconditional imitation" had finished in Russia, and that the country "could apply the fruits of education to its own needs better than its foreign teachers and clearly distinguish good from evil in the rest of Europe; it used the former, and was not afraid of the latter".[51] Uvarov's ideological programme was based on the bold assumption that Russia had already reached maturity, had transformed itself into a developed state and in some areas was already superseding its Western neighbours. The very concept of *narodnost'*, in which there was "something fresh and, so to speak, unworn out" to the contemporary ear, was meant to testify to Russia's maturity, its ability to move forwards on a par with the nations of Europe.[52]

Petr Pletnev, a professor of St Petersburg University, took it upon himself to support the doctrine developed by Uvarov. He showed the importance of the national principle in literature with reference to ancient Greek literature. According to Pletnev, the fruits of Greek literary culture, in all its richness and variety, merge into a "single image reflected in several mirrors", which is united by the common idea of civic consciousness.[53] However, Pletnev decided not to apply that measure to the history of Russian literature, referring instead to its national distinctiveness.[54] Uvarov's programme, which affirmed the unity of monarchy, the Orthodox faith, and national distinctiveness, had nothing in common with the Slavophiles' understanding of *narodnost'*.

---

50 The journal can be accessed online at http://www.runivers.ru/lib/book7643/450649/.
51 *ZhMNP*, 1, 1834, v–vi.
52 P. A. Pletnev, 'O narodnosti v literature. Rassuzhdenie, chitannoe v torzhestvennom sobranii Imp. SPB universiteta ord. prof. onogo Pletnevym', *ZhMNP*, 1, 1834, 2.
53 *Ibid.*, 3.
54 *Ibid.*, 18, 29.

Although the official ideology and the Slavophiles' views proclaimed the same principles, the spirit and meaning of the official programme and the Slavophiles' system were opposed to one another. The theory of official *narodnost'* was aimed at reinforcing state power; its main principle was autocracy, to which the principles of Orthodoxy and *narodnost'* were subordinated. By contrast, for Slavophiles who were not statists, the principles of true Orthodox faith and true *narodnost'* were definitive.

In a period of increased debate about what the national principle meant in Russia's culture and history, Uvarov had no intention of turning the ministry's official mouthpiece into a platform for discussions of society and politics.[55] It is therefore unsurprising that the works of Slavophiles such as Aleksei Khomiakov, the religious philosopher Ivan Kireevskii, and the brothers Ivan and Konstantin Aksakov, as well as others, failed to appear in the journal.

According to Uvarov's plan, the *Journal of the Ministry of Public Education* was to become an exemplary model of its kind for Russian journalists. It appealed to a wide audience, although it was first and foremost destined for the scholarly milieu—lecturers at institutions of higher education, teachers in gymnasiums and district schools—allowing them to follow successes in science and practical pedagogy in Russia and abroad in their own language. The print run in these years was 1,200 copies, and the number of compulsory subscribers reached 600.[56] The names of the voluntary subscribers were printed in the final issue of the year. From year to year the number of voluntary subscribers increased, and this served as the best evidence that Uvarov had managed to make the journal popular.[57]

---

[55] For Uvarov's relationship to polemics, see his letter to Mikhail Pogodin on 18 December 1840. M. Pogodin, 'Dlia biografii grafa Sergeia Semenovicha Uvarova', *Russkii arkhiv*, 12 (1871), column 2082.

[56] Ten exclusive copies were bound separately from the main print run and presented to the tsar, members of the imperial family, the Minister of Public Education and the head of department. See RGIA, coll. 1661, descr. 1, file 245, fol. 3. For Uvarov's circular obliging all educational institutions to subscribe to Zh MNP, see RGIA, coll. 742, descr. 2, file 1, fol. 76. There was a variable level of compulsory subscription: gymnasia took two copies, lyceums—three, and universities—four.

[57] The cost of an annual subscription was 30 rubles in St Petersburg, and 35 in all other cities of the Russian Empire.

In the 1830s and 1840s, different spheres of knowledge were represented in the journal, although the humanities were predominant, with history, philosophy, religion, Oriental studies, philology and jurisprudence taking pride of place.[58] The journal brought together works by the best lecturers of the Ministry of Public Education, who published their independent research in it: the most important lectures on their topics, works on the history of various disciplines, general reflections on the state of scholarship in Russia and Europe, accounts of research trips, reports on Russian and foreign scholarly publications, and so on.

Where possible, the *Journal of the Ministry of Public Education* aimed to review all scholarly books in the humanities published in Russia, as well as publishing regular thematic overviews of Russian and foreign periodicals. These periodicals came either from the publishers themselves or from the Chancery of the Main Censorship Administration, and served as a source of varied information on the state of education in Russia. These overviews were produced by the journal's employees, who were chosen personally by Serbinovich. As a rule, the journal's staff were capable young men who had recently completed university. People who knew several or rare languages were in particular demand. Contributors included the future editor of *Notes of the Fatherland* (*Otechestvennye zapiski*), Andrei Kraevskii, the publicist and education organiser Ianuarii Nemerov, the historian Ivan Tarnava-Borichevskii and Albert Starchevskii, a journalist and polyglot.

The editorial office received foreign newspapers and journals from Uvarov himself. The staff used all material from these publications that they found appropriate, sending it for translation or critical review. Every three months, the *Journal of the Ministry of Public Education* published detailed overviews of newspapers and journals broken down by category: general and Russian history, *belles lettres*, criticism, theory and history of literature and art, mathematics, natural sciences and medicine, and military science. These reviews were thorough and extensive, and were examined in detail by the editor. According to one of the journal's staff members, the reviews were written "expansively,

---

58 See the thematic indexes of *Ukazatel' k povremennym izdaniiam Ministerstva narodnogo prosveshcheniia s 1803 po iiun' 1864 goda* (St Petersburg: Ministerstvo narodnogo prosveshcheniia, 1865).

because Serbinovich had a penchant for pruning, and would delete a lot".[59]

The *Journal* had a particularly important role as a means for disseminating information about cultural life abroad. Although this was not stated explicitly at the time, it provided one of the few means of bypassing the normal obstacles imposed by the censors. According to the procedures laid down in the 1828 Statute on censorship, all printed materials from abroad were to be inspected by the Foreign Censorship Committee. The chairman of the Committee was the ultra-vigilant A. I. Krasovskii, who gave instructions to inspect even the printed scrap paper in which foreign books were packaged. Almost every time that one of the censors recommended approving a work for distribution in Russia, a supplementary annotation countered that "the chairman considers it more prudent to refuse". The Committee received foreign newspapers and journals by regular subscription, but very few of them made their way into the hands of Russian readers. The *Journal* provided its own channel for information from abroad, which it made still more accessible through rendering it in Russian.

The section on *belles lettres*, which reviewed literary works published in journals, was the least successful. At the end of the 1830s, literary reviews were sent to Boris Fedorov (1794–1875) for review: Serbinovich had complete faith in Fedorov's literary taste. A mediocre writer, and the object of mockery and epigrammes, Fedorov was a "retrograde and a true scourge of modern Russian literature, which he hated".[60] The journal's staff knew that Fedorov would edit and rewrite their reviews from start to finish.

Beginning in 1837, the *Journal of the Ministry of Public Education* printed advertisements and announcements for books published at home and abroad. Gradually, the bibliographic review content grew to the point that the editors created a separate section, "Reviews of books and journals". Reviewing all academic books in the humanities printed in Russia was painstaking work, and a thorough review could take up to six months to write. Books for review were given to specialists, but in the rare case when the author of a book under review happened to be on the journal's staff, he would review his own work: it was often

---

59 Starchevskii, 'Vospominaniia', 107.
60 Ibid.

difficult to find another specialist in the same narrow field. Starchevskii, for instance, had to write a "self review" on his two-volume *Historiae Ruthenicae Scriptores exteri saeculi XVI* (1841–42). The article was published under the surname of an acquaintance who had not even seen Starchevskii's work.[61]

The section "News and Miscellany" was notably diverse in its contents. It published bibliographic surveys, announcements of new foreign books, journalism, as well as information on new discoveries and inventions, or on travels, or on noteworthy developments in classical philology. Thanks to the *Journal of the Ministry of Public Education*, the Russian reader could become better acquainted with, for example, aspects of British life and history across a broad spectrum ranging from Newton to railways.[62]

Uvarov greatly valued his journal both for itself and for the uses to which it could be put. In his capacity as "education tsar", the *Journal* served as his means of promoting his education reforms. When he was appointed Minister of Public Education, a new university charter was in preparation, and Uvarov devoted considerable efforts to university reform. His "General Charter of Imperial Russian Universities", confirmed in July 1835, was an attempt to unify research and teaching, and to raise both the level of teaching and the quality of scholarly research.[63] Uvarov used the *Journal of the Ministry of Public Education* to show how his charter derived from the tradition of Western universities' legislative acts. Original and translated articles regularly appeared in the "News of foreign educational institutions" section. These articles were dedicated to the history and current state of university education in European countries. Particular attention was paid to the state of public education in Prussia, the structure of Prussian universities, and new

---

61 Ibid., 105.
62 See, for example, 'Tsennost' gornoi proizvoditel'nosti Anglii', *ZhMNP*, 1841, 86–91; 'Zheleznye dorogi v Anglii', 1856, Ch. LXXXIX, otd. VII, 122–24; 'Sravnenie anglichan s rimlianami', *ZhMNP*, 1846, XLIX, otd. VI, 222–24; D. Perevoshchikov, 'Otkrytiia N'iutona', *ZhMNP*, 1841, Ch. XXXII, otd. II, 1–68. For more detail see the *Ukazatel' k povremennym izdaniiam Ministerstva narodnogo prosveshcheniia*, pp. 9–10.
63 'Obshchii Ustav imperatorskikh rossiiskikh universitetov', *ZhMNP*, 8, 1835, XLIX–LXXXVII; 'Shtaty imperatorskikh rossiiskikh universitetov Sankt-Peterburgskogo, Moskovskogo, Khar'kovskogo i Kazanskogo', *ZhMNP*, 8, 1835, LXXXVIII–XCVII. For a list of articles, see 'Universitety otechestvennye', *Ukazatel' k povremennym izdaniiam Ministerstva narodnogo prosveshcheniia*, pp. 236–39.

forms of teaching in France. Several articles took English universities as their subject, in particular the history of Oxford.[64]

In the year leading up to the publication of the new charter, and continuing after it was implemented, Uvarov waged a campaign in support of disciplines that had previously seemed "dangerous" and subversive to the state. Relying on the authority of scholars, Uvarov tried to dispel fears about philosophy as a discipline of dubious reliability, and to highlight the benefits of studying law.[65] When Uvarov announced *narodnost'* as a cornerstone of education for the first time in 1832, he was trying not only to create a certain didactic effect, but also to attract students to study the history of their own country. Uvarov hoped that "harmless and thorough" lessons in Russian history would furnish young people with a kind of mental buttress "against the influence of so-called *European ideas,* which threaten us perilously".[66] The university charter of 1835 aided the institutionalisation of these areas of study, making Russian history a separate department for the first time, and establishing a new department dedicated to the history and literature of Slavonic dialects.

The pages of the *Journal of the Ministry of Public Education* presented historical research not only by university professors, but also by members of the Archeographic Commission, which was created by Uvarov in 1834 to extract from the archives and publish a full corpus of documents on Russian history. Historical articles took pride of place

---

64 'Universitety zagranichnye', *Ukazatel' k povremennym izdaniiam Ministerstva narodnogo prosveshchenii,* pp. 239–40. K. Morgenshtern, 'Sravnenie angliiskikh universitetov s nemetskimi', *ZhMNP,* 11, 1835, Ch. 8, otd. IV, 327–54; N. D. Brashman, 'Ob angliiskikh universtitetakh', *ZhMNP,* 4, 1843, Ch. XXXVIII, 1–30; 'Kratkaia istoriia Oksfordskogo universiteta i Oksforda kak goroda', *ZhMNP,* 10, 1844, Ch. XLIV, otd. IV, 1–18.

65 See, for example, A. A. Kraevskii, 'Sovremennoe sostoianie filosofii vo Frantsii i novaia sistema sei nauki, osnovyvaemaia Botenom', *ZhMNP,* 3, 1834, 317–77; A. S. Fisher, 'O khode obrazovaniia v Rossii i ob uchastii, kakoe dolzhna prinimat' v nem filosofiia', *ZhMNP,* 1, 1835, 28–68; V. Androsov, 'O predelakh, v koikh dolzhny byt' izuchaemy i prepodavaemy pravo politicheskoe i narodnoe', *ZhMNP,* 12, 1834, 367–85; K. O. Nevolin, 'O soedinenii teorii s praktikoiu v izuchenii zakonov i v deloproizvodstve', *ZhMNP,* 12, 1835, 445–75.

66 'S predstavleniem otcheta tainogo sovetnika Uvarova po obozreniiu im Moskovskogo universiteta i gimnazii, 4 dekabria 1832', *Sbornik postanovlenii po Ministerstvu narodnogo prosveshcheniia,* vol. 2, col. 517.

in the journal, and patriotism was no impediment to serious scholarly work.[67]

Uvarov's classicism also aimed to serve national interests. By insisting on the introduction of the Greek language into gymnasiums and universities, for instance, Uvarov aimed to highlight the Byzantine roots of Russian culture and hence to aid understanding of Russia's particular position in relation to Western cultures. Professors of the universities of Dorpat, Kharkov, and Moscow published articles in support of classical disciplines in the journal, explaining why studying the ancient past was useful.[68]

The permanent secretary of the Academy of Sciences, Pavel Fus, collected news of Russia's scholarly and educational establishments.[69] The journal's first issue included accounts of the work carried out by the Ministry of Public Education in 1833, and by two of the capital's higher research institutes: one about the activities of St Petersburg University for 1833–34 and a "Review of works by the Imperial St Petersburg Academy of Sciences, 1827–1833". In its second issue, the journal presented a "Review of works of the Russian Academy since its establishment up to 1833" by Fedorov. Apart from such reports, the journal also often published extracts from the minutes of meetings of the Academy of Sciences. This was a prime opportunity for President-cum-Minister Uvarov to present the Academy he had fostered in all its glory to the readers of the *Journal*—which meant to the whole of educated society.

---

67   See, for example, P. M. Stroev, 'Khronologicheskoe ukazanie materialov otechestvennoi istorii, literatury, pravovedeniia, do nachala XVIII stoletiia', *ZhMNP*, 1834, Ch. 1.2, 152–88; N. G. Ustrialov, 'Skazaniia kniazia Kurbskogo', *ZhMNP*, 1834, Ch. 3, 82–85; *idem*, 'Predpolozhenie ob izdanii russkikh letopisei i gosudarstvennykh aktov', *ZhMNP*, 1837, Ch. XIII, otd. II, 338–52; M. P. Pogodin, 'O vseobshchei istorii', 1834, Ch. 1, 31–44; *idem*, 'Otryvok iz rossiiskoi istorii dlia narodnykh uchilishch', *ZhMNP*, 1834, Ch. IV, otd. II, 386–400; *idem*, 'Povestvovanie o Moskovskikh proisshestviiakh po konchine tsaria Alekseia Mikhailovicha', *ZhMNP*, 1835, Ch. V, otd. II, 69–82; N. V. Gogol', 'Plan prepodavaniia vseobshchei istorii', *ZhMNP*, 1834, Ch. 1, 189–209. For a complete list of articles see *Ukazatel' k povremennym izdaniiam Ministerstva narodnogo prosveshcheniia*, pp. 90–95.

68   M. Rozberg, 'Glavnye svoistva grecheskoi i rimskoi slovesnstoi', *ZhMNP*, 7, 1834, 1–26; I. Kroneberg, 'Ob izuchenii slovesnosti', *ZhMNP*, 11, 1835, 253–89; I. M. Snegirev, 'O predmete i tseli drevnostei rimsikh i posobiiakh inostrannykh i otechestvennykh dlia izucheniia onykh', *ZhMNP*, 11, 1835, 301–13.

69   For a complete list of articles, see 'Uchebnye zavedeniia', *Ukazatel' k povremennym izdaniiam Ministerstva narodnogo prosveshcheniia*, pp. 242–46.

In 1835 the intellectual life of Russian universities was enlivened by the return of a group of young scholars from Germany, where they had been sent to finish their education, Uvarov was personally involved in the allocation of candidates to university departments, taking advantage of his right, as Education Minister, to appoint professors. Prior to departing for their new posts, each of these young scholars gave a lecture *pro venia legendi* (the lecture which demonstrated their professional credentials). These lectures took place publicly in the Academy of Sciences, and the *Journal of the Ministry of Public Education* published a detailed account of the events as well as the text of several lectures in full.[70]

The new university charter facilitated the rotation of personnel, since it limited the term of service to twenty-five years, and introduced the title of "emeritus professor", which allowed the ministry to retire older professors who had ceased to be active in scholarship, and to replace them with fresh cohorts, thus aiding the renewal and revival of Russian universities. The dismissal of nearly a quarter of the total number of professors was a painful process, and university bodies cautiously awaited the arrival of the new, younger guard. Thus Uvarov thought it wise to use the ministry journal to present this new generation to their senior colleagues. He used the *Journal* as an instrument with which to draw society's attention to the outcome of his policy: an improvement in the level of learning and scholarship in Russia.

The ministry's journal acted as a rich, living chronicle of the development of education and learning in Russia until Uvarov's retirement, which came soon after the revolutionary upheavals in Germany and Austro-Hungary in 1848–49. These events shook the Russian government, forcing it to change its priorities in state education policy. Uvarov's life's work was crushed before his eyes. With every means at his disposal he tried to protect the development of Russian education and learning from the harsh demands of the time, but he lacked the resources necessary for a serious struggle. According to Uvarov, he "was in the position of a man who, fleeing from a wild beast, throws pieces of clothing, one after another, to distract it, and is glad

---

70 'O probnykh lektsiiakh universtitetskikh vospitannikov, nedavno vozvrativshikhsiia iz-za granitsy', *ZhMNP*, 9, 1835, 507–33.

that he remains whole".[71] With the onset of a period of political reaction in 1849, there was nothing left to throw, and Uvarov retired.

In 1850, Platon Shirinskii-Shikhmatov (1790–1853), who saw "real enlightenment [*prosveshchenie*]" only in the light of the icon-lamp, became Minister of Public Education.[72] Under Shirinskii-Shikhmatov, the main emphasis of education policy was on religious education. The universities, so recently invigorated, were ostracised. The change of state education policy was reflected in the ministry's journal. Its annual State subsidy of 3,000 rubles was withdrawn, and this led to a deterioration of its contents. The journal shed its best authors and gradually fell into decline. It lost the "respect and trust of the reading and thinking public" which came to see it merely as "official drivel".[73]

---

[71] B. N. Chicherin, *Vospominaniia*, 4 vols (Moscow: Izd-vo Abashnikovykh, 1929), vol.1, p. 28.

[72] P. M. Kovalevskii, 'Vlasti prederzhashchie. U Chernysheva mosta', *Russkaia starina*, 2 (1909), 301.

[73] 'Otvet K. D. Ushinskogo na predlozhenie ministra E. V. Putiatina o vozvrashchenii k prezhnei programme zhurnala', *Arkhiv K. D. Ushinskogo*, vol. 1 (Moscow: Izdatel'stvo Akad. ped. nauk. RSFSR, 1959), p. 52.

V.
INFORMATION AND PUBLIC DISPLAY

11. Information in Plain Sight: The Formation of the Public Graphosphere

Simon Franklin

The "graphosphere" is the space of the visible word, the sum of the places where words are to be seen.[1] The graphosphere is therefore a multi-faceted, multi-functional phenomenon of culture. It is dynamic, both in its physical properties and in its interactions with its viewers and inhabitants. It can permeate many locations: domestic and institutional, official and informal, urban and rural. Over time it may change its size, its shape, its composition, its relative density, and its configuration of functions. It is a complex, multi-dimensional field of information and communication. The present chapter focuses on one set of its locations: public spaces, which here means places which are out of doors and openly accessible: streets, squares, external surfaces, but not interior spaces with public uses, such as public rooms. We will consider when, how, and to some extent why a public graphosphere emerged in Russia, the types of institutions and activities that facilitated or shaped (or inhibited) its formation, and the functions that its various components were intended to serve, as well as some of the ways in which it was perceived.

It is characteristic both of antiquity and of modernity that urban public spaces are saturated with visible words: signs, inscriptions, and

---

[1] Further on this concept see Simon Franklin, 'Mapping the Graphosphere: Cultures of Writing in Early 19th-Century Russia (and Before)', *Kritika*, 12. 3 (Summer 2011), 531–60.

so on. By contrast, the medieval city, across Europe, was outwardly mute. This was a difference in the very idea of the city. In the ancient city, visible writing was part of the fabric of the urban experience. Streets and squares were lined with inscriptions: formal and informal, funerary, commemorative, legislative, commercial, triumphal or devotional. The medieval city was more inward-facing. In medieval Rus, Byzantium, or early Muscovy, the space for the display of words was inside a church, with its inscribed wall-paintings and panel icons, its Gospel books in jewelled bindings, the wordily embroidered textiles covering the liturgical vessels or hanging beneath the sacred images, or draped over royal tombs.[2] Ecclesiastical interiors could be filled with visible words, but their graphospheric density did not extend into the streets. A few signs of writing might have been found clustered around church walls: on the occasional exterior wall paintings,[3] or, in a more transient context, on the icons, banners, and ceremonial vestments briefly paraded on feast-day processions. For the most part, however, public, open spaces were free of the visible words.

When, how, and why did signs of writing spread into the cityscape and, indeed, into the wider landscape? In Russia the transformation of the public graphosphere took place far later than in much of Europe. In the Renaissance city the stones spoke once more.[4] In Russia we only begin to see the faintest hints of a beginning of a process from the late fifteenth century, but little fundamental change — despite some vigorous attempts — until the late eighteenth and early nineteenth centuries. By the second half of the nineteenth century, in Jeffrey Brooks's evocation, "the city, with its shop signs and street names, window displays and price tags, newspapers and kiosks, announcements and bookstalls

---

[2] See, e.g., Charlotte Roueché, 'Written Display in the Late Antique and Byzantine City', in *Proceedings of the 21st International Congress of Byzantine Studies. London, 21–26 August 2006. vol. 1. Plenary Papers*, ed. by E. Jeffreys (Aldershot: Ashgate, 2006), pp. 235–53.

[3] M. A. Orlova, *Naruzhnye rospisi srednevekovykh khramov. Vizantiia. Balkany. Drevniaia Rus'*, 2nd ed. (Moscow: Severnyi palomnik, 2002); esp. pp. 193–250.

[4] On public inscriptions in the Renaissance see Armando Petrucci, *Public Lettering. Script, Power, and Culture*, transl. by Linda Lappin (London, Chicago: Chicago University Press, 1993), esp. pp. 16–51.

exhibited the written word to all who walked its streets".[5] How did such transformations come about? The question here is not about literacy. Obviously there may be links between graphospheric density and rates of literacy, but literacy rates are by no means the only variables, and, for present purposes, are not the most important variables.

Between the mid-fifteenth century and the mid-nineteenth century, the formation of the Russian graphosphere was not an evenly paced process. One can distinguish three phases. The first phase, roughly from the late fifteenth century to the late seventeenth century, is characterised by sporadic, uncoordinated and not widely conspicuous graphospheric activity on behalf of the Church and the state. The second phase, over the late seventeenth century and the early eighteenth century, was a period of fairly intense graphospheric initiatives by the state. The dynamics and the aims were, so to speak, top-down, as visible writing was introduced to further the causes of ideology, public information, and, to some degree, public education. The third phase began towards the middle of the eighteenth century but was not fully developed until the early nineteenth century. One of the principal actors was again the state, though now the purposes were largely administrative and fiscal. However, the crucial new catalyst for the spread of public writing was not an institution taking "top-down" decisions on the means of communication, but a "bottom-up" activity which generated its own powerful graphospheric demands: trade, commerce, private business. The three phases are not entirely distinct chronologically. In their movement and interrelations they are perhaps more like successive waves—linked at their troughs but separable at their peaks.

Phase One: Sporadic Inscription

Public inscription began to appear in Muscovy from the late fifteenth century, and for almost two hundred years was almost entirely restricted to three contexts: inscriptions on gravestones; inscriptions marking the completion or dedication of public buildings; and inscriptions on monumental bronze-cast cannons and bells.

---

5   Jeffrey Brooks, *When Russia Learned to Read. Literacy and Popular Culture, 1861–1917* (Princeton: Princeton University Press, 1985), p. 12.

For half a millennium after the first official conversion in Rus, Christian East Slavs were apparently content to bury their dead in unlabelled graves. In the early centuries the articulate lapidary marking of grave-sites, while not wholly unknown, was a rare exception.[6] A practice of producing inscribed commemorative stone crosses is suggested by a few survivals from the mid- to late fifteenth century.[7] As for grave-slabs themselves, a continuous tradition of their inscription begins from the 1490s. Over the following couple of centuries the practice became fairly widespread in major monastic cemeteries (and in church interiors) both in Moscow and elsewhere.[8] From the initial bare record of names, the inscriptions, on horizontal slabs, went through phases of increasingly informative formulae, adding the date according to the calendar of church festivals, the year, sometimes even the hour of death, as well as the lifespan and the social standing of the deceased. Eighteenth-century cemeteries adopted the whole range of rhetorical funerary genres that befitted an enlightened empire, including a rich variety of inscriptional forms and genres, and, from the latter part of the century, sculpted figurative monuments.[9]

What prompted the change in practice? The sources do not explain themselves.[10] Here we simply note that the proliferation of

---

[6] See Simon Franklin, 'On the Pre-History of Inscribed Gravestones in Rus', *Palaeoslavica*, 10 (2002), 105–21.

[7] A. V. Sviatoslavskii, A. A. Troshin, *Krest v russkoi kul'ture. Ocherki russkoi monumental'noi stavrografii* (Moscow: Drevlekhranilishche, 2000), pp. 158–63. (On the cross of Stepan Borodatyi: G. V. Popov, 'Belokamennyi krest 1462/1467 goda iz Borisoglebskogo monastyria v Dmitrove', in ΣΟΦΙΑ. *Sbornik statei po iskusstvu Vizantii i Drevnei Rusi v chest' A. I. Komecha* (Moscow: Severnyi palomnik, 2006), pp. 325–46.

[8] See L. A. Beliaev, *Russkoe srednevekovoe nadgrobie. Belmennye plity Moskvy i Severo-Vostochnoi Rusi XIII–XVII vv.* (Moscow: MODUS-GRAFFITI, 1996); *Russkoe srednevekovoe nadgrobie, XIII–XVII veka: materialy k svodu. Vypusk 1*, ed. by L. A. Beliaev (Moscow: Nauka, 2006).

[9] T. S. Tsarkova, S. I. Nikolaev, 'Epitafiia peterburgskogo nekropolia', in *Istoricheskie kladbishcha Sankt-Peterburga. Spravochnik-putevoditel'*, ed. by A. V. Kobak and Iu. M. Piriutko (St Petersburg: Izd. Chernysheva, 1993), pp. 111–29; S. O. Androsov, 'O pervykh figurativnykh nadgrobiiakh v Rossii', in *idem, Ot Petra I k Ekaterine II. Liudi, statui, kartiny* (St Petersburg: Dmitrii Bulanin, 2013), pp. 240–52.

[10] Daniel H. Kaiser, 'Discovering Individualism Among the Deceased: Gravestones in Early Modern Russia', in *Modernizing Muscovy: Reform and Social Change in Seventeenth-Century Russia*, ed. by Jarmo Kotilaine and Marshall T. Poe (London and New York: RoutledgeCurzon, 2004), pp. 433–59.

funerary inscriptions in cemeteries was one of the first processes as the graphosphere spread out from under the roof of the church or the scriptorium or the chancery, into the open air, exposed to the public gaze. However, cemeteries were "public" only in a limited sense. Though open to the elements, a cemetery was still enclosed, bounded: a designated, delineated space for the display of writing. This is still a very long way from the late antique lapidary inscriptions which lined the streets and addressed their civilised epigrams to any passer-by who cared to pause and contemplate.

The occasional practice of placing outward-facing inscriptions on buildings likewise dates from the end of the fifteenth century. The earliest known example was—and still is—on the Kremlin itself. The Kremlin's massive brick walls were built between 1485 and 1495 by a team of Italian architects including Antonio Gilardi, Marco Ruffo, and Pietro Antonio Solari. Above the main entrance to the Kremlin from Red Square, under the Frolov Tower (renamed the Spasskaia Tower in 1658), were two inscriptions carved on stone tablets, one on the inner façade (i.e. in effect above the exit from the Kremlin), the other on the outer façade (above the entrance from Red Square). Both recorded, in almost identical wording, the construction of the tower in 1491 by Solari on the orders of the Grand Prince Ivan III. Though the tablets agree on the year, they differ on the month: March in the outer inscription, July in the inner inscription. The exit inscription was in Slavonic, but the entrance inscription—the first and most publicly visible inscription—was in Latin.[11] For Solari this was normal, in the manner of equivalent inscriptions in contemporary Italy.[12] In Muscovy it was wholly exceptional. To a limited extent, the practice became naturalised. Several other equivalent inscriptions, in Slavonic, date from the early

---

11 D. A. Drboglav, *Kamni rasskazyvaiut… Epigraficheskie latinskie pamiatniki XV-pervaia polovina XVII v. (Moskva, Serpukhov, Astrakhan')* (Moscow: Izdatel'stvo Moskovskogo universiteta, 1988), pp. 12–16. See, however, D. A. Petrov, 'Monumental'nye nadpisi P'etro Antonio Solari v Moskve', *Voprosy epigrafiki*, 5 (2011), 322–34, for a different reading of the sequence of months.

12 See O. A. Belobrova, 'Latinskaia nadpis'' na Frolovskikh vorotakh Moskovskogo Kremlia i ee sud'ba v drevnerusskoi pis'mennosti', in *Gosudarstvennye muzei Moskovskogo Kremlia. Materialy i issledovaniia. Novye atributsii. Vypusk V* (Moscow: Iskusstvo, 1987), pp. 51–57.

sixteenth century.[13] Nor was the acquired custom restricted to the state, or to Moscow. Over the first half of the sixteenth century, carved stone or ceramic inscriptions marking the foundation or construction of churches can be found in the provinces, even in quite small settlements.[14] The tradition of ceramic inscriptions seems to have originated in Pskov in the late fifteenth century; several Moscow examples date from the seventeenth century.[15]

To treat bronze bells and cannon in the same context as buildings may seem incongruous, but they are brought together in the public graphosphere. Bells in a Russian bell-tower are somewhat liminal between exterior and interior. They are within the bell-tower, but Russian bell-towers were often little more than elaborate open-sided frames, in which the bells were visible. Although bells had been cast in Rus in earlier centuries, the proliferation of elaborately *inscribed* Muscovite bronze-cast bells dates from the sixteenth and seventeenth centuries.[16] Whether they were the grand, multi-ton monumental bells with details of their donors cast in quite large and visible bands of lettering around the shoulder and/or rim, or the smaller bells for market sale and subsequent inscription, they added to the thickening clusters of signs of writing on display on and around, rather than exclusively inside, the church.

The technology of casting cannons in bronze was brought to Moscow by Italian craftsmen in the late 1480s. Chronicles record the casting of a "great cannon" by the *friazin* Pavlin (Paolo), an event considered memorable enough to be recorded pictorially in the official, prestigious

---

13 A. V. Grashchenkov, 'Plita s latinskoi nadpis'iu so Spasskoi bashni i titul gosudaria vseia Rusi', *Voprosy epigrafiki*, 1 (2006), 16–25; A. G. Avdeev, 'Utrachennaia nadpis' 1530 g. o stroitel'stve kremlia v Kolomne: Opyt rekonstruktsii soderzhaniia', *Voprosy epigrafiki*, 2 (2008), 178–89.

14 G. G. Donskoi, 'Proklamativnaia funktsiia nadpisi na kolokol'ne Novospasskogo monastyria', *Voprosy epigrafiki*, 7. 2 (2013), 199–205; V. B. Girshberg, 'Nadpis' mastera Poviliki', *Sovetskaia arkheologiia*, 2 (1959), 248–49; A. G. Avdeev, 'Khramozdannye nadpisi XVI–XVII vv. Kostromy i kraia', *Kostromskaia zemlia*, 5 (2002), 158–65.

15 I. I. Pleshanova, 'Pskovskie arkhitekturnye keramicheskie poiasa', *Sovetskaia arkheologiia*, 2 (1963), 212–16; S. I. Baranova, *Moskovskii arkhitekturnyi izrazets XVII veka v sobranii Moskovskogo gosudarstvennogo ob"edinennogo muzeia-zapovednika Kolomenskoe-Izmailovo-Lefortovo-Liublino* (Moscow: MGOMZ, 2013), esp. e.g. pp. 75–77.

16 On inscribed bells, A. F. Bondarenko, *Istoriia kolokolov v Rossii XI–XVII vv.* (Moscow: Russkaia panorama, 2012).

and elephantine *Illustrated Chronicle* of the late sixteenth century.[17] The earliest surviving local cannon, by the master Iakov, dates (like the Kremlin tower inscriptions) from 1491. The mid-sixteenth century saw the casting of a series of enormous cannons which became, in effect, public monuments: in the 1550s by Kaspar Ganusov (over 19,000 kg) and Stepan Petrov (nearly 17,000 kg). These giants served on military campaigns in the early 1560s, but were later put on public display in Red Square, near the Frolov Gates (which bore Solari's inscription of 1491). Here they were joined by the most monstrous gun of all, Andrei Chokhov's "Tsar Cannon" (as it has come to be known) of 1586, weighing over 38,000 kg.[18] Chokhov's cannon was not even made to be fired. Its internal workings were never completed. Its function was to impress, and part of its impressive display was the eloquent cast decoration on its barrel, which included an equestrian representation of the Muscovite ruler, and two inscriptions (in Russian) declaring the patronage of the tsar and his wife, and the date of the cannon's manufacture by Chokhov. On the occasions that inscribed cannons were used in the field or on parade, they might be joined by an altogether more flimsy form of inscribed object: banners. Particularly grand and elaborate was Ivan IV's "Great Banner", commissioned in 1559–60.[19]

Few meaningful conclusions can be drawn from this period of sporadic public inscriptions. The functions seem to me mainly declarative or commemorative, noting a death, or the commissioning of the relevant structure or object. Some of the state inscriptions formed a graphospheric cluster around (and on) the entrance to the Moscow Kremlin. However, here and elsewhere we should make a distinction between visibility and legibility. Accessibility and ease of reading does

---

17 E.g. *Ioasafovskaia letopis'* (Moscow: Izdatel'stvo Akademii nauk SSSR, 1957), p. 126 (fol. 134v of the MS); *Litsevoi letopisnyi svod XVI veka. Russkaia letopisnaia istoriia. Kniga 17 1483–1502 gg.* (facsimile edition; Moscow: AKTEON, 2010), p. 73 (fol. 410 of the 'Shumilov' manuscript of the original).

18 E. L. Nemirovskii, *Andrei Chokhov (okolo 1545–1629)* (Moscow: Nauka, 1982); Sergei Bogatyrev, 'Bronze Tsars: Ivan the Terrible and Fedor Ivanovich in the Décor of Early Modern Guns', *Slavonic and East European Review*, 88. 1–2 (January/April 2010), 48–72.

19 Sergei Bogatyrev, 'The Heavenly Host and the Sword of Truth: Apocalyptic Imagery in Ivan IV's Moscow', in *The New Muscovite Cultural History. A Collection in Honor of Daniel B. Rowland*, ed. by Valerie Kivelson, Karen Petrone, Nancy Shields Kollmann, and Michael S. Flier (Bloomington: Slavica, 2009), pp. 77–90.

not seem to have been a criterion for those who commissioned and made many of the inscriptions. Few Muscovites would have been able to read Solari's Latin; but, equally, without exceptional eyesight, few would have been able to see distinctly the lettering on the bells in their bell-towers. And even if they had access to the towers, or if they bought one of the smaller portable bells, few would have found the bands of highly ornamental, quasi-cryptographic *viaz'* lettering simple to decipher. The *presence* of an inscription was plainer than its contents; as if that presence had its own eloquence, a visual communication irrespective of the individual's ability to decode its verbal information.

Phase Two: State Projects, Projections of the State

In May 1682 an uprising of the Moscow musketeers (the *strel'tsy*) installed Sofiia Alekseevna, elder half-sister of the nine-year-old future Tsar Peter I, as regent. As part of the settlement, Sofiia issued a decree, one of whose stipulations was that the actions of the *strel'tsy* were to be, in effect, retrospectively legitimised, and that they were not to be deemed rebels. The text of this decree was embossed onto two large brass plates, which were then fixed to what was described as a "pillar" — actually a kind of four-sided plinth or pedestal — on Red Square.[20] Whether or not this monumental decree-stand was intended to be permanent, it only survived for a few months. It was demolished with the next twist in political fortunes. However, the precedent did not go unnoticed, and was revived in the late 1690s by Peter, already as tsar. In March 1697 Peter set up another pedestal on Red Square, on which to display the heads of a group of failed (obviously) conspirators.

We do not know whether this graphic (in another sense) display was accompanied by a written text, but there is no doubt about the graphospheric function of Peter's next such monument, set up two years later, in 1699. The catalyst, as it had been in 1682, was a revolt of the *strel'tsy*, but on this occasion the revolt was catastrophically unsuccessful, the tsar's reprisals were harsh, wide-reaching, and prolonged, and the setting up of plinths with texts was an important

---

20 A. V. Lavrent'ev, 'Stareishie grazhdanskie monumenty Moskvy 1682–1700 gg', in idem, *Liudi i veshchi. Pamiatniki russkoi istorii i kul'tury XVI–XVIII vv., ikh sozdateli i vladel'tsy* (Moscow: Arkheograficheskii tsentr, 1997), pp. 177–202.

11. Information in Plain Sight: The Formation of the Public Graphosphere   349

device for promulgating the fate of the rebels. After the suppression of the revolt, Peter placed such plinths not only in Red Square, but in ten other locations around the city. Each column was four-sided, and to each side was fixed a cast-iron plate displaying lists of the names of the traitors. In the absence of any other free-standing public monuments, this was a major incursion into the Muscovite cityscape. Moreover, the "pillars" of 1699–1700 proved more durable than their predecessor from 1682. They stood throughout Peter's reign before being removed in 1727, before the coronation of Peter II. One of the cast iron plates survives to this day.[21]

These late-seventeenth-century structures were, in effect, monumental public notice boards. The monumental display of legislation was not unusual in the graphosphere of the antique city.[22] In Russia the monumentality turned out to be transient, but the function met what was increasingly felt by the authorities to be a regular need. In the second half of the seventeenth century, government decrees quite often specified the means by which they were to be promulgated. Traditional devices included public proclamation, and the distribution of handwritten copies to the relevant offices and regions. From the 1690s, the texts of some decrees begin to stipulate that, in addition to oral declamation and internal distribution, copies should be made for public display, to be posted on, for example, gate-posts, walls, and church doors.[23] These were, in a sense, a kind of official newspaper before newspapers.[24] From 1714 Peter decreed that all decrees of general applicability must be printed, not handwritten, and it became common for the texts to be produced in two formats: what one might call book-size, and poster-size. The book-sized versions, printed on both sides of the sheet, were for internal use, while the poster-sized versions, printed on one side only (i.e. as broadsides), were for display. The metallic messages on the plinths set up in Moscow in the wake of successive uprisings of the *strel'tsy* can be seen as early experiments in the visual

---

21   In the collections of the museum of the Novodevichi Monastery: see Lavrent'ev, 'Stareishie grazhdanskie monumenty', p. 178.
22   Also a widespread function of public inscriptions in the ancient world: see e.g. Roueché, 'Written Display', pp. 251–52.
23   Simon Franklin, 'Printing and Social Control in Russia 2: Decrees', *Russian History*, 38 (2011), 467–92 (esp. pp. 473–76).
24   On newspapers in Russia see Chapters 3 and 6 in the present volume.

projection of the authoritative word. However, although purpose-built monuments might have been felt to convey the importance of the message, public pronouncements generated by current events rarely retain their aura of urgency and currency. Paper, print and existing surfaces proved more effective (and, surely, more cost-effective) over time. The posting of paper copies of decrees from the late seventeenth and, especially, the early eighteenth century was perhaps the first device through which the word of the state contributed in a systematic and sustained way to the formation of a public graphosphere: initially in Moscow, then in St Petersburg, then throughout the empire.

As in the case of the earlier inscriptions, one might well wonder who, among a largely illiterate populace, was expected to read such notices. This was not the authorities' concern. The purpose was to make the text of decrees available, and to stress repeatedly in the texts themselves the principle that ignorance of the law would not be counted as an excuse. The expectation, presumably, was that further dissemination would still be oral. Those who could not read still had access to the text via those who could. And all could (or should) understand that words posted in public—especially printed words, since the technology of print was a state-controlled monopoly—carried the voice of authority. They were, indeed, the principal visible devices by which the tsar communicated information to his subjects.

For legislative announcements, the monumental form was abandoned, but the fashion for monumental public inscriptions persisted. It developed in different directions, for different purposes.

The monuments with the most dramatic effect on the cityscape and its graphospheric density were the towers, arches, gates and the like which Peter (and then several of his successors) ordered to be erected for festive occasions: for firework displays, or for triumphal entries of the tsar and his troops after military victories.[25] The earliest in the sequence were the fireworks and triumphal arch to mark the Azov campaign in 1696. The most elaborate were the multiple arches constructed in Moscow

---

25 D. D. Zelov, *Ofitsial'nye svetskie prazdniki kak iavlenie russkoi kul'tury kontsa XVII–nachala XVIII veka. Istoriia triumfov i feierverkov ot Petra Velikogo do ego docheri Elizavety* (Moscow: Editorial URSS, 2002), pp. 122–94; E. A. Tiukhmeneva, *Iskusstvo triumfal'nykh vrat v Rossii pervoi poloviny XVIII veka. Problemy panegiricheskogo napravleniia* (Moscow: Progress-Traditsiia, 2005).

to mark the victory at Poltava in 1709. All of them were prominently, and often copiously, inscribed, sometimes in Latin, sometimes in Cyrillic, sometimes in both scripts. These were very major projects for the projection of imperial prestige, both to an internal audience and to visitors. Rhetorical and explanatory descriptions of such festivities were written out in manuscript and printed as pamphlets, many of which included full details of all the inscriptions.[26] Engravings were commissioned, showing images of the triumphal and festive structures, including (in several cases) scrupulous renditions of the inscriptions.[27]

So, were public spaces in Moscow, and then in St Petersburg, thereby irrevocably transformed, turned into graphospheric simulacra of their counterparts in antiquity? No. The problem is that these structures were mostly temporary. They were erected quickly, for special occasions, generally in wood and with papier-mâché ornamentation, though painted to resemble marble. Then they disappeared. They were, in a sense, monumental ephemera, part of the decorations for one-off performances on a public stage. They served imperial ceremonial, not urban design. We know of them mostly by their reflection in other media: through printed descriptions and in engravings. Paper turned out to be more permanent than wood. A saturated public graphosphere was part of the aesthetic of urban space for Peter's engravers. They helped to create and to disseminate the image, but it was largely an illusion.

Such monumental ephemera, or ephemeral monuments, were not peculiarly Russian. Their transience should not be taken to imply that ceremonial graphospheric structures in Russia were uniquely or even unusually flimsy. On the contrary, ephemeral-monumental epigraphy (the oxymoronic phrase is suggested by Armando Petrucci)[28] was characteristically Western European. That was partly the point. In this, as in so many of his presentational initiatives, Peter was following European custom. Equivalent ephemeral monumental writing was common throughout Europe in the sixteenth and seventeenth centuries,

---

26 For texts see Tiukhmeneva, *Iskusstvo triumfal'nykh vrat*, pp. 154–275. For a list of printed accounts see Zelov, *Ofitsial'nye svetskie prazdniki*, pp. 140–48.

27 See the extensive illustrations in Tiukhmeneva, *Iskusstvo triumfal'nykh vrat*, between pp. 96 and 97; also M. A. Alekseeva, *Graviura petrovskogo vremeni* (Leningrad: Iskusstvo, 1990), pp. 72–75, 117–22; M. A. Alekseeva, *Iz istorii russkoi graviury XVII–nachala XIX v.* (Moscow, St Petersburg: Al'ians Arkheo, 2013), pp. 142–51, 188–94.

28 See Petrucci, *Public Lettering*, pp. 53–55.

as, indeed, was the concern to issue texts to record and explain the spectacle. The most immediate exemplars were probably Dutch. Among Russian translations from Dutch in the 1690s was a version of the detailed account of the triumphal entry of William of Orange into The Hague on 5 February 1691, including the translation of some 140 Latin inscriptions on the various ceremonial monuments.[29] William's parade was also captured in engravings by, among others, the physician Govert Bidloo, whose nephew Niclaas became physician to Peter. The early engravings of the Petrine festivities were made by Peter's Dutch engravers Adriaan Schoonebeck and Piter Pickaert and by their Russian pupils. Indeed, Schoonebeck's engraving of the firework spectacle following the Azov campaign of 1696 was most likely made while he was still in Holland, on the basis of the accounts of Russian envoys.

Peter's triumphal arches were durable in one respect. They set a fashion among Russia's rulers which lasted until the end of the eighteenth century, not just at parades to mark military victories but on more peaceable occasions such as coronations.[30] As for the inscriptions, their graphospheric functions were integral to the "top-down" creation of a quasi-classical urban aesthetic (once more, irrespective of whether viewers could read the Latin), but they also had more specific associations. They derived from the pan-European culture of emblems—illustrations with edificatory mottoes and captions—which Peter embraced and which retained popularity in Russia for much of the eighteenth century.

Peter's other initiative in the commissioning of inscribed monuments—antique statuary—was likewise both elegant and edificatory, though less bombastic and more solid. Peter worked on plans for his Summer Gardens from 1704. Antique statuary, ordered from abroad, was integral to the concept, and remained a characteristic feature of the gardens throughout many subsequent redesigns and

---

29 Yu. K. Begunov, '"Opisanie vrat chesti...": a Seventeenth-Century Russian Translation on William of Orange and the "Glorious Revolution"', *Oxford Slavonic Papers. New Series*, 20 (1987), 60–93. Begunov attributes the translation to Il'ia Kopievskii.

30 See e.g. A. N. Voronikhina, 'Triumfal'nye vorota 1742 g. v Sankt-Peterburge', in *Russkoe iskusstvo barokko. Materialy i issledovaniia*, ed. by T. V. Alekseeva (Moscow: Nauka, 1977), pp. 159–72; also Paul Keenan, *St Petersburg and the Russian Court, 1703–1761* (Basingstoke, New York, 2013), pp. 66–75.

remodellings.³¹ Mostly the inscriptions were simply labels identifying the figures represented in the sculptures, sometimes also the maker. Some, however, were more elaborate. Jacob von Stählin tells the story of a conversation between Peter and his Swedish garden designer. Peter said that he wished the garden to be educative, to "convert this place of mere amusement into a kind of school". The Swede assumed he meant that books—suitably protected—were to be left on the benches. Peter laughed, and explained his idea. One area was to consist of four fountains joined by alleys, and the fountains and the alleys were to be ornamented with figures from Aesop's fables. Moreover, "as the Czar knew that few people would be able to find out the meaning of these figures, and that a still smaller number would comprehend the instruction conveyed in the fables, he ordered a post to be placed near each of them: on these posts a sheet of tin was fastened, on which the fables and their morals were written in the Russian language".³²

Stählin's source for the story of Peter and the garden designer was apparently Aleksandr Lvovich Naryshkin (1694–1746), who was Director of the Imperial Buildings and Gardens from 1736—that is, more than a decade after Peter's death. This account may or may not reflect an actual conversation. However, it does catch one aspect of Peter's known intentions: that his parks and gardens should be places of education and edification as well as pleasure and contemplation, and that inscriptions were integral to this vision.³³

Among those who paid attention to the inscriptions was no less a commentator than Giacomo Casanova, who recorded his impressions of a visit in 1765. Casanova waxed supercilious not only about the poor quality of the statues but expressly about the ineptitude of the labelling: "As I walked about I marvelled at the statuary, all the statues being made of the worst stone, and executed in the worst possible taste. The names cut beneath them gave the whole the air of a practical joke. A

---

31 S. O. Androsov, 'Raguzinskii v Venetsii: priobretenie statui dlia Letnego sada', in *idem, Ot Petra I k Ekaterine II.*, pp. 44–78; James Cracraft, *The Petrine Revolution in Russian Imagery* (Chicago and London: University of Chicago Press, 1997), pp. 220–31.

32 J. Stählin, *Original Anecdotes of Peter the Great, Collected from the Conversation of Several Persons of Distinction at Petersburgh and Moscow* (London and Edinburgh: J. Murray, J. Sewell, W. Creech, 1788), pp. 249–52 (anecdote no. 75).

33 See e.g. D. S. Likhachev, *Poetika sadov. K semantike sadovo-parkovykh stilei. Sad kak tekst*, 2nd ed. (St Petersburg: Nauka, 1991), pp. 126–28.

weeping statue was Democritus; another, with grinning mouth, was labelled Heraclitus; an old man with a long beard was Sappho; and an old woman, Avicenna; and so on".[34] Most likely, Casanova was exaggerating for effect, but behind the specific points there perhaps lies a broader condescension regarding the use of such inscriptions in general, for he demonstrates that no self-respecting Venetian needs labels to help him identify the figures of antique statuary. Whether or not Casanova regarded inscriptions as, in principle, educative, he made it clear that he regarded the Russians as being in need of education.

Antique statuary, often inscribed, became a common feature of the grand parks that proliferated throughout the century: first the royal parks, then their aristocratic followers. Sometimes the intended educative function of inscriptions was further developed. For example, on Aleksandr Borisovich Kurakin's estate at Nadezhdino in Saratov province, the park itself, laid out in the 1790s, became the subject of an elaborate set of signs and captions. Kurakin explained that "on each path one will find several posts with placards of its name, so that visitors will be overwhelmed by ideas and corresponding sensations".[35] This was not just a matter of displaying evocative names. Kurakin's signs showed four-line iambic hexameter verses explaining how he wished each temple and path to be interpreted and experienced.[36]

Regarding the Petrine period of state-promoted expansion of the public graphosphere, two points are clear. In the first place, Peter shared and promoted a new — for Russia — sense of visible writing as intrinsic to urban public spaces. This is apparent both in the consistency with which he sponsored the public display of writing, and in the reflections of this graphospheric aesthetic in other media: the booklets that described and explained public inscriptions, the engravings that reproduced them on paper. Even book illustrations with no direct relation to urban space might use the trope of the inscribed building, such as the architectural

---

34 From the start of chapter 21 of the section 'In London and Moscow' in Casanova's *Memoirs*; cited from Arthur Machen's translation available at http://ebooks.adelaide.edu.au/c/casanova/c33m/index.html; see I. V. Riazantsev, *Skul'ptura v Rossii XVIII–nachala XIX veka* (Moscow: Zhiraf, 2003), pp. 412–18; and more broadly *ibid.*, pp. 396–451 on park statuary.

35 Cited in Andreas Schönle, *The Ruler in the Garden. Politics and Landscape Design in Imperial Russia* (Oxford, Bern, Berlin etc.: Peter Lang, 2007), p. 185.

36 Schönle, *The Ruler in the Garden*, pp. 185, 193–205.

allegory of mathematics created as a headpiece for Russia's first printed scientific textbook: Leontii Magnitskii's *Arifmetika*, printed in 1703.[37] Indeed, the *idea* of the inscribed city permeated many areas of elite culture. Peter subscribed to it and promoted it, but it did not begin with him. For example, the latter part of the seventeenth century saw the appearance, in Russia, of genres of "epigraphic" poetry. This was a literary conceit: verses that were ostensibly designed to be inscriptions, whether or not there was in fact anywhere for them to be inscribed.[38] Secondly, and in contrast, Peter did not complete the transformation, or even the formation, of the public graphosphere. The vision may have been there, but its translation into the urban landscape tended to be partial, transitory, or delayed. His most visible constructions—the inscribed celebratory and festive edifices—were temporary. His most stable and permanent innovations—park statuary—were, like inscribed gravestones, both open and enclosed, not fully part of the everyday city. Other projects were idiosyncratic and unrepeatable, such as his decision, in 1722, to turn one of his early boats into a public monument, by setting it on a pedestal with appropriate inscription and ensuring that its image as a monument was recorded in engravings.[39]

The tradition of inscribed monumental statuary in fully accessible public spaces began only towards the end of the century, with Peter as its subject rather than its patron: Falconet's "Bronze Horseman", unveiled in 1792 and inscribed in Latin and Russian; and the contrasting equestrian statue set up by the Tsar Paul in 1800. The latter is a curious temporal palimpsest. It had been commissioned from Carlo Rastrelli by Peter himself, and was cast under the direction of his son Francesco Rastrelli in the 1740s, but remained in storage until retrieved by Paul, who set it up on its pedestal, with a pointedly monolingual Russian inscription, outside his own newly built palace.

---

37 T. A. Bykova and M. M. Gurevich, *Opisanie izdanii, napechatannykh kirillitsei. 1689-ianvar' 1725 g.* (Moscow and Leningrad: Izdatel'stvo Akademii nauk SSSR, 1958), no. 25; reproduced in e.g. Alekseeva, *Graviura petrovskogo vremeni*, p. 65.

38 See L. I. Sazonova, *Literaturnaia kul'tura Rossii. Rannee Novoe vremia* (Moscow: Iazyki slavianskikh kul'tur, 2006), pp. 320–27.

39 Alekseeva, *Graviura petrovskogo vremeni*, pp. 86–89, 96.

Phase Three: Signs and the Shaping of Public Space

The second phase in the formation of the public graphosphere had been marked by a succession of acts of "top-down" communication, whether informative, celebratory or edificatory and educative. In the third phase, from the mid-eighteenth century, the state's interventions in the public graphosphere were of a very different type. Instead of communicating information *from* the ruler *to* those who frequented the relevant spaces, they focused on communicating information *on and about* the spaces, partly as aids to orientation for the users of those spaces, but partly also for the practical administrative purposes of the state itself. In their purposes and functions these graphospheric initiatives addressed some of the issues of information and communication that are already familiar from previous chapters in the present volume: postal routes, cartography and surveying, taxation. The particular inscriptions are varieties of what might loosely be termed signage: mileposts, street signs, house signs.

"Mileposts" here renders the Russian *verstovye stolby*, which mark not miles but versts. A verst (Russian *versta*) is 500 *sazhens*, which, in the system in place from the early eighteenth century, comes to almost exactly a kilometre (1.067 km). Some kind of route marking was essential and existed from ancient times, especially given the conditions in winter when snow obliterates so many features of the landscape. However, with specific regard to their inscriptions, the trail of legislation begins in the 1720s. The initiatives, therefore, are again Petrine, though some of the tasks and problems identified by Peter continued to be worked out subsequently for at least a hundred years.

On 7 August 1722 Peter instructed the Senate that they should arrange to measure the distance of the direct route from Moscow to Tsaritsyn (now Volgograd), and to set up "posts with inscriptions" (*stolby s nadpisiami*) along the way, "as has been done on the Novgorod and other roads". In addition, at the onset of winter, they were to arrange to measure the Moskva, Oka, and Volga rivers along the ice, and set up posts showing the distance between towns on the banks.[40] The measurements were

---

40 *Polnoe sobranie zakonov Rossiiskoi imperii*, Series 1 (1649–1825) (hereafter *PSZ* 1), no. 4071.

done in connection with the tsar's forthcoming journey to Azov. Route measurements and their markings became a recurrent theme in imperial legislation. Successive rulers accepted that mileposts were a necessity for the efficient administration of the empire. They were needed not for the convenience of curious travellers, but for the movement of people and goods on official business (and Russia's rulers strongly discouraged the movement of goods and people on unofficial business). However, mileposts were also a cause of administrative headaches. Stone posts were expensive to install; wooden posts, in Russia's climate, were expensive because of the need for regular maintenance and repair, and in the inscriptions it was difficult to sustain accuracy and consistency.

Such are the concerns and frustrations that are reflected in successive decrees. On 23 August 1739 the Senate complained that many of the mileposts around St Petersburg were rotted and their inscriptions had become illegible. New posts were to be set up in coordination with the *Iamskaia kontora*—the Office of Posts (in a different sense).[41] Here, and again in a series of decrees of the mid-1740s, we also find reference to the problem of inaccuracy as roads changed their courses, so that surveyors need to be sent to re-measure the roads and reposition the posts and recalibrate the inscriptions.[42] This was about money as well as time. On 16 August 1744 the empress complained to the Senate that the posts along the road from Moscow to Kiev indicated a total distance of 856 versts, but the charge for transport assumed a distance of 969 versts. On 27 November the Senate reported that their delegated surveyor had measured the route at 890 versts and had repositioned the posts.[43]

The inscriptions, too, were a recurrent theme: the techniques used to make them, their forms, information, shape, and location. Paint was the obvious medium, but in 1740 the Senate decided that in the long term it would be more economical to burn the lettering into the posts with specially made branding irons. In 1744 the inscriptions were to be painted again. In 1746 the Senate even specified the colours of the oil paints—scarlet and ochre. In 1760 it was decreed that inscriptions should be written on a triangular metal plate to be affixed to each post.[44] In the

---

41   *PSZ* 1, no. 7881.
42   *PSZ* 1, nos. 8909, 9016, 9031, 9073, 9092, all from 1744.
43   *PSZ* 1, nos. 9016, 9073.
44   *PSZ* 1, nos. 8147, 9348, 11127.

early nineteenth century Alexander I expressed periodic irritation with the state of the mileposts. In detailed legislation of 1803, 1817, and 1819 he specified their height, their design according to official drawings, and the exact wording and arrangement of the inscriptions: when they should state the distance from Moscow or St Petersburg, and when they should only give the distance between post stations. He complained not just of inconsistency, but of excess verbiage. His 1817 decree on roads is particularly informative, not just about mileposts, but about a wide range of roadside signage: labelled pointers at crossroads, border signs at administrative boundaries stating which region (*guberniia*) or district (*uezd*) one was entering or leaving; signs stating the tariff at toll bridges or ferries; and, at the entrance to every settlement, a post with a signboard stating the name of the settlement, who it belonged to, and the number of "souls" in its population, "as is the custom in Little Russia".[45] Alexander's "striped mileposts" (*versty polosaty*) became embedded in the Russian cultural imagination through their appearance in one of Pushkin's best known poems, "The Winter Road".[46]

Mileposts extend the graphosphere into the countryside; in long ribbons they inscribe the empire: in real space for the efficient operations of the post roads, in imagined and reconstructed space for the accurate reduction onto paper by cartographers.

Labelling of the city itself began later. On 8 May 1768 Catherine II instructed the St Petersburg police chief, Nikolai Chicherin, to "order that, at the end of every street and alley, signs (here *doski*) are to be attached bearing the name of that street or alley in the Russian and German languages; if any streets and alleys are as yet unnamed — please name them".[47] Catherine's street signs — only two of which survive to

---

[45] *PSZ* 1, nos. 21963 (article 4), 27180 (articles 15–23, 32–33), 27787 (articles 30, 31). For the approved drawings of the respective types of milepost see the supplement to *PSZ* 1: *Chertezhi i risunki k sobraniiu*, p. 50.

[46] A. S. Pushkin, *Sobranie sochinenii v desiati tomakh*, ed. D. D. Blagoi *et al.* (Moscow: Gosudarstvennoe izdatel'stvo khudozhestvennoi literatury, 1959–1962), vol. 2, p. 159, http://rvb.ru/pushkin/01text/01versus/0423_36/1826/0428.htm

[47] Cited in D. Iu. Sherikh, *Peterburg den' za dnem. Gorodskoi mesiatseslov* (St Petersburg: 'Peterburg–XXI vek', 1998), pp. 117–18. See also Ia. N. Dlugolenskii, *Voenno-grazhdanskaia i politseiskaia vlast' Sankt-Peterburga, 1703–1917* (St Petersburg: Zhurnal 'Neva', 2001), p. 278; S. Lebedev, *Nomernye znaki domov Peterburga. Zametki i nabliudeniia* (St Petersburg, 2010), http://www.liveinternet.ru/users/zimnyi/post285701342/

the present—were in marble. Thus began the process through which the very streets and houses became frames for the urban graphosphere. First the streets were inscribed, then the houses themselves: according to Catherine's *Charter for the rights and privileges of the towns of the Russian Empire* (*Gramota na prava i vygody gorodam Rossiiskoi imperii*), published on 21 April 1785, each building was to be allocated a street number, in order to facilitate the administrative task of drawing up lists of inhabitants,[48] though nothing is said here about the public display of such numbers. Finally, in 1804, in order to facilitate the administration of a new property tax, the authorities in St Petersburg required that the identifying information be made visible: above the entrances to all non-governmental buildings there were henceforth to be metal plaques stating not only the number and the district but the owner's name.[49] This sequence of measures on the systematic numbering of houses is roughly consistent with the chronology of equivalent legislation in parts of Western Europe. In France, for example, a requirement for universal house numbering was introduced in 1791, also for tax purposes.[50]

As in the case of mileposts, this process of inscribing the city with indications of its own physical and human geography, though undertaken for administrative reasons, also facilitated wider interactions and benefits. The city was now visibly indexed in the public graphosphere, and this "real space" index, too, could be transferred to paper, through the compilation of printed directories. St Petersburg's first address book was published in 1809 and was issued more or less simultaneously (by different publishers) in German, French and Russian. Its author, Heinrich Christoph von Reimers, acknowledged in his introduction the importance of the recent fact that, over the course of 1804, signs had been fixed on every house.[51] And, also like mileposts,

---

48 *PSZ* 1, no. 16187, in an annotation to article 63.
49 Heinrich von Reimers, *St. Petersburg am Ende seines ersten Jahrhunderts. Mit Rückblicken auf Entstehung und Wachsthum dieser Residenz unter den verschiedenen Regierungen während dieses Zeitraums*, vol. 2 (St Petersburg: F. Dienemann & Co., 1805), pp. 285–86.
50 David Garrioch, 'House Names, Shop Signs and Social Organization in West European Cities, c. 1500–1900', *Urban History*, 21 (1994), 37–38.
51 Heinrich von Reimers, *St.-Peterburgische Adress-Buch auf das Jahr 1809* (St Petersburg: A. Pluchart [1809]); *idem*, *Dictionnaire d'adress de St.-Pétersbourg pour l'anné 1809, avec un plan et guide des étrangers a St-Pétersbourg* (St Petersburg [1809]); *idem*, *Sanktpeterburgskaia adresnaia kniga na 1809 god* (St Petersburg: Schnoor [1809]), p. iii.

the reach of these street and house signs stretched beyond factual information, beyond documentation and into culture. For example, the writer Evgenii Grebenka, in a "physiological" sketch published in 1845, treats the house signs on the "Petersburg side" (the district on the unfashionable side of the Neva river) first as sources for the social composition of the population: "The Petersburg Side fell into decline and became a refuge for the poor", he writes. "If one seeks proof of this, one need only read the inscriptions on the gateposts of the houses". Many of the owners were civil servants of the fourteenth (i.e. the lowest) to the eighth grade, others were non-commissioned officers, clerks, firemen, court lackeys, retired musicians. Then, however, Grebenka digresses into an anecdote of the man who apparently chose to designate himself, on the sign at the entrance to his residence, as a "retired blackamoor" — a claim which the utterly fair-skinned resident justified on the grounds that it brought him a higher pension.[52] The sign thus becomes a locus of invention, a means of creative self-expression (despite periodic attempts to impose uniformity).[53]

Not that house signs yet met all practical demands. Once a letter had successfully reached St Petersburg along the network of long-distance post roads, how did it find its addressee within the city? Signage on streets and houses and flats ought to help, perhaps. However, one visiting Englishman was left frustrated. Edward Thompson, who published his *Life in Russia; or, the Discipline of Despotism* in 1848, complained that, when he tried to deliver a letter to a resident of a building just off Nevskii Prospekt, he was unable to do so, for there was no directory of residents of the 170 flats (though there may well have been names on the individual doors).[54] Even the government recognised the problem, and around the same time devised a bureaucratic solution. In 1851, in the second, expanded edition of *All Petersburg in Your Pocket*

Note that Reimers had recognised the usefulness of the measure as early as 1805; for statistical tables of Petersburg buildings and inhabitants that he published as part of his history of the city: von Reimers, *St. Petersburg am Ende seines ersten Jahrhunderts*, p. 318.

52 E. Grebenka, 'Peterburgskaia storona', in *Fiziologiia Peterburga* (Moscow: Sovetskaia Rossiia, 1984) pp. 109–110
53 One such attempt at regulation is cited by F. Distribuendi, *Vzgliad na moskovskie vyveski* (Moscow: I. Smirnov, 1836), pp. 61–62.
54 See A. G. Cross, *St Petersburg and the British. The City through the Eyes of British Visitors and Residents* (London: Frances Lincoln Ltd., 2008), p.146.

11. Information in Plain Sight: The Formation of the Public Graphosphere   361

by Aleksei Grech, readers were informed that now, if they wanted to find out where anybody lived, they had only to go to the "Bureau of Addresses" (*adresnyi stol*): "a new and highly useful institution, which can be used by private individuals who wish to find out anybody's place of residence".[55]

Important and resonant though it undoubtedly was, the state's administrative contribution to the formation of the urban graphosphere came to be massively overshadowed by the proliferation of a different kind of sign, generated not by an institution, but by an activity: not "top down", but "bottom up". The activity was trade. Its graphospheric contribution was in the spread of shop signs.

The spread of trade signs and shop signs cannot be mapped precisely either in time or space. The process can be approximately imagined through a succession of three types of evidence: legislation, illustration, and description. The trail of legislation seems to start towards the middle of the eighteenth century. Illustrations become informative from approximately the second and third decades of the nineteenth century, while in the 1830s and 1840s such signs became objects of documentary description, literary evocation, and even quasi-philosophical contemplation.

The trail of legislation about commercial signage begins in the 1740s and 1750s, and it relates both to the location of signs and to aspects of their contents. Where trade spilled over from its designated locations (markets, trading rows), the signs of its presence were not always welcome. On 2 December 1742, Empress Elizabeth issued a decree on the construction of railings on the canal embankments. And, while on the subject of urban orderliness and sightliness (this was the same day on which she ordered the expulsion of all Jews from the empire), Elizabeth added to the decree an instruction that inns and taverns should be banned from the main embankments, and that in the same locations fruit traders should be prohibited from setting up stalls under

---

55 Aleksei Grech, *Ves' Peterburg v karmane: spravochnaia kniga dlia stolichnykh zhitelei i priezzhikh, s planami Sanktpeterburga i chetyrekh teatrov*, 2nd expanded and corrected ed. (St Petersburg: N. Grech, 1851), pp. 3–4. The first edition had been published in 1846. Note that Grech was aware that such directories needed constant updating: three supplements were published in 1852 alone (to 20 January, 25 May, and 15 November).

awnings at the ground-floor or basement street entrances to buildings.[56] Ten years later Elizabeth returned to the topic. In a decree of 14 October 1752 she reaffirmed the restrictions of 1742, and she further specified, significantly for our purposes, that she took exception not merely to signs of trade but to trade signs. The new decree stipulated that "along these streets there should be no signs (*vyveski*); lots of such signs, of various trades, are now visible even opposite the court of Her Imperial Majesty; signs are permitted on the street along the Moika".[57] This is the first legislation about trade signs, indicating that they were already becoming quite numerous and prominent, and for the empress a nuisance when they cluttered her view.

Also in the late 1740s we find the first legislation on wording. It relates to establishments which sold alcohol and tobacco. On 8 November 1746 the Senate ordered that hostelries (*kabaki*) in Moscow and St Petersburg must not display boards with the words "official drinking house" (*kazennyi piteinyi dom*). There was no objection to the designation "drinking house"; it was the word "official" that was to be deleted.[58] Clearly this was not enough to rein in the self-promoting commercial imagination, and in 1749 the Board of Revenue (*Kamer Kollegiia*) issued an order banning all excess graphic elements from signs advertising hostelries and tobacco shops. Henceforth they were to use only the prescribed wording: "In this house drinks are sold", "in this house tobacco is sold".[59]

Catherine II took a different approach. She accepted that a zonal restriction, with a blanket ban in specified areas, was damaging to trade, so in March 1770 she rescinded Elizabeth's decree of 1752. However, she did not thereby abandon all attempts to impose her own sense of civic decorum. Instead of a general ban, she regulated the form. In a decree which was to be generally applicable to both St Petersburg and Moscow, she stipulated that trade signs made of wood or canvas

---

56 *PSZ* 1, no. 8674, articles 3–5.
57 *PSZ* 1, no. 10032. Note also the slightly earlier decree of Anna Ioannovna, dated 9 November 1739, allowing merchants to build permanent shops in specified locations, but forbidding unauthorised trading from houses and basement stalls: *PSZ* 1, no. 7940.
58 *PSZ* 1, no. 9350.
59 G. V. Esipov, *Tiazhelaia pamiat' proshlogo. Rasskazy iz del Tainoi Kantseliarii i drugikh arkhivov* (St Petersburg: A. S. Suvorin, 1885), p. 307.

were permissible either when fixed flat to walls, or when suspended from a protruding arm not exceeding one *arshin* in length.[60] Decency required that there should be no signs advertising men's underwear, or funeral services, and there were to be no paper or leather signs attached to fences or shutters (that is, "proper" fixed signs were acceptable, random posters were not).[61] This is consistent with Catherine's broadly facilitative legislation on urban trade. For example, in successive decrees of 28 June and 8 July 1782 she overturned previous restrictive legislation and permitted merchants throughout the empire to trade from shops in their houses rather than just in designated markets and trading rows. In principle these decrees all but abandoned a restrictive principle of urban zoning for retail trade in favour of facilitating the autonomous spread of private shops.[62]

The implication of this sequence of decrees is that on-street painted trade signs became increasingly familiar features of the urban landscape during the third quarter of the eighteenth century. For this early period, however, we have little direct evidence regarding what was actually displayed on such signs. The likelihood is that they were principally pictorial, rather than verbal: pictures on boards representing the type of goods sold, or the type of services offered.[63] The presence of some inscriptions is plausible. By the time that signs became objects of illustration and description, pictorial and verbal elements were mixed and matched to taste.

Paintings, drawings and engravings of the cityscape, by both Russians and foreigners, are a feature of the first half of the nineteenth century. Their coverage is neither consistent nor systematic, but in some cases

---

60 On restrictions on protruding or hanging signs in various Western European countries see Garrioch, 'House Names, Shop Signs and Social Organization', 37.
61 PSZ 1, no. 13421.
62 PSZ 1, nos 15451, 15462; 28 June and 8 July 1782; on earlier decrees forbidding merchants to trade from their houses see e.g. PSZ 1, no. 7940, of 9 November 1739. Broadly on Catherine's policies on trade and merchants see Isabel de Madariaga, *Russia in the Age of Catherine the Great* (London: Weidenfeld and Nicolson, 1981), pp. 299–303, 470–77.
63 See Alla Povelikhina and Yevgeny Kovtun, *Russian Painted Shop Signs and Avant-garde Artists* (Leningrad: Aurora Art Publishers, 1991), pp. 11–26; also the summary of the early history of signs in Sally West, *I Shop in Moscow: Advertising and the Creation of Consumer Culture in Late Tsarist Russia* (DeKalb: Northern Illinois University Press, 2011), pp. 21–25; A. V. Sazikov and T. V. Vinogradova, *Naruzhnaia reklama Moskvy. Istoriia, tipologiia, dokumenty* (Moscow: Russkii Mir, 2013), pp. 11–18.

the contrasts between consecutive depictions of the same or equivalent spaces is sufficient to serve as evidence for a rough chronology of graphospheric change. With regard to the main thoroughfares of St Petersburg, they suggest that the decisive proliferation of inscribed shop signs took place over the first couple of decades of the century. We can compare, for example, the views of Nevskii Prospekt around 1800, by the Swedish artist Benjamin Patersen, with scenes from the panorama of Nevskii Prospekt in the mid-1820s by Vasilii Sadovnikov, which in the early 1830s was turned into an influential and much-celebrated series of lithographs. Patersen's St Petersburg is not completely sign-free; his view of Palace Square from the bottom end of Nevskii Prospekt shows a red sign in French in the right foreground. However, his long perspective view down the central part of Nevskii Prospekt, from Gostinyi Dvor on the left, is utterly wordless.[64] This is in stark contrast with the equivalent scenes in Sadovnikov's panorama.[65] By the 1820s Petersburg's most fashionable street had become saturated with signs.

To what extent did such signs spread beyond St Petersburg's most fashionable street? To follow them further we have to move beyond legislation and illustration. From the 1830s onward, street signs became objects of description in several genres: articles and essays, correspondence, and literature.

A vivid account of what one might call "off-street" signs is given in a sketch called "Nooks and Crannies of Petersburg" (*Peterburgskie ugly*), by Nikolai Nekrasov, which appeared in a collection of essays and stories about the city published in 1845 under the general title *The Physiology of Petersburg*. In search of accommodation, Nekrasov's narrator turns into the inner courtyard of a large building, where his "eyes encountered a patchwork of signs, which had been attached to the building just as carefully on the inside [i.e. in the courtyard] as on the outside [i.e. facing the street]". The signs advertised anything from coffins to tin plates to the services of a certified midwife. Each sign displayed three things: the relevant designation in words (the narrator is amused by some

---

64 *Sankt-Peterburg v akvareliakh, graviurakh i litografiiakh XVIII–XIX vekov: iz sobraniia Gosudarstvennogo Ermitazha*, compiled by G. A. Miroliubova, G. A. Printseva, and V. O. Looga (St Petersburg: Arka, 2009), pp. 67–69 (from the engraving by Gabriel Ludvig Lory), 189–191.

65 See the detailed analysis by Katherine Bowers in Chapter 12 of the present volume.

idiosyncratic phraseology, here in non-standard Russian rather than in French); a hand pointing towards the entrance to the relevant apartment or stall; and an explanatory picture, such as a boot, scissors, a samovar with a broken handle, a sausage, an item of furniture, and so on.[66]

Shop signs seem to have proliferated in central Moscow over roughly the same period as in St Petersburg. On 27 August 1833 Aleksandr Pushkin wrote a letter from Moscow to his wife, Natalia, in St Petersburg. It was her birthday, and the poet was chatty and upbeat. "Important news", he wrote, "the French shop signs, destroyed by Rostopchin in the year that you were born, have reappeared on Kuznetskii Most".[67] Count Fedor Rostopchin had been the military governor of Moscow at the time of Napoleon's invasion of 1812.[68] However, in Moscow during the early 1830s, shop signs were by no means limited to Kuznetskii Most. The first (to my knowledge) attempt at systematic description is an engaging pamphlet about Moscow signs, published in 1836, whose author used the unlikely-sounding name of Fedor Distribuendi.[69] Distribuendi describes twenty-five varieties of what he calls "ordinary" signs, with brief information on their design and on their usual inscriptions. With the exception of clothes shops, most of the signs noted by Distribuendi are in Russian.

Shop signs appear quite regularly in essays and stories of the period. For some they are simply the background to the bustling life of the city, others are rhetorically indignant at what they regard as the culturally demeaning prominence of French.[70] One strand of such descriptions relates to signage in general, as an urban phenomenon. Curiously (in view of the evidence for the actual spread of signs), according to this

---

66 *Fiziologiia Peterburga*, p. 132.
67 Pushkin, *Sobranie sochinenii v desiati tomakh*, vol. 10 (1962), p. 135.
68 For a satirical allusion to brash signs on foreign shops on Kuznetskii Most on the eve of the Napoleonic invasion see Konstantin Batiushkov's 'Stroll through Moscow' ('Progulka po Moskve') written in late 1811 or early 1812, in K. N. Batiushkov, *Sochineniia v dvukh tomakh*, vol. 2 (Moscow: Khudozhestvennaia literatura, 1989), p. 288.
69 Distribuendi, *Vzgliad na moskovskie vyveski*.
70 For Moscow in this perspective see e.g. I. T. Kokorev, 'Publikatsii i vyveski', in *idem*, *Moskva sorokovyh godov. Ocherki i povesti o Moskve XIX veka* (Moscow: Moskovskii rabochii, 1959), pp. 61–76 (esp. pp. 73, 74). On St Petersburg: E. I. Rastorguev, *Progulki po Nevskomy prospektu* (St Petersburg: Tipografiia Karla Kraiia, 1846), repr. in *Chuvstvitel'nye progulki po Nevskomu prospektu*, ed. by A. M. Konechnyi (St Petersburg: Petropolis, 2009), esp. pp. 138–40.

view, signs — street signs, house signs, shop signs — are sometimes taken as a distinguishing feature of the graphosphere of St Petersburg, by contrast with that of Moscow. Indeed, the two cities are even characterised in terms of this contrast. In an article entitled "Petersburg Notes for 1836", Nikolai Gogol wrote: "Moscow is a warehouse. It piles bale upon bale. It is completely oblivious to the ordinary customer. Petersburg has spread itself piecemeal, has dissipated into stalls and shops to lure the ordinary customer. Moscow says 'if the buyer needs something, he'll find it'. Petersburg thrusts its signs in one's face. [...] Moscow is one big market; Petersburg is a well lit shop".[71] Vissarion Belinskii picked up this theme in his essay "Petersburg and Moscow", with which *The Physiology of Petersburg* opens. Moscow looks inwards on itself; St Petersburg faces outward. Moscow is for Muscovites and their families; St Petersburg is for the public and for visitors. Moscow is uninterested in helping you find your way around. To find a flat in Moscow is "pure torment", whereas in St Petersburg the doors will often display "not only the number but also a bronze or iron plaque with the name of the occupant".[72] Thus, for Gogol and Belinskii, the fact that St Petersburg was a city of visible words was taken to be indicator of an aspect of its urban modernity.

In a way, the communicative dynamic of the graphosphere had been reversed. In the initiatives of Peter I the public graphosphere was created as a means of projecting information and images from and about the state. By the mid-nineteenth century, the public graphosphere had expanded as a set of reference points for orientation within and across the spaces themselves. In the early eighteenth century the translations of graphospheric phenomena into other media (engravings, printed explanations) were complementary devices to amplify and explain the message. By the mid-nineteenth century, the translations of the graphospheric phenomena into other media — in maps and plans, tax registers, urban directories of businesses and residents — served practical purposes both for the state administration and for private convenience. Under Peter I the graphosphere was, at least in part, formed to project cultural ideas of public space. By the mid-nineteenth

---

71 N. V. Gogol, *Polnoe sobranie sochinenii v 14 tomakh*, ed. by N. F. Bel'chikov and B. V. Tomashevskii (Moscow and Leningrad: AN SSSR, 1952), 8, p. 179.

72 *Fiziologiia Peterburga*, p. 56.

century, cultural ideas of public space were being formed to reflect perceptions of the graphosphere. Most of the earlier initiatives were either deliberately transient (the "ephemeral monuments") or they faded with the fashions that had engendered them. By the mid-nineteenth century the public graphosphere had taken on many of the features that it retains to the present.

12. Experiencing Information: An Early Nineteenth-Century Stroll Along Nevskii Prospekt

Katherine Bowers[1]

Nevskii Prospekt has long been St Petersburg's famous boulevard; it was where Imperial Russian high society went to see and be seen, as well as home to all the best shops: confectionaries, vintners, haberdashers, bootmakers, swordmakers, modistes, milliners. Thanks to the eighteenth- and nineteenth-century mania for urban depiction, in artists' renderings and writers' sketches we have "snapshots"—in a sense—of the street's life, giving insight into its appearance before the development of photography. In the 1820s work of artist Vasilii Sadovnikov, for example, Nevskii Prospekt is celebrated; its stately buildings, grand monuments, and bridges depicted elegantly under an idyllic pale blue sky. His remarkable watercolours painstakingly

---

1   This research was made possible through support from the University of Cambridge and the Hampton Fund at the University of British Columbia. An earlier version of this chapter was presented at the Humanities and Social Sciences seminar at Darwin College, Cambridge, in October 2014 and I am grateful to those present for their helpful feedback. I am indebted to Connor Doak, Tatiana Filimonova, Simon Franklin, and Alexander M. Martin for their constructive comments on earlier drafts of this chapter. Additionally, I wish to thank Viktoria Ivleva, with whom I consulted on several research queries about nineteenth-century Russian trade cards and shopping arcades. The images from *Panorama* that illustrate this chapter appear with permission from the State Russian Museum, St Petersburg, and I thank Yulia Khodko for her assistance in obtaining them.

reproduce every building along each side of the famous street, from the Admiralty to the Anichkov Bridge.[2] In 1830 and 1835, respectively, publisher and art patron Andrei Prévost commissioned two masters who shared a common surname, Ivan and Petr, both Ivanov, to lithograph Sadovnikov's watercolours. The monochromatic lithographs were then coloured by hand with watercolour paint and published in a collection called *Panorama of Nevskii Prospekt* (*Panorama Nevskogo Prospekta*).[3]

Panorama is made up of two continuous lithographed scrolls mounted on bands of linen: "The Left, Sunny Side of Nevskii Prospekt" (P. Ivanov, 1835), and "The Right, Shady Side of Nevskii Prospekt" (I. Ivanov, 1830). Beginning at Palace Square, the scroll records buildings along the "sunny" side of the street, crosses the thoroughfare at the Anichkov Bridge, and records buildings along the "shady" side back to the Square. By rolling the scroll, nineteenth-century viewers could "walk along" the street, pausing as often as they liked to study each individual building and monument. The quality of the images is high, given Sadovnikov's noted precision and *Panorama*'s immense dimensions of approximately 7.1 metres by 26.4 centimetres per street side.[4]

Writing in the 1830s, one reviewer called it a "masterly lithographic scroll" and another commented, "This is, so far, the best likeness of our beautiful Nevsky Prospekt".[5] St Petersburg's noted architects Carlo Rossi and Auguste de Montferrand praised *Panorama*, and many residents bought copies of the scroll, despite its ungainly length, to use as

---

2   Only two fragments of the original watercolour scrolls exist, one in the National Library of Russia, St Petersburg, and the other in the National Pushkin Museum, St Petersburg. Together they comprise only about a fifth of the complete *Panorama*. Additionally, Sadovnikov's preparatory sketches in ink have been preserved in the State Russian Museum, St Petersburg, and in the State Museum of the History of St Petersburg.

3   When describing Sadovnikov's work here and throughout, I refer to V. S. Sadovnikov, *Panorama of Nevsky Prospect: From the Collection of the Russian Museum*, ed. by Nataliia Shtrimer (Leningrad: Aurora Art Publishers, 1993). This edition consists of a good quality reproduction of the scroll broken up into coloured plates. The 1974 edition, also published by Aurora Art Publishers, is a smaller scale black and white reproduction of the original lithographs and some of the image details are difficult to make out.

4   In the original announcement, in *Literaturnaia gazeta*, no. 15 (1830), the dimensions are noted: "around ten arshins long and six vershoks wide" (*okolo 10 arshin dlinoiu i 6 vershkov shirinoiu*).

5   I. Kotel'nikova, 'Introduction', in *Panorama of Nevsky Prospekt* (Leningrad: Aurora Art Publishers, 1974), p. 8.

decorations or gifts.⁶ The work caused a stir both because of its precision and the unique visual look at the city it provided. Early nineteenth-century feuilletons and physiological sketches enabled readers to "experience" urban space, taking them on verbal "strolls".⁷ The scroll's depiction of the famous street was based on a similar concept; it allowed viewers in St Petersburg and elsewhere in the Russian Empire to "visit" and "take in" its notable perspectives, fashionable façades, and famous monuments, as well as its service class, consumer culture, and popular storefronts, from their homes in a uniquely visual way which omits many of the aspects of urban experience including smells, sounds, and bustle.

The word *Panorama* in the title, deliberately chosen by Prévost, is a commercial gimmick, meant to evoke the popular entertainment of the panorama, a handheld device that enabled viewers to traverse a rendered landscape.⁸ Contemporary scholars have connected the material experience of viewing the *Panorama* with a kind of virtual reality, an imagined journey along the fashionable thoroughfare. Art historian Tatiana Senkevitch suggests that Sadovnikov's *Panorama* could also "be pushed simultaneously through two special boxes with glass windows—the viewer was situated between them... [giving] an impression of simulating an imaginary carriage ride through the city".⁹ Julie Buckler observes that the inclusion of objects like shop signs and the "chance encounters and particulars of dress and posture" of recognisable members of St Petersburg society "rendered the Prospect very much of its moment".¹⁰ Buckler views the material form of the

---

6   Kotel'nikova, 'Introduction', p. 32.
7   Julie A. Buckler describes several of these works in the context of the Nevskii Prospekt literary tradition in *Mapping St. Petersburg: Imperial Text and Cityshape* (Princeton: Princeton University Press, 2005), pp. 83–88.
8   For more information about the development of both the panorama and Sadovnikov's *Panorama*, see Tatiana Senkevitch, 'The Phantasmagoria of the City: Gogol's and Sadovnikov's Nevsky Prospect, St Petersburg', in *The Flâneur Abroad: Historical and International Perspectives*, ed. by Richard Wrigley (Newcastle upon Tyne: Cambridge Scholars Publishing, 2014), pp. 171–74. Senkevitch's study uses Sadovnikov's *Panorama of Nevskii Prospekt* and Gogol's story 'Nevskii Prospekt' to explore notions of vision, perception, spatial dynamics, architectural and urban planning history, and the imagined city.
9   Senkevitch, 'The Phantasmagoria of the City', p. 176.
10 Buckler, *Mapping St. Petersburg*, p. 84.

scroll as instrumental in creating "a more 'local' sense of street life".[11] In this sense, *Panorama* provides an intriguing case study of the nineteenth-century public graphosphere as it was visualised contemporaneously. In this chapter—and in the spirit of *Panorama*'s original use—I will embark upon a visual "stroll" down Nevskii Prospekt, but I will focus not on imperial monuments or elegant palaces, but on commercial enterprise and, in particular, on shop signs.

In the previous chapter, Simon Franklin introduced the graphosphere and gave a broad overview of its formation and many functions. In this chapter, I will use Sadovnikov's *Panorama* as a case study that enables close observation of the minutiae of shop signs, their placement, arrangement, contents, and aesthetic. Shop signs had been regulated by a series of imperial decrees throughout the eighteenth century, as Franklin describes. Initially, official regulations were restrictive, but eventually urban zoning laws were relaxed, which allowed for mixed commercial and residential spaces and, as a result, flourishing small enterprise. As trade grew, so too did the proliferation of shop signs. Eventually, by the 1820s, as can be seen in *Panorama*, signs were a regular feature of urban space. Franklin draws the distinction between signs generated by state institutions and those generated by commercial activity; as he notes, this proliferation was "not 'top down' but 'bottom up'".[12]

Scholars typically date the decline of St Petersburg's "purity" in architecture to the moment when Nicholas I broke with convention and allowed the rapid construction of plain buildings to house the growing imperial bureaucracy.[13] However, even before the proliferation of "bureaucratic classicism" in the 1830s and its destabilisation of the ideological power inherent in imperial structures, growing commercial enterprise encroached on the neoclassical purity of the seat of power. Buckler observes that Sadovnikov's work, in its representation of "high and low, distanced and near", is able to provide "a sense of urban space as a whole".[14] The tension between trade and authority comes

---

11   Ibid.
12   See Simon Franklin's chapter in the present volume.
13   Buckler, *Mapping St Petersburg*, p. 29.
14   Ibid., p. 84.

to the fore in Sadovnikov's watercolours precisely because Nevskii Prospekt is so grand—it is a space that reflects imperial vision with its monuments and palaces—but, at the same time, is host to intense commercial enterprise, which necessarily aims mainly to communicate with potential customers.

The urban public graphosphere present along Nevskii Prospekt, as seen in Sadovnikov's watercolours, sheds light on the complicated, often conflicting relationship between commercial enterprise and imperial authority in the first half of the nineteenth century. While the graphosphere portrayed is limited to a single notable street and, therefore, by no means gives a comprehensive overview of urban space, it nonetheless proves productive. This captured graphosphere demonstrates how commercial enterprise and imperial authority are juxtaposed through their representation in information technologies.

Sadovnikov's Perspective

V. S. Sadovnikov was a serf born on the estate of Princess Natalia Golitsyna in 1800; both he and his older brother Petr were educated from childhood through the Golitsyn family's patronage. Vasilii became a landscape painter known for his attention to detail while Petr became a celebrated architect. While studying as a child in the studio of architect Andrei Voronikhin, Sadovnikov met landscape painters Maksim Vorob'ev and Aleksei Venetsianov, who exerted influence on his development as an artist. In the 1820s he had a series of popular successes with his watercolours, *Views of St Petersburg and Surrounding Areas* (*Vidy Peterburga i okrestnostei*) (1823–27) and the series of late 1820s watercolours that became *Panorama* (1830–35); these works emerged with the help of the Imperial Society for the Encouragement of Artists (*Obshchestvo pooshchreniia khudozhnikov*), which supported the work of talented serfs. Notably, the society's salon is visible on our "stroll", and we will see it when we come to figure 12 of the present chapter; the salon sign prominently features the year of its founding, 1826, and its name in both French and Russian. In the 1830s, the *Panorama* scroll could be purchased in this building!

In 1838 Sadovnikov received the title *"svobodnyi neklassnyi khudozhnik"* (free unclassed artist) from the Academy of Arts and also his freedom from bondage.[15] At the time, he was already a well-known artist thanks to his two watercolour series, *Views* and *Panorama*. In the announcement of the publication of *Panorama* in 1830, he is referred to as "*g Sadovnikov*" (Mr Sadovnikov), a title atypical for a serf. At his death in 1879, Sadovnikov was widely considered a master of both landscape and genre painting.[16]

Sadovnikov's training as an artist comes through in the spatial composition of *Panorama*. The central element of the scroll is the line of buildings; these draw the viewer's attention first. Above them is the limpid blue sky, below, the street, populated by small figures. In comparison to the figures, however, the architecture dominates. In this sense, the scroll demonstrates the result of the imperial project that began in the first half of the eighteenth century, the transformation of Nevskii Prospekt into "an unbroken chain of related ensembles".[17] Yet, these watercolours do not just depict imperial pomp; they also show glimpses into the life of the street.

Sadovnikov's experience of aristocratic society as an outsider may inform *Panorama* in that its population includes passers-by from all classes. From high-ranking noblemen wearing dress uniforms and fashionable society ladies to members of the lower classes such as tradesmen, peddlers, servants, and labourers, all can be seen along Sadovnikov's Nevskii. Even some specific, recognisable individuals (including Pushkin) stroll along Sadovnikov's boulevard. Similarly, Sadovnikov focusses on the commercial aspects of the street, particularly its residents' gastronomic and sartorial pursuits. Fashionable artists of the time such as T. A. Vasiliev, A. Martynov, K. P. Beggrov, and many others depicted St Petersburg's neoclassical façades, grand squares,

---

15 The designation of "free unclassed artist" was granted with a small silver medal from the Imperial Academy of Arts and could be given to artists unaffiliated with the Academy. In Sadovnikov's case, his medal was granted for being self-taught and practicing perspective landscape painting independently. The designation of "classed", "unclassed", or "free unclassed" artist from the Academy was required at that time to work professionally as an artist. For more information on serf artists' classifications during this period, see Richard Stites, *Serfdom, Society, and the Arts in Imperial Russia: The Pleasure and the Power* (New Haven: Yale University Press, 2008), pp. 325–27.

16 For more on Sadovnikov's life and works, see O. Kaparulina, *Vasilii Semonovich Sadovnikov* (St Petersburg: Palace Editions, 2000).

17 Yuri Egorov, *The Architectural Planning of St Petersburg*, trans. by Eric Dluhosch (Athens, OH: Ohio University Press, 1969), pp. 204–05.

and elegant bridges as grand architectural studies; in comparison, Sadovnikov's St Petersburg has a striking energy. His scenes invite the viewer to experience urban space, to "feel the spirit of the age".[18]

Shop Signs Along the Sunny Side

Our stroll begins with a view of Palace Square; Rastrelli's grand Winter Palace is visible behind the immense Alexander Column. The Column, a monument to the victory over Napoleon in 1812, was designed by architect Auguste Montferrand and does not appear in Sadovnikov's original watercolours; it was raised between 1830 and 1834. Throughout the scroll, there are some chronological discrepancies as the lithographers updated the original rendering of the street to reflect new noteworthy sights and businesses. Notable, too, is the sense of movement given by populating the street scene with individual figures going about their business. Here, a company of soldiers marches across the square while passers-by look on, ladies stroll, boys chase each other at play, and a group of dogs frolicks. This vibrancy sets the *Panorama* apart from the static engraved images of urban space that had become popular in the eighteenth century.

This initial introduction to Nevskii Prospekt is saturated with the emblems of empire: grand displays of wealth, power, and glory, as well as attention to the square's ensemble of palace and monument. St Petersburg itself represents a grand imperial building project, an exercise in authority in the sense of the moderation and control of public space. Here, in the home of the tsar and the headquarters of the military forces, the empire's might is apparent not only in the company of soldiers marching past, but also in the neoclassical façades and spatial composition of the square. As historian William Craft Brumfield has succinctly articulated, "The architecture of St Petersburg—grandiose, overpowering at times, obsessed with rational design—remains the clearest statement of purpose that Imperial Russia ever made: to measure, to build, to impose order at any cost".[19]

---

18 Kotel'nikova, 'Introduction', p. 32.
19 William Craft Brumfield, 'St Petersburg and the Art of Survival', in *Preserving Petersburg: History, Memory, Nostalgia*, ed. by Helena Goscilo and Stephen M. Norris (Bloomington: Indiana University Press, 2008), p. 1.

Figure 1: View of Palace Square.

As we move down Nevskii Prospekt away from Palace Square along the left, sunny side of the street in the perpetual afternoon of Sadovnikov's watercolours, commercial displays such as shop signs and storefronts begin to appear. Senkevitch argues that moving along Nevskii activates "the kinesthetic command of the observer by imposing on him/her a certain hegemony of visual order enforced by the rhetoric of architectural spaces".[20] However, the commercial spaces that confront us sharply contrast with the stately ensemble of the Square, and interrupt the "hegemony of visual order" that the imperial architecture imposes. While still neoclassical and grand, the façades here host a proliferation of shop signs mixing languages, scripts, and images. Signs spell out names in both Cyrillic and Latin scripts—for example: "Formann/Форманъ" or "Elers/Елерсъ". Images, too, begin to appear in addition to the words.

In his 1858 travel account, Théophile Gautier remarks on the wonders of the multilingual and image-rich signage on Nevskii Prospekt:

> But perhaps you don't know Russian, and the form of the characters means nothing more for you than an ornamental design or a piece of embroidery? Here to the side is the French or German translation. You still haven't understood? The obliging sign pardons you for not recognising any of these three languages; it even assumes that you might be completely illiterate, and presents a lifelike depiction of the goods for sale in the shop it is advertising. Sculpted or painted bunches of golden grapes indicate a wine merchant; further along glazed hams, sausages, tongues, tins of caviar designate a food shop; high boots, ankle boots, naïvely presented galoshes, say to feet that don't know how to read: 'Enter here and you will be shod'; crossed gloves speak an idiom intelligible to all.[21]

The mix of Russian, French, German, Italian and even English and Dutch is not surprising, given Nevskii's typically elite and cosmopolitan clientele.[22] Nearly all the signs are at least bilingual.

---

20 Senkevitch, 'The Phantasmagoria of the City', p. 169.
21 Théophile Gautier, *Voyage en Russie*, Vol 1 (Paris: 1867), pp. 124–25. The translation I use appears in Alla Povelikhina and Yevgeny Kovtun, *Russian Painted Shop Signs and Avant-Garde Artists*, trans. by Thomas Crane and Margarita Latsinova (Leningrad: Aurora Art Publishers, 1991), p. 23.
22 On Russian elites, luxury, and Western European connections, see Alexander M. Martin, *Enlightened Metropolis: Constructing Imperial Moscow, 1762–1855* (Oxford: Oxford University Press, 2013), pp. 161–67.

Figure 2: Formann and Elers.

The images that appear in addition to the words lend decoration, but also have a utilitarian purpose. The literate minority of St Petersburg could frequently read all three languages, and lower-level monolingual literacy existed at this time as well, but, as Gautier observes, shopkeepers took no chances of missing out on potential customers, and therefore often included visual depictions.[23] These could be aimed at illiterate servants, for example, sent to pick up or purchase goods.

Along Nevskii, shop signs are typically mounted flush to the buildings, and include images as well as text as in, for example, a storefront with images of scissors denoting a tailor or a craftsman's shop sign showing an array of canes and umbrellas or mathematical instruments. This style of signage was the result of mingling and exchange between eighteenth-century Western European merchants and Russian merchants in the capital. In antiquity, shop signs had been emblematic (as we know from those found in Pompeii, for example).[24] In medieval Western Europe, signs in the form of frescoes and murals gave way to painted shop signs as secular art developed.[25] In Jean Fouquet's 1458 illuminations, for example, painted shop signs can already be seen (fig. 3). However, scholars have not found literary or pictorial evidence of signboards in fifteenth-century Russia, even as late as the seventeenth century. One of the earliest known examples of Russian advertising appears in a late seventeenth-century wood cut print depicting Moscow that shows goods were hung outside the shop so customers would see them (fig. 4).[26] Commercial signs in Russia continued to develop visually

---

23 On advertising and the development of guild and shop signs in eighteenth- and early nineteenth-century Russia, see Eleonora Glinternik, *Reklama v Rossii XVIII–pervoi poloviny XX veka* (St Petersburg: Avrora, 2007), pp. 12–51. On advertising in Imperial Russia, see Sally West, *I Shop in Moscow: Advertising and the Creation of Consumer Culture in Late Tsarist Russia* (DeKalb: Northern Illinois University Press, 2011).

24 On advertising in antiquity, see V. V. Uchenova and N. V. Starykh, *Istoriia reklamy: detstvo i otrochestvo reklamy* (Moscow: Smysl, 1994), pp. 9–20.

25 On the development of signs in Western Europe, the classic study is Jacob Larwood and John Camden Hotten, *The History of Signboards from the Earliest Times to the Present Day* (London: John Camden Hotten, 1867), especially pp. 1–44. See also Uchenova and Starykh, *Istoriia reklamy*, pp. 21–37 for a history of advertising in medieval Western Europe more broadly.

26 Adam Olearius, *Vermehrte Newe Beschreibung Der Muscowitischen vnd Persischen Reyse, So durch gelegenheit einer Holsteinischen Gesandschafft an den Russischen Zaar vnd König in Persien geschehen* (Schleswig: Johan Holwein, 1656), p. 224. Olearius describes merchant culture and trade in seventeenth-century Moscow.

rather than textually until the influx of German, Dutch, French and English merchants in the eighteenth century, and the Western European commercial traditions they brought with them.

Figure 3: Jean Fouquet, *Boccace écrivant le De Casibus* (1458).

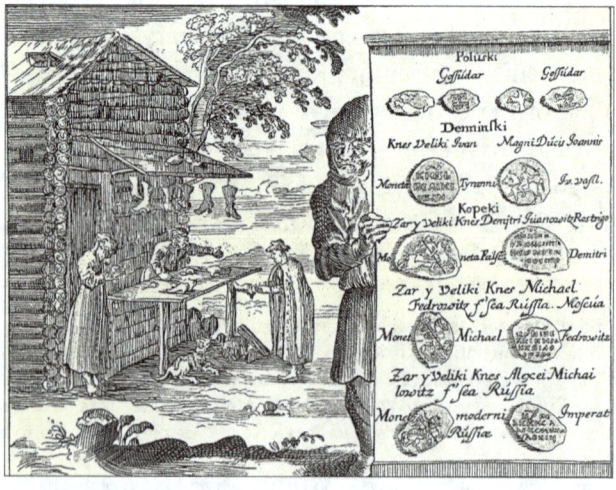

Figure 4: A bootmaker's stall, from Adam Olearius's *Vermehrte Newe Beschreibung Der Muscowitischen vnd Persischen Reyse* (1656).

The signs on Nevskii Prospekt appeal to a clientele with a taste for the fashionable and elegant, and are a far cry from what you would see on a typical Russian urban street at this time. The Nevskii signs project information about the quality or exclusivity of the businesses they advertise. Reassuring to consumers, signs featuring a single glove or boot in profile are common, and modelled after guilds' Western European-style heraldic banner signs.[27] Introduced into Russia during the reign of Peter the Great, but based on the medieval Western European model, merchant and craft guilds stood for quality and consistency of goods.[28] During Catherine II's reign, guilds began using their signs as advertising. Consumers would have recognised the form of guild signs in these shop signs, meant to assure them of good service. One of the most famous of these banner signs is that of the guild of German bakers, symbolised by a golden pretzel held aloft by two lions (fig. 5). We see its echo in the shop signs along Nevskii, a golden-coloured pretzel appears several times over the course of our stroll, but without its lions; the guild's heraldic image has come to represent a bakery, generally (fig. 6). These images visibly demonstrate that the importation of Western culture was not confined to the neoclassical architecture that lined St Petersburg's streets, but also played a significant role in the development of commerce.

Figure 5: Symbol of the Bakers' Guild, East Frisian Island of Juist (Lower Saxony, Germany).

---

27 Povelikhina and Kovtun, *Painted Shop Signs and Avant-Garde Artists*, pp. 16–17. Povelikhina and Kovtun's work is not a history of shop signs, but a study of the ways nineteenth-century and earlier painted shop signs influenced Russian avant-garde artists. Their introduction to the volume gives a history of the development of the shop sign in Russia.

28 For more information about the introduction and development of guilds in Russia, see Roger P. Bartlett, *Human Capital: The Settlement of Foreigners into Russia* (Cambridge: Cambridge University Press, 1979), pp. 147–49. For information about St Petersburg guilds, specifically, see George E. Munro, *The Most Intentional City: St Petersburg in the Reign of Catherine the Great* (Cranbury: Rosemont Publishing, 2008), pp. 215–24.

Figure 6: A pretzel on a bakers' sign from the *Panorama*.

Figure 7: Cakes, mathematical instruments, and wigs.

Figure 8: Coats, frocks, and musical instruments.

Storefronts with signs featuring only images tend to represent goods that speak for themselves. A dry goods merchant has no sign, only enormous gleaming sugar loaves in his windows. Similarly, a vintner has hung a bunch of grapes above his door and includes no other decoration. These examples are much more reminiscent of earlier signs, which tend towards universal emblems. Similarly, some specialty shops include signs that describe the variety of goods for sale in one store. A musical instrument dealer features a wide array of musical instruments on his shop sign (fig. 8), while a scientific instruments dealer includes images of his specialised stock: abacuses, rulers, compasses and protractors, and other instruments (fig. 7). These enormous signboards seem merely decorative at first glance, but have a utilitarian function. Art historians Alla Povelikhina and Yevgeny Kovtun suppose that, "For a Russian, a detailed and evocative depiction of the complete choice of merchandise, instruments, or goods for sale in a shop was especially understandable, for he preferred seeing the actual product to hearing about it or, even more, to reading about it, since he may have been illiterate or unwilling to take the trouble".[29] Whether or not their claim that these pictorial lists are a particularly Russian tendency is accurate, there can be no doubt about their efficacy as information technology. These image-only signs convey information to a broad audience, seeking to advertise and sell to as many passers-by as possible.

A dedicated advertising campaign can be seen in the decoration of Rode's large store (fig. 9), located at the corner of Nevskii Prospekt and Malaia Millionnaia (a name used to refer to the top of Bolshaia Morskaia until the middle of the nineteenth century). Whereas other buildings we have passed feature a proliferation of signs placed with little system to proclaim and advertise the many businesses housed within and tucked away in their courtyards, this storefront features a uniform façade with large windows with lamps between each, multiple entrances, and signs neatly spaced, symmetrically arranged, and placed with some view to neoclassical aesthetics. Rode's signs are a variety of shapes: diamonds, rectangles, and some half-circle, half-square. Some are in French, some in Russian, and some feature images of the goods within: gentlemen's frock coats, hats, and dress swords. A large, ornate sign above the main

---

29   Povelikhina and Kovtun, *Russian Painted Shop Signs and Avant-Garde Artists*, p. 17.

entrance on the corner of Nevskii and Malaia Millionnaia proudly displays RODE/РОДЕ in enormous capital letters. The careful placement of signs here echoes the "grand spatial composition" of the building's location on the corner of two major avenues, while no one can be in doubt of either what goods are for sale or their quality.

Advertising using images was common, but signs featuring only text tended to be for more exclusive locales along Nevskii, those where representative images would either be superfluous or considered vulgar. Continuing our "stroll", just before Police Bridge,[30] the first cast iron bridge in the city, an elegant confectioner's shop has wide windows and broad steps, and presents a good prospect of the canal (fig. 10). Its signs wrap around, proclaiming, on the Nevskii Prospekt side, "С. Волфъ и Т. Беранже", then over the door at the corner "Café Chinois", and on the far side "S. Wolf et T. Béranger". This particular confectionary was famous at the time as a favourite café of Petersburg literary society; Pushkin would eat his last meal at Wolf and Béranger before setting off to his fatal duel in January 1837, and the premises would become part of the legend surrounding the famous poet. Notably, for passers-by unable to read, this building offers no picture to show what it contained. Its façade features elegant iron railings and stonework; its signs display the name prominently in multiple languages, but only the "Café Chinois" sign on the building's corner offers a clue, and, to get it, one must understand French, that tea comes from China, and that one has cakes with tea. In their signage, Wolf and Béranger make a statement about their elite premises, further demonstrated by their use of only "tasteful" advertising—no gauche signs picturing food here! For the same reason, the elite hotels we have passed—the Hotel London and Hotel Demuth—feature little to no signage, and that with text only, when present.

Bookshops, presumably presupposing literacy in their clients, tend to feature text-only signs. Across the Moika, on the corner of Nevskii and Bolshaia Koniushennaia, there is another large commercial operation: that of early nineteenth-century publishing mogul Aleksandr Smirdin (fig. 11). The lithographs depict Smirdin's thriving business, with large signs declaring the offices of the innovative *Library for Reading* (*Biblioteka dlia chteniia*).

---

30 Now called Green Bridge, the bridge held the name Police Bridge from 1768–1918.

Figure 9: Rode's shop.

Figure 10: Wolf and Béranger.

Figure 11: Smirdin's *The Library for Reading*.

Sadovnikov's watercolours could not have depicted Smirdin's shop and printing house in the 1820s as it did not yet exist, but by 1835, as P. Ivanov was creating the lithographed scroll, the business's omission would have been a glaring one, and the scroll has been updated accordingly. I. Kotelnikova suggests that the 1820s watercolours from the "sunny" side of the street were updated to reflect notable sights, but the "shady" side watercolours — closer in time to Sadovnikov's original watercolours — were not.[31]

The first mass-circulation journal, *The Library for Reading* had a subscription base of 5000 by its second year, 1835. The journal was a monthly publication aimed at a broad middle-class readership, not just at the elite. Similarly, Smirdin's bookshop on Nevskii Prospekt catered to a broad clientele, reflecting his business model.[32] Large placards wrap around the building's corner, with text in French and Russian. On the structure's façade, most signs only give information in Russian. Signs wrap the building just under its balcony, and also appear in a second row, on either side of the central balcony. Below, a basement shop also has its own sign. On the other side of the building, just before the church, signs again wrap around the corner.

The contrast with Bellizard's bookshop, passed earlier, is obvious. Smirdin's operation occupies the majority of the building and includes multiple imprints of his business; their various signs mark and advertise the bookshop and the journal, but, also, as an ensemble give off a united sense of activity and industry. Bellizard's sign simply labels his bookshop, showing its location to passers-by,[33] but we must consider that Bellizard operates a relatively small bookshop and does a limited amount of publishing. Smirdin, on the other hand, is one of the most successful and influential of the St Petersburg publishers.

---

31 Kotel'nikova, 'Introduction', p. 65.
32 For more about *The Library for Reading* and Smirdin's publishing model, see V. G. Berezina et al., *Istoriia russkoi zhurnalistiki XVIII–XIX vekov* (Moscow: Vysshaia shkola, 1963), pp. 169–74, p. 295. Melissa Frazier has analysed the journal's impact on readers and writers of its era with a focus on its editor, Osip Senkovskii; see Frazier, *Romantic Encounters: Writers, Readers, and the 'Library for Reading'* (Palo Alto, CA: Stanford University Press, 2007). For a literature review of sources on various aspects of Smirdin's business, see George Gutsche, 'Dinner at Smirdin's: Forces in Russian Print Culture in the Early Reign of Nicholas I', in *The Space of the Book: Print Culture in the Russian Social Imagination*, ed. by Miranda Remnek (Toronto: University of Toronto Press, 2010), pp. 74–75.
33 As I mentioned earlier, the *Panorama*'s most famous passer-by is Pushkin, who can be seen walking past Bellizard's shop in Figure 12.

Figure 12: Bellizard's bookshop.

His premises' use of signage, like Rode's, tells a great deal about his business. Smirdin's profusion of signs renders his operation unmissable and unmistakable. His large building, its prominent location, and the fact that multiple businesses operate under its auspices (publishing, book selling, editing, journalism, etc.) all promote a sense of confidence and durability, something that many other publishers operating in Petersburg at the time did not have.

Shopping Arcades from the Shady Side

As we complete the stroll to the Anichkov Bridge and cross Nevskii to head back towards Palace Square, let us pause for a moment to reflect on the avenue's history. The stroll along Nevskii so far has been characterised by a profusion of signs and goods, however, this informational deluge was not always characteristic of the street. In the city's original plan, Nevskii Prospekt was not designated as a main shopping thoroughfare; rather, it was planned as a route for travellers entering the city by land, a main artery linking the wooden Admiralty—the heart of the city—with the Aleksandr Nevskii Monastery. However, it remained largely unbuilt into the eighteenth century. A plan in 1739 to construct a central market—the unrealised Mytnyi dvor—in the area shows the neighbourhood's shift to a more commercial and utilitarian design. However, Nevskii's prospects changed in the 1740s when a period of building activity transformed the street.

Empress Elizabeth chose the avenue for two building projects. Right now, from our position at the Anichkov Bridge, we stand before the first, the Anichkov Palace, built to commemorate her ascension to the throne, constructed between 1741 and 1754. The second was her own timbered Winter Palace, a temporary residence located back towards the present-day Palace Square that the empress inhabited while the now-famous stone Winter Palace designed by Rastrelli was constructed. Similarly, along the Fontanka in the neighbourhood near Nevskii, Elizabeth constructed her splendid summer palace.[34] While neither Elizabeth's winter nor summer palace survived even to the end of her

---

34   Buckler, *Mapping St Petersburg*, p. 82.

successor's reign, their location, as well as that of the Anichkov Palace, resulted in an increase in the street's value for both residents and those seeking commercial enterprise.

Figure 13: Elizabeth's summer palace, 1756.

Anxious to preserve the baroque complex she had become so fond of, in the 1740s and 50s Elizabeth passed several decrees affecting businesses and their shop signs in St Petersburg.[35] Franklin goes into detail about decrees in his chapter in this volume, so I mention them only briefly here. In December 1742, she decreed that taverns and unsightly fruit and vegetable stands should be removed from the city's main streets.[36] In October 1752, she went on to order that no shop signs of any kind should remain on main streets,[37] complaining, "There are a multitude of them for various trades, visible right opposite Her Majesty's very

---

35 For a somewhat subjective version of this narrative, see P. Antonov, 'Vyveski', *Neva*, 4 (1986), 183–88 (p. 186).
36 *Polnoe sobranie zakonov Rossiiskii imperii*, Series 1 (1649–1825) (hereafter *PSZ* 1), no. 8674. For more details about these decrees, see Franklin's discussion in Chapter 11 of the present volume.
37 *PSZ* 1, no. 10032.

courtyard".[38] These decrees had a significant impact on the appearance of St Petersburg's streets. The result was the opulent look the empress desired on the capital's grand boulevards (in decrees made later in October 1752, for example, she includes detailed descriptions of neoclassical monuments and canals she desires to construct). At the same time, however, these decrees reduced revenue for the many businesses along them. Shop signs seemed distasteful, markers of commerce and trade, which Elizabeth saw as vulgar.

Possibly as a result of this, Elizabeth spearheaded the planning and construction of Gostinyi dvor, one of the earliest closed shopping arcades in the world (fig. 14). While closed shopping structures had existed in the Roman Empire, and the sixteenth-century Grand Bazaar in Constantinople provides a good example of them, Gostinyi dvor set out to enclose "avenues" lined with shops and stalls within a single façade, thus isolating commercial enterprise to certain areas and controlling the graphic display along Nevskii Prospekt. Gostinyi dvor — the "merchants' yard", which literally includes the word "gost", meaning "guest" or, then, "foreign merchant", in its name — was intended for foreign merchants, as were the so-called Nuremberg Stalls, one of the original shopping arcades along Nevskii, a row of stalls within the architectural arches of St Catherine's Church dating from the 1780s (although designed from the 1760s onward), which we passed on our way to the Anichkov Bridge and can spy looking North and across the street from where we stand. From the words "guest" and "Nuremberg" we infer they host non-Russian merchants, although in practice both Russian and non-Russian tradesmen sold goods in them. Walking back up Nevskii, this time on the shady side of the street, we pass another planned commercial arcade, the Privy Cabinet Building. Dating from the early nineteenth century, it was planned with commercial space below and residential space above. Compared to the earlier façades we passed along Nevskii Prospekt, these are strangely empty of commercial signs, more closely tied into the neoclassical aesthetic vision.

---

38   Antonov, 'Vyveski', p. 186; the translation of this quotation is from West, *I Shop in Moscow*, p. 22.

Figure 14: Gostinyi dvor.

While Elizabeth's distaste for public signs and obstructed façades no doubt shaped the cityscape and helped spearhead the grand shopping arcade in Russia before many Western European countries adopted the model (the Gostinyi dvor predates even most Parisian arcades!), her decrees regulating commercial space did not stay in effect for long. Possibly recognising the difficulty of convenient trade if shops could not advertise their wares on their storefronts and artisans were consigned to the alleys and courtyards, Catherine II revoked Elizabeth's decrees in March 1770. She added the stipulation, however, that the text and images on the signs meet the standards of *"pristoinost'"* (decency).[39] Signs that suggested topics that polite conversation did not allow were forbidden: for example, depictions of men's undergarments or funeral accoutrements. Catherine's reversal of Elizabeth's decrees resulted in the increased proliferation of shop signs on the capital's main boulevards in the last decades of the eighteenth century. In this narrative we see a good example of the tension between the neoclassical aesthetics that represent authority in Elizabeth's eyes and the need for information technology for trade.

Figure 15: Passazh exterior, 1848.

Looking back across the street from the Privy Cabinet Building, a fairly typical Nevskii view of neoclassical palace façades can be seen. In fact, these were demolished in 1848 to make way for another commercial building project. In their place, the Passazh shopping arcade was constructed. Whereas, in the Nuremberg Stalls, or the shopping arcades

---

39 *PSZ* 1, no. 13421.

across the street, goods would have been largely lined up for view and sold that way, a more traditional model dating back to bartering, in the Passazh elite stores advertised their wares with signs, just as they did along Nevskii Prospekt itself. However, by the middle of the nineteenth century, the shopping arcade had become popular not because of imperial decree, but because of its benefits for merchants and consumers. Intriguingly, while some of the earliest shopping arcades feature on Nevskii Prospekt, the structures are much more closely associated with London and Paris, where they had their heyday in the 1820s and quickly passed out of fashion with the rise of the new department stores.[40] In Russia, where department stores did not appear until the second half of the nineteenth century, the shopping arcade continued to thrive. While the old Gostinyi dvor was cramped, dark, and packed with crowds of people, the new Passazh allowed for a more pleasant shopping experience.

Figure 16: Passazh interior, 1850s.

Here, passing the many public buildings along the right, shadowed side of Nevskii Prospekt—for example the Public Library or the Grand Theatre—there is little in the way of signage, aside from

---

40 Anneleen Arnout, 'Something Old, Something Borrowed, Something New: The Brussels Shopping Townscape, 1830–1914', in *The Landscape of Consumption: Shopping Streets and Cultures in Western Europe, 1600–1900*, ed. by Jan Hein Furnée and Clé Lesger (London: Palgrave Macmillan, 2014), p. 172.

images representing imperial power or simply a chiselled name. A statue of Minerva, Roman goddess of wisdom, adorns the library roof, overlooking the theatre square, a referential nod to the activity within the building. These institutions do not need to advertise; they all assume knowledge on the part of those seeking them out. Similarly, the construction of Gostinyi dvor, which we are just approaching now, also represents imperial authority: the attempted regulation of both commercial enterprise and its attendant array of signs and advertising. Those using the shopping complex would expect and need signs to understand what is for sale, but these are confined entirely within. The side facing Nevskii was known as the "Cloth Line" for the types of goods sold there, but only two small signs around the building's corner suggest this activity. The sole sign that appears on the outer façade is the imperial eagle.

All along Nevskii Prospekt, the imperial double-headed eagle adorns pharmacies and notary public offices. In these examples we see the manifestation of authority as information technology, in the form of the imperial crest. This symbol of empire above a business marks that these premises are part of a state monopoly and carry the weight of legal authority behind them. However, they also underscore the proliferation of imperial power throughout the city, visibly demonstrating authority while asserting control over some commercial enterprises.

While the lack of shop signs in some areas exposes the tension between authority and the development of the commercial graphosphere, authority vis-à-vis information technologies is most clearly seen just beyond Gostinyi dvor, in the tower built onto the arcade housing silver traders, Silver Row. In *Panorama*, the tower looks like mere architectural embellishment, but it too had its function. On the next block, in the distance, the outline of the optical telegraph can be seen atop a building. The Silver Row tower was also part of this semaphore line, which represented cutting edge information transfer in the early nineteenth century. Brought into regular use by Napoleon, the optical telegraph was operated by manipulating the two antennae into a series of signs. An operator used a telescope to observe the signs, reproduced them at his own station, and thus passed the message on to the next station. The system worked well, enabling message transmission over hundreds of kilometres in minutes. By 1839, the network stretched from St Petersburg to Warsaw, and a message could be sent along the entire route and decoded in under an hour.[41] The silhouette of the optical telegraph spied from Nevskii Prospekt is as telling as the imperial eagles over the notary public and apothecaries' doors; it enforces authority and imperial omnipotence on a grand scale. Designed purely for official, bureaucratic use, the optical telegraph represents information technology as authority controlling the most efficient means of communication.

As we complete the stroll, we end on the steps of the Hotel London, overlooking Palace Square once more, the gold spire of the Admiralty shining above a troop of marching soldiers and several perambulating ladies wearing colourful hats and cloaks. The optical telegraph has taken us far afield from the public graphosphere, but it emphasises the importance of Nevskii Prospekt not just as a grand boulevard featuring imperial façades, fashionable shops and cafes, and public monuments, but as an information conduit, an encapsulated graphosphere. As the optical telegraph's presence emphasises Nevskii's role as a grand boulevard, so too does it emphasise the limitations of Sadovnikov's watercolours as a source for capturing urban experience.

Looking Beyond Nevskii Prospekt

While *Panorama* projects a precise view of the street's buildings populated with lively and whimsical characters, as a piece of urban representation it also has its limitations. Common aspects of St Petersburg life are omitted: chilly and inclement weather, the gloomy darkness of winter, the dirt of the streets, the noise of urban bustle, and the strong smells. Some omissions would be difficult to convey in two-dimensional printed format, of course, particularly those of an auditory or olfactory nature. Sadovnikov's additions of carriages, animals, goods, and people do suggest motion, noise, and smells, and invite the viewer to imagine these omnipresent elements of urban life. However, the experience of Nevskii Prospekt without the rattle of carriages, the noise of the crowds, the sound of horse hoofs on the street, or the pungent and intense smells of urban space is already an incomplete, partially imagined one.

---

41   On the optical telegraph in Russia, see D. I. Kargin, 'Opticheskii telegraf Kulibina', *Arkhiv istorii nauki i tekhniki*. Trudy instituta istorii nauki i tekhniki. Seriia 1. Vypusk 3 (Leningrad: Izdatel'stvo Akademii nauk SSSR, 1934), pp. 77–103.

More important than the limitations of medium, however, is *Panorama*'s inherent limitation: its scope. On our stroll, we turned back at the Fontanka, and for good reason: even just across the river, still in view of the Anichkov Palace, the street's grandeur deteriorates. Astolphe de Custine observes in his 1839 *Letters from Russia*,

> A little below the bridge of Aniskoff [...] The superb city created by Peter the Great, and beautified by Catherine II and other sovereigns, is lost at last in an unsightly mass of stalls and workshops, confused heaps of edifices without name, large squares without design.[42]

Custine's view of the city is one that serves as a counterpoint to Sadovnikov's. Custine's travel memoir praises some aspects of St Petersburg, but his overall impression is unfavourable. Sadovnikov's watercolours, on the other hand, deliberately omit less than pleasing urban scenes; an "unsightly mass" would not be in keeping with the scroll's aesthetic. And, indeed, Sadovnikov's gaze turns back at the Anichkov Bridge. While Nevskii Prospekt—or at any rate its fashionable section—is meticulously documented by artists like Sadovnikov, the little we know about street signs elsewhere paints a very different image of the experience of the public graphosphere.

Most of the information scholars have about off-boulevard street signs from this period comes from physiological writing. One anonymous author, writing in *Literaturnaia gazeta* in 1845, notes: "I would go out to see other signs beyond the gate [...] where [...] they just say 'En trence to eatery' or 'To restrunt', while above it the painter had, with a free hand, shown a ham with a paper frill, a suckling pig, a plate full of meat pies, fresh eggs, huge cutlets, tea with a Chinese figurine, i.e. whatever you might want".[43] These misspellings and the freedom of the signmakers off the grand boulevards shows both the potential of the public graphosphere—the sign's message is more important than its grammar or language—and its relative freedom. Intriguingly, there are misspelled signs apparent in Sadovnikov's *Panorama* as well—in some cases French is misspelled, and in some cases Russian is—but the artist documents them by rote. The *Literary Gazette* writer, on the other hand, revels in them as a unique expression of free spirit.

---

42 Astolphe de Custine, *Letters from Russia*, the 1843 translation edited and introduced by Anka Muhlstein (New York: New York Review Books Classics, 2002), p. 215.

43 Anonymous, Appendix to 'Zapiski dlia khoziaev', *Literaturnaia gazeta* (1845), quoted in Povelikhina and Kovtun, *Russian Painted Shop Signs and Avant-Garde Artists*, p. 23.

It is within this atmosphere that the tradition of wordplay and folk painting in shop signs developed, sidestepping the grand boulevards and augmenting the previously largely graphic examples. In his *Tales of Belkin*, in "The Undertaker" (*Grobovshchik*, 1830), Pushkin, for example, gives an example of a street sign:

> Over the gate hung a sign depicting a plump cupid with a downturned torch in his hand and bearing the inscription: 'Plain and painted coffins sold and upholstered here. Coffins also let out for hire and old ones repaired'.[44]

Pushkin's imagined sign is nothing like the signs on Nevskii. Its image is not utilitarian, but more suggestive. The language of the sign is playful, and intended to be so—Pushkin ironises it in his story, but this kind of playful language was prized on street signs off the grand boulevards at this time.

One of the best records of street signs from this period appears in the journal *Illustration* (*Illiustratsiia*) in 1848, in the article "Petersburg Shop Signs" by an anonymous contributor known only by the initial "T".[45] This admirer of street signs from the non-affluent areas of the capital extols their "primitive character", and points out the humour and folk traditions that frequently crop up among them. In one example, the anonymous author relates:

> The sign of Smekayev's tobacco shop depicted the following scene: on one side a gentleman was sitting at a small round table holding a glass in his hand, on the other a lady was handing the man a pipe and trying to take his glass away. Underneath was the quatrain clearly showing a knowledge of folk ways:
>
> *Have a smoke instead of wine,*
> *A pipe will make you feel so fine,*
> *I guarantee you'll get so stewed,*
> *You'll swear you'd drunk a pint or two.*

In the windows of hairdressers and barbershops, ladies and men's busts were displayed with a sign saying: 'We cut hair, and comb and shave—have yourself bled according to the latest journal'.[46]

---

44 Alexander Pushkin, 'The Undertaker', *Tales of Belkin and Other Prose Writings*, trans. by Ronald Wilks (London: Penguin Classics, 1998), p. 33.
45 'T', 'Peterburgskie vyveski', *Illiustratsiia*, 30. 4–7 (28 August 1848), 81–82.
46 'T', 'Peterburgskie vyveski', p. 81. Translation adapted from that in Povelikhina and Kovtun, *Russian Painted Shop Signs and Avant-Garde Artists*, p. 28.

The irony of these snippets—"you'll swear you'd drunk a pint or two" or "have yourself bled according to the latest journal"—recalls Pushkin's fictional shop signs, which play on fashion and good-natured humour. This inventive language evokes the tradition of *lubok*, woodcuts which predate the influx of Western European models of shop signs found on the grand boulevards.[47] It is these so-called "eccentric" signs that fascinate this anonymous physiological voyager-author, and they provide a different set of information about urban life and experience than the neoclassical façades and fashionable, elegant signs we see in Sadovnikov's watercolours.

"T" gives a short history of shop signs in Russia, which aligns with the graphosphere observed along Nevskii in *Panorama*. According to "T", signs originally captured the act of trading in addition to images of the goods for sale themselves. He observes:

> Thus, over a fabric shop there would be a picture of a merchant standing in front of a pretty purchaser. Inn signs often show Russian men sitting in orderly fashion at a table laid with a tea set or with *zakuski* (savoury snacks) and decanters; painters paid particular attention to the figure, making them pour out and drink tea in very grand poses which were not, of course, usual to the *habitués* of such places.[48]

For a physiological writer, the history of signs is of interest as it is a history of urban communication. "T" stresses the central role of information transfer, commenting:

> Now the figures were replaced simply by objects which speak for themselves—the tea set, snacks and decanters; fabric shops have signs which depict various kinds of material, and others give only the merchants name.[49]

These "speaking" signs sound very similar to those found along Nevskii.

"T", however, is less interested in these standard signs. His passion is for the "eccentric" signs—not just the misspelled ones, or those

---

47   For an overview of *lubok* as advertising material, see Uchenova and Starykh, *Istoriia reklamy*, pp. 52–53. Iurii Lotman also provides insight on the folk tradition of the *lubok* within the commercial realm in 'Khudozhestvennaia priroda russkikh narodnykh kartinok', in *Narodnaia graviura i fol'klor v Rossii XVII–XIX vv.*, ed. I. E. Danilova (Moscow: Sovetskii Khudozhnik, 1975), pp. 257–58.
48   'T', 'Peterburgskie vyveski', 81.
49   *Ibid.*

featuring folk humour. Some of those collected in the article show his *bonhomie*: he takes pleasure in the small details of signs, treating them as artworks ("Beer-stalls had signs with bottles of beer, foaming as the cork pops"[50]), while emphasising their communicative meaning ("We also find the inscription 'Sale for consumption on the premises', indicating that beer, porter, and honey could be drunk in the shop itself".[51]). Depicted through "T"'s marvelling eyes, the signs come whimsically to life: a coachman in a blue kaftan doffs his cap to passers-by; grocery shops have exotic views of China taken from tea chests, evoking distant lands; and, perhaps most amazing of all, "Meat shops showed not only bulls, rams, and chickens eating lush grass, but also the slaughter itself. On one sign of this type (in Spassky Lane) the artist painted all the letters of the inscription from different cuts of meat".[52] These signs clearly demonstrate the creative liberty that emerged in advertising as merchants worked to discover ways to outstrip competition and communicate their message to customers in the most attractive way possible—even if that way involves spelling out your business name with different meat cuts.

The signs we have seen on Nevskii in Sadovnikov's watercolours seem to show a definite progress along Western European models, but these off-boulevard signs seem derived from folk traditions or pre-eighteenth-century depictions of goods for sale. From these descriptions, we can see the limitations of using a resource such as Sadovnikov's scroll exclusively to gain an understanding of the scope of the public graphosphere, which sprawled well beyond *Panorama*'s bounds. While Sadovnikov's watercolours do provide some insight, one must go off-boulevard like the anonymous physiological author to sketch in additional details and strands, and, even then, the experience remains incomplete.

In 1835, a reviewer was inspired by the scroll to proclaim, "Nevsky Prospekt is without a doubt the finest street in the world, for its regularity and its remarkable length and breadth, as well as for the beauty and majesty of its buildings [...] a poet could confidently proclaim Nevsky

---

50   *Ibid.*
51   *Ibid.*
52   *Ibid.*

Prospekt the soul of St Petersburg".[53] This reading of *Panorama* emerges from the work's inherent aristocratic point of view. The "regularity, remarkable length and breadth, beauty and majesty of buildings" all toe the imperial line. Furthermore, these remarks resemble Custine's comment on St Petersburg architecture, "The line and rule figure well the manner in which the absolute sovereigns view things".[54] The public graphosphere, however, resists categorisation and containment, and, similarly, complicates the imperial perspectives and rectilinear prospects typically associated with St Petersburg's planned design.

Refractions and Reflections

For those who viewed *Panorama of Nevskii Prospekt* in 1835, the scroll provided a new way of sharing urban life with others, of capturing a slice of the elegant street, featuring neoclassical façades, modish shops and even a glimpse of cutting edge technology such as the optical telegraph or celebrities like Pushkin. An anonymous visitor to St Petersburg in the 1840s called Nevskii Prospekt "a kind of picture gallery",[55] conflating city with artistic object, just as the scroll creates art out of urban experience. Viewers at the time would have been conscious of this way of seeing the city; just before the optical telegraph, the scroll itself includes the "Rotunda", the home of Madame la Tour's Panorama (recognisable by its distinctive lantern). This popular attraction on Bolshaia Morskaia Street was one of the first panoramas, on display here in the 1820s. Madame La Tour's allowed visitors to experience cutting-edge nineteenth-century optical entertainment such as panoramas, cosmoramas, and an attraction called the "theatre of light" — early forerunners of the cinematograph.[56]

---

53 A review of *Panorama of Nevksii Prospekt* that appeared in *Severnaia pchela*. Quoted in Kotel'nikova, 'Introduction', p. 8.
54 Custine, *Letters from Russia*, p. 213.
55 Quoted in West, *I Shop in Moscow*, p. 23, who cites Povelikhina and Kovtun, *Russian Painted Shop Signs and Avant-Garde Artists*, p. 23, who provide no citation.
56 See Nataliia Shtrimer's annotations to *Panorama of Nevsky Prospekt* (1993), 'The Left, Sunny Side' Card 11 for more information on the Panorama of Madame la Tour.

Figure 17: Madame La Tour's Panorama and the Optical Telegraph.

In another account of Nevskii Prospekt from 1835, Nikolai Gogol writes of the street as a "great mixer" in his story that bears the street's name. His subject matter is grittier than Sadovnikov's idealised cityscapes, dealing as it does with prostitution, poverty, suicide, and crime; he begins his story with an ironic exclamation that echoes that of the anonymous *Panorama* reviewer: "Nothing could be finer than Nevsky Prospect, at least not in St Petersburg; it is the be-all and end-all. It positively gleams and sparkles—the jewel of our capital!"[57] Gogol's characters' urban experience differs from that of the figures in Sadovnikov's watercolours: Gogol's "Nevskii Prospekt" features a grotesque ultimate scene in which the devil lights the lamps along the avenue, surrounded by darkness, with occasional dim lights illuminating the dull yellow fog. Gogol knew of *Panorama*, and even sent a copy to his mother, although his representation of the city differs greatly from Sadovnikov's limpid blue skies. Still, in giving his mother the scroll, Gogol not only sent home a souvenir of his life in the capital, but also passed along one experience of Nevskii Prospekt, enabling his mother, too, take a "stroll".

For us, viewing the scroll nearly two hundred years later, *Panorama* provides a rare visual account of Russian urban space in the 1820s. However, for our discussion of Sadovnikov, Nevskii Prospekt, and the public graphosphere, it is prudent to mention the limitations of using works like *Panorama* to draw conclusions about early nineteenth-century shop signs. The information we glean from our "stroll", is constrained by the fact that, typically, only beautiful, grand, or historical urban spaces were subjects of artworks during this period. Sadovnikov does illustrate a deeper perspective at cross streets, allowing the viewer to look beyond the famous boulevard, which suggests the city beyond Nevskii Prospekt, but the street remains the central focus. Some works existed that depicted street life if not street signs, like, for example, the monthly anthology "Magic Lantern", which came out at the same time as *Panorama*. The full title is "Magic Lantern, or a Spectacle of St Petersburg's Travelling Sellers, Masters, and Other Folk Craftsmen, Depicted with a True Brush in their Real Clothes and Presented Conversing with One Another, Commensurate

---

57 Nikolai Gogol, 'Nevsky Prospect', *Plays and Petersburg Tales*, trans. by Christopher English (Oxford: Oxford University Press, 2009), p. 3.

With Each Person and Title".[58] This detailed description's emphasis on veracity ("a True Brush", "their Real Clothes") and the lower classes going about their daily business anticipate the trend of physiological depictions of slums and lower class areas, demonstrating the relatively new notion that representations of the lower classes were necessary for a complete and authentic picture of urban life. In the next decades, as the technology of photography developed alongside physiological writing, a much broader and more intricate picture of the public graphosphere becomes possible.

---

58 For more information about 'Magic Lantern', see Solomon Volkov, *St Petersburg: A Cultural History* (New York: Simon & Schuster, 1997), pp. 60–61.

Selected Further Reading

Alef, Gustave, 'The Origin and Early Development of the Muscovite Postal Service', *Jahrbücher für Geschichte Osteuropas*, New Series, 15. 1 (March 1967), 1–15.

Alekseeva, M. A., *Iz istorii russkoi graviury XVII–nachala XIX v.* (Moscow and St Petersburg: Al'ians Arkheo, 2013).

Anisimov, Evgenii V., *Podatnaia reforma Petra I* (Leningrad: Nauka, 1982).

Antonov, P. A., 'Vyveski', *Neva*, 4 (1986), 183–88.

Bagrow, Leo, *A History of the Cartography of Russia up to 1600*, and *A History of Russian Cartography up to 1800*, both ed. by Henry W. Castner (Wolfe Island, ON: The Walker Press, 1975).

Bauer, Volker, and Holger Böning, eds., *Die Entstehung des Zeitungswesens im 17. Jahrhundert: Ein neues Medium und seine Folgen für das Kommunikationssystem der Frühen Neuzeit* (Bremen: Edition Lumière, 2011).

Becker, Peter, '"Kaiser Josephs Schreibmaschine": Ansätze zur Rationalisierung der Verwaltung im aufgeklärten Absolutismus', *Jahrbuch für europäische Verwaltungsgeschichte*, 12 (2000), 223–54.

Beliaev, L. A., ed., *Russkoe srednevekovoe nadgrobie, XIII–XVII veka: materialy k svodu. Vypusk 1* (Moscow: Nauka, 2006).

Behringer, Wolfgang, *Im Zeichen des Merkur. Reichspost und Kommunikationsrevolution in der Frühen Neuzeit*. Veröffentlichungen des Max-Planck-Instituts für Geschichte, Bd. 189 (Göttingen: Vandenhoeck & Ruprecht, 2003).

Berkov, P. N., *Istoriia russkoi zhurnalistiki XVIII veka* (Moscow: Izdatel'stvo Akademii nauk SSSR, 1952).

Blair, Ann M., *Too Much to Know: Managing Scholarly Information before the Modern Age* (New Haven: Yale University Press, 2010).

Bogoslovskii, Mikhail, *Oblastnaia reforma Petra Velikogo. Provintsiia 1719–27* (Moscow: Universitetskaia tipografiia, 1902).

Bondarenko, A. F., *Istoriia kolokolov v Rossii XI–XVII vv.* (Moscow: Russkaia panorama, 2012).

Borodkin, L. I., and Iu. Petrov, eds., *Ekonomicheskaia istoriia. Ezhegodnik 2013* (Moscow: Rossiiskaia politicheskaia entsiklopediia, 2014), pp. 89–127.

Brown, Peter B., 'How Muscovy Governed: Seventeenth-Century Russian Central Administration', *Russian History,* 36 (2009), 459–529, https://doi.org/10.1163/009428809x12536994047659

Buckler, Julie, *Mapping St Petersburg: Imperial Text and Cityshape* (Princeton: Princeton University Press, 2005).

Burmistrova, L. P., *Provintsial'naia gazeta v epokhu russkikh prosvetitelei (Gubernskie vedomosti Povolzh'ia i Urala 1840–1850 gg.)* (Kazan: Izdatel'stvo Kazanskogo universiteta, 1985).

Chechulin, N. D., *Ocherki po istorii russkikh finansov v tsarstvovanie Ekateriny II* (St Petersburg: Senatskaia tipografiia, 1906).

Chernyshev, V. A., *Konnye povozki i ekipazhi v Rossii X–XIX vekov* (St Petersburg: Fort, 2007).

Collins, Daniel, *Reanimated Voices. Speech Reporting in a Historical-Pragmatic Perspective* (Amsterdam and Philadelphia: John Benjamins, 2001), https://doi.org/10.1075/pbns.85

Cracraft, James, *The Petrine Revolution in Russian Imagery* (Chicago and London: University of Chicago Press, 1997).

Cross, Anthony, *By the Banks of the Neva: Chapters from the Lives and Careers of the British in Eighteenth-Century Russia* (Cambridge: Cambridge University Press, 1997).

Dickinson, Sara, *Breaking Ground: Travel and National Culture in Russia from Peter I to the Era of Pushkin* (Amsterdam: Rodopi, 2006).

Distribuendi, F., *Vzgliad na moskovskie vyveski* (Moscow: I. Smirnov, 1836).

Dixon, Simon, *The Modernisation of Russia, 1676–1825* (Cambridge: Cambridge University Press, 1999).

Dooley, Brendan, ed., *The Dissemination of News and the Emergence of Contemporaneity in Early Modern Europe* (Farnham, Surrey and Burlington, VT: Ashgate Publishing, 2010).

Droste, Heiko, ed., *Connecting the Baltic Area: The Swedish Postal System in the Seventeenth Century* (Stockholm: Södertörns högskola, 2011).

Dumschat, Sabine, *Ausländischer Mediziner im Moskauer Rußland* (Stuttgart: Franz Steiner Verlag, 2006).

Eisenstein, Elizabeth L., *The Printing Press as an Agent of Change* (New York and Cambridge: Cambridge University Press, 1979).

Esin, B. I., and I. V. Kuznetsov, *Trista let otechestvennoi zhurnalistiki (1702–2002)* (Moscow: Izdatel'stvo Moskovskogo universiteta, 2002).

Franklin, Simon, 'Mapping the Graphosphere: Cultures of Writing in Early 19th-Century Russia (and Before)', *Kritika*, 12. 3 (Summer 2011), 531–60, https://doi.org/10.1353/kri.2011.0036

Franklin, Simon, 'Printing and Social Control in Russia 2: Decrees', *Russian History*, 38 (2011), 467–92, https://doi.org/10.1163/187633111x594560

Garrioch, David, 'House Names, Shop Signs and Social Organization in West European Cities, c. 1500–1900', *Urban History*, 21 (1994), 20–48.

Gatrell, Peter, 'Economic Culture, Economic Policy and Economic Growth in Russia, 1861–1914', *Cahiers du Monde Russe*, 1 (1995), 37–52.

Glinternik, Eleonora, *Reklama v Rossii XVIII–pervoi poloviny XX veka* (St Petersburg: Avrora, 2007).

Goldenberg, L. A., 'Russian Cartography to ca. 1700', in *The History of Cartography*, vol. 3, pt. 2, *Cartography in the European Renaissance* (Chicago: University of Chicago Press, 2007), http://www.press.uchicago.edu/books/HOC/HOC_V3_Pt2/HOC_VOLUME3_Part2_chapter62.pdf

Golubinskii, A. A., 'Stepan Khrulev: Sud'ba zemlemera', in *Rus', Rossiia, Srednevekov'e i Novoe vremia*, vypusk III, Tret'i chteniia pamiati akademika RAN L.V. Milova (Moscow: Orgkomitet Chtenii pamiati akademika RAN L. V. Milova, 2013), pp. 404–10.

Gnucheva, V. F., *Geograficheskii departament Akademii nauk XVIII veka* (Moscow: Izd-vo AN SSSR, 1946).

Griesse, Malte, ed., *From Mutual Observation to Propaganda War. Premodern Revolts in Their Transnational Representations* (Bielefeld: Transcript Verlag, 2014), https://doi.org/10.14361/transcript.9783839426425

Gromova, L. P., ed., *Istoriia russkoi zhurnalistiki XVIII–XIX vekov* (St. Petersburg: Izdatel'stvo Sankt-Peterburgskogo universiteta, 2003).

Gurliand, I. Ia., *Iamskaia gon'ba v moskovskom gosudarstve do kontsa XVII veka* (Iaroslavl: Tipografiia Gubernskogo Pravleniia, 1900).

Harms, Wolfgang, *Das illustrierte Flugblatt in der Kultur der Frühen Neuzeit: Wolfenbüttler Arbeitsgespräch 1997* (Frankfurt am Main: Peter Lang, 1998).

Hartley, Janet, *Russia, 1762-1815: Military Power, the State and the People* (Westport: Praeger, 2008).

Herberstein, Sigmund Freiherr von, *Notes Upon Russia*, 2 vols, Elibron Classics Reprint of the 1852 publication by the Hakluyt Society (Adamant Media, 2005), https://archive.org/details/notesuponrussiab02herbuoft

Hobart, Michael E., and Zachary S. Schiffman, *Information Ages: Literacy, Numeracy, and the Computer Revolution* (Baltimore: Johns Hopkins University Press, 2000).

Il'iushina, T. V., 'Ot bussoli do astroliabii', *Nauka v Rossii*, 3 (2007), 97–101.

Jones, Robert E., *Provincial Development in Russia: Catherine II and Jacob Sievers* (New Brunswick: Rutgers University Press, 1984).

Kahan, Arcadius, *The Plow, the Hammer and the Knout: An Economic History of Eighteenth-Century Russia* (Chicago: University of Chicago Press, 1985).

Kationov, O. N., *Moskovsko-Sibirskii trakt i ego zhiteli v XVII–XIX vv.* (Novosibirsk: NGPU, 2004).

Keuning, Johannes, 'Nicolaas Witsen as a Cartographer', *Imago Mundi*, 11 (1954), 95–110, https://doi.org/10.1080/03085695408592063

Kiselev, Mikhail, 'State Metallurgy Factories and Direct Taxes in the Urals, 1700–50: Paths to State Building in Early Modern Russia', *Kritika: Explorations in Russian and Eurasian History*, 16. 1 (Winter 2015), 7–36, https://doi.org/10.1353/kri.2015.0012

Kivelson, Valerie, *Cartographies of Tsardom: Maps and their Meanings in Seventeenth Century Russia* (Ithaca, NY: Cornell University Press, 2007).

In Russian: Kivel'son, Valerii, *Kartografii tsarstva: Zemlia i ee znacheniia v Rossii XVII veka* (Moscow: Novoe literaturnoe obozrenie, 2012).

Kivelson, Valerie, *Desperate Magic: The Moral Economy of Witchcraft in Seventeenth-century Russia* (Ithaca and London: Cornell University Press, 2013), https://doi.org/10.7591/9780801469381

Kollmann, Nancy Shields, *The Russian Empire 1450–1801* (Oxford: Oxford University Press, 2017), https://doi.org/10.1093/acprof:oso/9780199280513.001.0001

Kochegarov, Kirill A., *Rech' Pospolitaia i Rossiia v 1680–1686 godakh. Zakliuchenie dogovora o Vechnom mire* (Moskva: INDRIK, 2008).

Kotel'nikova, I., 'Introduction', in *The Panorama of Nevsky Prospect* (Leningrad: Aurora Art, 1974), pp. 7–78.

Kotilaine, Jarmo, and Marshall Poe, eds., *Modernizing Muscovy: Reform and Social Change in Seventeenth Century Russia* (London and New York: Routledge Curzon, 2004), https://doi.org/10.4324/9780203507032

Kozlovskii, Ivan P., *Pervye pochty i pervye pochtmeistery v moskovskom gosudarstve*, 2 vols. (Warsaw: Tip. Varshavskogo uchebnogo okruga, 1913).

Kudriavtsev, A. S., *Ocherki istorii dorozhnogo stroitel'stva v SSSR: Dooktiabr'skii period*, 2 vols (Moscow: Dorizdat, 1951).

Kulomzin A. N., 'Finansovye documenty tsarstvovaniia Imperatritsy Ekateriny II', *Sbornik Rossiiskogo Imperatorskogo Obshchestva*, vol. 28 (St Petersburg: tip. V. Bezobrazova i Komp., 1880).

Küng, Enn, 'Postal Relations between Riga and Moscow in the Second Half of the 17th Century', *Past. Special Issue on the History of Estonia* (Tartu-Tallinn: National Archives, 2009), 59–81.

Kusov, V. S., *Chertezhi zemli russkoi XVI–XVII vv.* (Moscow: Russkii mir, 1993).

Kusov, V. S., *Izmerenie zemli: Istoriia geodezicheskikh instrumentov* (Moscow: Dizain. Informatsiia. Kartografiia, 2009).

Larwood, Jacob, and John Camden Hotten, *The History of Signboards from the Earliest Times to the Present Day* (London: John Camden Hotten, 1867).

Le Donne, John P., *Absolutism and Ruling Class. The Formation of the Russian Political Order, 1700–1825* (Oxford: Oxford University Press, 1991).

Lincoln, W. Bruce, *Nicholas I: Emperor and Autocrat of All the Russias* (Bloomington: Indiana University Press, 1978).

Liseitsev, D. V., N. M. Rogozhin, and Iu. M. Eskin, *Prikazy Moskovskogo gosudarstva XVI–XVII vv. Slovar'-spravochnik* (Moscow and St Petersburg: Tsentr gumanitarnikh initsiativ, 2015).

Lyubichankovski, Sergei V., 'The State of Power in the Late Russian Empire: The English-American Historiography of the Second Half of the XXth-Early XXIst Centuries', *Proceedings of the Samara Scientific Center of the Russian Academy of Sciences*, 2 (2007), 342–47.

Maier, Ingrid, 'Newspaper Translations in Seventeenth-Century Muscovy. About the Sources, Topics and Periodicity of *Kuranty* "Made in Stockholm" (1649)', in *Explorare necesse est. Hyllningsskrift till Barbro Nilsson*, Acta Universitatis Stockholmensis, Stockholm Slavic Studies, vol. 28 (Stockholm: Almqvist & Wiksell, 2002), 181–90.

Maier, Ingrid, and Wouter Pilger, 'Polnische Fabelzeitung über Sabbatai Zwi, übersetzt für den russischen Zaren', *Zeitschrift für slavische Philologie*, 62. 1 (2003), 1–39.

Mamonov, N. E., *Materialy dlia istorii meditsiny v Rossii*, 4 vols (St Petersburg: M. M. Stasiulevich, 1881).

Man'kov, A. G., ed., *Inostrannye izvestiia o vosstanii Stepana Razina. Materialy i issledovaniia* (Leningrad: Nauka, 1975).

Marker, Gary, *Publishing, Printing, and the Origins of Intellectual Life in Russia, 1700–1800* (Princeton: Princeton University Press, 1985).

Marks, Stephen G., *The Information Nexus: Global Capitalism from the Renaissance to the Present* (Cambridge: Cambridge University Press, 2016), https://doi.org/10.1017/cbo9781316258170

Martin, Alexander M., *Enlightened Metropolis: Constructing Imperial Moscow, 1762–1855* (Oxford: Oxford University Press, 2013), https://doi.org/10.1093/acprof:oso/9780199605781.001.0001

Martin, Welke, 'Rußland in der deutschen Publizistik des 17. Jahrhunderts (1613–1689)', *Forschungen zur osteuropäischen Geschichte*, 23 (1976), 105–276.

McConnell, Allen, *Tsar Alexander I: Paternalistic Reformer* (New York: Crowell, 1970).

Mironov, Boris N., *Rossiiskaia imperiia: ot traditsii k modernu*, vol. 2 (St Petersburg: Dmitrii Bulanin, 2014).

Ogloblin, Nikolai, 'Voevodskie vestovye otpiski XVII v. kak material po istorii Malorossii', *Kievskaia starina*, 12 (1885), 365–416.

Orlova, Galina, 'Biurokraticheskaia real'nost'', *Obshchestvennye nauki i sovremennost'*, 6 (1999), 96–106.

Petrucci, Armando, *Public Lettering. Script, Power, and Culture*, trans. by Linda Lappin (London and Chicago: Chicago University Press, 1993).

Petrukhintsev, N. N., 'Tsarstvovanie Anny Ioannovny: problemy formirovaniia vnutripoliticheskogo kursa (1730–1740)' (Dokt. dissertation, Moskovskii gosudarstvennyi universitet, 2001).

Pettegree, Andrew, *The Invention of News: How the World Came to Know about Itself* (New Haven and London: Yale University Press, 2014).

Pisar'kova, Ludmila F., 'Rossiiskaia biurokratiia v epohu Petra I', *Otechestvennaia istoriia*, 1 (2004), 18–41.

Postnikov, A. V., *Karty zemel' rossiiskikh: ocherk istorii geograficheskogo izucheniia i kartografirovaniia nashego otechestva* (Moscow: Nash dom and L'Âge d'Homme, 1996). In English: Postnikov, A. V., *Russia in Maps: A History of the Geographical Study and Cartography of the Country* (Moscow: Nash dom and L'Âge d'Homme, 1996).

Postnikov, Alexey and Marvin Falk, *Exploring and Mapping Alaska: The Russian America Era, 1741–1867*, trans. by Lydia Black (Fairbanks: University of Alaska Press, [2015]).

Povelikhina, Alla, and Yevgeny Kovtun, *Russian Painted Shop Signs and Avant-Garde Artists*, trans. by Thomas Crane and Margarita Latsinova (Leningrad: Aurora Art, 1991).

Presniakov, A. E., *Emperor Nicholas I of Russia: The Apogee of Autocracy, 1825–1855*, ed. and trans. J. C. Zacek (Gulf Breeze: Academic International Press, 1974).

Redin, D. A., *Administrativnye struktury i biurokratiia Urala v epokhu petrovskikh reform (zapadnye uezdy Sibirskoi gubernii v 1711–1727 gg.)* (Ekaterinburg: Volot, 2007).

Remezov, S. U., *Chertezhnaia kniga Sibiri, sostavlennaia tobol'skim synom boiarskim Semenom Remezovym v 1701 godu*, ed. by A. A. Drazhniuk, *et al.*, 2 vols. (Moscow: PKO "Kartografiia", 2003).

Remezov, S. U., *Khorograficheskaia kniga Sibiri*. MS Russ 72 (6). Houghton Library, Harvard University, Cambridge, MA, ff. 5v–6, http://pds.lib.harvard.edu/pds/view/18273155?n=10&imagesize=1200&jp2Res=.25&printThumbnails=no

Remnek, Miranda, ed., *The Space of the Book: Print Culture in the Russian Social Imagination* (Toronto: University of Toronto Press, 2010), https://doi.org/10.3138/9781442686441

Rey, Marie-Pierre, *Alexander I: The Tsar Who Defeated Napoleon* (DeKalb: Northern Illinois University Press, 2012).

Riasanovsky, N. V., *A Parting of Ways: Government and the Educated Public in Russia, 1801–1855* (Oxford: Clarendon Press, 1976).

Riazantsev, I. V., *Skul'ptura v Rossii XVIII–nachala XIX veka* (Moscow: Zhiraf, 2003).

Ruban, Anatolij and Ekaterina Basargina, eds., *Russische klassische Altertumswissenschaft in der Zeitschrift des Ministeriums für Volksaufklärung* (St Petersburg: Bibliotheca Classica Petropolitana and Nestor-Verlag, 2012).

Sadovnikov, V. S., *Panorama of Nevsky Prospect: from the Collection of the Russian Museum*, ed. by Nataliia Shtrimer (Leningrad: Aurora Art Publishers, 1993).

Sazikov, A. V., and T. V. Vinogradova, *Naruzhnaia reklama Moskvy. Istoriia, tipologiia, dokumenty* (Moscow: Russkii Mir, 2013).

Sedov, P. V., *Zakat Moskovskogo tsarstva. Tsarskii dvor kontsa XVII veka* (St Petersburg: Dmitrii Bulanin, 2008).

Shamin, Stepan M., *Kuranty XVII stoletiia. Evropeiskaia pressa v Rossii i vozniknoveniia russkoi periodicheskoi pechati* (Moscow and St Petersburg: Al'ians-Arkheo, 2011).

Shevtsov, V. V., *"Tomskie gubernskie vedomosti" (1857–1917 gg.) v sotsiokul'turnom i informatsionnom prostranstve sibiri* (Tomsk: Tomskii gosudarstvennyi universitet, 2012).

Silverstein, Adam J., *Postal Systems in the Pre-Modern Islamic World* (Cambridge: Cambridge University Press, 2007), https://doi.org/10.1017/CBO9780511497520

Smith-Peter, Susan, 'The Russian Provincial Newspaper and Its Public, 1788–1864', *Carl Beck Papers 1908* (2008), https://doi.org/10.5195/cbp.2008.145

Tiukhmeneva, E. A., *Iskusstvo triumfal'nykh vrat v Rossii pervoi poloviny XVIII veka. Problemy panegiricheskogo napravleniia* (Moscow: Progress-Traditsiia, 2005).

Uchenova, V. V. and N. V. Starykh, *Istoriia reklamy* (Moscow: Smysl, 1994).

Velychenko Stephen, 'The Size of the Imperial Russian Bureaucracy and Army in Comparative Perspective', *Jahrbücher für Geschichte Osteuropas*, New Series, 49. 3 (2001), 346–62.

Vigilev, A. N., *Istoriia otechestvennoi pochty*, 2nd ed. (Moscow: Radio i sviaz', 1990).

Waugh, Daniel C., 'The Best Connected Man in Muscovy? Patrick Gordon's Evidence Regarding Communications in Muscovy in the 17th Century', *Journal of Irish and Scottish Studies*, 7. 2 (2014 [2015]), 61–124.

Waugh, Daniel C., *The Great Turkes Defiance: On the History of the Apocryphal Correspondence of the Ottoman Sultan in Its Muscovite and Russian Variants*, with a foreword by Dmitrii Sergeevich Likhachev (Columbus: Slavica Publishers, 1978).

Waugh, Daniel C. and Ingrid Maier, 'How Well Was Muscovy Connected with the World?', in *Imperienvergleich: Beispiele und Anätze aus osteuropäischer Perspektive. Festschrift für Andreas Kappeler*, ed. by Guido Hausmann and Angela Rustemeyer, Forschungen zur osteuropäischen Geschichte, Bd. 75 (Wiesbaden: Harrassowitz, 2009), 17–38.

Weller, Toni, ed., *Information History in the Modern World. Histories of the Information Age* (Basingstoke: Palgrave Macmillan, 2011), https://doi.org/10.1533/9781780631318

West, Sally, *I Shop in Moscow: Advertising and the Creation of Consumer Culture in Late Tsarist Russia* (DeKalb: Northern Illinois University Press, 2011).

Whittaker, C. H., *The Origins of Modern Russian Education: An Intellectual Biography of Count Sergei Uvarov, 1786–1855* (DeKalb: Northern Illinois University Press, 1984).

Witzenrath, Christoph, 'Literacy and Orality in the Eurasian Frontier: Imperial Culture and Space in Seventeenth-Century Siberia and Russia', *Slavonic and East European Review*, 87. 1 (2009), 53–77.

Wortman, Richard S., *Scenarios of Power: Myth and Ceremony in Russian Monarchy from Peter the Great to the Death of Nicholas I* (Princeton: Princeton University Press, 1995).

Zakharov, V. N., Y. A. Petrov and M. K. Shatsillo, *Istoriia nalogov v Rossii. IX–nachalo XX v.* (Moscow: ROSSPEN, 2006).

List of Figures

1. Early Mapping: The Tsardom in Manuscript

1. Willem Janszoon Blaeu, *Tabula Russiae* (1635). Map and inset of the city of Moscow based on Isaac Massa's maps. Image in the public domain. Wikimedia, https://commons.wikimedia.org/wiki/File:Willem_Janszoon_Blaeu._Tabula_Russiae_ex_autographo,_quod_delineandum_curavit_Foedor_filius_Tzaris_Borois_desumta._MDCXIIII.jpg 25

2. Isaac Massa, *Russiæ, vulgo Moscovia, Pars Australis* [The Southern part of Russia, aka Muscovy], from *Theatrum Orbis Terrarum, sive Atlas Novus in quo Tabulæ et Descriptiones Omnium Regionum*, ed. by Willem and Joan Blaeu (1645), from the collection of the University of California. Image in the public domain. Wikimedia, https://commons.wikimedia.org/wiki/File:Blaeu_1645_-_Russiæ_vulgo_Moscovia_pars_australis.jpg 25

3. Isaac Massa, *Caerte van't Noorderste Russen, Samojeden, ende Tingoesen Landt* [Map of the Northern-most Russian, Samoyed, and Tungusic land, as copied from the Russians] (1610), from *A Short History of the Beginnings and Origins of These Present Wars in Moscow under the Reign of Various Sovereigns down to the Year 1610 by Isaac Massa*, translated and with an introduction by G.[eorge] Edward Orchard, Toronto [u.a.], 1994. Image in the public domain. Wikimedia, https://commons.wikimedia.org/wiki/File:Massa_-_Caerte_van't_Noorderste_Russen,_Samojeden,_ende_Tingoesen_Landt.jpg 26

4. Map of Moscovia, Sigismund von Herberstein (1549). Image in the public domain. Wikimedia, https://commons.wikimedia.org/wiki/File:Herberstein-Moscovia.jpg 27

5. Drawing of the Lands of the River Solonitsa (1533). Reproduced from A. V. Postnikov, *Russia in Maps: A History of the Geographical Study and Cartography of the Country* (Moscow: Nash dom and L'Âge d'Homme, 1996). Image © RGADA, all rights reserved. 29

6. Map of Aleksin (1671). RGADA, coll. 1209, Aleksin stlb. 31 494, fol. 115. Image © RGADA, all rights reserved.   32

7. Signatures on obverse of a map of lands along the Kamenka and the Urshma rivers in Suzdal Province. RGADA, coll. 1209, Suzdal' stlb. 27955, ch. 1, l. 73b. Image © RGADA, all rights reserved.   35

8. Map of the lands along the river Lakhost near the village of Tolstikova in Suzdal Province. RGADA, coll. 1209, Suzdal' stlb. 28043, Ch. 1, fol. 142. Image © RGADA, all rights reserved.   36

9. Map of the land along the river Sem Kolodezei in Iurev Polskoi Province, 1670-72. "The ploughed land of the uninhabited arable field Tiapkova". RGADA, coll. 1209, Iur'ev Pol'skoi, stlb. 34253, Ch. 1, fol. 132. Image © RGADA, all rights reserved.   37

10. Borovsk, RGADA, coll. 192, descr. 1, Kaluzhskaia guberniia, no. 1. Image © RGADA, all rights reserved.   38

11. Borovsk, satellite view from Google Maps (2017). Imagery © DigitalGlobe, Map data © Google, all rights reserved.   38

12. Martin Waldseemüller, *Universalis cosmographia* (1507), detail. Image in the public domain. Library of Congress, http://hdl.loc.gov/loc.gmd/g3200.ct000725C   41

13. S. U. Remezov's copy of the Godunov map of 1666-67, from his *Chorographic Sketch Book*. Image in the public domain. Houghton Library, Harvard University (Semen Ul'ianovich Remezov, *Khorograficheskaia kniga* [Chorographic Sketch-book of Siberia]. MS Russ 72 (6).).   44

14. Kamchatka. Map of Kamchatka included in S. U. Remezov's *Working Sketch Book*. Image in the public domain. Russian National Library, St Petersburg (Ermitazhnoe sobranie, no. 237, Sluzhebnaia chertezhnaia kniga Remezova, fol. 102v.).   47

15. S. U. Remezov, *Map of All Siberia*. Image in the public domain. Houghton Library, Harvard University (Bagrow Collection, MS Russ 72 (3).).   48

16. Map of a segment of the Tura River, from S. U. Remezov's *Working Sketch Book*. Image in the public domain. Houghton Library, Harvard University (Semen Ul'ianovich Remezov, *Khorograficheskaia kniga* [Chorographic Sketch-book of Siberia]. MS Russ 72 (6), Ch. 25, f. 48.).   55

2. New Technology and the Mapping of Empire: The Adoption of the Astrolabe

1. Unknown artist. Plan of 1699 of the environs of Kolomna. (1799), Fragment, RGADA, coll. 1209, descr. 77, columns Kolomna, file 25186, fol. 43–44. Image © Aleksei Golubinskii, CC BY-NC 4.0.   62

2. Franciscus Fiebig/Franziskus Viebig. A universal astrolabe (semicircumferentor) with compass. (Middle of the seventeenth century). From *Rossiia i Gollandiia: prostranstvo vzaimodeistviia. XVI–pervaia tret' XIX veka* (Moscow: Kuchkovo pole, 2013), p. 311. Image in the public domain.   64

3–1 Depiction of an astrolabe (circumferentor) on the *Plan of the city of Tver with its villages*. Unknown artist (last quarter of the eighteenth century), RGADA, coll. 1356, descr. 1, file 6057. Image © Aleksei Golubinskii, CC BY-NC 4.0.   64

3–2 Depiction of an astrolabe (circumferentor) on the *Plan of the city of Vesegonsk with its villages*. Unknown artist (last quarter of the eighteenth century), RGADA, coll. 1356, descr. 1, file 6027. Image © Aleksei Golubinskii, CC BY-NC 4.0.   64

3–3 Depiction of an astrolabe (circumferentor) on the *Plan of Tver Province*. Unknown artist (last quarter of the eighteenth century), RGADA, coll. 1356, descr. 1, file 5949. Image © Aleksei Golubinskii, CC BY-NC 4.0.   64

4. The Surveying Process. Fragment from the *Map of Iaroslavl Province*. Unknown artist (last quarter of the eighteenth century), RGADA. coll. 1356, descr. 1, file 6735. Image © Aleksei Golubinskii, CC BY-NC 4.0.   65

5. Unknown artist. *Cercle, demicercle et cercle avec une rose de boussole d'arpenteur*. From *Recueil de planches sur les sciences, les arts libéraux et les arts méchaniques avec leur explications*, vol. 1. (1765–72), Neuchâtel, 1779. Image in the public domain.   67

6. Fragment from the *Plan of the city of Klin with its villages*. Unknown artist (last quarter of the eighteenth century), RGADA, coll. 1356, descr. 1, file 2463. Image Image © Aleksei Golubinskii, CC BY-NC 4.0.   73

4. How was Western Europe Informed about Muscovy? The Razin Rebellion in Focus

1. An (invented) portrait of a turbaned Razin with a marshal's baton in his right hand from a German-language pamphlet (1671). The Royal Library, Copenhagen. Photo by Ingrid Maier, public domain. — 127

2. Coloured drawing of Razin's execution (originally from Moscow), 1671, 400 x 310 mm. The Swedish State Archives, Stockholm. Photo by Ingrid Maier, public domain. — 139

3. Folding plate, printed in London (1672). The British Library. Photo by Daniel C. Waugh, public domain. — 141

8. Bureaucracy and Knowledge Creation: The Apothecary Chancery

1. The Apothecary Chancery today (2015). Photo by Clare Griffin, CC BY-NC 4.0. — 258

2. An illuminated page from Josephus's *Antiquities of the Jews*, Brother Maciej and Master of the Lady with Unicorn (1466). From the collection of the National Library of Poland. Image in the public domain. Wikimedia, https://en.wikipedia.org/wiki/File:Josephus_Antiquitates_Iudaice.jpg — 273

3. Herbal Page (*ca.* seventeenth century). The Library of the Russian Academy of Sciences, coll. 17, descr. 4, file 12. Photo by Clare Griffin, CC BY-NC 4.0. — 278

10. Communication and Official Enlightenment: The *Journal of the Ministry of Public Education*, 1834–1855

1. V. A. Golike, *Portrait of Count S. S. Uvarov* (1833). Image in the public domain. Wikimedia, https://commons.wikimedia.org/wiki/File:Golike_Vasily_Portrait_of_Count_Sergey_Uvarov_(1833).jpg — 320

12. Experiencing Information: An Early Nineteenth–Century Stroll Along Nevskii Prospekt

1. View of Palace Square, from V. S. Sadovnikov, *Panorama of Nevskii Prospect* (1830–35). © State Russian Museum, St Petersburg, all rights reserved.   376

2. Formann and Elers, from V. S. Sadovnikov, *Panorama of Nevskii Prospect* (1830–35). © State Russian Museum, St Petersburg, all rights reserved.   378

3. Jean Fouquet, *Boccace écrivant le De Casibus* (1458). Bayerische Staatsbibliothek München (Cod. Gall. 6, fol. 10). Image in the public domain. Wikimedia, https://commons.wikimedia.org/wiki/File:De_Casibus.jpg   380

4. A bootmaker's stall, from Adam Olearius's *Vermehrte Newe Beschreibung Der Muscowitischen vnd Persischen Reyse, So durch gelegenheit einer Holsteinischen Gesandschafft an den Russischen Zaar vnd König in Persien geschehen* (1656). Image in the public domain. Wikimedia, https://commons.wikimedia.org/wiki/File:Olearius_russian_coins.gif   380

5. Sign of the Bakers' Guild, East Frisian Island of Juist (Lower Saxony, Germany). Image © 4028mdk09, CC BY-SA 3.0. Wikimedia, https://commons.wikimedia.org/wiki/File:Symbol_des_Bäckerhandwerks.JPG   381

6. A bakers' sign, from V. S. Sadovnikov, *Panorama of Nevskii Prospect* (1830–35). © State Russian Museum, St Petersburg, all rights reserved.   382

7. Cakes, Mathematical Instruments, and Wigs, from V. S. Sadovnikov, *Panorama of Nevskii Prospect* (1830–35). © State Russian Museum, St Petersburg, all rights reserved.   383

8. Coats, Frocks, and Musical Instruments, from V. S. Sadovnikov, *Panorama of Nevskii Prospect* (1830–35). © State Russian Museum, St Petersburg, all rights reserved.   384

9. Rode's shop, from V. S. Sadovnikov, *Panorama of Nevskii Prospect* (1830–35). © State Russian Museum, St Petersburg, all rights reserved.   387

10. Wolf and Béranger, from V. S. Sadovnikov, *Panorama of Nevskii Prospect* (1830–35). © State Russian Museum, St Petersburg, all rights reserved.   388

11. Smirdin's *The Library for Reading*, from V. S. Sadovnikov, *Panorama of Nevskii Prospect* (1830–35). © State Russian Museum, St Petersburg, all rights reserved.   389

12. Bellizard's bookshop, from V. S. Sadovnikov, *Panorama of Nevskii Prospect* (1830–35). © State Russian Museum, St Petersburg, all rights reserved.   391

13. M. I. Makhaev, *View of Elizaveta Petrovna's Summer Palace* (1756). From the collection of the State Hermitage Museum, St Petersburg. Image in the public domain. Wikimedia, https://commons.wikimedia.org/wiki/File:Summer_Palace_St_Petersburg.jpeg   393

14. Gostinyi dvor, from V. S. Sadovnikov, *Panorama of Nevskii Prospect* (1830–35). © State Russian Museum, St Petersburg, all rights reserved.   395

15. V. S. Sadovnikov, *View of the Passazh* (1848). Image in the public domain. Wikimedia, https://commons.wikimedia.org/wiki/File:Passazh_department_store_(Sadovnikov).jpg   396

16. Pavel Semechkin, *Interior of the Passazh in St Petersburg* (1850s). Image in the public domain. Wikimedia, https://en.wikipedia.org/wiki/File:Semechkin.jpg   397

17. Madame La Tour's Panorama and the Optical Telegraph, from V. S. Sadovnikov, *Panorama of Nevskii Prospect* (1830–35). © State Russian Museum, St Petersburg, all rights reserved.   405

Index

Admiralty College (*Admiralteistv-Kollegiia*) 65–66, 370, 399
advertisement 126, 128, 192–193, 198, 203, 206, 208–209, 332
Aesop 353
Afinogenov, Gregory 45, 48, 57
Aleksei Mikhailovich, Tsar 43, 50, 59, 79–80, 82, 85, 88 89, 105, 147, 216–217, 238, 243, 266–267, 280, 306, 308, 322, 330, 373
Alexander I, Tsar 12, 168, 182, 194–196, 209, 312–314, 317, 322, 358
Allsen, Thomas 156–158, 172
Ambassadorial Chancery (*Posol'skii prikaz*) 18, 81–82, 85, 86–87, 90, 92, 95, 100, 110, 120, 124, 136–137, 139, 148, 238–239, 245, 260
ambassadorial reports (*stateinye spiski*) 80–81, 88
America 41, 80, 188
Amsterdam 54, 86, 99, 117
Andrusovo, Truce of 90, 101
Anichkov Bridge 370, 392, 394, 400
Apothecary Chancery (*Aptekarskii prikaz*) 56, 68, 255–257, 258, 259–272, 274–277, 279–285
Archangel (Arkhangelsk) 85, 162–163, 223, 291, 293
Asia 19, 26, 46, 54–55, 93
Asiatic 10, 320

Astrakhan 116, 121–122, 132–133, 137, 145, 157, 204, 237, 241–244, 246
astrolabes 15, 60–61, 63–71, 73–74
Atlas of the Russian Empire (1792) 74
Atlas of the Russian Empire by V. P. Piadyshev (1821–1827) 74, 179
Auditing Office 300, 302
Austria, Austrian 53, 56, 99, 288, 294
autopsy 266, 279–281
Azov 105, 120, 166, 218, 350, 352, 357

Bagrow, Leo 26, 31, 33, 40, 42–45, 51, 56–57, 59
Baltic, sea and region 85, 90, 99, 106, 146–147, 159, 162, 164
banners 342, 347, 381–382
Bariatinskii, Prince Iurii 135
Basargina, Ekaterina 17
Behringer, Wolfgang 77, 108, 177
Belgorod 136, 238, 242, 244, 248, 250, 291, 293, 299
Bellizard 390, 391
bells 183, 217, 228, 343, 346, 348
Beloozero Province 30, 218
Berlin 94, 115, 118, 120, 143
Bezobrazov, Andrei Ilich 218–220
Bible 12–13, 23, 271–272, 275–277
Bidloo, Govert and Niclaas 352
Bills, Dr Valentine 268, 274
Black Sea 24, 42
Blaeu, Willem and Joan 25, 52, 54
Boelau, Gustav 72

Bogdanov, Andrei P. 103, 276
Book of the Great Sketch Map (*Kniga Bol'shomu chertezhu*) 39–40, 43
Boris Godunov, Tsar 39, 44
Borovsk 35, 38–40
Boterbloem, Kees 55–56
Bowers, Katherine 17, 364
Braunschweig 118
Bremen 77, 79, 89, 113, 115, 119, 128–129
Britain, British 59–60, 70, 73–74, 140, 174, 288, 294, 333
Brown, Peter B. 12, 257, 260, 261, 264, 265
Byzantium, Byzantine 277, 335, 342

cannon 343, 346–347
cartography 26–27, 29, 31, 33, 40, 42–43, 45, 49, 54, 59, 64
Casanova, Giacomo 353–354
Caspian Sea 121, 237
Catherine I, Empress 189
Catherine II, Empress 71, 73, 178–179, 181, 186, 189–191, 308, 312, 314, 318–319, 358, 362–363, 381, 396, 400
Catholic, Catholics 105, 107, 119, 191, 327
censorship 13, 24, 56, 112, 187, 192, 197, 210, 316, 324, 332
Chaadaev, Petr 324–325
Chancery for Ukrainian Affairs (*Malorossiiskii prikaz*) 82
Charles I, King 87
Charles VI, Holy Roman Emperor 282
Charles XI, King 49, 131
Charmantier, Isabelle 262–263, 272
Chekin, Leonid S. 35, 38–39
Chernyi Iar 243–244
Chernyshev, Count Petr Grigorievich 66, 68, 70, 327
Chicherin, Nikolai 358
Chief Directorate of Educational Institutions 314–317, 319
Chief Surveying Chancery 71–73, 194

China, Chinese 14, 28, 47, 48–49, 54–55, 57, 157, 386, 400, 403
Chokhov, Andrei 347
Christ 230, 233
Christian IV, King of Denmark 266
Christina, Queen of Sweden 99, 114, 146
chronicles (*letopisi*) 103, 116, 215, 221, 226–229, 233
Chudovskii, Evfimii 230
Church 13, 18, 101, 218, 222, 224, 229, 231, 233, 247–249, 257, 277, 343, 394
Chyhyryn 102, 220
Collins, Daniel E. 275
Collins, Samuel 270–271, 275–277
Cologne 115, 122, 126
comets 103–104, 229–230
commercial
  enterprise 372–373, 393, 394, 398
  signs 394
  space 372, 377, 394, 396
Committee of Ministers 198, 199, 201–202, 206–207, 313
Constantinople 188–189, 394
Copenhagen 119, 126, 129
correspondence 84, 93, 95, 100, 114–116, 131–132, 137, 145–147, 149–150, 155, 162, 168–169, 175–176, 180, 194, 199, 216–257, 294, 302, 327, 364
Cossacks 16, 46, 99, 113–114, 120, 122, 125, 136, 138, 144–146, 178, 218, 220, 237–250. *See also* Don Cossacks
couriers 79, 81, 85, 120, 132, 145, 155, 159, 161–162, 174–175, 239
Crimea 24, 40, 79, 238
Cronman, Lieutenant Colonel Fritz 49–50
Crummey, Robert O. 102, 264–265, 280
Custine, Astolphe de 53, 400, 404
customs registers (*tamozhennye knigi*) 215, 234–236
Cyrillic script 13, 129, 142, 351, 377

Daniel (Bible) 276–277
Danish 85, 87, 91, 266–267, 270
Danzig 68, 85, 94, 120, 122, 124
Decembrists 322–323
Delisle, Joseph-Nicholas 61–63
Demidova, N. F. 144, 258
Denmark 42, 99, 266
Department of Public Education 316
Derzhavin, Gavril 201
Deutsche Presseforschung 113, 115, 119, 128
Diarium Europæum 128
Distribuendi, Fedor 360, 365
Dixon, Simon 255, 301, 304, 307, 309
Dmitriev, Aleksei 68
Don Cossacks 114, 120, 122, 125, 138, 145, 218, 240, 245. *See also* Cossacks
Don (river) 238–241, 244, 247, 250–251
Dormition Cathedral 228, 230
Dorpat 315, 328, 335
Droste, Heiko 90–91, 124, 130, 132, 136, 143, 147, 157
Dutch 24, 54, 56, 84, 89, 92–100, 107, 113–114, 120–121, 126, 128, 134, 148–149, 162, 246, 274, 352, 377, 380

education reform 312, 314–317, 321, 323–325, 329, 333–336
Elizabeth, Empress 69, 72, 191–192, 361–362, 392–396
emblems 352, 375, 385
Engelhardt, Andreas 267, 275, 283
England, English 8, 15, 24, 57–58, 60, 65–66, 69–70, 72, 81, 86–88, 91, 99–100, 104, 106–107, 114, 117, 121, 134, 141–142, 149, 177, 188, 209, 223, 274, 334, 377–378, 380
engraving 99, 127–128, 141–142, 197, 351–352, 364
Enlightenment 311–312, 323–324, 326–327
Esin, B. I. 186, 201, 208, 210
Euler, Leonhard 63

Eurasia, Eurasian 10, 41, 43, 49, 61
eyewitness 42, 118, 125, 129, 140, 142, 144–145, 223, 225, 228, 242, 245
Falconet, Étienne 355
Falk, Marvin 43, 49–51, 56
Fedor Alekseevich, Tsar 83, 104, 230
Fedorov, Boris 332, 335
Fedorov, Vasilii 306
Fermor, General Lieutenant William 72
feuilletons 371
Fick, Heinrich 164–165, 175
Filaret, Patriarch 266
Filimonatus, Justus 85
Finland 155, 179
Fouquet, Jean 379, 380
France 14, 60, 66, 117, 176, 334, 359
Franklin, Simon 40, 372, 393–394
French 14, 50, 61–63, 86, 149, 176–177, 274, 312, 320, 325, 359, 364–365, 373, 377–380, 385–387, 390, 400
Frolov Tower (Spasskaia Tower) 345
Fustov, Ivan Eremeev 223–225

gardens 352–353
Gascoigne, Charles 72
Gautier, Théophile 377–379
General Land Survey 61, 64–65, 71, 73
General Map of Siberia 48, 50–51
German, Germans 51, 87, 90, 94–98, 100, 115, 117–118, 120–121, 126–131, 133, 146–150, 162, 188, 195, 220, 223, 231, 265, 274–275, 281, 308, 320, 322, 358–359, 377–381
Germany 87, 115, 148–149, 336, 381
Godunov map 43–46, 48–51
Godunov, Petr Ivanovich 43–46, 48–51
Goethe, J. W. 321
Gogol, Nikolai Vasilievich 335, 366, 371, 406
Golitsyn, Aleksandr Mikhailovich 69–70, 373

Golitsyn, Prince Vasilii Vasilevich 216, 220
Golosov, Timofei 224–225
Golubinskii, Aleksei 15
Google Earth 38
Gordon, Patrick 92–93, 107, 219–220
Gostinyi dvor 364, 394–396, 397–398
Graman, Dr 275
gravestones 343, 355
Great Britain 60, 70
Grebenka, Evgenii 360
Grech, Aleksei 361
Greek 274, 321–322, 329, 335
Greflinger, Georg 119–126, 128–129
Griesse, Malte 116, 121, 127, 221, 237
Griffin, Clare 16
Grishov, August Nathanael 63
Grundel-Helmfelt, Simon 122, 125, 130
Gubernskie vedomosti 185, 200–207, 210
guild signs 381
Gurliand, I. Ia. 158–159, 161
Gustavus Adolphus, King 157
Gutenberg, Johannes 13

Habermas, Jürgen 111
Hamburg 68, 79, 86, 91, 94, 100, 104, 106, 111, 114–116, 118–120, 122–128, 142, 150, 209, 223, 228, 230
Hartley, Janet 309
Heesen, Anke Te 262–263
Herberstein, Sigmund von 26–27, 27, 42–43, 52–53, 175
Herzen, Aleksandr 210, 320
Higgs, Edward 8
Hippocratic corpus 272
Hirsvogel, Augustin 42, 53
Holland 95, 99, 114, 117, 352
Hollandtsche Mercurius 128
Holy Roman Empire 117, 126
Holy Synod 13, 327
Horn, Bengt 131–132, 138
Hornhausen 87, 231

Horn, Johann van 107
horse relay system (*iamskaia gon'ba*) 16, 89, 90, 160, 179, 234, 236, 239
Hughes, Lindsey 186, 216, 260
Hungary 99, 336
Huttenbach, Henry R. 45
Hyslop, John 156

Iakov, cannon master 347
Iakovlev, Kornei 120, 136, 138, 144–146
iamshchiki (relay communities) 161, 181–183
Iaroslavl 65, 158, 204, 221, 234–235
Illustrated Chronicle 347
Imperial Society for the Encouragement of Artists (*Obshchestvo pooshchreniia khudozhnikov*) 373
information technology 61, 187–188, 193, 196, 199, 207, 210–211, 256–257, 262–263, 265, 268, 277–279, 282–285, 373, 385, 396, 398–399
Iona, Bishop 227, 229
Islam 105, 157
Istoma, Gregory 42, 53
Istomina, E. G. 176–177
Italian 274, 345–346
Italy 88, 90, 189, 345
Ivan III, Grand Prince 160, 162, 345
Ivan IV, Tsar 30, 40–41, 249, 347
Ivanov, Ivan 370
Ivanov, Petr 370, 390

James II and VII, King 107
Jan Kazimierz, King 100
Jenkinson, Anthony 43, 54
Jenkins, Sir Lionell 104, 106, 223
Jensen, Claudia 113, 260
Jesuits 48
Jews 100–101, 271, 273, 361
Josephus, Flavius 271, 273
Journal of the Ministry of Public Education 17, 315–316, 325, 329–336

Kagalnik 120
Kamchatka 47, 63, 155
Karamzin, Nikolai 53, 287, 318, 320, 324, 327
Kazakova, N. A. 52
Kazakov, Gleb 113, 127, 139–140
Kazan 121, 135, 159, 166, 175, 204, 226, 232–234, 238, 245, 291, 293, 304, 315
Kazan Court, Chancery of (*Prikaz Kazanskogo dvortsa*) 238, 245
Kharkov 315, 335
Khitrovo, Iakov Timofeevich 242–243
Khlopova, Mariia Ivanovna 266
Khlynov (Viatka, Kirov) 226–228, 230–234
Kholmogory 234
Kiev 166, 204
Kilburger, Johann 91, 94
Kilburger, Philipp 116, 150
Kireevskii, Ivan 330
Kirill-Belozerskii Monastery 28, 30
Kirilov, Ivan Kirilovich 61
Kivelson, Valerie 15, 60
knowledge circulation 257, 263, 274, 282
Koch (von Kochen), Christoff 91, 125, 130–139, 143–151
Kolesnikov, Nikifor Ivanov 244–245
Kollmann, Nancy Shields 249–250, 347
Koludarov, Petrushka 224–225
Königsberg 93–94, 115, 120
Korchmina, Elena 16
Korobov, Colonel 298
Korolenko, Vladimir 182–183
Korotoiak 137, 239, 243–244
Kostroma 296–297
Kotoshikhin, G. K. 258–259
Kovtun, Yevgeny 363, 377, 381, 385, 400, 401, 404
Kozlov 248, 259
Kozlovskii, I. P. 89, 91–93, 109, 159, 162

Kraevskii, A. A. 331, 334
Kremlin 30, 40, 50, 54, 81–82, 85, 87, 94, 106–107, 109, 148–149, 230, 241, 244, 246, 249, 282, 345, 347
Krusbjörn, Peter 85
Kulibin, Ivan Petrovich 72
Kulishki 223–225
Kurakin, Aleksandr Borisovich 354
kuranty 18, 78, 81–84, 86, 88, 94–96, 98–106, 108–112, 120–121, 134–135, 185, 214, 221, 223, 230–231, 252, 260, 276
Kusov, V. S. 29, 33, 40, 63, 66
Kuznetskii Most 365

Latin 51, 54, 97, 115, 122–123, 126, 188, 256, 271, 274–277, 281, 345, 348, 351–352, 355, 377
Le Donne, John P. 287, 289, 309
Lemberg 120, 122
L'Estocq, Jean Armand de 69
letters (*poslaniia, gramotki*) 80, 88, 91, 100, 102, 104, 110, 114–115, 119–125, 129–132, 134–136, 138–139, 142, 150, 155, 161–162, 169, 171, 176, 215–220, 236, 240–241, 247–248, 252, 275, 386, 403
Levin, Eve 255, 261
Liatskoi, Ivan 43, 53
Lichifinus, Andreas 270–271, 275
Likhachev, Fedor Fedorovich 264
Linnaeus, Carl 262, 272
literacy 216, 259, 280, 284, 343, 379, 386
lithograph 364, 370, 386
Lithuania 53, 90, 120
London 91, 99–100, 113–114, 140–142, 223, 228, 230
Loptunov, Andrei 257, 263, 264, 268, 274, 279, 282
Lotman, Iurii 173, 402
Louis XIV 8
Lübeck 68, 107

Madame la Tour 404
Magnitskii, Leontii 355
Maier, Ingrid 15, 18, 83, 91, 100, 148, 162, 214, 236, 246, 260
Man'kov, A. G. 116–117, 127, 128, 142
manuscript/scroll 18, 24, 40, 51, 53, 56–57, 84, 94, 109–112, 114, 117–118, 163, 198, 213, 222–223, 231, 262–263, 280, 282–284, 347, 351, 370–375, 390, 400, 403–406
maps 15, 23–24, 26–51, 53–58, 60–65, 72–74, 160, 179, 234, 366
Marker, Gary 13, 186, 216
Marks, Steven G. 8, 11
Marselis, Leonhardt 90, 95
Marselis, Peter 85, 121
Martynov, Ivan 316–318
Massa, Isaac 24–26, 84
  Notes upon Russia 26
Matveev, Artamon Sergeevich 124, 136, 139, 147–149
Mercator, Gerhard 52–53
Miechowita, Maciej 42–43, 52
Mikhail Fedorovich Romanov, Tsar 40, 266
mileposts 356–359
Military College 296, 300, 302–303, 305
Military Service Appointment Chancery (*Razriadnyi prikaz*) 238, 241–242, 250–251
Military Service Chancery (*Razriadnyi prikaz*) 256–257, 264–265, 268, 279, 282
Miloslavskii, General Ivan 135, 283
ministerial periodical 315
Minister of Public Education 319, 322–325, 330, 333, 337
Ministry of Finance 203
Ministry of Internal Affairs 179, 195, 199, 201, 203, 205, 315
Ministry of Public Education, Minister of Public Education 17, 311, 314–319, 322, 325, 327–328, 331, 335
Ministry of Religious Affairs 318

miracles 88, 103, 215, 219, 227, 230–233
Mironov, Boris N. 288, 294, 309
Mirskii, M. B. 68, 70, 261–262
Mittwochischer Mercurius 118
Mogilev, Grigorii 68
Monastery Chancery 185, 188
Mongol Empire 156–158, 172
Montferrand, Auguste de 370, 375
monuments 17, 156, 343–344, 346–352, 355, 367, 369–373, 375, 394, 399
Morgan, Francis 71
Morozov, M. 133
Moscow 13, 14, 18, 23–24, 30, 38–40, 42, 46–47, 49–51, 53, 56, 65–66, 70, 73, 78, 81, 83–88, 91–97, 99–101, 105–107, 109, 114–120, 122–126, 128–132, 134–143, 145–147, 149–150, 158–160, 162, 164–166, 169, 171, 174–179, 182–183, 185, 187–189, 191–193, 195, 200, 203, 209, 217–218, 220–223, 225, 227, 230–234, 237–239, 241–250, 255, 257, 266, 291, 293, 296–297, 299, 302, 306, 315, 318, 324, 326, 335, 344, 346–351, 356–358, 362, 365–366, 379
Moscow Print Yard 14, 18
Moscow University 13, 64, 70, 188, 193, 324–325
Moscow Vedomosti 188, 209
Moskva, river 74, 145
Müller, Gerhard Friedrich 63
Münster 33, 87, 100
Murom 171–172
Muscovy, Muscovites 10–16, 24–28, 31, 33–34, 36, 39–43, 46, 48–49, 51–53, 56–57, 77–95, 97, 99, 101–112, 113–116, 118–125, 130–131, 133–136, 138, 140–142, 146–151, 160–162, 167, 185, 214–216, 220, 223, 226, 230–231, 233, 236–239, 241–242, 245–246, 249–250, 252, 256–257, 260–261, 267–268, 270, 275, 277, 279, 282–284, 342–343, 345–349, 366

Musketeers' Chancery 267–268
Muslims 54, 178

Nadezhdin, Nikolai 324–325
Napoleon Bonaparte, Emperor 73, 317, 365, 375, 398
Napoleonic Wars 70, 196
narodnost', culture of 323–325, 329–330
Narva 91, 115, 122, 125, 130–132, 134, 136–137, 139, 146–147, 149–150, 180
Naryshkin, Aleksandr L'vovich 353
Nekrasov, Nikolai 364
Netherlands 60, 86–87, 99–100, 148
Neva 59, 71–72, 188, 360, 393
Nevolin, K. O. 261–262, 334
Nevskii Prospekt 17, 360, 364, 369–375, 377, 380, 385–386, 390, 392, 394–399, 400, 404–406
news 15–16, 77–90, 93–103, 105–112, 113–126, 129–138, 146–151, 188–190, 192, 195–200, 202–203, 205–206, 208–210, 213–223, 225–234, 236–247, 249, 251–252, 317–318, 325–326, 335, 365
newspapers, Dutch 15, 82, 86, 92–94, 96, 98–99, 106, 113–114, 120, 134, 148, 246
newspapers, European 79–80, 83–84, 86–87, 90, 93–96, 103, 111, 113–114, 116–117, 130, 146–147
newspapers, German 15, 86, 92, 94, 96, 100, 106, 114–116, 118–119, 122, 126–128, 130, 146–148, 150, 223
newspapers, Russian 15–16, 18–19, 77, 80, 82–84, 96, 101, 108, 111, 112, 114, 117–118, 128, 133–135, 149, 185–212
Nicholas I, Tsar 182, 196–197, 199, 201, 204, 207, 210, 322–323, 372
Nicholas Velikoretskii, Saint, icon of 227, 230–231
Nikon, Patriarch 247, 277
Nizhnii Novgorod 204, 238, 295

Nordischer Mercurius 116, 119–129, 142, 150–151
Notes of the Department of Public Education 319
Notes Upon Russia 42
Novgorod 12, 85, 91, 120–121, 124–125, 131–135, 147, 149–150, 160, 166, 216–217, 221–223, 225–227, 233, 245, 291, 293, 306, 356
Novikov, Nikolai 186, 209
Novokshchenov, Dmitrii Mikhailovich 298
Nyen 139

Oglodaev, Petr 235
Oglodaev, Roman 117, 126, 235
Oka, river 356
O'Neill, Kelly 179
optical telegraph 398–399, 404
orality, oral communication 80, 214, 263, 278, 280–282, 285
Ordinariæ Relationes 122–123
Ordin-Nashchokin, Afanasii Lavrent'evich 88–90, 107, 136
Øresund customs duty 69
Orthodox Church, Russian 101, 105, 191, 206, 247, 327, 329, 330
Orthodoxy 191, 323, 325, 330
Oslo 119, 129
Ostolopov, Nikolai 318
Ottoman, Ottoman Empire 14, 34, 79, 88, 99–102, 104, 200, 282. *See also* Turks
Ozeretskovskii, Nikolai 316
Oznobishin, Mikhail 243–244

Pacific Ocean 41–42
Padua 142, 270
Palace Square 364, 370, 375–377, 392, 399
Palmquist, Eric 51
Panorama of Nevskii Prospekt (Panorama Nevskogo Prospekta) 369–375, 382, 390, 398–400, 402–406
Panov, Eufimka 224
Panov, Vikulka 224

paper technology 256, 262–263
paperwork 201, 225, 262, 310
Passazh 396–397
passports 190, 198, 205
Paul I, Tsar 91, 127, 130, 180, 195, 311–313, 355
Pavlin (Paolo) *friazin* 346
Penza 242–243, 304
Periodic Publication of the Successes of Public Education 316–317
Persia 230, 238, 244–245
Peter II, Tsar 349
Peter I (the Great), Tsar 12, 63, 68, 77, 82, 95, 98, 105, 107, 111–112, 159, 164, 166–168, 178, 185–190, 208, 218–219, 262, 289, 300, 313, 348, 348–349, 351–353, 356–366, 381, 400
Petersburg Academy of Sciences 13, 59, 61, 63, 66–69, 71–72, 188–193, 195–196, 208, 261, 280, 314, 317, 321–322, 328, 335–336
"Petersburg side" 360
Petrine 59, 61, 68, 111, 163, 170–171, 208, 227, 352–354, 356
Petrucci, Armando 342, 351
Pettegree, Andrew 79, 117, 147, 213
photography 369, 407
physiological sketch 371
Physiology of Petersburg, The 364, 366
Piadyshev, V. P. 74, 179
Pickaert, Piter 352
Piechocki, Katharina N. 42–43
Pipes, Richard 188
Pisarkova, Ludmila 288
Plavsic, Borivoj 264
Poe, Marshall T. 52, 280, 344
Pogodin, Mikhail 233, 330, 335
Poland, Polish 42, 52, 54, 88, 90, 92–94, 99–101, 108, 120, 134, 136–137, 146, 155, 182, 218, 258, 260, 277
Polibin, Mikhail 279
Polo, Marco 156, 270
Poltava 351

Pommering, Karl 85
Popov, Semen 227, 229–230
Popp, Franz Ludwig 67
post, Habsburg Imperial 78
Postnikov, A. V. 27, 30–31, 40, 43, 45, 49–51, 53, 56
post, Russian 16, 121, 155–182, 203–204, 217
post, Swedish 90, 157, 177
Povelikhina, Alla 363, 377, 381, 385, 400–401, 404
Prévost, Andrei 370–371
printing 8, 12–14, 16, 19, 123, 126–127, 140, 185–186, 188, 191, 193, 195–197, 200, 203–204, 256, 390
Privy Chancery (*Prikaz tainykh del*) 88–90, 238
Prokofev, Mishka 218, 222
Protestant 87, 105, 231
provincial
  newspapers. See Gubernskie vedomosti
  publishing 19
  reform 164, 178, 189
Prussia 70, 116, 288, 294, 333
Pskov 85, 120, 125, 131, 133, 147, 149, 181, 218, 346
Ptolomy, Ptolemaic 41–43
Pushkin, Aleksandr Sergeevich 312, 358, 365, 370, 374, 386, 390, 401–402, 404

Randolph, John 16
Rastrelli, Carlo 355
Rastrelli, Francesco 355, 375, 392
Razin, Frol ("Frolko") 138, 140, 142–145
Razin, Stepan ("Stenka") 16, 18, 91, 113–123, 125–130, 132–146, 148–150, 227, 236–248, 250–251
Redin, Dmitrii 159, 174–175
Red Square 144, 148, 233, 345, 347–349
Reimers, Heinrich Christoph von 359–360

Reissig, Kornelius Khristianovich 72
Relay Chancery 161, 163, 169–172, 178, 181
Remezov, Semen Ulianovich 44–51, 53–57
Reval 91, 130, 132, 138, 147
Riga 85, 89–91, 93–94, 116, 120–121, 123–124, 135, 150, 159, 162–163, 182, 195
roads 17, 31–32, 34, 38–40, 155–156, 158, 160–162, 173–178, 181–182, 234–235, 356–358, 360
Roche, Daniel 177
Rodes, Johan de 114, 130, 146
Romodanovskii, Grigorii Grigor'evich 136–137, 145, 220, 242, 244–248, 250
Rossi, Carlo 370
Rostopchin, Count Fedor Vasil'evich 365
Ruban, V. G. 172, 179
rumour 8, 16, 80, 117, 133, 136, 145, 213–215, 225, 233, 238, 243, 251
Rus 72, 100, 158, 342, 344, 346
Russian Empire 10–11, 13–14, 60–62, 74, 155–156, 158–160, 163, 168, 175, 178, 183, 186–187, 191, 196, 200, 202, 288, 296, 302, 304, 306, 325, 330, 369, 371, 375, 379
Russian State Academy 317
Russo-Turkish War 70

Sadovnikov, Vasilii 364, 369–377, 390–391, 399–400, 402–403, 406–407
Saratov 115, 137, 243, 354
Schibli, Roland 83–84, 87
Schoonebeck, Adriaan 352
Senate 13, 61–62, 66, 69, 71, 73, 164–165, 171–172, 188–196, 198–200, 202, 204–205, 207, 294–295, 300, 302, 304–305, 308, 314, 356–357, 362
Senkevitch, Tatiana 371, 377
Serbinovich, Konstantin 327, 331–332
Shabbetai Zevi 100–101, 104

Shafirov, Petr 163, 165
Shamin, Stepan M. 82–84, 88, 94–95, 98, 100, 102–104, 106–107, 109, 121, 223, 229–230, 236, 246
Sheremetev, Fedor Ivanovich 265–266
Shishkov, Aleksandr 318–319
shopping arcades 369, 394–397
shop signs 17, 342, 361, 364–366, 371–372, 377, 379–382, 385, 393–394, 396, 398, 401–402, 406
Shuvalov, Petr Ivanovich 69
Siberia, Siberian 15, 24, 39–41, 43–51, 53–56, 159, 174, 182, 224, 291, 293
    Siberian Chancery 46, 56, 224
    Western Siberia 41, 43–44
Simbirsk 116, 132–134, 137, 237, 306
Simmel, Georg 160
Simonov, V. I. 86, 94, 115
Slavonic 12, 24, 52, 88, 111, 142, 263, 277, 334, 345, 347, 352
Smirdin, Aleksandr 386–390, 392
    Library for Reading 386–387, 389–390
Smith, Alison K. 16
Smith-Peter, Susan 201, 210, 415
Smolensk 174–175, 181–182, 290–291, 293
Sofiia Alekseevna, regent 348
Sokolov, Petr 319
Sokolovskii, M. K. 261
Solari, Pietro Antonio 345, 347–348
Soll, Jacob 8, 11
Solonitsa, river 29–30
Solvychegodsk 234–235
Sotnikova, S. I. 33
Soviet 117, 128, 158, 208, 210
    Soviet Academy of Sciences 117
Spain 28, 87
Spalskoi, Petr 68
Spasskaia Tower. *See also* Frolov Tower
Stählin, Jacob von 353
Starchevskii, A. V. 327, 331–333

statues 353–355, 398
Stepanov 296–297
Stockholm 51, 85–87, 91, 113, 120–121, 130–132, 134, 139, 146–147, 149, 276
Storch, Heinrich 173, 175
St Petersburg 17, 59, 61, 63–64, 68, 70, 72, 164–166, 168, 172, 175, 180, 185, 187–189, 191–193, 195, 198–200, 203, 205, 208–209, 296, 311, 315, 326, 329–330, 350–351, 357–360, 362, 364–366, 369–372, 374–379, 381, 390–394, 399–401, 404–406
St Petersburg Vedomosti 188, 205, 208
Stralsund 128, 223
street signs 17, 356, 358, 364, 366, 400–401, 406
Struys, Jean 175
Stryjkowski, Maciej 260
Sweden, Swedish 49, 51, 77, 85, 87, 89–91, 93, 99, 107, 113–115, 120–122, 124–125, 130–137, 141–142, 146–150, 157, 164, 185, 189, 258, 262, 353, 364
Swedish residents in Moscow. *See also* Koch, Krusbjörn, Pommering
Sweeden, Johann van 89–90
Symes, Carol 33
Synod 318, 327

Tambov 156, 181, 201, 241–243, 304, 307
Tataria, Tartars 40–41, 54, 56, 101–102, 157
Thirty Years War 87
Thompson, Edward 360
Tiapkin, Vasilii 92, 94
Time of Troubles (*Smutnoe vremia*) 252
Tiriutin, Filip 67–68
tobacco 362, 401
Tobolsk 44, 46–51, 53, 54, 174–175
Tolmacheva, Marina 48, 54–55
Toropets 257, 279
translation 11, 24, 26, 51–52, 78, 81–87, 92–98, 100–102, 105, 107, 109, 120–123, 134, 139, 142, 148–149, 222, 260, 274–277, 284, 316–317, 322, 331, 352, 354–355, 366, 377–378, 394, 400
triumphs 342, 350–352
Tsaritsyn (Volgograd) 136–137, 145, 237, 239–241, 243–244, 246, 356
Tura, river 55–56
Turks 83, 92, 101–102, 104, 137, 189, 238. *See also* Ottoman, Ottoman Empire
Tver 125, 143, 306
Ukraine, Ukrainian 40, 82, 93, 99, 101, 104, 110, 120, 136–137, 159, 178–179
Uliana 223–225
Unkovskaya, Maria 261–262, 269, 276
Urals, mountains 39–40, 174, 226, 234
Ustiug 234–235
Ustiug Chronicles 228–229
Uvarov, Count Sergei 17, 319–331, 333–337

Valdemar, Count 266–267, 281
Vedomosti 82, 107, 111–112, 185–189, 205, 208–210, 227. *See also Gubernskie vedomosti*; *See also Moscow vedomosti*; *See also St Petersburg vedomosti*
Velikii Ustiug 234, 236, 279
Velychenko, Stephen 288, 294
versts 49, 155, 170, 178, 181, 235, 356–357
Vesti-Kuranty. *See kuranty*
Viatka 88, 226, 229, 231–234, 304. *See also* Khlynov
Viazemskii, Procurator General Aleksandr 180
viaz' letters 348
Vienna 26, 53, 100, 102
Vigilev, A. N. 158–159, 162–163, 176
Vignon, Pierre 62
Vilna (Vilnius) 90, 92–94, 116, 120, 150, 162–163, 315
Vinius, Andrei 55–56, 90, 92–93, 99, 163, 219

Vladimir 171–172
voevoda 132–133, 218, 294
Volga, river 132, 134, 145, 217, 237–239, 243, 251, 356
Volgograd 237, 356
Vologda 217–218, 221, 234–235, 305
von Staden, Nicolaus 121, 123–124, 135
Vorob'ev, Maksim 373
Voronezh 137, 238, 241, 244, 291, 293, 304, 307
Vorotynskii, Prince Ivan Alekseevich 50, 232, 266, 279

Waldron, Peter 309
Waldseemüller, Martin 41–42
Warsaw 89, 120, 188, 399
watercolours 369–370, 373–377, 390–391, 399–400, 402–403, 406
Waugh, Daniel C. 15–16, 54–55, 99, 111–112, 137, 141, 145, 148, 162–163, 260
Weickhardt, George G. 265
Welke, Martin 114–115, 117–120, 127–128

Western Europe, Western European 10–15, 28, 85, 108, 113–114, 116, 119, 130, 135, 146, 148, 208, 220, 252, 262, 269, 312, 321, 359, 379
Westminster Treaty (1756) 60, 70
White Sea 85, 159, 221
William of Orange 107, 352
Winter Palace 375, 392
witchcraft 255–256, 267–269, 274, 279, 281
Witsen, Nicholas 50, 56
Wöchentliche Zeitung auß mehrerley örther 86, 127
Wolf and Béranger 386, 388
Wolf, Friedrich 321
Working Sketch Book (Sluzhebnaia chertezhnaia kniga Sibiri) 46
Wyche, Sir Peter 91, 104, 106, 223, 228, 230

Zhukovskii, Vasilii 320
Zlata Baba, Golden Woman 54

This book need not end here...

At Open Book Publishers, we are changing the nature of the traditional academic book. The title you have just read will not be left on a library shelf, but will be accessed online by hundreds of readers each month across the globe. OBP publishes only the best academic work: each title passes through a rigorous peer-review process. We make all our books free to read online so that students, researchers and members of the public who can't afford a printed edition will have access to the same ideas.
This book and additional content is available at:
https://www.openbookpublishers.com/product/636

Customize

Personalize your copy of this book or design new books using OBP and third-party material. Take chapters or whole books from our published list and make a special edition, a new anthology or an illuminating coursepack. Each customized edition will be produced as a paperback and a downloadable PDF. Find out more at:
https://www.openbookpublishers.com/section/59/1

Donate

If you enjoyed this book, and feel that research like this should be available to all readers, regardless of their income, please think about donating to us. We do not operate for profit and all donations, as with all other revenue we generate, will be used to finance new Open Access publications.
https://www.openbookpublishers.com/section/13/1/support-us

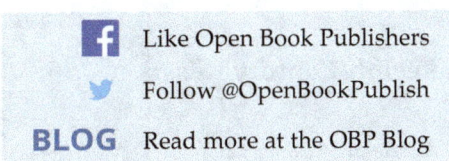

Like Open Book Publishers

Follow @OpenBookPublish

BLOG   Read more at the OBP Blog

You may also be interested in:

Twentieth-Century Russian Poetry
Reinventing the Canon

Katharine Hodgson, Joanne Shelton and Alexandra Smith (eds.)

https://www.openbookpublishers.com/product/294

In the Lands of the Romanovs
An Annotated Bibliography of First-hand English-language Accounts of the Russian Empire (1613-1917)

Anthony Cross

https://www.openbookpublishers.com/product/268

 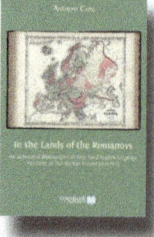

Beyond Holy Russia
The Life and Times of Stephen Graham

Michael Hughes

https://www.openbookpublishers.com/product/217

 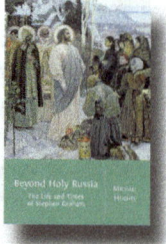

A People Passing Rude
British Responses to Russian Culture

Anthony Cross (ed.)

http://www.openbookpublishers.com/product/160

Women in Nineteenth-Century Russia
Lives and Culture

Wendy Rosslyn and Alessandra Tosi (eds.)

http://www.openbookpublishers.com/product/98

 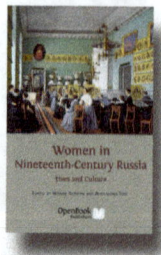

www.ingramcontent.com/pod-product-compliance
Lightning Source LLC
Chambersburg PA
CBHW072117290426
44111CB00012B/1684